lonely planet

100 WEEKENDS IN EUROPE

INTRODUCTION

When compared to its immediate neighbours, Africa and Asia, Europe seems very small indeed. And yet, what a variety of landscapes, what a diversity of languages, what a multiplicity of atmospheres, experiences and feasts for the senses on this compact continent! The shores of the Aegean Sea are a far cry from the Swiss lakes, the Irish coast or the beaches of Sicily. The streets of Cardiff, Madrid, Vilnius and Ljubljana vibrate with an energy at once familiar yet very dissimilar. The flavours of your meal will have little in common whether enjoyed in a Sardinian trattoria, a Viennese cafe or a British pub.

And it's here, to discover and experience this cultural and natural profusion, that Europe's modest size is a gift. All it takes is one train journey to change the scenery, and two or three hours by plane to reach most corners of the continent. With these 100 weekends, Lonely Planet aims to redefine the map of Europe and direct your gaze towards a discreet area you hadn't noticed before: do you know of Gozo and Zadar? Have you ever thought of playing Robinson Crusoe on Ingmar Bergman's island, taking an architecture course in Riga, going back in time in Minho? Many of these escapades are well-kept secrets. Europe offers such a wealth of unexpected excursions that we asked our authors to select the ones they considered most outstanding and worthy of sharing: this map is then unfolded, and it's they who accompany you, as close friends would do, recommending that little restaurant in Porto they discovered by chance, that hidden

courtyard in Venice, or passing on the tip to go skiing in Sarajevo, probably the most affordable winter sports resort in Europe.

We also wanted you to discover the hidden and unexpected sides of unmissable destinations that you already knew, or thought you knew. Ibiza, the party capital of the world? Yes, but also the magnetic, alternative epicentre of European hippie culture. Amsterdam, home of Rembrandt, whose canals are a UNESCO World Heritage site? Yes, but also an open-air laboratory for architecture and contemporary art. London, Prague or Berlin certainly have some surprising wonders in store for you.

Each of these weekends is also a starting point: you'll find three or four must-see or surprising experiences, as well as ideas for extending your trip if you have the time. A weekend in Vienna can take you to Bratislava, an hour away by train; a weekend in the form of a Scottish road trip, to the Isle of Skye; a weekend in Ghent, to the Belgian coast.

And, of course, this book of inspiration remains a guide: for each destination, our practical information (where to stay, when to go, how to get there) will help you get organised, while sidebars shed light on an aspect of the history and culture of your destination. The most beautiful journeys are often those we wouldn't have thought of spontaneously: this book will give you the push you need to make them happen.

CONTENTS

MAP KEY

Southern Europe

- 01 Madrid
- 02 Galicia
- 03 The Basque Country
- 04 Catalonia
- 05 Barcelona
- 06 Mallorca
- 07 Ibiza
- 08 Between Granada & Almería
- 09 Seville to the Costa de la Luz
- 10 The Minho
- 11 From Ericeira to Nazaré
- 12 Faro & the Algarve
- 13 Madeira
- 14 Andorra
- 15 Rome & Lazio
- 16 Around Viterbo
- 17 The Venice lagoon
- 18 From Verona to Lake Garda
- 19 Piedmont delights
- 20 Umbria's hilltop towns
- 21 The island of Elba
- 22 The Bay of Naples
- 23 Puglia, from Bari to beaches
- 24 Lecce, Salento & southern Puglia
- 25 Eastern Sicily
- 26 Southern Sardinia
- 27 Malta
- 28 Gozo
- 29 Zadar & North Dalmatia
- 30 Split & South Dalmatia
- 31 Sarajevo
- 32 Montenegro
- 33 Athens & Aegina
- 34 Messinia
- 35 Thessaloniki & Halkidiki
- 36 Corfu & Paxi
- 37 Crete
- 38 Rhodes & Symi
- 39 İstanbul
- 40 Cyprus

Western Europe

- 41 Alsace
- 42 Bordeaux
- 43 Finistère
- 44 Grenoble & the Alps
- 45 Limoges & the Limousin
- 46 The Loire Valley
- 47 Nice & the Côte d'Azur
- 48 Brussels
- 49 Liège & the Hautes Fagnes
- 50 Flanders
- 51 Ghent
- 52 Amsterdam
- 53 Rotterdam
- 54 Luxembourg
- 55 Berlin
- 56 Hamburg
- 57 Baden-Württemberg
- 58 Stuttgart to Lake Constance
- 59 Bavaria
- 60 Lucerne
- 61 Fribourg
- 62 Lausanne
- 63 Graubünden

Central and Eastern Europe

- 64 Warsaw
- 65 Kraków
- 66 Prague
- 67 Plzeň & Bohemia
- 68 Budapest & the Danube
- 69 Vienna
- 70 Salzburg & the Wolfgangsee
- 71 Innsbruck & the Austrian Tyrol
- 72 Ljubljana
- 73 Cluj-Napoca, in the heart of Transylvania
- 74 Sofia & the Balkans

Northern Europe

- 75 South London
- 76 Brighton
- 77 Oxford
- 78 Northwest England
- 79 Between Bristol & Bath
- 80 The Channel Islands
- 81 Cardiff
- 82 Glasgow
- 83 The Scottish Highlands
- 84 The Cairngorms
- 85 Dublin & Wicklow
- 86 Southern Ireland
- 87 Belfast
- 88 Zealand
- 89 The Faroe Islands
- 90 Stockholm Archipelago
- 91 Bohuslän
- 92 Gotland & Fårö
- 93 Swedish Lapland
- 94 Around Oslo
- 95 The fjords of western Norway
- 96 The Helsinki archipelago
- 97 Tallinn Bay
- 98 Riga
- 99 Vilnius
- 100 Reykjavík's surroundings

THE 100 WEEKENDS AT A GLANCE

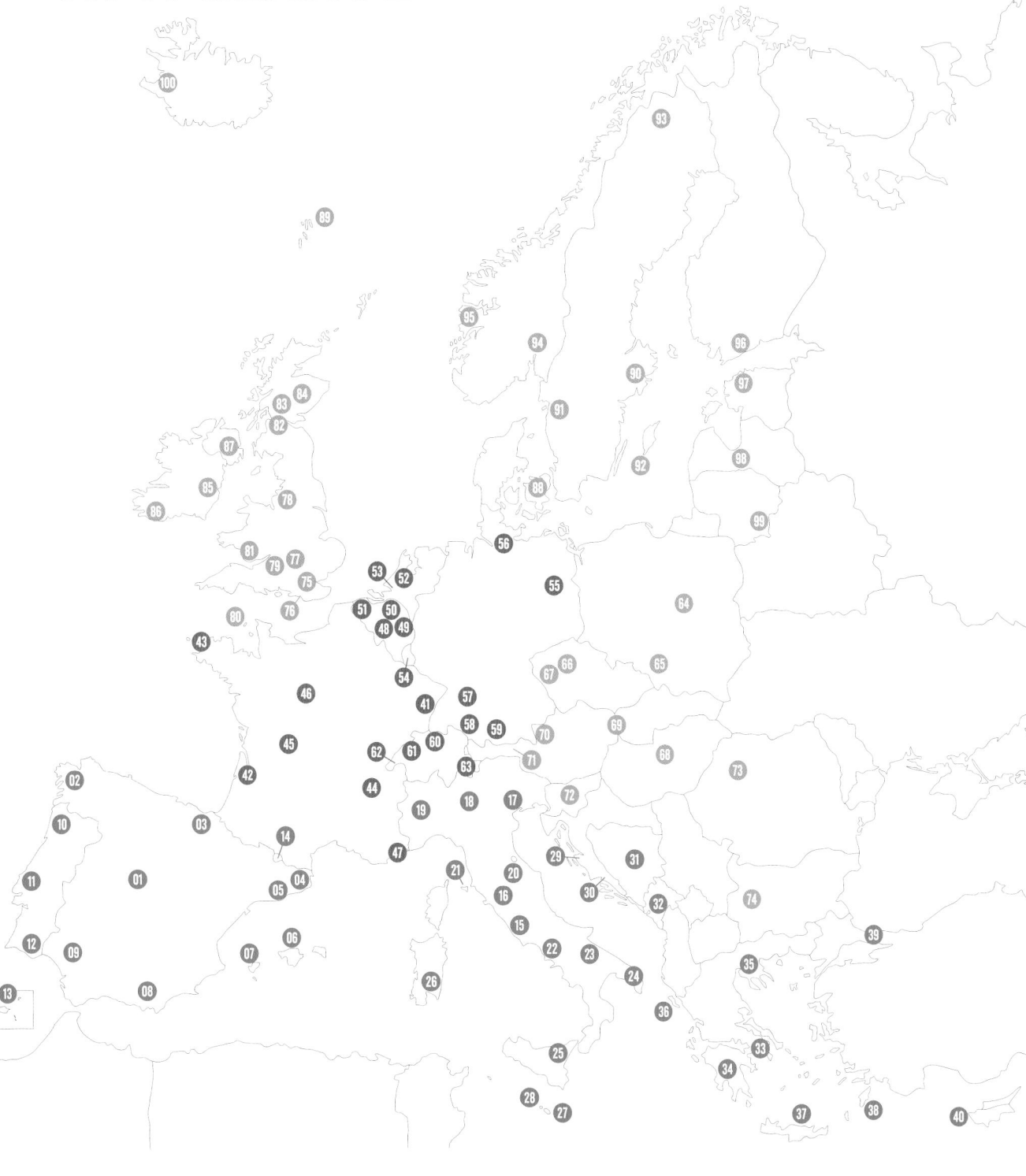

Southern Europe

01

SPAIN

Trace Madrid's history
THROUGH THE ARTS

With its abundance of world-renowned monuments and museums, **Madrid is the beating heart of Spanish culture;** its architecture, cinema, music and galleries offering a guided tour through the centuries. Built in 1734, the 2800-room **Palacio Real** bears witness to the splendour of the Spanish monarchy; the flamboyant **Plaza Mayor** (left) was the scene of brutal autos-da-fé during the Inquisition. Near the **Parque del Buen Retiro** (overleaf), the headline **Museo del Prado** (museodelprado.es) is a window on Spanish history. Paintings such as Velázquez's famous *Las Meninas* offer an immersion in royal life, while Goya's *The 2nd and The 3rd of May* illustrate the city's 1808 revolt against Napoleon's occupation. Other must-sees include Bosch's *Garden of Earthly Delights* and works by El Greco and Rubens. The journey through time continues at the **Museo Thyssen-Bornemisza** (museothyssen.org), which brings together the greats of European art from the 13th century right up to the present day. Finish off at the **Centro de Arte Reina Sofía** (museoreina-sofia.es), dedicated to the 20th century, to admire Picasso's moving *Guernica*.

Marvel at L'Escorial

Built in the 16th century, the majestic palace and monastery complex of San Lorenzo de El Escorial is a true gem of Renaissance architecture. Must-sees run from an impressive painting by El Greco in the basilica to the sumptuous library, the painted ceilings of the Salas Capitulares (featuring works by Titian, Tintoretto and Bosch), and the marble tombs of the Panteón de los Reyes (Royal Crypt), where almost every sovereign since Carlos I is laid to rest. The complex is reachable by train in an hour from Madrid's Atocha station.

See street art in Lavapiés

One of the city's oldest barrios (districts), Lavapiés is now a temple to counterculture and street art. Lose yourself in the labyrinth of alleyways in search of the most beautiful pieces, with rich pickings along Calle Santa Isabel and Calle de los Embajadores. Continue on to La Tabacalera, a former tobacco factory reincarnated as a cultural centre and managed by a local grassroots collective. Take in changing exhibitions dedicated to urban art, then head down to the basements, where the walls are covered in colourful graffiti.

Marvel at modern art at Matadero Madrid

In the south of the city, within a vast building that once housed Madrid's cattle market and slaughterhouse, this dynamic contemporary arts centre (mataderomadrid.org) is an extraordinary multipurpose space that hosts avant-garde events – from theatre performances and dance shows to exhibitions devoted to photography, architecture, fashion, literature and cinema. After your visit, take a stroll in the riverside Madrid Río park, much loved by Madrileños.

Embrace movida in Malasaña

In 1975, when Franco's death put an end to 40 years of dictatorship and Spain began its transition into a democracy, Madrid's Malasaña district became the heart of the *movida* movement that swept the country – an unbridled exploration of creative freedom that saw an explosion of new music and art in the city. This hedonistic era was perhaps best expressed in the films of arthouse director Pedro Almodóvar; today, you can still see echoes of *movida* in the spicy fashions of designer Ágatha Ruiz de la Prada. Follow in the footsteps of this creative frenzy with a dive into Malasaña's thrift stores, and in legendary bars like El Penta, Madrid me Mata or La Vía Láctea.

MORE TIME?

TEMPLO DE DEBOD Rebuilt block by block in the middle of Madrid, this temple to Amun was gifted to Spain after being saved from the rising waters of Lake Nasser in southern Egypt. It's a magical place to watch the sun set over the Spanish capital.

ANTIGUA ESTACIÓN DE ATOCHA The imposing 19th-century metal and glass structure (opposite) now houses a lush, light-filled tropical garden, with more than 500 species of plants.

ESTACIÓN DE CHAMBERÍ First opened in 1919, this 'ghost station' offers an atmospheric window into the early days of the Madrid metro. It's replete with restored original elements, from furniture and ticket counters to ceramic advertising panels.

PEDRO ALMODÓVAR

The renowned Madrid-born director has shot a dozen films in the capital. With *Pepi, Luci, Bom* (1980), which followed the chaotic lives of three Madrileña women, and the exploration of a nymphomaniac singer in *Labyrinth of Passion* (1982), Almodóvar established himself as the ambassador of the *movida* movement, before adopting a darker approach at the turn of the millennium. Joyously transgressive, several of his films – including *Women on the Verge of a Nervous Breakdown* (1988), *All About My Mother* (1999) and *The Skin I Live In* (2011) – have been awarded Goyas (the Spanish Oscars), as well as winning several BAFTAs, Golden Globes and Academy Awards.

PRACTICALITIES

HOW TO GET THERE

Trains from destinations around Spain and from Paris (nine hours) run to Madrid's Atocha station. The city's Barajas Airport is an international hub, with numerous flights from destinations worldwide.

WHERE TO STAY & EAT

The Spanish capital offers a wide range of accommodation, from value-for-money family hotels in the Retiro district to stylish (and more expensive) establishments in Las Letras. Budget travellers might head to the Generator Madrid (staygenerator.com), with dorms and rooms in the heart of Malasaña. In the evenings, fill up on tapas in the bars on Calle de la Cava Baja, in the La Latina district, and on Calle de Ponzano in Chamberí. Other highlights of Madrid's culinary scene include the many covered markets, such as the Mercado San Miguel (mercadodesanmiguel.es) and the Mercado de la Cebada (mercadodelacebada.com).

EVENTS

On 15 May, Madrid celebrates its patron saint, San Isidro. Crowds flock to the centre of town to witness the colourful procession that heralds a week of cultural happenings across the city. From August to September, neighbourhood festivals, such as those of San Cayetano in Lavapiés, or San Lorenzo and La Paloma in La Latina, are excellent opportunities to mingle with Madrileños.

SPAIN

Discover Galicia
BETWEEN LAND & SEA

Tucked into the extreme northwest of Spain, Galicia is a land of character, strongly marked by its Celtic roots. Dotted with small fishing ports, its 1200km (746 miles) of **rugged**, jagged **coastline** offer a spellbinding landscape. The hilly interior is greener, with a multitude of peaceful villages alongside a scattering of cultured cities; among the latter, **Santiago de Compostela** holds a special place. With its labyrinth of narrow streets and medieval atmosphere, this is a place that oozes spirituality. Each day, the grand square of Praza do Obradoiro plays host to the emotional arrival of pilgrims who have walked the **Camino de Santiago** to the city's soaring, richly ornate **cathedral** (see page 17). Elsewhere, the **Museo do Pobo Galego** (Museum of the Galician People; museodopobo.gal) and the **Museo das Peregrinacións** (Pilgrimage Museum) give the lowdown on local culture and the Camino. There's plenty to tantalise your taste buds, too: head to the **Mercado de Abastos** (mercadodeabastosdesantiago.com) to sample delicious local produce every morning.

Hike in Cabo Fisterra

There's great hiking along the length of the Galician coastline, but Cabo Fisterra on the remote Costa da Morte is particularly alluring. Especially beautiful as a sunset-watching spot, this immense rocky promontory, overlooked by a lighthouse, has a definite 'end of the world' feel – appropriately so, as this is journey's end for many Compostela pilgrims, who ritually burn their hiking gear here to mark the end of their walk. To hike to the cape, follow the 3.5km (2.2-mile) trail along the wild coast from the town of Fisterra, which is reachable by car or bus.

Admire Galicia's Atlantic archipelago

Nestled in Parque Nacional de las Islas Atlánticas de Galicia, and ringed by glorious white-sand beaches, lie the paradisical Illas Cíes. This island trio is home to a wealth of birdlife (terns, cormorants, petrels, shearwaters and auks are year-round residents); and as well as swimming and snorkelling, you can hike from deserted coves to breathtaking viewpoints. You can get to the islands via a 45-minute ferry crossing from Vigo.

Climb the majestic Monte Pindo

The coastal village of O Pindo is the starting point for a remote but rewarding hike of moderate difficulty. To reach the summit of the 'Celtic Olympus' (inset), you'll have to pick your way through an extraordinary tableau of granite formations. At the top, the views open up, revealing a splendid 360-degree panorama of the ocean and bay below. Public transport to O Pindo is limited; renting a car is the best way to get here.

Discover Pontevedra

This important former port, where Christopher Columbus' ship *Santa María* was built, still features a lively pedestrianised Old Town, where the Edificio Sarmiento and Sexto Edificio collections of the Museo de Pontevedra (museo.depo.gal) include Galician art, ceramics and jewellery. Pontevedra is also a good jumping-off point for excursions into the estuaries of the Rías Baixas. In the Ría de Pontevedra, you can visit the Combarro *hórreos* (raised granary houses; see previous page), the popular seaside resort of Sanxenxo, and search out a host of remote beaches.

MORE TIME?

LUGO Take a turn atop Lugo's imposing 2.2km-long (1.4-mile), 15m-high (49ft) wall, built by the Romans in the 3rd century. Within the walls, the highlight of the historic Old Town is the 12th-century Catedral de Santa María, an architectural mishmash, with an ultra-Baroque high altar surrounded by colourful stained-glass windows. **A CORUÑA** This buzzing beachside city, with a fine food scene and lively nightlife, is overlooked by the Torre de Hércules lighthouse; climb its 234 steps for coastal views. Find art by Rubens, Goya and Picasso at the Museo de Belas Artes (museobelasartescoruna.xunta.gal).

GALICIAN CUISINE

From sea bass to turbot and langoustines to oysters, seafood is the soul of traditional Galician cuisine. On regional menus, look out for the famous *pulpo á feira* (boiled octopus with garlic and paprika) and *vieiras á galega* (breaded scallops). Other specialities include sweet, melt-in-your-mouth Padrón peppers and cheeses like the semi-soft Tetilla. The local wine – including some sublime Albariño – is also well worth seeking out.

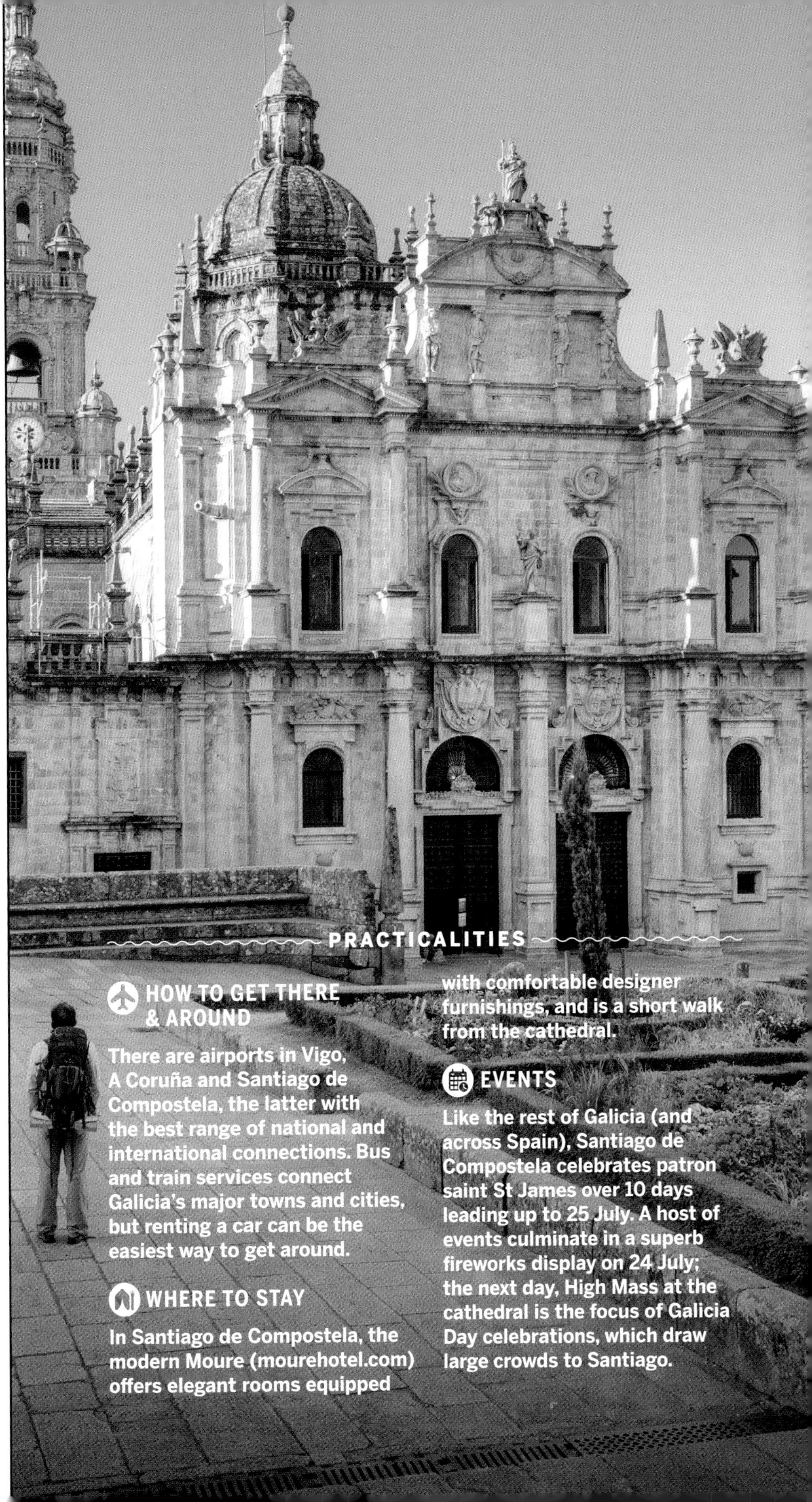

PRACTICALITIES

✈ HOW TO GET THERE & AROUND

There are airports in Vigo, A Coruña and Santiago de Compostela, the latter with the best range of national and international connections. Bus and train services connect Galicia's major towns and cities, but renting a car can be the easiest way to get around.

🏠 WHERE TO STAY

In Santiago de Compostela, the modern Moure (mourehotel.com) offers elegant rooms equipped with comfortable designer furnishings, and is a short walk from the cathedral.

📅 EVENTS

Like the rest of Galicia (and across Spain), Santiago de Compostela celebrates patron saint St James over 10 days leading up to 25 July. A host of events culminate in a superb fireworks display on 24 July; the next day, High Mass at the cathedral is the focus of Galicia Day celebrations, which draw large crowds to Santiago.

ATLANTIC OCEAN

Cape of Matxitxako

Bay of Biscay

MUNDAKA

GETXO

BILBAO

GUERNICA

HONDARRIBIA

FRANCE

GETARIA

PASAIA

Nervión

Urdaibai Biosphere Reserve

SAN SEBASTIAN

SPAIN

SPAIN

03

Explore Euskadi
BETWEEN BILBAO & SAN SEBASTIÁN

With its world-renowned architecture and dynamic dining scene, the Euskadi (Basque Country) capital of Bilbao is a worthy gateway to the coastline west towards San Sebastián, about an hour's drive away. In the city itself, Frank Gehry's iconic **Museo Guggenheim Bilbao** (guggenheim-bilbao. eus) sparked the regeneration of the Ensanche district, and the compact **Casco Viejo** (Old Town) offers an atmospheric counterpart, but it's just a short hop from the city centre to the stunning surrounding coast. Northwest of Bilbao, **Cabo de Matxitxako** is Euskadi's most northerly point; nearby, the much-photographed islet of **San Juan de Gaztelugatxe**, accessible by a snaking stone pathway from the mainland, served as Dragonstone castle in *Game of Thrones.* There's more astonishing scenery all the way to San Sebastián (see page 21), where the **San Telmo Museoa** (santelmomuseoa. eus) explores Basque history and culture; and a slew of dining options in the **Parte Vieja** (Old Town) are a gourmand's delight, whether you opt for the local tapas (*pintxos*; overleaf) or a Michelin-starred meal.

Surf the legendary 'left' at Mundaka

Euskadi's wonderful waves have long been renowned in the surfing world, and the breaks at Mundaka – a fishing port at the mouth of a river, where a sandbar forms fast, hollow waves – are particularly legendary. Surfers flock in to brave Mundaka's legendary 'left'; those not up to the challenge can watch the spectacle from the town's harbour walls. Experienced surfers and beginners alike will find other good places to catch a wave along the coast: head for Zarautz, Sopelana or the beaches of San Sebastián.

Take the metro to the cliffs

Living just a few stops from the ocean is a city dweller's dream – and one that's realised in Bilbao, where the metro can whisk you to the mouth of the Ría del Nervión and the pretty town of Getxo in under 30 minutes. This small seaside resort, with its dapper fishers' quarter and opulent mansions, is attractive enough for a wander, but it's worth striking out from the centre to follow the long promenade that runs along the beaches and climbs up to cliffs overlooking the Cantabrian Sea. Take a look, too, at the UNESCO-listed Puente Bizkaia (puente-colgante.com), built in 1893 between Getxo and Portugalete as the world's first transporter bridge: a gondola suspended from the main structure glides cars and passengers silently over the waters of the Nervión.

Birdwatch in the Urdaibai Reserve

Centred on the Mundaka Estuary (see previous page) north of Gernika, and extending down to the sea over some 220 sq km (85 sq miles) of constantly evolving water flows, mudflats, marshes and forests, the Urdaibai Biosphere Reserve is an important stopover for migratory birds. The impressive Urdaibai Bird Center (birdcenter.org), close to the village of Gautegiz-Arteaga, operates hides throughout the reserve; head to Cabo de Matxitxako to see a wealth of seabirds. The local tourist boad (turismourdaibai.com) also has details of outdoor activities in Urdaibai, from mountain biking to hiking and kayaking.

Follow the art trail in San Sebastián

Also known by its Basque name, Donostia, San Sebastián is an open-air museum of contemporary art; tracking down the sculptures scattered around its streets is an excellent way to get to know the city. Among the most imposing are Eduardo Chillida's *The Comb of the Wind*, at the western end of the hallowed La Concha beach; and Jorge Oteiza's *Empty Construction*, which stands on the Paseo Nuevo. There are dozens of others to discover; the tourist office website (sansebastianturismoa.eus) has a downloadable map detailing locations across the city.

MORE TIME?

GERNIKA East of Bilbao, Gernika was made famous by Picasso, whose anti-war painting *Guernica* recalls the bombing of this anti-Franco stronghold by Hitler's Condor Legion in 1937. An earthenware reproduction of his masterpiece can be seen at the Museo de la Paz (Peace Museum; museodelapaz.org).
PASAIA AND HONDARRIBIA Heading east, toward the French border, Pasaia is home to the Albaola Foundation (albaola.org), which traces the history of the port's whaling industry. Pushing on a further 20km (12 miles), Hondarribia (Fuenterrabía in Castilian) faces across the estuary to Hendaye, and has a definite Gallic air to its fortified centre and handsome plazas.

ESKADI'S TXAKOLI

Once considered a rather vulgar, inferior tipple, Txakoli is now one of Euskadi's most celebrated wines. This easy-drinking, slightly sparkling dry white, low in alcohol and with a fruity, citrus aroma, is made with grapes grown in the Gipuzkoa region, and some of the best Txakoli hails from the hillsides surrounding the comely fishing village of Getaria. Txakoli can be drunk as an aperitif or as an accompaniment to *pintxos*, with waiters pouring it from height to release its subtle flavours. To discover more, arrange a tasting at one of the local wineries (via getariakotxakolina.eus).

PRACTICALITIES

HOW TO GET THERE

Bilbao International has flights from all across Europe; the airport in San Sebastián has connections with major Spanish cities. Getting to Bilbao by rail can be a slow business, though new high-speed links are slated.

WHERE TO EAT

While undeniably delicious, *pintxos* are more of a light bite than a full-blown meal; more substantial Basque specialities include *kokotxas* (fish stew), and *bacalao al pil pil*, (salt cod in a garliky, spicy sauce). For a gastronomic splurge, book well ahead for three-Michelin-starred Azurmendi (azurmendi. restaurant) or one-starred Eneko (eneko.restaurant) in Larrabetzu, near Bilbao; in San Sebastián, try three-starred Arzak (arzak.es).

04

Follow the Dalí trail
IN CATALONIA

Born in the Catalonian village of Figueres in 1904, Salvador Dalí **became the best-known exponent of the Surrealist movement, his iconic artworks known the world over.** A printmaker, painter and sculptor, with an equal curiosity for cinema and photography alongside a ferocious talent for self-promotion, **Dalí** left his eccentric mark on the **Catalan hinterland** and the **Costa Brava**. Pick up the Surrealist trail in Figueres at the inimitable **Teatre-Museu Dalí** (left), which he designed in every detail to exhibit his work; today, it's one of the most popular museums in all of Spain. Then discover the easterly outcrop of **Cadaqués** and the little hamlet of **Port Lligat**, where **Dalí** lived out his romance with his wife and muse, Gala, for almost half a century, his work inspired by the singular rocky landscapes of the surrounding area. Finally, make a beeline for the elegant and surprising **Girona**, some 40km (25 miles) south of Figueres and the largest city in northern Catalonia; wander the medieval ramparts, take in the monumental cathedral and explore the 12th-century Jewish quarter.

Delve into Dalí's world at his 'Theatre-Museum'

In the early 1970s, at the suggestion of the Figueres mayor, Dalí transformed the former municipal theatre into the extravagant Teatre-Museu Dalí (salvador-dali.org). With red walls studded with concrete croissants and topped by a vast glass dome, it's an appropriate final resting place for the master of Surrealism, who lies in a crypt beneath the former stage. The 1500 works include the Mae West Room and the *Rainy Taxi* installation, a statue-topped Cadillac that 'rains' on the mannequins inside; and paintings from *Soft Self-Portrait with Fried Bacon* to mind-bending *The Image Dissapears* and the monstrous *Portrait of Picasso*.

Stroll between art & reality in Cadaqués

'I am inseparable from this sky, from this sea, from these rocks', wrote Dalí, who had an enduring love affair with Cadaqués, the village and its surrounds featuring in many of his paintings. Nestled in a rocky bay dotted with alluring pebble beaches and secluded coves, and with a mix of Modernista and traditional homes spreading back from the coast, the village was the birthplace of Dalí's father, and the artist spent holidays here as a child and teen before buying his Port Lligat home. Changing exhibitions at the small Museu de Cadaqués are often centred around his works.

Discover the Dalís' sanctuary in Port Lligat

If Figueres' Teatre-Museu is the mask that this complicated showman presented to the world, the Casa Museu Dalí is an intimate glimpse of the artist unadorned. He and his wife, Gala, lived in this seaside home outside Cadaqués from 1930 to 1982, transforming it from a simple fishers' cottage into a labyrinthine complex of whitewashed buildings, adorned with Dalí-esque touches like a bejewelled taxidermied polar bear and giant eggs scattered around the grounds. Book well ahead for the guided tour, which takes in Dalí's workshop, the bedroom and the Oval Room.

Admire the surreal landscapes of Cap de Creus

Spreading inland across the cape from Cadaqués and Port Lligat, the rugged, lunar-like landscapes of Parc Natural del Cap de Creus (opposite) were a major inspiration for Dalí's work. The best way to immerse yourself in this bewitching landscape, pummelled by the Tramontana winds, is to hike a section of the GR 92. The route passes through almost all the municipalities in the park – Llançà, El Port de la Selva, Cadaqués, Roses, Palau-Saverdera and Paut – as well as winding through the birding hot-spot of Parc Natural dels Aiguamolls de l'Empordà.

MORE TIME?

GIRONA With its arcaded houses and secret passageways, it's no wonder Girona (inset) served as a suitably medieval location for the filming of *Game of Thrones*. Stroll the restored Roman walls for views over the historic centre, take in displays on the city's Jewish community at the Museu d'Història dels Jueus, and visit the immense cathedral, flanked by a grand 86-step staircase.
PARC NATURAL DE LA ZONA VOLCÀNICA DE LA GARROTXA With around 40 extinct cones swathed in beech forest, this stunning reserve is a surprising corner of Catalonia, just 37km (23 miles) west of Figueres and ideal for exploring on foot or by bike; the park wesbite (parcsnaturals.gencat.cat) has more info.

CATALONIA'S CAGANER

Spend any time in Catalonia and you'll likely come across the region's caganer (poopers), irreverent ceramic figurines depicting a person defecating. Originally created as shepherds or peasants, and intended for Christmas nativity scenes (they're thought to bring good luck and prosperity in the year ahead), caganer have latterly evolved, modelled on everyone from the Pope to politicians and pop stars. They're sold in souvenir shops throughout Catalonia; to see traditional examples, visit the Museu del Joguet in Figueres (mjc.cat).

~~~ **PRACTICALITIES** ~~~

🚆 HOW TO GET THERE

Figueres makes an excellent base, with Renfe train connections (renfe.com) from Girona in under 30 minutes, Barcelona (one to two hours), Marseille and Lyon (around four hours) or Paris (five and a half hours). Buses also run to Cadaqués; journey time is about an hour.

ℹ️ GOOD TO KNOW

Figueres' Teatre-Museu Dalí is crowded in high season, when it's best to avoid visiting at weekends if possible. Be sure to book tickets early for both the Teatre-Museu and Port Lligat's Casa Museu Dalí; tour-group numbers for the latter are limited to eight people.

📅 EVENTS

In mid-May, during the Temps de Flors flower festival (tempsdeflors.girona.cat), the whole of Girona is decked out in fantastical floral arrangements.

MONISTROL
DE MONTSERRAT

To Gérone &
Tossa de Mar

Montserrat

Montseny
Massif

BARCELONA

PENEDÈS

BALEARIC SEA

SPAIN

05

Uncover a different side of
BARCELONA

Promising sea, sun, exceptional museums, world-renowned architecture, a lively nightlife and a diverting food scene, beautiful Barcelona could never be described as undiscovered.
Most visitors kick off their time here by seeking out the extravagant buildings designed by Antoni Gaudí – including the famous **Sagrada Família** (sagradafamilia. org) and the **Park Güell** (parkguell. barcelona) – then moving on to the fabulous **Museo Picasso**, and the **Fundació Joan Miró** on the flanks of view-rich **Montjuïc**.

Must-see neighbourhoods include the cobbled streets of the **Barri Gòtic** (left), the refined, bohemian atmosphere of **El Born**, the terraces of hipster **El Poble-Sec** or **Sant Antoni**, or the narrow streets of **La Barceloneta** for seafood feasts. And decamping to the beach for a day of sun and swimming is nothing short of obligatory. But beyond the big-hitter barrios and headline sights, there's always something new to see and experience, from seeking out street art and sampling local cava at a tapas bar to heading out of the city to marvellous Montserrat.

Track street art from Raval to Poblenou

Gaudí may take all the headlines, but Barcelona's thriving arts scene promises plenty of alternative diversions. For the best crop of street art (inset), head to the diverse districts of El Raval – where a blood-red mural by Keith Haring adorns a concrete wall near the entrance to the MACBA contemporary art gallery – and El Poblenou; other works are scattered throughout the city. You can discover them independently, or take a tour with outfits like Street Art Barcelona (streetartbcn.com), which also runs graffiti workshops and collective street-art events.

Take to the skies in a hot-air balloon

If you're in need of respite from the perenially crowded streets of central Barcelona, consider seeing Catalonia from above via a flight in a hot-air balloon. A number of operators – such as Globus Barcelona (globusbarcelona.com) – offer balloon trips of varying lengths, providing fantastic aerial views of the Catalan capital (when conditions permit) and surrounding sights, from the heights of Monserrat and the Montseny massif to the beaches of the Costa Brava. Most provide snacks and a glass or two of cava to toast your trip in fine style.

Soak up heavenly views in Montserrat

A mountain, monastery and natural park 50km (31 miles) northwest of Barcelona, Monsterrat is at the heart of Catalan identity. Venture out on the trails that range around its slopes to enjoy panoramic views stretching as far as the Pyrenees, then visit the Benedictine Monestir de Montserrat, established in the 11th century and rebuilt in the 19th and 20th centuries. Its basilica is the draw for those paying homage to Catalonia's patron, the 12th-century La Moreneta sculpture. The complex is 725m (2379ft) up the mountain, and is reachable by cable car and cog railway from Monistrol de Montserrat.

Taste cava in the Penedès

Move over, Champagne: the fizz of choice in Barcelona is cava. This sparkling wine is produced in the Penedès region, less than an hour from the Catalan capital. As well as cava, the vineyards that stretch between the Mediterranean and the Montserrat massif also produce fine reds and whites. Take a trip along the Penedès Wine Route (penedesturisme.cat) for tours and tastings at local wineries, accompanied by tasty tapas.

MORE TIME?

BUNKERS DEL CARMEL Just east of Parc Güell in the El Carmel district, take a climb up to the Rovira del Carmel bunkers to enjoy unique 360-degree views of the city (opposite), particularly beautiful at sunset. Built in 1930 to defend the city from aircraft fire during the Spanish Civil War, they also house a small museum.
TOSSA DE MAR This pretty Costa Brava town, a favourite of painter Marc Chagall, is a little better-preserved than some of its neighbours. Its hilltop Old Town, with the remains of a castle, is enchanting, even more so (perhaps especially) out of season.

LA RAMBLA

Running from Plaça de Catalunya to the sea, Barcelona's emblematic avenue owes its name to the Arabic word *ramla*, meaning 'muddy area' – a reference to the culvert that ran here during the Middle Ages, when what's now La Rambla was outside the town. This open sewer was covered with a stone pavement when Barcelona expanded; convents and monasteries were established, only to be destroyed or seized by the state in the 19th century and replaced by many of the buildings that still stand here – such as the Mercat de la Boqueria and the Gran Teatre del Liceu. Today, the city's tourist epicentre is often referred to in the plural, due to its five neighbourhood sections.

🅟 HOW TO GET THERE

Flights from Europe and around the world land at El Prat Airport, 17km (10.6 miles) southwest of Barcelona, from where there are buses to Plaça de Catalunya in the city centre. Direct high-speed train services link Barcelona Sants Station with several Spanish cities, as well as Paris, Lyon and Marseille.

🅦 WHERE TO EAT

Though it's thronged with locals and tourists alike, the Mercat de La Boqueria (boqueria. barcelona) is still full of charm, with long queues forming at stands selling local produce – cheeses, charcuterie, vegetables – inside this metal-framed, Modernista-style covered market on La Rambla. Some of the merchants run cafes and restaurants offering tapas, seafood and drinks, but you'll need to be patient to find a seat.

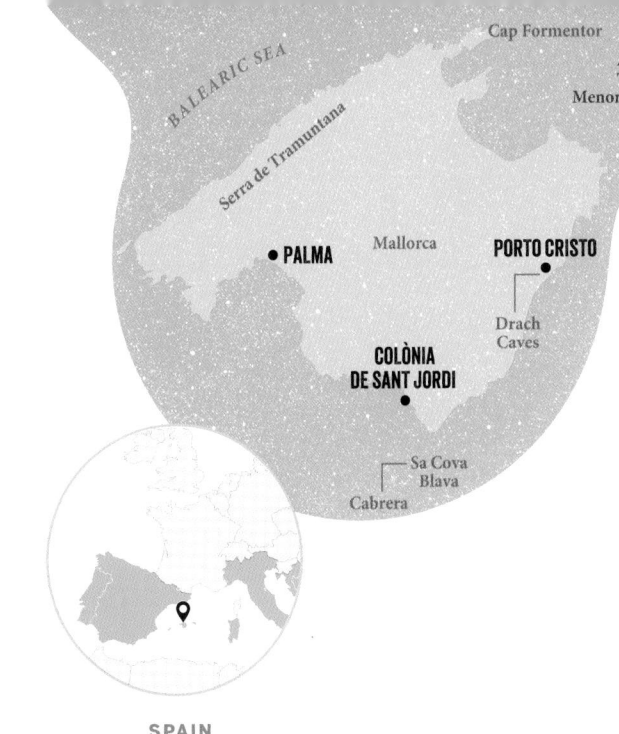

BALEARIC SEA

Cap Formentor

To Menorca

Serra de Tramuntana

● PALMA   Mallorca   PORTO CRISTO

Drach Caves

COLÒNIA DE SANT JORDI

Sa Cova Blava

Cabrera

SPAIN

06

Take the pulse of the MEDITERRANEAN IN MALLORCA

Sitting pretty in the **Mediterranean Sea off the Iberian Peninsula's northeast coast, the Balearics bring together islands with very different atmospheres.** If Ibiza is famous for its parties, neighbouring Formentera is known for its gentle way of life and white sandy beaches; if Menorca surprises with the extraordinary richness of its UNESCO Biosphere Reserve, Mallorca manages to deliver all of the above, concentrated in one little island. Though it's best-known for its glorious beaches, Mallorca is one of **the Mediterranean's great nature destinations**. Beyond the idyllic coastline and captivating resorts lies the UNESCO World Heritage **Serra de Tramuntana**, its **gnarly limestone peaks** and sheer cliffs plunging into translucent waters. The rural landscapes are gorgeous too, dotted with vineyards and carob, olive and almond orchards, the latter erupting in a cloud of blossom each spring; while the capital, **Palma, offers culture, nightlife and a knockout cathedral**. Mallorca's attractions are manifold; if you can, visit in mid-season to enjoy the island without the summer crowds.

Find portside perfection in Palma

With its honey-coloured buildings stretching back from the Badia de Palma, Mallorca's capital is a handsome introduction to the island. Headline attraction is the splendid Catedral de Mallorca (opposite; catedraldemallorca. org), built on the water in Catalan Gothic style – it's a sight to behold, especially at sunset. Other highlights include the Palau de l'Almudaina (patrimonionacional. es), official residence of the Spanish monarchy, and the Convent de Santa Clara (clarisaspalmamallorca.wordpress. com), built in the 16th and 17th centuries, where the nuns sell sweet treats like *rollitos de anís* (aniseed rolls) to visitors.

Tour & taste along Mallorca's wine route

One of the best ways to get to know Mallorca is to stay in traditional fincas, delightful agricultural estates offering accommodation to visitors; many of the island's bodegas – wineries that offer tastings – also have rooms to rent. Plot a route between them by following a wine route around the island through the villages of Algaida, Sineu, Santa Eugènia, Binissalem and Santa Maria del Camí. And don't forget to try the local Hierbas, a traditional liqueur made with aniseed and other Mallorcan aromatics.

Indulge in Mallorcan nightlife

Party people from all over the world flock to Palma's clubs, beach bars and pubs year-round. In the buzzing Santa Catalina district, enjoy a drink while sampling regional specialities like *pa amb oli* (bread seasoned with olive oil and tomato, and topped with cured ham and cheese) or the famous *sobrasada* (a spicy sausage). Lined with bars and restaurants overlooking the harbour, seafront Paseo Marítimo is another popular spot.

Go underground at Porto Cristo

They're no secret, but even given the crowds of visitors, it's well worth heading to the family resort of Porto Cristo to explore the Coves del Drac (cuevasdeldrach. com). During the hour-long tour, you'll admire stalactites and stalagmites illuminated by a beautiful light show, and take a turn in a boat on an underground lake.

Marvel at the works of Miró & Barceló

Overlooking the sea, away from Palma's centre, the Fundació Pilar i Joan Miró (miromallorca.com) is set in the former home of the Catalan painter, engraver, sculptor and ceramist, who lived here from 1956 until his death in 1983; visit his studio and see pieces from the 6000-plus collection of his works. But Miró isn't the only big name in the Mallorcan art scene: renowned painter, draughtsperson, sculptor and ceramist Miquel Barceló was born here in 1957, and you can see his work in Palma's cathedral, where he designed the interior of the Capella de Sant Pere.

MORE TIME?

CAP DE FORMENTOR The foothills of the Serra de Tramuntana meet the sea at the end of narrow Cap de Formentor (see previous page), Mallorca's northeastern tip. The winding road along the peninsula's coast offers lovely views of jagged peaks overhanging the waves, and sheer cliffs enclosing superb stretches of sand; it's a great place for some secluded beachtime.

ILLA DE CABRERA The largest of the 19 uninhabited islands that make up the Balearic Islands' only national marine park, Cabrera is a haven of peace. Access is limited to no more than 300 visitors every day; boat trips to the island from Colònia de Sant Jordi stop at the magnificent sea cave of Sa Cova Blava.

A CYCLISTS' PARADISE

Whether you're a serious cycling enthusiast, an intermediate or a weekend peddaller, Mallorca offers a multitude of possible routes. For the more athletically inclined, the Serra de Tramuntana offers challenging gradients. For a scenic seaside cycle, head out from Palma along the bay towards the south of the island, where you'll reach the small seaside resort of Colònia de Sant Jordi after 64km (40 miles). Bike rental is available in Palma and other main towns, and several companies organise all-expenses-paid cycling tours.

HOW TO GET THERE

Numerous low-cost seasonal flights from European destinations arrive at Palma International Airport, just 8km (5 miles) from Mallorca's capital. Boat travel is also an option, with several ferry companies operating between various towns on the Spanish coast (Alicante, Barcelona, Dénia and Valencia) and the island. From France, Corsica Ferries crosses from Toulon to Alcúdia in northeast Mallorca three times a week.

EVENTS

Staged over the last weekend before Lent, Mallorca's Carnival sees parades, street parties and live music in towns across the island, with the biggest events in Palma. One of Mallorca's most popular festivals, celebrating Palma's patron saint, the Festa Sant Sebastià takes place in January, with two weeks of cultural activities, sporting events and shows.

BALEARIC SEA

PORT DE
SANT MIQUEL

SANT CARLES
DE PERALTA

SANT ANTONI
DE PORTMANY

SANTA GERTRUDIS
DE FRUITERA

Ibiza

IBIZA (EIVISSA)

Es Vedrà

Parc Natural
de Ses Salines

To
Formentera

SPAIN

07

Discover the unexpected
IN IBIZA

The most famous of the Balearics is, paradoxically, the most misunderstood. It may be overshadowed by the party-hard reputation of its **iconic clubs** and world-class **DJ residencies** during the summer, but there's far more to Ibiza than just dancefloors and sunset chill-out bars. On the island's sublime **beaches**, you carve out a space in the sand even at the peak of high season; in the interior, discover whitewashed hamlets and organic vineyards. **Archaeological remains** such as the Necròpolis del Puig des Molins and the fortified Dalt Vila uncover

Ibiza's foundation by the Phoenicians, its occupation by the Moors and its battle against pirates; of more recent settlers, the hippy crowds that descended in the 1960s and 1970s have left their own mark in the island's alternative, **boho-cool spirit**. The same intimate, magnetic atmosphere reigns over Ibiza's smaller neighbour, **Formentera**, beach paradise of choice for lovers of seclusion by the sea. Whether you're in search of clubbing heaven or an island idyll where you can stay on agritourism farms and feast on fresh seafood, Ibiza and Formentera will deliver.

Explore the heart of Ibiza in Eivissa

In the historic capital of Ibiza Town (Eivissa in Catalan), head to the Upper Town of Dalt Vila to climb the 25m-high (82ft) ramparts, dating from the 16th century, then stroll through the cobbled streets of this UNESCO-listed fortified hilltop. Founded by the Phoenicians, Dalt Vila (opposite) has an exceptional heritage: medieval houses; the excellent Museu d'Art Contemporani (eivissa.es/mace), housed in a 17th-century gunpowder store; and, at the top of the hill, the elegant cathedral and the semi-ruined Castell d'Eivissa.

Reconnect with Ibiza's hippy heyday in the north of the island

There are three good reasons to visit the north of Ibiza: it's the least populated and most rural part of the island, its secluded coves are magnificent and relatively deserted even in high season, and it's in these villages that the hippy spirit lives on. To soak up the bohemian vibes, head to the beaches of Benirràs or Aigües Blanques (the latter a clothing-free zone); browse the stalls in the huge hippy market at Sant Carles de Peralta; and stroll through Santa Gertrudis, a whitewashed village of low-slung houses incorporating fine-art galleries, craft shops, boutiques and excellent cafe-restaurants.

Cool off in the island's caves

During the hottest hours of the day, take refuge underground to cool off and enjoy the spectacle offered by the island's caves. Around 20km (12 miles) north of Eivissa, turn east just before **Port de Sant Miquel** and drive around the promontory to reach the Cova de Can Marçà (inset), a former smugglers' hideout on the cliffside that's now been dramatically illuminated by coloured lights. On the west side of the island, in Sant Antoni, Cap Blanc is the only aquarium in the world housed in a natural cave, the Cova de ses Llagostes. Boardwalks over the tanks allow you to view the inhabitants, from groupers and wrasse to starfish and moray eels. Injured birds and marine animals, particularly sea turtles, are cared for before being reintroduced into the wild. In southern Ibiza, near the former quarry named in the 1970s as Atlantis for the chiselled shapes in the rocks, you can hike to the undeveloped Cova de Buda in about 30 minutes; the trail starts at Torre des Savinar.

Find fabulous beaches & super sunset spots

Ibiza is home to some of the most beautiful beaches in Spain, and perhaps in all of the Mediterranean. The western shores deliver unforgettable sunsets: head for the three sandy coves of Platges de Comte, from where you can admire the offshore Illa des Bosc. In the south, the island's main gay beach, Es Cavallet, is a stretch of immaculate white sand; while Platja de Ses Salines, set against imposing dunes, is one of Ibiza's most popular strips of sand. Family-friendly to its north, boho to its south, Salines offers a view of the glistening pink marshes at dusk.

MORE TIME?

FORMENTERA From May to October, a ferry leaves every 20 to 30 minutes (less often between November and April) from Ibiza Town for La Savina on Formentera. When you land on this 20km-long (12-mile) island, with just three villages, you might think there's nothing to do – but this low-key feel is the main draw. The UNESCO-listed Parc Natural de Ses Salines promises bird-rich marshes, saltpans and cliffs, while the white-sand beaches (the limpid waters come courtesy of offshore seagrass meadows) take on a sublime dimension along the Trucador Peninsula.

MYSTICAL ES VEDRÀ

A crag of rock off Ibiza's southwest coast, rising to a height of 382m (1253ft), Es Vedrà (see page 34) has long inspired myths. Some say it was the haunt of the sirens who, in Homer's *Odyssey*, tried to lure Odysseus to a watery grave. Others claim an association with Tanit, the Phoenician goddess of fertility, while a Carmelite priest is said to have seen the Virgin Mary appear here in the late 19th century. Another tall tale bestows Es Vedrà with a magnetic field so strong it renders compasses useless, and it's also claimed to be a hotspot for UFO sightings. Access to the island is prohibited; observe it from afar at the viewpoint signposted from Torre des Savinar.

(see page 34)

PRACTICALITIES

☀ WHEN TO GO

Ibiza is overcrowded during the summer season when the humidity can be very high. In spring and autumn, accommodation rates drop and water temperatures are pleasant.

🛫 HOW TO GET THERE

Budget operators offer direct flights to Ibiza Airport from London, Paris and other European cities.

🏠 WHERE TO STAY

Some 30 farmhouse hotels await you on the island: try the likes of Can Pere Sord (canperesord.com), with a spectacular hilltop location; Can Pujolet (canpujolet.com), an 18th-century finca; and Atzaró (atzaro.com), the ultimate in country luxury.

GRANADA
Parque Nacional
de Sierra Nevada
Mulhacén
Tabernas
Desert
BUBIÓN
CAPILEIRA
PAMPANEIRA
ALMERÍA
ALBORAN SEA

SPAIN

08

Take a culture trip
IN GRANADA &
ALMERÍA PROVINCE

Granada is best known for its Alhambra, the sublime legacy of Moorish rule in Andalucía between the 8th and 15th centuries. But this city in southern Spain has much more to offer than just its peak-framed palace. Its rich architectural heritage includes *cármenes*, private houses of Moorish origin, whose high walls conceal superb terraced gardens. You can visit them in the **Albaicín** (left), the old Islamic quarter, with its maze of cobbled streets and miradors (lookouts) offering unparalleled views over to the Alhambra. Don't underestimate the nightlife in this student city, which has no shortage of places to enjoy a **flamenco show**. Just outside Granada, the **Sierra Nevada** delights nature lovers and outdoor enthusiasts, some taking up the challenge of climbing the highest peak on the Spanish mainland, the 3479m-high (11,414ft) **Mulhacén**, or skiing in Europe's most southerly resort. In **Almería** region, you can make like a cowhand in the Western-themed parks of the Tabernas Desert, or take the coast road to the west or east of the province's eponymous city to explore a wild coastline.

Explore Granada's ancient cave houses

Granada's Sacromonte quarter offers superb views over to the Alhambra, but it has its own cultural draws. The area was once a stronghold of the Roma community, many of whom lived in homes built in the naturally abundant caves of the Sierra Nevada foothills here; the earliest date back to the 16th century. You can explore several cave homes, furnished in traditional style, at the Museo Cuevas del Sacromonte (sacromontegranada. com); flamenco shows in the Granaína style are also staged in several Sacromonte caves. For more underground allure, head to the catacombs and underground chapels of the 17th-century Abadía del Sacromonte (abadiasacromonte. com).

Go Wild West in the Tabernas Desert

Some 30km (19 miles) north of the city of Almería, this scrubby desert may well seem familiar, having served as the setting for several of Sergio Leone's spaghetti westerns, as well as episodes of *Game of Thrones*. With mocked-up Western-style towns and saloon bars, the Fort Bravo and Oasys MiniHollywood theme parks here offer an immersive dive into the Wild West of the silver screen, complete with cancan shows and staged shootouts.

Hike in the Sierra Nevada

Those snowcapped peaks that provide the backdrop to Granada's Alhambra are just a small part of the Parque Nacional Sierra Nevada, home to Iberian ibex and a wealth of plant species. Hikers take on multiday itineraries across this mighty mountain range; its lower southern reaches, peppered with picturesque white villages, are known as the Alpujarras (opposite). The villages of Pampaneira, Bubión and Capileira are popular starting points for hikes of varying length and difficulty.

Discover Andalucía's other Moorish fortress

Granada's richly decorated Alhambra (inset) is deservedly famous, but the Almería region's 10th-century Alcazaba is another magnificent Moorish marvel. Perched on a hilltop, it was once among the most powerful citadels in Spain, and is divided into distinct compounds: the lower Primer Recinto is notable for its lush gardens, laced with mini canals; the upper Tercer Recinto was added by Catholic Monarchs. Bonus: the tour is free!

MORE TIME?

COSTA TROPICAL South of Granada and west of Almería city, this stretch of cliffs, coves and eye-stretching beaches is a watersports paradise. You'll find all the facilities you need for diving, sailing and waterskiing in the coastal resorts of Almuñécar, Salobreña, Motril, Castell de Ferro and La Rábita.

PARQUE NATURAL DE CABO DE GATA-NÍJAR For a wilder coastline and a taste of windswept isolation, head east from Almería city to this stunning natural park in Andalucía's southeastern corner, with 340 sq km (131 sq miles) of volcanic cliffs, salt flats and hidden, sandy beaches.

TEA AT THE TETERÍAS

Unsurprisingly, Andalucía's 800 years of Moorish rule left a legacy that extends beyond headline sights like the Alhambra. Granada is still home to many *teterías*, Arabic teahouses with soft lighting and plush cushions that make them supremely relaxing places to enjoy mint tea and sweet pastries, as well as Middle Eastern meze; some also offer *cachimba* (shisha) pipes. You'll find several of these *teterías* – as well as shops selling clothing, rugs and homewares imported from Morocco – on Calle Calderería Nueva in the Albaicín district.

~ PRACTICALITIES ~

🖫 HOW TO GET THERE

The airports in Granada and Almería are served by direct flights from London, Paris and other European hubs, as well as domestic services within Spain.

📅 EVENTS

In June and July, Granada hosts the prestigious Festival Internacional de Música y Danza (granadafestival.org), with classical music concerts in venues all around the city as well as live flamenco and world-music shows. In November, it's the turn of the Festival Internacional de Jazz (jazzengranada.es). The Feria de Almería takes place in the port city over nine days in late August, with parties, concerts, fairground rides and exhibitions.

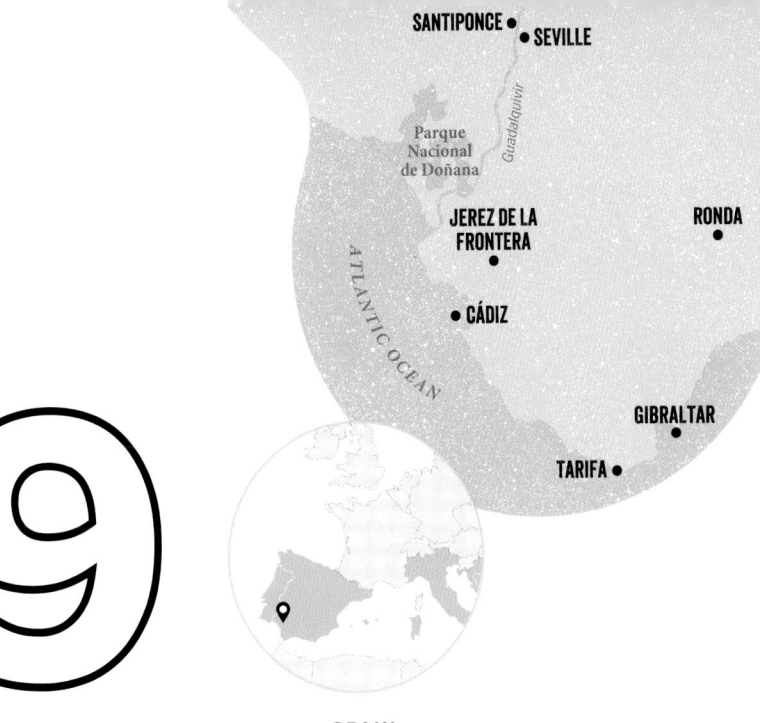

SANTIPONCE • • SEVILLE

Parque
Nacional
de Doñana

Guadalquivir

ATLANTIC OCEAN

JEREZ DE LA
FRONTERA
•

RONDA
•

• CÁDIZ

GIBRALTAR
•

TARIFA •

SPAIN

09

Be bedazzled by
SEVILLE & THE COSTA DE LA LUZ

The home of flamenco, **this sun-drenched corner of Andalucía, in the very south of Spain, is simply spell-binding.** Thanks to its rich cultural and architectural heritage, Seville (left) is the region's standout city. Topped by the mighty Giralda bell tower, its awe-inspiring **Gothic cathedral** is the world's largest, while the magnificent **Real Alcázar** (Royal Palace; alcazarsevilla.org) is a feast of Mudéjar architecture, and the **Museo de Bellas Artes** has paintings by Murillo, El Greco and Velázquez. Then head south for about 100km (62 miles) to

discover the sherry capital of **Jerez de la Frontera**, enjoying tastings in the *tabancos* and taking in an equestrian show before heading on to **Cádiz**, a port city with a beautiful seafront promenade, inviting beaches, a captivating Old Town, a Roman theatre and a diverting food scene. Finally, set off to admire the wild beauty of the **Costa de la Luz**, its Atlantic shores facing over the Strait of Gibraltar to Morocco. With a smaller visitor footfall than Andalucía's Mediterranean coast, this **windswept 'coast of light'** is one of Europe's top destinations for windsurfers and surfers.

Walk in the footsteps of the Romans in Itálica

Santiponce, just northwest of central Seville, holds the extensive site of Itálica (italicasevilla. org), founded in 206 BCE as the first Roman city in Spain. With its wide paved streets, temples and mansions – such as the Casa del Planetario (House of the Planetarium) – sporting well-preserved mosaic floors (inset), it's a spectacular sight. The highlight is the superb amphitheatre, which could seat up to 25,000 spectators.

Peek at pink flamingos in the Parque Nacional de Doñana

Spreading back from the Atlantic coast southwest of Seville, covering some 543 sq km (210 sq miles) in the heart of the Guadalquivir Delta, this UNESCO World Heritage-listed national park is an oasis of biodiversity. Its wetlands, beaches, dunes and woodlands provide a habitat for pink flamingos and hordes of migratory birds, as well as herds of deer and wild boar and smaller numbers of endangered but elusive Iberian lynx. Vehicle access is forbidden beyond the visitor centres, but you can enjoy beautiful hikes, or take part in organised tours in off-road vehicles, bookable through approved agencies such as Doñana Nature (donana-nature.com) or Doñana Reservas (donanareservas.com). Don't forget your binoculars!

Marvel at an equestrian or flamenco show in Jerez

The capital of Andalucían equestrian culture, Jerez de la Frontera is home to the Real Escuela Andaluza del Arte Ecuestre (realescuela.org), where shows see the horses put through their paces to music. Jerez is also the cradle of flamenco (though Seville and Cádiz lay an equal claim); the *bulería* style was born here, in the Roma barrios of Santiago and San Miguel. It would be remiss to visit without taking in a live show in one of the *peñas* (private clubs) or *flamenco tablaos* along Calle Francos in Santiago.

Tame the wind in Tarifa

The southernmost town on the Costa de la Luz, Tarifa (opposite) is the meeting point of the Mediterranean and the Atlantic, and a magnet for watersports enthusiasts. The atmosphere is relaxed in the 'Windy City', with its winding whitewashed streets and walled Old Town giving it a Moroccan air. By day, take your pick from windsurfing, kitesurfing and surfing at nearby Punta Paloma or Playa de Valdevaqueros; by night, leave the waves behind to chill out in Tarifa's bohemian bars and eateries.

PUEBLOS BLANCOS Established between the 13th and 15th centuries, these fortified 'white villages' on the one-time Moorish-Christian border, high up in the northeast of Cádiz province, stand testament to a turbulent history. Wind your way through whitewashed streets in Arcos de la Frontera, El Bosque or Grazamela.
RONDA Some 130km (80 miles) southeast of Seville and built on a dramatic mountain gorge carved by the Río Guadalevín, Ronda was a favourite haunt of Alexandre Dumas, Ernest Hemingway and Orson Welles. Enjoy spectacular views from the Puente Nuevo.

MORE TIME?

GIBRALTAR

Since capturing it in 1704, the UK has controlled this limestone outcrop of the Andalucían coast, which was officially ceded by Spain in 1713. At 426m (1398ft) high and some 5km (3 miles) long, Gibraltar lies just under 50km (30 miles) northeast of Tarifa, but it cultivates its British side, replete with tearooms and pubs; legend has it that if the Barbary macaques that inhabit the upper reaches of the 'Rock' disappear, so will the Brits. Despite its official status as a British Overseas Territory, Gibraltar enjoys a degree of autonomy: though it's no longer part of the EU post-Brexit, Gibraltar joined the Schengen area in 2021, so European nationals need only present ID at the border.

PRACTICALITIES

🚉 HOW TO GET THERE

Around 10km (6 miles) north of the city, Seville Airport has flights from most European capitals; the airport in Jerez handles domestic flights.

📅 EVENTS

Staged over 10 days in February, Carnival in Cádiz is a hugely popular event, with masked *murgas* parades and processions, concerts and dancing and singing in the streets, plus comedy, street theatre and puppet shows. Seville's famous Feria de Abril takes place two weeks after Easter, with six days of horse-drawn-carriage parades, feasts and *sevillana* dancing. During the Bienal de Flamenco, held in September on even-numbered years, the great names of flamenco come together to perform in Seville.

10

Uncover Portugal's history
IN THE MINHO

The fertile Minho region, Portugal's far north, is a source of national strength and character. Some 50km (31 miles) northeast of Porto, the medieval village of **Guimarães** (overleaf) was the birthplace, in 1110, of Portugal's first independent king, Afonso I, and thus of the Portuguese kingdom. Today, visiting heads of state stay at the Gothic **Paço dos Duques de Bragança** (Palace of the Dukes; pacodosduques.gov.pt). Continuing northwest, Minho capital **Braga** holds the title of oldest city in the country, founded over 2000 years ago by the Romans and nicknamed the 'Portuguese Rome' for its many religious monuments, including its ancient **Sé** (cathedral). The location of Braga's **Museo dos Biscaínhos** (museudosbiscainhos.gov.pt), in an 18th-century aristocrat's palace with lovely gardens, is as much of a draw as the displays, while the **Centro Interpretativo das Memórias da Misericórdia**, in the rococo **Palácio do Raio** (scmbraga.pt), is a riot of blue azulejo tiles. Northeast of Braga, **Parque Nacional da Peneda-Gerês** preserves peaks, valleys and lush forests, as well as a smattering of traditional granite villages.

Climb to the Bom Jesus do Monte pilgrimage site

The neoclassical church of Bom Jesus do Monte watches over the city of Braga from its hilltop perch, 5km (3 miles) to the east. To reach it, pilgrims – the most zealous ascending on their knees – climb the 580 steps of its Escadaria do Bom Jesus do Monte (see previous page), a sumptuous, zigzagging baroque staircase embellished with chapels, fountains and sculptures. Its stages represent the five senses and the virtues of faith, hope and charity. The less devout can also get to the top via a 19th-century funicular railway.

Marvel at the espigueiros

The Parque Nacional da Peneda-Gerês (opposite) is home to scores of little villages where traditional life still holds strong, and where you can see 18th-century *espigueiros*: diminutive granite granaries set on stilts, with crosses at each end to ward off evil spirits. Ventilated by slits in the walls, they were used to store corn away from marauding pests. The village of Soajo has 24 hillside-perched *espigueiros*; a few kilometres further on, Lindoso is home to an even more impressive group, with some 60 *espigueiros* adjoining the medieval castle.

Tour 'Little Tibet'

Framed by the magnificent terraced fields that give it its surprising nickname, the village of Sistelo is a hikers' paradise. Experienced walkers head out on the steep Trilho das Brandas de Sistelo, a 9km (5.6-mile) walk that offers views of the mountains, where *cachenas* (long-horned cows) and wild *garrano* horses (an ancient Portuguese breed) graze freely. For those put off by steep slopes, the 2km (1.2-mile) Trilho dos Passadiços tracks through forest and across a series of wooden bridges. Visit the Arcos de Valdevez tourist office for more info.

Dip into natural pools in Peneda-Gerês

Spreading across 703 sq km (271 sq miles) of northern Portugal, Parque Nacional da Peneda-Gerês is one of the country's best-kept secrets, with lush green mountains and crystal-clear pools where you can enjoy a refreshing dip. Easily accessible from the N308-1, the Cascata da Portela do Homem offers delightful swimming in clear turquoise waters. Nearby, a path leads to the Mata da Albergaria waterfalls through a magnificent forest of ancient trees. Near the village of Xertelo, the Cascata das Sete Lagoas offers seven natural pools of varying depths.

MORE TIME?

GEIRA ROMANA This Roman road once linked Portugal to Spain; today, it offers the opportunity to hike in the heart of nature in the Parque Nacional da Peneda-Gerês. The route is still lined with well-preserved milestones, and explanatory panels give insights into its history along the way.

VILA DO GERÊS This popular spa town is the perfect place to relax in thermal pools after a hike in the national park, and its pretty gardens are home to a small lake where you can go boating.

VINHO VERDE

A speciality of the Minho, Vinho Verde (meaning 'green wine') owes its name not to its colour, but to its youthfulness. Bottled early, it is often slightly sparkling. The best-known Vinho Verde wines are light, fresh whites, made with grapes grown on climbing or hanging vines, freeing up space for other crops such as cereals or fodder. A few pergola vineyards can still be seen in the area today. For more on the region, visit the Vinho Verde website (vinhoverde.pt), which also has details of the Vinho Verde Wine Route. The Vinho Verde Interpretation Center in Ponte de Lima, some 40km (25 miles) northeast of Braga, offers tasting sessions.

~ PRACTICALITIES ~

HOW TO GET THERE

The international airport in Porto has direct flights from most European capitals, as well as New York and Toronto. Cars can be hired at the airport or in Porto itself to reach Braga, an hour's drive away.

WHERE TO STAY & EAT

For a splurge, try the Vila Galé Collection Braga (vilagale.com), with palatial rooms in a former hospital and convent dating to 1508; or the contemporary suites at at Tea 4 Nine. When it's time to eat, opt for vintage-themed Retrokitchen's comforting plates.

Elsewhere, Portugal's historic pousadas (pousadas.pt) are a great choice: in Guimarães, there's the Pousada Mosteiro, a one-time monastery converted into a hotel; close to the national park, Pousada Caniçada-Gerês has incredible views. Also in Gerês, Hotel Carvalho Araújo (hotelcarvalhoaraujo.com) offers well-appointed rooms. Visiting Soajo, you can enjoy regional specialities at Saber ao Borralho.

EVENTS

In June, Braga is lit up for the lively São João festival, with music, folk dancing and parades.

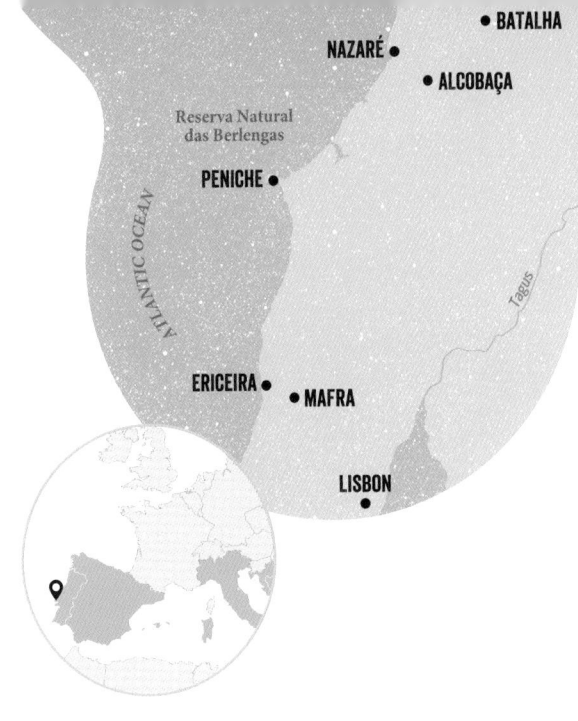

PORTUGAL

11

Explore the coast
BETWEEN ERICEIRA & NAZARÉ

With its long Atlantic shoreline, Portugal is a land sprinkled by sea spray and lulled by the surf. North of Lisbon, in the swathe of coast between Ericeira and Nazaré, the days unfold to the rhythm of the waves: the residents of pretty fishing villages share their long sandy beaches with surfers from all over the world, and cook up the catch of the day in seafood restaurants. With its many surf schools, **Ericeira** is the ideal place to get started. Beginners will prefer the gentler breaks at **Foz do Lizandro** and **Praia do Sul**, while experienced surfers head to **Ribeira d'Ilhas** and **Praia dos Coxos**, the scene of the biggest international competitions. Following the coast 85km (53 miles) north, the port of **Peniche** stands on a rocky promontory, overlooking the relentless rollers of **Praia dos Supertubos**. Another 65km (40 miles) on, **Nazaré** is one of Portugal's most picturesque coastal villages, its cobbled lanes running down towards the beach. Offshore, the legendarily huge breakers that roll in here during the winter months attract big-wave **surfers** and crowds of spectators.

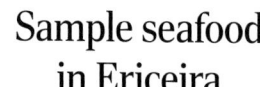

Set sail for the Berlengas archipelago

Just 15km (9 miles) offshore of Peniche, the islands of the Reserva Natural das Berlengas are an important nesting site for seabirds and migratory species. The only visitable island is Berlenga Grande, 45 minutes by ferry from Peniche, where you can hike the east coast to a lofty lighthouse and the impressive 16th-century fort of São João Baptista (opposite). From the main dock, boat rides head around the coast, taking in the Cova do Sonho (Dream Cave), and there's fantastic swimming and snorkelling in the limpid waters of Carreiro do Mosteiro beach. Bring a picnic, as dining options are limited.

Watch surfers brave the waves in Nazaré

Imagine a mountain of moving water, a tiny surfer towed by a Jet Ski and a sublime swoop on the swell before the wave breaks in a deafening crash – this is surfing in Nazaré, home of some of the largest waves on Earth. In winter, the breakers here can reach 30m (98ft) in height, the equivalent of an eight-storey building; and in 2020, in front of a stunned audience, noted big-wave surfer Sebastian Steudtner set a new record here for the highest wave ever surfed – 26.2m (86ft). The cliffside fort of São Miguel Arcanjo (inset) makes a spectacular viewpoint for watching the bold and the brave take on the challenge of besting Steudtner's record.

Enjoy beachtime & boats in Nazaré

There's more to Nazaré than just its monster waves. At the foot of the historic centre, the town's wide, cliff-backed beach is ideal for an afternoon of idleness: rent one of the colourful cabanas on the sand if you need some shade, take invigorating dips in the Atlantic and watch the intrepid surfers in the distance. Nazaré is primarily a fishing village, and at the end of the beach, you'll see colourful traditional boats pulled up on the shore. And after a day by the sea, ride the funicular up to the Promontório do Sítio to enjoy heady views.

Sample seafood in Ericeira

With a gorgeous coastline and renowned surf breaks, the fishing village of Ericeira is also famed for its seafood. It's a popular getaway spot for *lisboêtas*, who escape the hustle and bustle of the capital for a few days of sun, sea and feasting. Menus here are dictated by whatever the boats bring in, from freshly hauled crab and shrimp to just-netted fish. Wander through the old centre around Praça da República to find a table, or head for the beach and its Clube Naval, a no-frills cafe popular with fisherfolk.

MORE TIME?

PALÁCIO NACIONAL Mafra's monumental baroque palace is home to no fewer than 1200 rooms, including the stone-clad Blessing Room and a vast barrel-vaulted library.

MARVELLOUS MONASTERIES A 12th-century Gothic masterpiece, Alcobaça's Mosteiro de Santa Maria complex (mosteiroalcobaca. gov.pt) holds an austere and vast church, its long, narrow nave lined with oversized pillars; splendid tombs commemorate Dom Pedro I and his lover, Inês de Castro, protagonists in the country's most tragic love story. Some 20km (12 miles) northeast, the Gothic Mosteiro da Batalha (mosteirobatalha.gov.pt) features a gloriously detailed interior.

FISHING THE TRADITIONAL WAY

Typical of the Portuguese coast, *Arte-Xávega* is an artisanal fishing technique in which nets are cast from wooden boats close to the shore, and then hauled back on to the sand by oxen, with the fish sold immediately on the beach. Tractors have replaced oxen these days, but you can still see things done the traditional way in Nazaré, where the local fishers stage regular demonstrations.

~~~~~ PRACTICALITIES ~~~~~

☼ WHEN TO GO

Beginner surfers will prefer the period between May and September. From September to April, the swell becomes more powerful, whipped up by winds that delight big-wave surfers.

🛢 HOW TO GET THERE

Lisbon's Humberto Delgado Airport is Potrugal's primary international hub, served by direct flights from across Europe and destinations worlwide. Car rental is available at the airport or in Lisbon itself.

⛺ WHERE TO STAY & EAT

In Ericeira, opt for the sea-view Laneez Ericeira Surf House (laneezericeira.com) or the luxurious Aethos Ericeira (aethos.com). For food, don't miss Costa Fria's inventive dishes. In Peniche, try the Mercearia d'Alegria (merceariadalegria.pt). Nazaré's Zulla Surf Village (zulla.pt) has private and shared rooms, and its own surf school. La Rosa dos Ventos is a family-run restaurant serving excellent fish and seafood, all super-fresh.

Serra de Monchique

PORTIMÃO

ALVOR

LAGOS

LAGOA

SILVES

CARVOEIRO

ALBUFEIRA

FERRAGUDO

Algar de Benagil

OLHÃO

FARO

ATLANTIC OCEAN

PORTUGAL

12

Combine nature & culture

IN FARO &
THE ALGARVE

Situated in the extreme south of Portugal, the Algarve capital of Faro – said to bask in sunshine for 300 days of the year – is a city steeped in history. Encircled by medieval ramparts, its **Cidade Velha** (Old Town) is best accessed via the neoclassical Arco da Vila gateway. Then stroll to the **18th-century Sé** (cathedral), where the tower affords lovely views across the walled town and estuary islands, and take a look at the nearby Museu Municipal, housed in a 16th-century former convent. On your way out, admire the Jardim Manuel Bívar, buy sardines at Conserveira de Portugal, then enjoy a cinnamon-laced Dom Rodrigo, an Algarve speciality, in one of the town's tearooms. History and pastries digested, consider taking a **boat trip** to admire the coast between Faro and **Lagos**, or booking a dolphin-watching cruise between the marina in **Albufeira** and **Carvoeiro** (left) – the best time to see them is from May to October. More comfortable on land? Rent a bike in Faro and follow one of the 40-odd signposted routes from the city, heading west to **Alvor** or east to **Olhão**.

See the Algarve coast from a hot-air balloon

From Lagos – an hour's drive or two hours by train from Faro – Algarve Balloons (algarveballoons.com) offer a different way to see the sights: a bird's-eye view of the region from the basket of a hot-air balloon. Flights skirt along the coastline, taking in the cliffs, sandy beaches and turquoise waters below; conditions depending, you might drift over Faro and its stocky cathedral, or the russet-coloured roofs and of Silves, crowned by the terracotta turrets of a Moorish-era castle. Departing around dawn, the hour-long flights include transport back from the landing spot; allow around four hours in total.

Hike the Seven Hanging Valleys Trail

The gentle 5.7km (3.5-mile) Percurso dos Sete Vales Suspensos runs east along the ocean and the karst cliffs between Praia de Vale Centeanes and Praia da Marinha. Sights along the way include the chapel of Senhora da Rocha, the Alfanzina Lighthouse, built in 1920, Benagil Beach – you'll peek into its famous caves (opposite), which are only accessible from the water – and the the rock arches near Praia da Marinha. Leave early in the morning to avoid the crowds and the heat, and bring swimming gear for mid-hike dips. The closest access point to Praia de Vale Centeanes is the town of Lagoa, 60km (37 miles) west of Faro.

Visit Portimão's state-of-the-art museum

Around an hour an a half by train or an hour's drive from Faro, Portimão is home to the ultramodern Museu de Portimão (museudeportimao.pt). Housed in a 19th-century fish cannery, its displays trace local history, with a particular focus on the fishing industry that has contributed so much to the region; the fascinating recreation of the cannery is a highlight.

Take a stroll in Alvor

About 75km (47 miles) west of Faro, Portimão's neighbour, Alvor, is one of the oldest towns in the Algarve. Take a wander through the historic centre, then hit the sands of its 3.5km-long (2-mile) beach. Winding around the headland to the west of the town, a 5km (3-mile) boardwalk threads through the Ria de Alvor Nature Reserve, where the salt marshes and mudflats provide a habitat for numerous bird species.

Enjoy fresh fish in Olhão

Located 10km (6 miles) east of Faro, Olhão is the Algarve's biggest fishing port, with a busy harbour and, unsurprisingly, some great restaurants serving fresh-off-the-boat fish. Its flat-roofed, Moorish-influenced architecture and North African feel make it an alluring place to explore, and it's especially lively during the Saturday morning produce market, with stalls ranged along the waterfront.

MORE TIME?

SERRA DE MONCHIQUE Rising up to the 773m-high (2536ft) Mt Picota, this forest-clad range offers some excellent hiking and mountain biking; routes span out from the hamlet of Monchique, suitable for beginners and experienced riders and walkers.
VICENTINE COAST In the west of the Algarve, this wild slice of coast (inset) with its dramatic black cliffs is protected as a natural park. Just below the river-straddled town of Aljezur, Praia de Monte Clérigo is a laid-back surfers' hangout; to the southwest, Praia da Arrifana promises more breaks and a picturesque offshore rock stack.

THE PORTUGUESE CATAPLANA

Just as the Chinese have the wok and the Spanish the paella pan, so the Portuguese have the *cataplana*, a concave, two-handled liddled pan, usually made of copper or brass, that's used for stewing or steaming food on the stove or in the oven, and as a serving dish. But *cataplana* is also the name of the Algarve's speciality dish; there are many recipes and variations, but essentially it's a delicious seafood stew, often laced with spicy sausage and served with rice or crusty bread.

🅿 HOW TO GET THERE

Faro International Airport is 4km (2.5 miles) west of the city, with flights from Europe, the UK and the US.

🏨 WHERE TO STAY & EAT

In Faro, the conveniently located Hotel 3HB (3hb.com) offers comfortable rooms, a spa, a pool with a view and big terrace. You'll also find good-value hotels in Portimão and Alvor. In Almancil, 13km (8 miles) northwest of Faro, the seafront 2 Passos (restaurante2passos.com) offers reliably good fish, seafood and steaks. In Faro, Tertúlia Algarvia (tertulia-algarvia.pt) shines a light on local produce, from fish and seafood to Algarve-reared chicken, pork and beef and carob-laced desserts.

📅 EVENTS

From 29 December until 1 January, the Medieval Festival in Paderne, 35km (22 miles) northwest of Faro, sees the town dressed as it would have looked in the Middle Ages, with local people donning period garb and selling era-appropriate food and drink, plus live music, sword-fighting displays and parades. In nearby Loulé, 17km (10.5 miles) from Faro, the pre-Lenten Carnival is the oldest such event in Portugal, with Brazil-esque costume parades and floats bedecked with giant puppets satirising Portuguese public figures.

VILA BALEIRA •
• Porto Santo

Madeira
CURRAL
DAS FREIRAS • ⌐ Pico do Arieiro

• FUNCHAL

Cape Girão

Ilhas
Desertas

PORTUGAL

13

Discover tropical Europe
IN MADEIRA

An isolated island archipelago, out in the Atlantic
off the coast of Morocco,
**this little piece of Portugal
promises a slice of the exotic.**
Geologically dramatic, swathed
in subtropical greenery and with
a year-round mild climate, the
volcanic main island of Madeira is
the big draw. Although very busy,
Funchal, the capital, is well worth a
visit; highlights include its 16th-cen-
tury Sé (cathedral), as well as the
historic Praça do Município, the Art
Deco Mercado dos Lavradores, and
the floor-to-ceiling azulejos of the
Convento de Santa Clara. Madeira's
rugged interior is ideal for **hiking**.
Enjoy breathtaking panoramic views
from **Miradouro dos Balcões** and
the 1820m (5971ft) **Pico do Arieiro**,
one of the island's highest points.
The island's loftiest sea cliffs, the
Cabo Girão rise almost 600m
(1970ft) above sea level; take in the
coast from the vertigo-inducing
glass-floored viewing platform. And
don't forget to try the **local specialities** – such as *espada* (black
scabbardfish) with fried bananas, or
espetadas, marinated beef kebabs
– as well as visiting a local winery to
sample sweet Madeira wine, ideal as
an accompaniment to dessert.

Swim in volcanic pools

Madeira isn't renowned for its beaches. The sand at Praia da Calheta or Praia de Machico was imported from Morocco and the western Sahara, but both beaches offer excellent swimming and watersports nonetheless. However, many prefer to swim in a more natural setting, taking a dip in the many coastal rock pools of this volcanic island, which fill with seawater as the waves and tides roll in; some are well equipped with staircases, terraces and so forth. Top spots include the lava pool at the resort of Porto Moniz (opposite) on the north coast, or Funchal's Complexo Balnear Doca do Cavacas.

Explore Madiera's levadas

Latticing across Madeira, the island's 2500km (1553 miles) of narrow irrigation canals, known as *levadas*, have carried water to the most remote corners since the 15th century. The *levadas* also offer a wonderful way to get out into the heart of the island: a network of well-maintained hiking trails (inset) runs alongside them, taking walkers into beautiful and varied landscapes, sometimes snaking through tunnels and over bridges. The routes vary in difficulty: Funchal's tourist office (visitmadeira.com) can help to organise hikes independently, or you can join a guided tour.

Luxuriate in lofty gardens

The Jardins Botânicos da Madeira (see previous page; telefericojardimbotanico.com), on this 'island of eternal spring', is a marvel. Perched high above Funchal, and spread over some 8 hectares (20 acres) of gently sloping land, it's home to more than 2000 plants and trees from all over the world, some of them endangered. Nearby, the Monte Palace Tropical Garden has more exotic flora alongside fountains, grottoes, sculptures and follies. Both gardens are reachable by cable car; the two routes each offer spectacular views of Funchal and the surrounding coastline from their upper stations.

Go door-to-door in Zona Velha

Since 2011, as part of the Projecto Arte Portas Abertas (Open Doors to Art Project; arteportasabertas. com), local artists and creative residents have been decorating the dilapidated doors of old houses and abandoned stores in this old quarter of Funchal. Take a stroll through the streets (especially Rua de Santa Maria) to discover this unique street art. You can also enjoy the vibrant nightlife of the Zona Velha, which the project has helped to revitalise.

MORE TIME?

PORTO SANTO Reachable by boat in about an hour and a half, this small island in the Madeira archipelago is famous for its 8km (5 miles) of fine, wild sandy beach. In the capital, Vila Baleira, the Casa Museu Colombo is reputed to have been the home of Christopher Columbus, whose father-in-law was governor here.
ILHAS DESERTAS These three small, uninhabited islands to the southeast of Madeira are a protected area; take a boat trip with Ventura (venturadomar.com) to discover their marine- and birdlife.

MORE THAN MADEIRA

Madeira's famous sweet wine is well worth tasting, and there's no shortage of places to do so, including producers Pereira D'Oliveira (doliveiras.pt) and Henriques & Henriques (henriquesehenriques. pt). But don't miss out on sampling typical drinks such as *poncha* (punch), made with potent *aguardente de cana* (sugar-cane spirit); the classic Pescador version is made with just lemon and sugar (or sometimes honey), while the Regional adds orange juice. Other local tipples include *ginja*, a cherry-based liqueur produced in Curral das Freiras and sometimes served in a chocolate cup; or the island's Coral and Zarco beers.

⌇ PRACTICALITIES ⌇

🗘 HOW TO GET THERE

Named after the island's most famous son, Cristiano Ronaldo Madeira International Airport, in the east-coast city of Santa Cruz, has direct flights from most European capital cities; as well as New York's JFK, and Toronto in Canada.

📅 EVENTS

The island's pre-Lenten Carnival is the biggest festival in Madeira, with around two weeks of celebrations – costumed processions, street shows – centred on Funchal. The Festa da Flor (April or May) sees an explosion of colour, with parades of flower-bedecked floats.

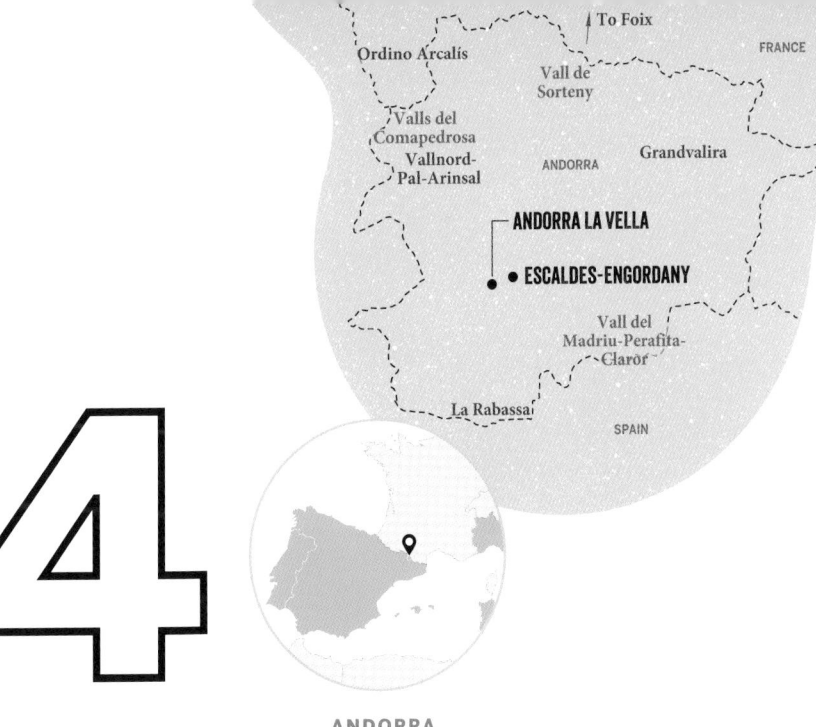

ANDORRA

14

Find summer & winter fun
IN ANDORRA

Located in the heart of the Pyrenees between France and Spain, 185km (115 miles) from Toulouse and about the same from Barcelona, the small, discreet principality of Andorra is best known to its regional neighbours for its bargainous shopping.** It's true that a visit to the capital, Andorra la Vella, to buy perfumes, electronics and spirits at reduced prices at its vast open-air **Shopping Mile** mall, is almost obligatory for many. But Andorra has many other natural assets: this tiny territory of just 468 sq km (181 sq miles) features 65 **peaks** topping 2500m (8202ft), and some 300km (186

miles) of **ski slopes**. With its three resorts – **Grandvalira**, the largest; **Vallnord-Pal-Arinsal** and **Ordino Arcalís** – it's a paradise for **winter-sports** enthusiasts, with skiing and tobogganing, snowshoeing and snowmobiling. But the principality is just as welcoming when the snow is gone, with beautiful **walks** in nature parks, such as **Comapedrosa** (left; comapedrosa.ad) and **Sorteny** (sorteny.ad). There are cultural draws, too: in **Andorra la Vella**, pay a visit to the graceful former parliament building, **Casa de la Vall**; and the collection of vintage cars, motorbikes and bicycles in the **Museu Nacional de l'Automòbil**.

Pamper yourself at the spa

Want to relax your muscles after a day's hiking? Head for Caldea (caldea.com), reputed to be the largest thermal spa in southern Europe, with the naturally heated waters in its pools maintained at around 32°C (90°F). It comprises three areas: Likids has a playroom, a pool and a wellness area for young children, while Thermoludic is family-friendly, with an indoor lagoon dotted with Jacuzzis and an outdoor 'panoramic' pool, plus a hammam, Roman baths and aqua-massage. Inúu is adults only, with more pools, saunas, indoor and outdoor Jacuzzis and relaxation areas, as well as therapy rooms, where you can indulge in massages, beauty treatments and the like.

Hike in a pristine valley reserve

Occupying nearly 10% of Andorra's entire land area, the 42-sq-km (16-sq-mile) Vall del Madriu-Perafita-Claror (madriu-perafita-claror.ad) is a protected valley, listed by UNESCO as a World Heritage Site. Its cliffs, Alpine meadows, rivers and lakes – some 30 in all, including Lac de la Nou and Lac Blau, both renowned for their beauty – provide a habitat for all kinds of wildlife (you're sure to come across marmots, foxes and mouflons) and offer a fabulous backdrop for hiking. The network of trails link five high-mountain refuges, where you can spend the night during an extended trek.

Mush through the mountains on a dogsled ride

You don't have to travel to a Scandinavian country to try your hand at mushing. At an altitude of over 2000m (6562ft), Grandvalira is the largest ski resort in the Pyrenees, and several operators here offer dogsled rides (inset). Swishing along by day behind a team of happy huskies delivers wonderful mountain scenery, but booking one of the evening mushing excursions offers an extra touch of magic.

Book a ticket to ride & dine

Skis are not the only way to explore Andorra's mountains. Gicafer Nature run sightseeing trips up into the slopes around the Ordino Arcalís resort in an all-terrain caterpillar vehicle; snowshoeing and quad-biking excursions are also available. Afterwards, enjoy mountain cuisine with a breathtaking view over the valley at the Borda de la Coma restaurant.

MORE TIME?

NATURLAND This mountain adventure park in the La Rabassa area offers a wide range of activities year-round, from mountain biking, pedal-karting, ziplining and horseback riding to the Tobotronc, the world's longest alpine toboggan, which runs for over 5km (3 miles) through the forest. Once the snow falls, winter activities include Nordic skiing, sledging, sleigh-touring and taking a spin on a MoonBike, an ultralight electric snowmobile. Visit the Naturland website (naturland.ad) for more information.

BOUNTIFUL BORDAS

To discover Andorra's mountain cuisine, there's nothing better than a visit to a *borda*. In the past, grain and fodder were stored on the upper floors of these buildings, while the first floor housed livestock. Many have now been converted into restaurants serving typical local dishes, such as *trinxat* (a sort of hash pancake of cabbage, mashed potatoes, leeks and bacon), *escudella* (a warming meat and vegetable stew), meats cooked *a la pedra* (stone-grilled), and local charcuterie such as *llonganissa* and *botifarra* sausages.

~ PRACTICALITIES ~

HOW TO GET THERE

With no airpoirt or train stations within the principality, getting to mountain-bound Andorra can be tricky. The nearest train station – L'Hospitalet-près-l'Andorre – is 11km (7 miles) from Andorra's northeast border in the Ariège, with services from Toulouse (home of the nearest airport). Buses run from the airport and Toulouse Matabiau station to Andorra la Vella (andbus.net) in around three hours, and Barcelona in around four hours.

WHERE TO EAT

In Andorra la Vella, La Borda Estevet (bordaestevetandorra. com) is one of the best *bordas* in Andorra. You'll enjoy seasonal cuisine, with rustic specialities alongside Mediterranean dishes.

15

ITALY

CERVETERI •
Lago di Bracciano
Tiber (Tevere)
• TIVOLI
• ROME
OSTIA •
• CASTEL GANDOLFO
Lazio
Appian Way
SABAUDIA •

Cross through the centuries
IN ROME & LAZIO

With its haunting ruins, awe-inspiring art and buzzing street life, Italy's charismatic capital is rightly proud of its past – and what a past it is. The city's **Roman-era remains range** from the **Colosseum**, the 50,000-seat arena where gladiators fought, to the sprawl of ruins in the **Roman Forum** (left) and the mighty temple of the **Pantheon**. There's far more to Rome than its ancient sites, of course, and the sumptuous array of buildings from the following centuries are overflowing with artistic riches, from the spectacular **Vatican Museums** and **Sistine Chapel**, the latter home to Michelangelo's ceiling frescoes and his *Last Judgement*; to hallowed **St** Peter's Basilica** or the **Museo e Galeria Borghese** and its Renaissance treasures. Then there are exuberantly decorated squares, such as **Piazza di Spagna** with its sparkling Spanish Steps; elegant **Piazza Navona**; or **Piazza di Trevi**, with its famous baroque fountain. And after a day of seeing the sights, enjoy an aperitivo on a terrace in the historic centre, or at night out in the boho **Trastevere** district on the banks of the Tiber. Beyond Rome, however, the wider delights of the **Lazio region** beckon: **Etruscian and Roman remains** and fabulous Renaissance villas adorned with refined **Italian gardens**, plus volcanic lakes, sweeping beaches and protected parks that promise swimming, hiking and cycling.

Relive antiquity at Ostia Antica

The evocative ruins of ancient Rome's seaport lie at the mouth of the Tiber, 35km (22 miles) southwest of the city. One of Lazio's highlights, this once-prosperous trading centre was gradually abandoned as Rome's fortunes changed. Beautifully preserved by a covering of silt, Ostia Antica gives a Pompeii-esque window into daily life in ancient Rome. Don't miss the Porta Marina gate and the Terme di Nettuno (Baths of Neptune) with their exquisite mosaics. There's also a 4000-seat amphiteatre and the Thermopolium, an ancient cafe complete with a bar and fragments of its original frescoed menu.

Taste Renaissance refinement in Tivoli

Tuscany is not the only guardian of Renaissance treasures. Tivoli, 30km (19 miles) northeast of Rome, is home to the Villa d'Este. Its incomparable terraced gardens are emblematic of 16th-century Italian landscaping, listed as a World Heritage Site and embellished with fountains and grottoes. Stepping back through the centuries, ruined Villa Adriana, 5km (3 miles) from Tivoli, was the country estate of the Roman emperor Hadrian.

Get active at Lago Di Bracciano

About an hour's train ride or drive north of Rome, Lago di Bracciano is the second-largest Lazio lake. Motorboats are prohibited and it's renowned for the cleanliness of its waters. Swimming is pleasant in summer, and you can also enjoy windsurfing and canoeing, or cycling the path around the shore. While you're here, you can make forays out to the nearby medieval towns of Bracciano, with its 15th-century Castello Odescalchi (inset), as well as Trevignano Romano and Anguillara Sabazia.

Visit an Etruscan 'city of the dead'

Just outside the modern city of Cerveteri, the Necropoli di Banditaccia was once part of the Etruscan settlement of Caisra, first established in the 9th century BCE. Now a UNESCO World Heritage Site, the necropolis is organised like a town, with streets, squares and terraces of tumuli, circular tombs cut into the earth and capped by turf. Some of the 2000 or so tombs here, like the 6th-century Tomba dei Rilievi, retain traces of painted reliefs; others remain bare. Note that you can buy a combined ticket that covers Banditaccia and the Necropoli di Tarquinia (see page 72), some 50km (31 miles) further north, home to 200 frescoed tombs.

MORE TIME?

CASTEL GANDOLFO Roughly 20km (12 miles) southeast of Rome, in the heights of the Colli Albani (Alban Hills), Castel Gandolfo is one of the prettiest of the 13 Castelli Romani towns. Tour its imposing Palazzo Apostolico, former papal summer residence, surrounded by superb gardens.
SABAUDIA Travel 80km (50 miles) southeast of Rome to laze on one of Lazio's most beautiful beaches, a surfing hot spot that's lined with dunes on one side and cliffs on the other, and explore the Parco Nazionale del Circeo on foot or by bike.

ALONG THE VIA APPIA

One of the oldest roads in the world, the Via Appia's (Appian Way) construction began in 312 BCE to link Rome with present-day Brindisi in Puglia; it was completed in 190 BCE. This ancient *regina viarum* ('queen of roads') is beautifully preserved, and offers wonderful walking and cycling. Arrowing south from Rome, the route is flanked by monuments and milestones and surrounded by flat-topped pine trees and green fields, and passes interesting sites, churches, catacombs and Roman remains, such as the vast Villa di Massenzio and its Roman racetrack; and the towering, once-lavish Villa dei Quintili.

PRACTICALITIES

🅿 HOW TO GET THERE

Rome has two airports: Leonardo da Vinci International in Fiumicino, 30km (19 miles) southwest of the city, has flights from destinations worldwide, while Giovan Battista Pastine in Ciampino, 15km (9 miles) southeast, has services from all over Europe with budget carriers.

🅝 WHERE TO EAT

One of the delights of strolling around Rome is indulging in street food, such as *suppli*, the Roman equivalent of Sicilian *arancini* (meat- and mozzarella-filled rice balls served with tomato sauce); as well as *fiori di zucca* (courgette-flower fritters); *coppiette* (spiced strips of dried pork) or just a classic slice of thin-crust pizza. For a sweet touch, opt for *maritozzi*, bread rolls filled with *panna* (sweetened cream).

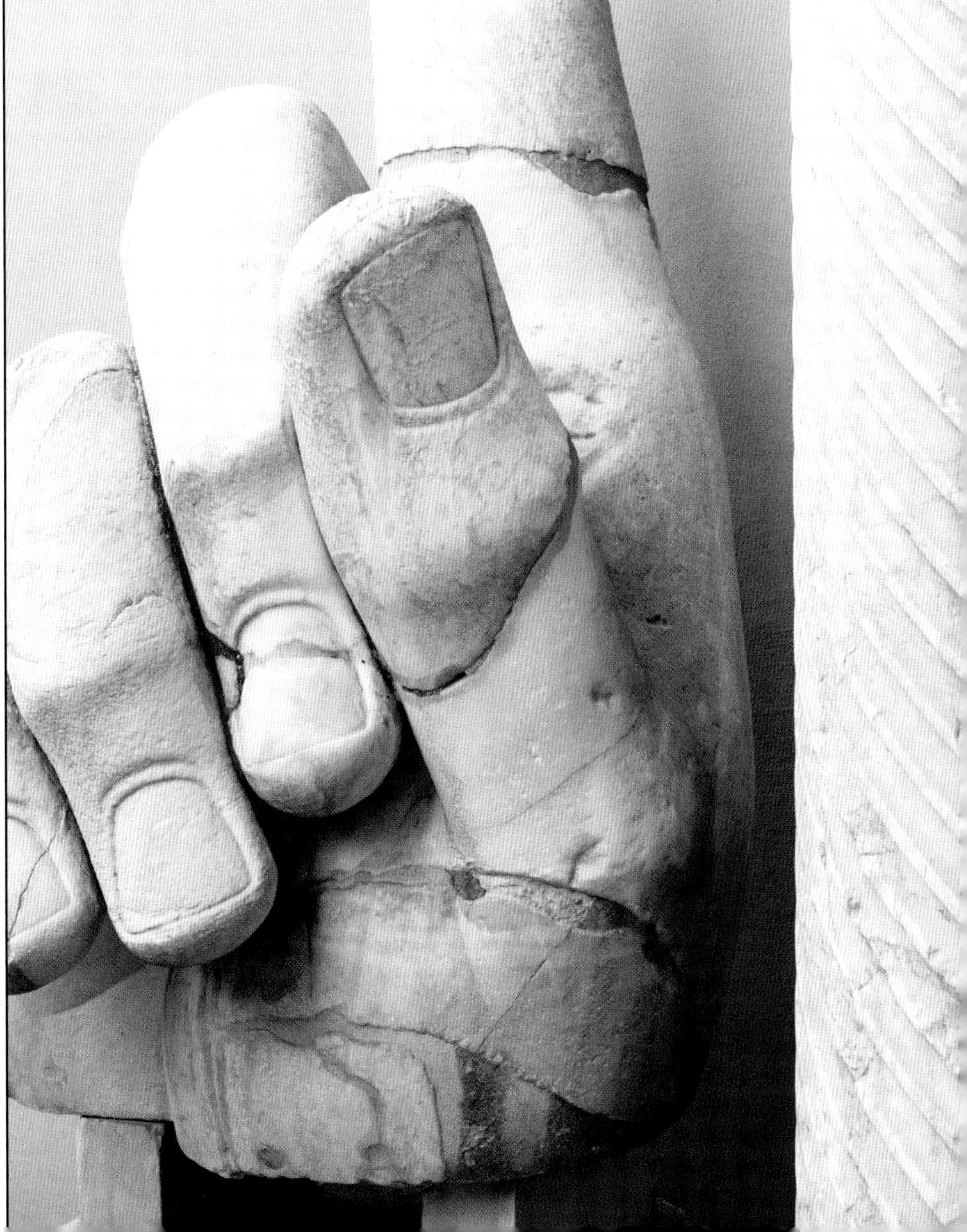

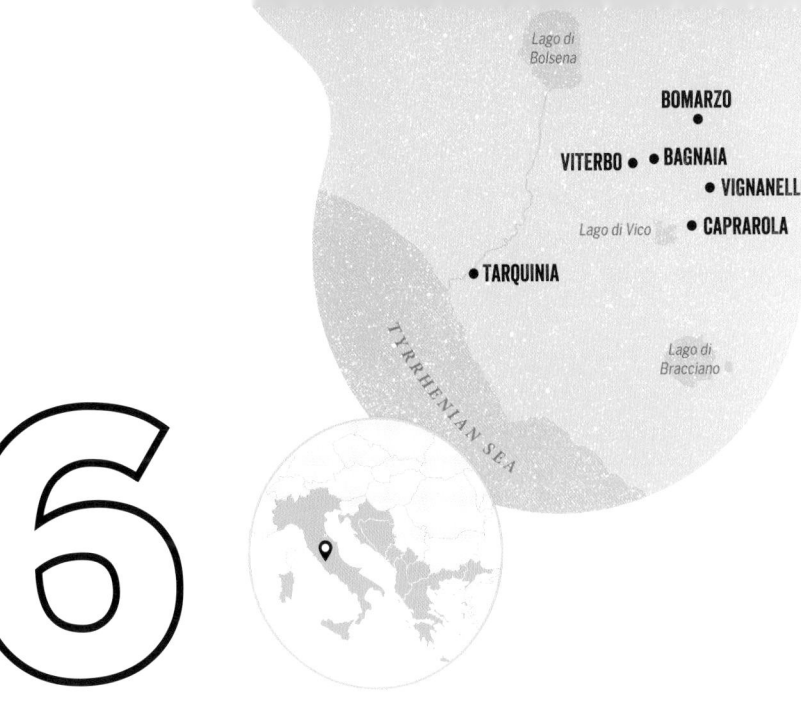

Lago di Bolsena

BOMARZO

VITERBO ● ● BAGNAIA

● VIGNANELLO

Lago di Vico ● CAPRAROLA

● TARQUINIA

TYRRHENIAN SEA

Lago di Bracciano

16

ITALY

Discover a secret Italy
AROUND VITERBO

Nestled in northern Lazio, between the Tyrrhenian Sea and the Tiber Valley, the region around the city of Viterbo has (largely) remained under the radar of visitors. Yet it holds myriad treasures: fabulous **Renaissance castles and gardens** or the grand papal buildings of **Viterbo**, as well as Roman **amphitheatres** at Ferento and Sutri, picturesque **villages** and dramatic hilltop settlements such as **Civita di Bagnoregio** (left), and a wealth of **Etruscan remains**, from the UNESCO-listed necropolis sites at Tarquinia and Cerveteri to the city ruins of Vulci and Norchia. There are **natural attractions** aplenty too: in a mosaic of landscapes that alternates between mountains and olive groves, vineyards and vast plains, you can **bathe in the hot springs at** Bullicame, Carletti, Bagnaccio and San Sisto; go canoeing, fishing or birding in **volcanic lakes**; or head into the hills to enjoy **hiking trails** through the beech forests. The local **cuisine** is another drawcard: sample freshwater fish from the lakes or local delights such as *zuppa di ceci e castagne* (chickpea and chestnut soup) and *acquacotta* (a rustic broth enriched with bread and egg) – and don't forget fine **local wines** such as Montefiascone's Est! Est!! Est!!!

Admire a Mannerist masterpiece in Caprarola

Some 20km (12 miles) southeast of Viterbo, Caprarola is home to the lordly Palazzo Farnese (inset), a 16th-century gem commissioned by Cardinal Alessandro Farnese, the future Pope Paul III (1534–1549). Its distinct pentagonal design, internal circular courtyard and extraordinary columned staircase are the work of Antonio da Sangallo, with later modifications by one of Renaissance Italy's finest Mannerist architects, Giacomo Barozzi da Vignola. The interior frescoes are spectacular, and it's well worth making time to explore the formal gardens, with their fountains and French-style parterre.

Stroll through ravishing Renaissance gardens

In Bagnaia, the Villa Lante (opposite), also designed by Vignola, has a very different look to the Palazzo Farnese. Here, the buildings feel like a mere ornament to the garden, which features fountains, an ingenious water cascade and, at the bottom, a perfectly manicured parterre. In Vignanello, Castello Ruspoli features a beautifully maintained formal garden, first laid out in 1611. The region's most eccentric 16th-century garden is Bomarzo's Parco dei Mostri (Park of Monsters), aka the Sacro Bosco, brainchild of Count Vicino Orsini, and scattered with sculpted animals, ogres, giants and dragons.

Discover Viterbo's medieval marvels

Known as the 'City of the Popes', Viterbo had its heyday between 1257 and 1281, when it was a favoured papal residence. Transport yourself to the heart of the medieval city in Piazza San Lorenzo, overlooked by a fantastic ensemble of buildings, including Palazzo dei Papi and the Cattedrale di San Lorenzo. Then lose yourself in the maze of alleyways in the San Pellegrino district, its houses flanked by external staircases (*profferli*), arcades and towers.

Visit Viterbo's lakes

Of the two volcanic lakes near Viterbo, Bolsena is the larger and offers a wide range of activities – sailing, kayaking, fishing, birdwatching – as well as beautiful villages such as Bolsena, Capodimonte and Montefiascone along its shoreline. Surrounded by the Monti Cimini and a protected nature reserve, Lago di Vico is for nature lovers. Hiking trails thread into the hills around the lake, taking in the wild slopes of Monte Fogliano and Monte Venere.

Explore an Etruscan realm of the dead

The Necropoli di Tarquinia (also known as Monterozzi) dates to the 7th century BCE and comprises about 6000 tombs, some 200 of which are adorned with fabulous frescoes. Full of life and colour, they depict banqueting, hunting and fishing. Of the 20 or so tombs open to the public, one of the most beautiful is the Tomba dei Leopardi, with a rich banquet scene complete with dancers and musicians. End your Etruscan adventure at the superb Museo Archeologico Nazionale Tarquiniense in the pretty medieval town of Tarquinia.

MORE TIME?

CIVITA DI BAGNOREGIO Accessible via a footbridge, this dramatic medieval village (see previous page) is perched on a tufa escarpment that gradually crumbles into the Valle dei Calanchi.
VIA FRANCIGENA To explore the region, follow the Via Francigena, the medieval pilgrimage route from Canterbury in England to Rome. Stages 38 to 42 link Acquapendente to Sutri via Lake Bolsena, Viterbo and Vetralla. The route's website (viefrancigene. org) details walking and cycling itineraries.
NECROPOLI DI BANDITACCIA Listed as a UNESCO World Heritage Site, this Etruscan necropolis near Cerveteri contains some 2000 tombs, many still covered by tumuli.

TUSCIA & BEYOND

The corner of northern Lazio around Viterbo has a storied history, and one that's possible to trace through the region's burial sites and forts, palaces and grand villas. This was once at the centre of Tuscia, the historical heartland of the Etruscans, whose civilisation reached its apogee in the 6th century BCE and whose legacy lives on in the area's fortresses and necropolis sites. Conquered by the Romans then the Germanic Lombards, the region later became a papal state, with a succession of popes resident at the palazzo built for them in Viterbo. In the 16th and 17th centuries, palaces were built in Viterbo, Bomarzo, Caprarola, Bagnaia and Vignanello.

PRACTICALITIES

📖 HOW TO GET THERE & GET AROUND

Rome's two airports have flights from Europe and around the world; from the city centre, Viterbo is about an hour and a half's drive to the northwest. Direct trains also run between Rome and Viterbo; journey time is about an hour and 40 minutes. It's a 40-minute drive from Viterbo to Tarquinia.

🛏 WHERE TO STAY

At the end of a long pine-lined road, and surrounded by olive groves and fields, Tenuta di Paternostro (tenutadipaternostro.it), near Vetralla, offers five chic suites in the heart of a working farm that also offers equine therapy and wellness retreats.

📅 EVENTS

Among Tuscia's traditional festivals, the most famous is the annual procession of the Macchina di Santa Rosa, an illuminated 30m-high (98ft) tower built to honour Viterbo's patron saint. On the evening of 3 September, a hundred men — known as Facchini di Santa Rosa — carry the *macchina* through the town; it's a grand spectacle that's included in UNESCO's Intangible Cultural Heritage of Humanity list.

17

ITALY

Seek out secret havens

IN THE VENICE LAGOON

Venice unfurls its beauty in a lagoon facing the Adriatic, from which it is protected – sometimes insufficiently – by a few tongues of land. The splendours of Serenissima are hardly a secret, but this is a city whose reputation is well deserved. You'll be wowed by the waterfront **Palazzo Ducale** and the unforgettable **Basilica di San Marco**, by the majesty of the **Grand Canal** and its many marble-covered palaces, and by the artistic wealth of the city's churches and museums, with treasures by Tintoretto, Titian, Canaletto and Veronese. And despite the crowds, there's always something to dazzle as you navigate through the narrow streets and over the bridges that span the canals. But there's more to enjoy beyond the headline sights: hop on a vaporetto (waterbus) to explore the less-frequented islands of the Venetian lagoon, such as **San Giorgio Maggiore** (left), with its gracious Benedictine abbey church designed by Palladio; or the beaches of **Lido**. **Murano** is known for its traditional glassblowing workshops, while the brightly painted buildings of **Burano** hold shops selling handmade lace and some superlative seafood restaurants.

Learn the art of glassblowing in Murano

The days when Venice's glassblowers were stripped of their property or executed for treason if they left the city are long gone – but the tradition of glassblowing endures on Murano, where it has been honed to a fine art (opposite) since the 13th century. Today, master glassmakers still ply their trade in the island's workshops, many open to the public, and you can learn more about Murano glass in the Museo del Vetro. Set in the Palazzo Giustinian, its displays give the lowdown on manufacturing traditions and include a fine collection of local glassware.

Take a fishing tour from Burano

The island of Burano is best-known for its brightly painted houses and lacemaking industry, but it's also a great place to take to the water on a fishing expedition. The island's San Marco Fishermen's Cooperative has put together a 'pescatourism' programme (pescaturismoburano.it) offering fishing trips around Burano and neighbouring Torcello aboard traditional boats, with lots of local lore thrown in. Try your hand at crabbing or throwing out a net.

Explore the lagoon by kayak

Gondolas are great, but kayaks (inset) offer a more sustainable way to see the sights of the Venice Lagoon, taking in secluded and picturesque spots, such as Lio Maggiore, Lio Piccolo or Lazzaretto Nuovo. Operators such as Venice Kayak host tours ranging from two hours to a full day, pitched at beginner, intermediate and advanced paddlers; night tours and customised itineraries are also offered.

Birdwatch at Ca'Roman

Just south of Lido, the 11km-long (7 mile) island of Pellestrina is popular with Venetians who come here to recharge their batteries and leave the tourist crowds behind. In addition to three fishing villages, it has the Ca'Roman Natural Reserve (lipu-uk.org), a breathtaking dune area that's home to a rich variety of birds; the 100 or so resident and migratory species include kingfishers, golden orioles, cirl buntings and black-headed and herring gulls.

MORE TIME?

PADUA Less than an hour from Venice, this medieval city is home to a few Renaissance wonders of its own. Must-sees include the Giotto frescoes in the Cappella degli Scrovegni (best booked in advance), and the anatomy theatre at Palazzo Bo, dating to 1595.
PROSECCO HILLS In the foothills of the Dolomites in Veneto, the hills between Conegliano and Valdobbiadene are covered with vineyards that produce premium Prosecco, Italy's sparkling white wine and a key component of the Aperol Spritz. Take the 'Prosecco Route' (coneglianovaldobbiadene.it) and treat yourself to tasting sessions in the historic cellars of local wineries.

FINDING FORTUNY

Marcel Proust's novel *In Search of Lost Time* waxes lyrical over dresses by the legendary designer Mariano Fortuny y Madrazo (1871–1949), but Proust was not his only fan. Though born in Spain, Fortuny settled in Venice, where he founded a textile company. His Art Nouveau designs were beloved by models, actresses and society belles, from Isadora Duncan to Peggy Guggenheim (his uncorseted Delphi-goddess frocks are sought after by vintage buyers with big budgets), and his work set the standard for bohemian chic in both clothing and interiors. Pick up clutches and cushions at the Fortuny factory and boutique on Giudecca island, or learn more at Museo Fortuny.

～～～ PRACTICALITIES ～～～

🅿 HOW TO GET THERE & GET AROUND

Served by flights from Europe and worldwide, Venice's Marco Polo Airport is on the mainland just north of Venice. Buses run to Piazzale Roma in the city; you can also opt for a shuttle or a water taxi. Vaporetti (passenger boats) are the easist way to move around the lagoon. Single tickets are expensive but multi-day passes are available.

🅰 WHERE TO STAY

To immerse yourself in the Venetian atmosphere, rent a room in an old house via sites such as Airbnb. In summer, opt to stay on Lido; it's less expensive than central Venice and has great beaches and outdoor pools.

18

Taste la dolce vita
IN LAKE GARDA & VERONA

With its beguiling palette of greens and blues, the Verona province is a feast for the eyes. Straddling the Veneto, Lombardy and Trentino-Alto Adige regions, the area's landscapes range from olive-planted valleys and vineyards to the mountain-flanked waters of lovely **Lake Garda**. With its mild climate and cool, clear waters, Italy's largest lake is a paradise for **outdoor sports enthusiasts** and lovers of what the Italians call *far niente* **(doing nothing)**. Several towns feature a **notable** architectural heritage, including **Peschiera del Garda,** with its UNESCO-listed Venetian fortress, or **Salò**, a friendly seaside resort with fine palazzo and cathedral. Some 25km (15.5 miles) east of Garda's southern shore, **Verona** offers a wealth of beautiful buildings. Though best known for its *Romeo and Juliet* connection, with visitors lining up for snaps on the balcony of the **Casa di Giulietta**, the **historic centre** also promises pretty cafe-thronged piazzas; a vast Roman Arena (overleaf) that still serves as the venue for the city's summer opera festival; and the Museo di Castelvecchio, housed in a battlemented bridge over the Adige River.

Hike the lakeshore from Riva del Garda

Spreading back from Lake Garda's northern shore, charming Riva del Garda is the ideal setting for a quiet lakeside break. Its narrow streets and shady squares are overlooked by the imposing 12th-century Bastione, a chalk-white fortress clinging to sheer cliffs above the west edge of town, and reachable via a steep 2.5km (1.6-mile) hike. East of Riva, you can take a gentle lakeshore amble right at the water's edge, while to the west, the 10km-long (6-mile) Strada del Ponale walking and cycling trail delivers superb views over Garda.

Try windsurfing at Torbole

A hub for watersports, Lake Garda is a popular playground for lovers of windsurfing and kitesurfing. Favourable winds in the lake's northern corner – the morning breeze is known as the *pelèr*, while the afternoon wind is the *ora* – create the ideal conditions to skim across the water here (opposite), with the mountans that rise up from the shore offering a superbly scenic backdrop. Beginners and experienced wind- and kitesurfers alike can head for Torbole, just east of Riva del Garda, where a number of sailing schools offer lessons and equipment rentals.

Fall in love with the Sirmione Peninsula

Pretty as a picture and known as the 'Pearl of the Lake', this narrow strip of land on the southern shores of Lake Garda is a magnet for visitors. To avoid the high-summer crowds, it's best to explore the resort town of Sirmione (sirmionebs.it) out of season, enjoying beautiful lake views, medieval Rocca Scaligera and the impressive Roman-era ruins of the Grotte di Catullo.

Take to the water on a Lake Garda cruise

From most of Garda's lakeside towns, you can board a boat to cruise across its waters to gorgeous villages like Limone, Malcesine, Sirmione or Bardolino. There are endless possible itineraries, but make sure you include a stop at the privately owned island of Isola del Garda, just offshore of Salò, with its glorious gardens and sumptuous neogothic Venetian villa.

Soar above Monte Baldo from Malcesine

Nature lovers and thrill-seekers are in for a treat in Malcesine (see previous page), on Garda's northeast shore, where you can enjoy the experience of paragliding down to the lake from Monte Baldo. The Malcesine paragliding club (paraglidingclubmalcesine. it) rents out equipment and offers tandem paragliding lessons. To get to the takeoff points, some 1800m (5900ft) above the water, ride the cable car up from Malcesine, which presents ravishing views.

MORE TIME?

BERGAMO Lombardy's masterpiece, the magnificent city of Bergamo has some seriously dazzling architecture, and the Venetian ramparts of the Città Alta offer a majestic panorama of the city and the surrounding plain.

MANTUA In the Po Valley, and flanked by the waters of lakes Inferiore and Superiore, Mantua is home to several gardens, the splendid Palazzo Te and the Renaissance Palazzo Ducale, where the Camera degli Sposi (Bridal Chamber) of the Castello San Georgio is adorned with superb frescoes.

BUON APPETITO

In this land of gastronomy, it's no surprise that Lake Garda and its surrounds promise some special culinary delights. Fresh lake-caught fish is at the top of local menus, served grilled, in fish risottos or in dishes such as *bigoli* pasta with sardines. Olive oil, citrus fruits, mountain cheeses, capers, truffles and honey are other headline local ingredients. Last but not least, the area around Bardolino on Garda's southeast shore is known for its wonderful wines, and several wineries here offer tours and tastings.

 ## HOW TO GET THERE & GET AROUND

Verona Airport has direct flights from around Italy and elsewhere in Europe. From the airport, you can take a bus or train to Peschiera del Garda, on the shores of the lake. Several bus and ferry lines (navigazionelaghi. it) serve the towns on Lake Garda's shoreline.

WHERE TO STAY

Garda's lakeside towns offer endless accommodation possibilities. In Verona, stay in the historic centre for easy access to the Roman Arena and Piazza delle Erbe.

EVENTS

Verona stages one of Europe's oldest carnivals, known as the Bacanal del Gnoco and held over the last weekend before Lent. The summer Verona Opera Festival (arena.it) has been making music lovers' hearts beat faster for over a century. The city shines brightly at Christmas, too, when many festive events take place.

Parco Nazionale
Gran Paradiso

FRANCE

ITALY

Abbaye de
Sacra di
San Michele

PO

PO

● TURIN   *PIEDMONT*

BARBARESCO ┐   ● ASTI

ALBA   │

BRA ●   │

BAROLO ●

PO

ITALY

Learn locavore lore
IN PIEDMONT

Home of the Slow Food movement and some very famous wines, Piedmont is the perfect place for a gourmet weekend. Situated at the foot of the Italian Alps, between the plains of the Po Valley – Europe's largest rice-growing region – and the fertile hills of the Langhe (left), Piedmont is known for its **local produce** – arborio rice, hazelnuts, white truffles – as well as a host of artisanal cheeses and superlative **red and white wines**, such as Barolo, Barbaresco and Asti spumante. But any stay here begins in **Turin**, Piedmont's ancient capital (and a short-lived capital of Italy in the late 19th century). This city of elegant treelined boulevards was once the stronghold of the powerful House of Savoy, whose palaces and grand royal buildings form a '**Crown of Delights**' around modern Turin. After visiting these jewels, as well as the **Museo Egizio** (museoegizio. it), which houses the largest collection of Egyptian treasures outside Cairo, take time to enjoy a luxe hot chocolate in one of Turin's Art Deco cafes. There's much to discover in the surrounding region, dotted with **beguiling historic towns** such as Alba, Bra, Asti, Barolo and Barbaresco, plus **prestigious wineries** and **restaurants** that put the farm-to-fork precept into practice. And beyond the food and wine, there's also hiking in the wildlife-rich **Parco Nazionale Gran Paradiso**.

Tour Turin's Crown of Delights

Known as the *Corona di Delizie* (Crown of Delights), these grand structures scattered around central Turin date from the 17th and 18th centuries, when the city was the seat of the Dukes of Savoy. Eleven of the 14 main buildings are UNESCO World Heritage Sites, including the lavish Palazzo Reale (museireali.beniculturali.it/palazzo-reale) in the heart of Turin. Further out from the centre, the Villa della Regina in Torino (turismotorino.org) is surrounded by lovely Italian gardens overlooking the city, while the Reggia di Venaria Reale (lavenaria.it) is a baroque pile with gardens worthy of Versailles and exhibits on the Savoy dynasty.

Make time for some Slow Food in Bra

Founded by Bra native Carlo Petrini in 1986, the Slow Food movement champions produce that is grown locally, sustainably and according to fair-trade principles – as well as promoting the simply delicious, with an emphasis on regional recipes and specialities. Today, Bra is a hub for locavore gastronomy. Rather than mega-supermarkets, the historic centre is dominated by family-run grocery stores that shut down twice a week for a 'slowdown'. It also hosts the Mercato della Terra di Bra farmers market. To sample some sublime Slow Food cooking on its home turf, head to Bra's Osteria del Boccondivino (boccondivinoslow.it).

Taste the 'King of Wines'

At the Savoy court, Barolo was known as the 'King of Wines and the Wine of Kings', and this regal title still rings true. Bold, full-bodied Barolo is made with nebbiolo grapes, an ancient variety grown on the sunny hillsides around Langhe, to the southeast of Bra. This village of ochre-coloured houses is dominated by the Castello Falletti, where the Museo del Vino a Barolo (wimubarolo.it) gives the lowdown on local viticulture. To arrange tastings and vineyard tours, head to Barolo's Agrilab Wine Tasting Tour (barolowinetastingtour.com).

Take the truffle trail in Alba & Asti

Capital of the Langhe region, Alba is famous for its truffles (opposite), and its annual fair (fieradeltartufo.org) attracts fans every weekend from October to December. For its part, Alba's neighbour, Asti – producer of the sparkling white wine – puts on its own truffle fair every November.

Recharge your batteries in Parco Nazionale Gran Paradiso

This venerable park has a history dating back to 1856 and the reign of Victor Emmanuel II, who declared it a royal hunting reserve in order to preserve the ibex that are now its symbol. Classified as a national park in 1922, and then divided between Valle d'Aosta and Piedmont, Gran Paradiso adjoins the Parc National de la Vanoise in France. With its forests, waterfalls and high-altitude lakes, it's a hikers' paradise; visit the park website (pngp.it) for more information on trails. Watch for ibex, chamois, marmots, ermine, snow partridges and golden eagles.

MORE TIME?

BARBARESCO Nestled in vineyard-swathed hills some 10km (6 miles) northeast of Alba, Barbaresco (above) is topped by an 11th-century tower that gives superlative views over the surrounding wine country. The village's Enoteca Regionale del Barbaresco (enotecadelbarbaresco.it) organises tastings of local wines.
SACRA DI SAN MICHELE Said to have inspired Umberto Eco's novel *The Name of the Rose*, this austere Gothic-Romanesque abbey (sacradisanmichele.com) in the Val di Susa, 14km (9 miles) northwest of Turin, has occupied its brooding spot atop Monte Pirchiriano since the 10th century. You can drive or take a bus up to the car park below, from where it's a short but steep hike up to monastery itself.

CHOCOLATE CITY

Turin has a long association with all things cacao. The city can claim to having invented the wrapped chocolate bar, as it was here, in 1865, that chocolatiers Caffarel produced the first bar of *gianduiotto*, a typically Turinese concoction laced with ground Langhe hazelnuts. Today, the town maintains its status as Italy's capital of chocolate with the Cioccolatò fair (cioccola-to.events) in November. Enjoy delicious chocolate drinks in historic Turin cafes such as Torino, open since 1903; Caffè Al Bicerin (opened 1763), named for its flagship blend of chocolate, coffee and cream (photo above); or Caffè Fiorio (1780), which serves a sublime bittersweet hot chocolate.

HOW TO GET THERE & GET AROUND

Turin Airport (aeroportoditorino.it) is in Caselle, 16km (10 miles) northwest of the centre, with flights from around Italy as well as European capitals and the UK. Fast trains (TGV and Frecciarossa) from Paris and Lyon also run to Turin's Porta Susa station, and a regular rail service links Turin's Stazione Porta Nuova with Alba and Bra. Renting a car in Turin is another easy way to reach local attractions. But to fully appreciate the Italian way of life, slow the pace by riding a Vespa or an electric bike; rentals are available from Langhe Experience (langhe-experience.it) in Alba.

EVENTS

With a wealth of fresh produce on offer in shops and markets and cooked up in local restaurants, harvest season (August to October) is an exhilarating time to explore Piedmont. Staged in September in even-numbered years, Turin's Terra Madre Salone del Gusto (terramadresalonedelgusto.com) is a celebration of the Slow Food movement. Also in September, Asti stages the Festival delle Sagre di Asti, dedicated to fine food and wine; and the Palio di Asti, a frenetic bareback horse race – see Visit Asti (visit.asti.it) for more on both events.

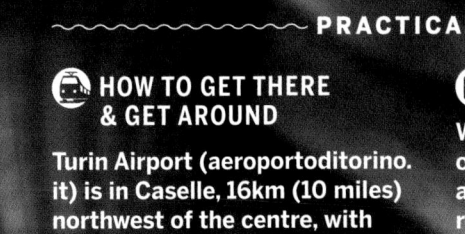

20

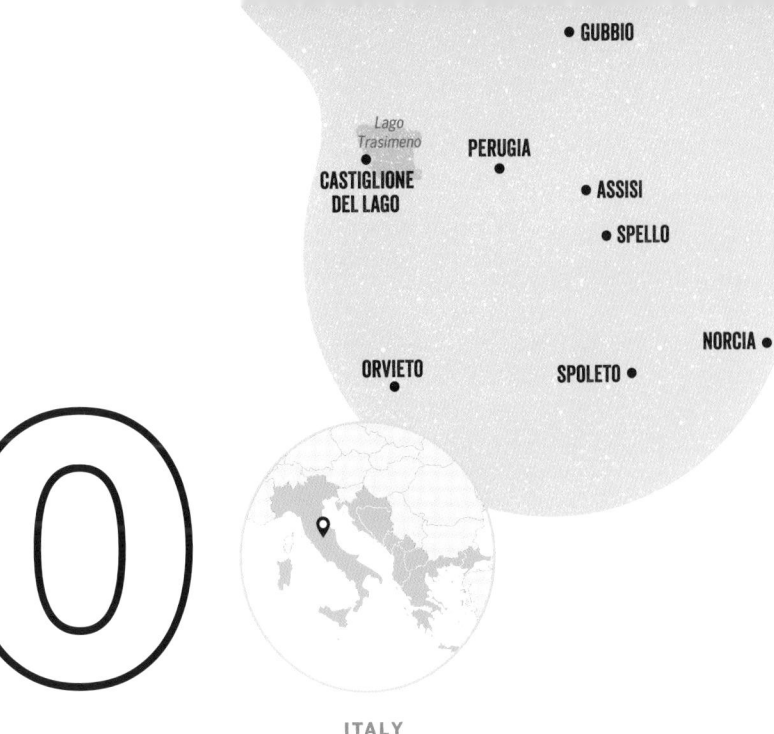

GUBBIO

Lago
Trasimeno · PERUGIA
· CASTIGLIONE · ASSISI
DEL LAGO
· SPELLO

NORCIA ·

· ORVIETO
SPOLETO ·

ITALY

Explore Italy's green heart
IN UMBRIA

R ight in the centre of Italy, Umbria enjoys relative isolation from outside influences. This region of gentle mountains, hilltop towns and lush green valleys laced with centuries-old vineyards and olive groves is a place where local traditions persist. With no access to the sea (though it does have the beautiful **Lake Trasimeno**), Umbria is nicknamed *il cuore verde dell'Italia* (the 'green heart of Italy'). Discovering the characterful towns around **Perugia**, its capital, promises a rejuvenating stay that will uplift the soul and delight the senses. A student town renowned for its nightlife, Perugia is built on two hills, and holds a host of fine heritage buildings. Its neighbour, **Assisi** (left), a city-museum built into a hillside, offers art, culture and a host of sites associated with its patron saint, the animal-loving Francis. Smaller hilltop towns include **Gubbio, Spoleto,** the magnificently perched **Orvieto** (overleaf) and flower-filled **Spello**, occupying a a rocky outcrop on Monte Sabino and one of Italy's most beautiful villages. This fertile region is also renowned for its produce, with **Norcia's black truffles** adding earthy flavour to local salamis, hams and cheeses.

Pucker up in Perugia

Perugia is as famous for its 2.8km-long (1.7-mile) city walls and universities as it is for its Baci chocolates. Invented here in 1922, Baci are wrapped in words of love (*baci* means 'kisses' in Italian) and filled with *gianduja* and a single whole hazelnut. To get the lowdown on how they're made, visit Casa del Cioccolato (perugina.com). Beyond Baci, Perugia's other wonders are mostly contained in its Old Town: Rocca Paolina, a 16th-century fortress, and the Palazzo dei Priori, home to the Galleria Nazionale dell'Umbria and its important collection of 3000-plus works, from paintings to sculpture.

Go underground & overgound in Orvieto

Dramatically situated atop a giant butte of rock, Orvieto, 80km (50 miles) southwest of Perugia, was originally an Etruscan settlement. Start by visiting the underground city carved out of the tufa rock, accessible via the ancient wells of Pozzo della Cava and the Pozzo di San Patrizio (opposite). Then change your perspective and take the funicular (near the station) up to Piazza Cahen, from where it's a short walk to the Duomo (1290), a UNESCO-listed jewel of Italian Gothic, with an astonishing facade and frescoes by Fra Angelico and Luca Signorelli decorating the San Brizio chapel.

Follow in the footsteps of St Francis in Assisi

Comprising two separate churches, the 13th-century Basilica di San Francesco complex is the crowning glory of Assisi's UNESCO-listed historic centre. The Gothic Basilica Superiore is best-known for its celebrated cycle of Giotto frescoes, which depict the life of Francis of Assisi, born here in 1181. The older Basilica Inferiore holds paintings by Cimabue, Pietro Lorenzetti and Simone Martini, as well as the much-venerated Cripta di San Francesco, home to the tomb of St Francis. To visit further sites associated with Francis' life, head off on foot from central Assisi to the Eremo delle Carceri, a 4km (2.5-mile) walk east. This monastery on the slopes of Monte Subasio is set around caves where the saint and his followers prayed. Some 1.5km (1 mile) southeast of Assisi, the Chiesa di San Damiano is where St Francis is said to have heard the voice of God in 1205, and later wrote his *Cantico delle Creature* (*Canticle of the Creatures*).

On land & water at Lago Trasimeno

A splash of deep blue in the hilly Umbrian landscape, 20km (12 miles) northwest of Perugia, Lago Trasimeno (lagotrasimeno. net) offers a wealth of outdoor pursuits, from hiking, horseback riding and cycling to watersports (information from the sailing club: cvcastiglionese.it), as well as simply lazing on lakeside beaches. On the shores of the lake, visit the frescoed Palazzo della Corgna and the Rocca del Leone in the charming town of Castiglione del Lago, from where ferries run to Isola Polvese, the largest of the lake's three islands; Isola Maggiore can be reached from Tuoro sul Trasimeno.

MORE TIME?

SPELLO Linked to Perugia and Assisi by regular trains, Spello's highlight is the frescoed Chiesa di Santa Maria Maggiore.
GUBBIO Located 18km (11 miles) north of Assisi, Gubbio's landmark sight is the Basilica di Sant'Ubaldo, perched on Monte Ingino and reachable via the fun Funivia Colle Eletto, a sort of glorified ski lift.
SPOLETO Hill-set Spoleto, with its photogentic Duomo and medieval fortress, lies 40km (25 miles) south of Assisi.

THE BLACK TRUFFLES OF NORCIA

Sniffed out by specially trained dogs in the forests of southeastern Umbria between November and March, the delectable black truffles harvested around the small town of Norcia are renowned among aficionados of these premium fungi. Gourmands with deep pockets snap up nuggets of 'black gold' at Norcia's Thursday market; Castelluccio lentils are a more affordable option and still 100% local. Held over two weekends in late February and early March, Norcia also hosts an annual truffle fair (nero-norcia. it) featuring tastings, cooking demonstrations and lots of local produce, from cheese to charcuterie.

~ PRACTICALITIES ~

HOW TO GET THERE

San Francesco d'Assisi Airport is around 12km (7.5 miles) east of central Perugia, with flights from around Italy, Europe and the UK. Alternatively, fly to Rome's Fiumicino airport, from where regular Sulga buses (sulga.it) run to Perugia from Terminal C; journey time is around three and a half hours. Trains from Rome to Perugia take around two hours.

HOW TO GET AROUND

Trains from Perugia run to Assisi, 25km (15.5 miles) away; and Orvieto, 80km (50 miles) away via Lake Trasimeno.

EVENTS

Don't miss the Umbria Jazz Festival (umbriajazz.it), featuring rock, pop and blues as well as jazz; it's staged in Perugia in July and Orivieto in December. In Gubbio, on 15 May, the Corsa dei Ceri (Feast of the Candles; ceri.it) features teams of *ceraioli* (strong men) carrying imposing stylised wooden candles, crowned with the statue of their patron saint, to the summit of Monte Ingino.

• PISA

LIVORNO •

Parco Archeologico di
Baratti e Populonia

PIOMBINO •

Monte
Capanne
• PORTOFERRAIO

Elba

Pianosa

ITALY

21

Travel through Tuscany
FROM PISA TO ELBA

The slice of Tuscany between Pisa and the offshore island of Elba offers an enticing mix, combining culture, history and the sybaritic pleasures of the seaside. The journey begins in **Pisa**. After an obligatory sweep around the signature sights of the **Piazza dei Miracoli** – the **famous Torre Pendente (Leaning Tower)**, the Battistero (Baptistry) and the Duomo – next stop is the coastal town of **Piombino**; around an hour and a half from the city by train or car, this is the departure point for ferries to **Elba** (left). As you approach the island capital of **Portoferraio** from the sea, and the 16th-century walls of Forte Falcone come into view, you'll get a first taste of Elba's varied charms. Covering some 224 sq km (86.5 sq miles), Elba is no mere speck in the sea, and Italy's third-largest island (after Sicily and Sardinia) has a huge amount to see and do. Its steep, winding roads lead to a generous sprinkling of **medieval hilltop villages**, while the coastline delivers both broad resort beaches and **hidden coves** reachable only from the sea. Elba's maquis-swathed hinterland, meanwhile, promises exhilarating **hikes** on a network of trails such as the **Grande Traversata Elbana** (GTE), which winds across the central spine of the island from end to end. And after a day of sea, sights and hikes, wind down at Elba's seafood restaurants and enjoy fine island-made wines.

Get a bird's-eye view of the Tuscan Archipelago

Looming large over western Elba, the island's highest peak is the 1018m (3340ft) Monte Capanne. Thankfully, Capanne's upper reaches are accessible to all via a chairlift that departs from the inland town of Marciana. Its bright-yellow cages glide slowly up the slopes, with plenty of time to take in the unravelling views of Elba on the way. And at the top, there's a fabulous panoramic perspective over the entire Tuscan Archipelago: Pianosa, Gorgona, Capraia and Montecristo.

Explore the Elba coastline by sea-kayak

Elba is home to a number of expansive, easily accessible sandy beaches – such as those fronting the coastal towns of Procchio and Lacona – but some of the best seaside spots take a little more effort to get to. Sea kayaking is a wonderful way to explore the coastline, giving access to the smallest of coves, peeking into caves and pitching up on pristine shores for a swim (opposite). Numerous operators in Marciana Marina, Marina di Campo and Capoliveri offer courses and guided paddles, from day trips to overnight excursions with cooking and camping on the beach.

Walk in the footsteps of Napoleon

For history buffs, Elba is chiefly notable for its association with Napoleon Bonaparte, who was exiled here for 300 days, between May 1814 and February 1815. It was an exile in fine style, however, as you'll see when visiting the two palatial buildings that served as his island homes, both now open as museums. The Villa dei Mulini in Portoferraio has Empire-style furnishings, a splendid library, Italianate gardens and an unbeatable sea view; the Villa San Martino, 5km (3 miles) away, holds a grand Egyptian room. Napoleon's presence made its mark on Elba, and islanders commemorate his time here with a Mass in his memory every 5 May. It's held in the Chiesa della Misericordia, where a small exhibition includes his death mask.

Take to two wheels on Pianosa

It's hard to imagine that this postcard-perfect island off the southwest coast of Elba was first a penal colony and, until 1988, a high-security prison. Today, Pianosa is part of the Parco Nazionale dell'Arcipelago Toscano, with visitors flocking in to enjoy its unspoilt nature and crystal-clear waters, and to explore its Roman ruins and former prison houses. As it's relatively flat, Pianosa is ideal for cycling; bike rental is available on the island. To get here from Elba, hop on a boat from the south-coast town of Piombino.

MORE TIME?

PARCO ARCHEOLOGICO DI BARATTI E POPULONIA On the mainland, just opposite the island of Elba, this extensive site holds some of Tuscany's finest Etruscan remains. Trails link key sights, such as the Necropoli di San Cerbone, the Monastery of San Quirico and the Acropoli di Populonia.

LIVORNO Just 25km (15.5 miles) south of Pisa, and marking the beginning of Tuscany's Etruscan Coast, this lively port city features a historic quarter latticed with canals and a beautiful belle époque waterfront. Climb to the top of the Fortezza Nuova to enjoy the view over the beautiful Piazza della Repubblica.

ELBA'S FAMOUS WINES

Dubbed the 'island of good wine' by Pliny the Elder, Elba has a long tradition of viticulture. Winemaking here is very much an active pursuit today; you'll see terraces of vines flanking hillsides and valleys in all corners of the island. With its own DOC (Denominazione di Origine Controllata), Elba is known for its white wines, and the family-owned Arrighi winery (arrighivigneolivi. it) produces some of the best. You can visit for tours and tastings of their wines, which include the unique Nesos, a 'marine wine' made with grapes that have been immersed in the sea in baskets for five days, which removes the 'bloom' from the skin and allows for quicker drying, thus preserving the grapes' delicate aroma.

PRACTICALITIES

HOW TO GET THERE

Pisa Airport has numerous international connections. The cheapest and most convenient way to reach Elba is to take a ferry from Piombino (with Toremar, Moby, Elba Ferries or Blu Navy) to the island's capital, Portoferraio, or to Rio Marina; journey time to both is around an hour.

WHERE TO EAT

For some of the best seafood on Elba, sidestep the tourist-oriented seaside restaurants and head inland. In Marciana, L'Osteria del Noce (osteriadelnoce.com) offers splendid views from its terrace, and reasonably priced, creative cuisine.

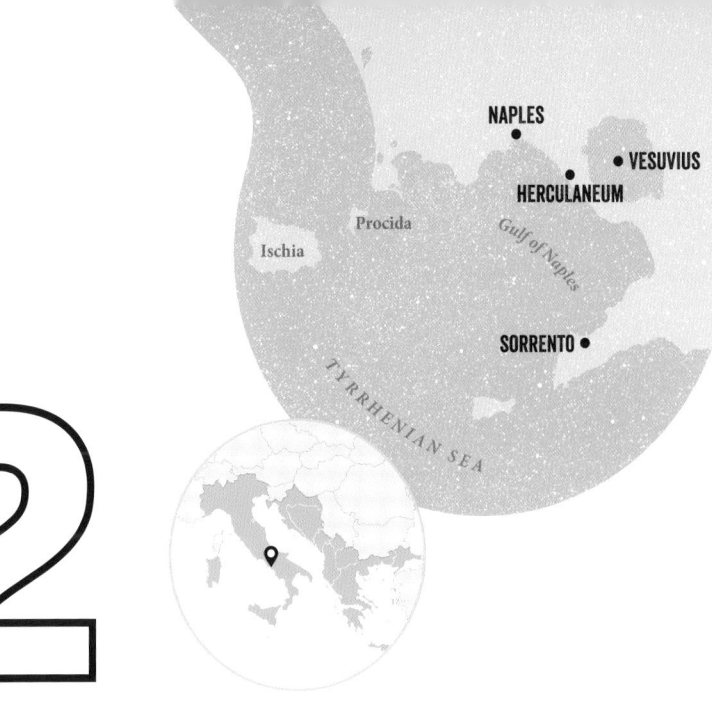

22

ITALY

Plot a route around the
GULF OF NAPLES

I taly's third-largest city, Naples is both chaotic and cultured, opulent and gritty, exuberant and understated, with architectural gems around every corner. But despite its many draws, many visitors skip the city entirely, making instead for the Amalfi Coast or Pompeii – and this is a mistake. Culture plays an important role in this busy city, from the vast array of centuries-spanning works at the **Museo di Capodimonte** (capodimonte.cultura.gov.it) to the **Museo Archeologico Nazionale** (mann-napoli.it), home to one of the world's finest collections of Greco-Roman artefacts. Naples (left) has a rich architectural heritage, too: stroll the lively streets of the UNESCO-listed **Centro Storico** (historic centre), home to the famous **Cappella Sansevero**, or the atmospheric **Quartieri Spagnoli**, with its washing-strung balconies and old-school pizzerias. Elegant Piazza del Plebiscito in more upscale **San Ferdinando** makes for a striking contrast, as does the *lungomare* (seaside promenade) in the middle-class districts of **Santa Lucia** and **Chiaia**. From the waterfront, funiculars sweep up to **Vomero**, which affords views of the island-scattered Gulf of Naples. The best of the destinations here – bar busy and expensive Capri – include **Procida** and **Ischia**, the latter linked by causeway to the island fortress of **Castello Aragonese**.

Climb the slopes of an active volcano

Looming menacingly over the bay, 12km (7.5 miles) southeast of Naples, Vesuvius is infamous for the 79 CE eruption that devastated Pompeii. This simmering volcano has since erupted a further 30 times (most recently in 1944), and is closely monitored. Today it forms the centrepiece of the Parco Nazionale del Vesuvio (parconazionaledelvesuvio.it), with nine hiking trails that can be explored on foot or on horseback. Buses from Naples, Pompeii and Herculaneum run to the foot of the volcano. The ascent, between hardened lava flows, is not too arduous, and from the 1281m-high (4203ft) summit the crater is impressive – as is the panorama over the Apennine Mountains and the Gulf of Naples.

Descend into Naples' underground city

A silent world of caves, catacombs and ancient ruins lies beneath the city's bustling streets. Explore them by way of tours taking in sites such as the Catacombe di San Gennaro, which contain early Christian burial chambers; and the Galleria Borbonica, a 19th-century tunnel built to link the Palazzo Reale to the barracks and used as an air-raid shelter during WWII. Beneath the Basilica of San Lorenzo Maggiore, underground passages hold a sprawl of extraordinary Greco-Roman ruins; the on-site museum provides illuminating background.

Take a dip in thermal waters

The beaches on the island of Ischia – such as Baia di San Montano and Spiaggia dei Maronti – are renowned as the most beautiful in the Bay of Naples. But visitors also come here for the thermal waters of this volcanic island, visiting spas or the hundred-odd natural hot springs like the Baia di Sorgeto, which are free to access year-round. You can also take the waters at thermal baths, such as Negombo, with beautifully landscaped outdoor pools and a hammam.

Wonder at Procida

The village of Corricella (opposite) is the main reason to visit the island of Procida; with its pretty, colourful houses arranged like an amphitheatre facing the sea, it's one of the Bay of Naples' most enchanting harbours. This photogenic locale has served as the location for several films, including blockbuster *The Talented Mr Ripley* and *Il Postino* (*The Postman*). While you're here, explore the island by bike, or see Procida from the sea in a rented *gommone* (dinghy).

MORE TIME?

HERCULANEUM A short way northwest along the coast from Pompeii, this ancient town was destroyed by an earthquake in 62 CE; following the eruption that did for Pompeii, it was submerged in a 16m-thick (52ft) sea of mud that essentially fossilised it. The frescoes and mosaics (inset) are virtually intact.
SORRENTO For a taste of the Amalfi Coast (which deserves a weekend of its own), stop off at Sorrento, less than an hour's drive from Naples, and barely more by train. This elegant cliff-set coastal resort, with its beautiful squares and luxury hotels, is famous for its lemons, used to make its signature Limoncello liqueur.

PIZZA & BEYOND

As with any stay in Italy, the business of eating well is an essential component of your Bay of Naples weekend. The city is the birthplace of pizza, and you're sure to taste some delicious rounds of cheesy heaven here. There are pizzerias all over Naples, and everyone has their favourite spot, but Starita (pizzeriestarita. it) and Gino Sorbillo (sorbillo.it) are reliable choices. Other standouts of the local cuisine include Ischia's fresh-caught fish cooked *all'acqua pazza* ('in crazy water' – poached in a flavoured broth) or the island specialty, *coniglio all'ischitana*, rabbit stewed over a wood fire.

~ PRACTICALITIES ~

🛢 HOW TO GET THERE

Naples Airport has flights from across Europe and the UK with low-cost airlines, and services from Canada and the US. Ferries and hydrofoils run from Naples to Procida (journey time is 35 minutes to an hour and a half) and Ischia (50 minutes to an hour and a half); water shuttles run between the two islands (15–30 minutes).

📅 EVENTS

A nighttime procession of decorated boats, fireworks and a mock fire at the Castello Aragonese are the main events of Ischia's annual Festa di Sant'Anna celebrations, held on 26 July.

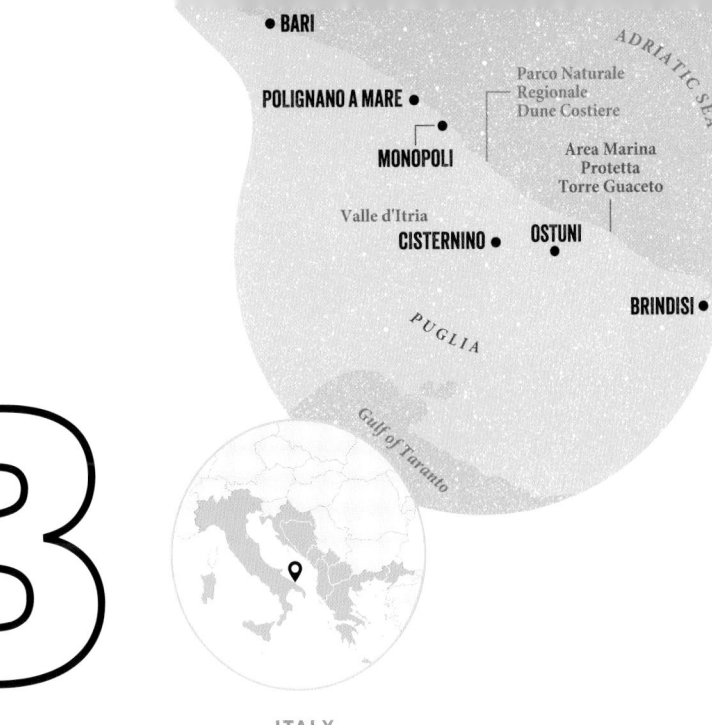

ITALY

23

Journey around Puglia
FROM BARI
TO THE BEACHES

One of Puglia's key charms is its authentic, friendly and festive atmosphere. Traditions are alive and well here, as seen in enduring events, such the Sant'Oronzo festival in **Ostuni**, a riot of processions, dancing and music. In **Bari Vecchia** (old Bari), residents still prepare orecchiette (the name means 'little ears') outdoors, pulling a table out of the kitchen to watch the world go by as they shape Puglia's most famous pasta by hand. The charm of this southern-most corner of the Italian peninsula also lies in its **landscapes**, with the blues of the sea alternating with the greens of the olive trees, the gold of the wheatfields, the grey of the drystone walls, the red of the earth and the whitewashed glare of the **hilltop villages**. Everywhere, history has left traces of successive conquerors, from the Greeks to the Normans to the Spanish – but in Puglia, there's no need to rush around the sights. Breathe in the seductive **atmosphere** as you savour a cup of coffee in a square of blond stone, swim at the glorious beaches, or wander a maze of medieval alleyways before coming upon a breathtaking view from hill-town ramparts.

Feel the heartbeat of Bari's Old Town

A major port since the Crusades, Bari has preserved its historic heart, the Bari Vecchia. This maze of alleyways, courtyards and medieval squares is an atmospheric place for a wander, with cooking smells wafting from open doorways, and locals playing cards at tables set up in the street. Notable buildings include the Castello Svevo, dating from the 12th century and with tower-topped bastions added in the 16th. The Pugliese-Romanesque Basilica di San Nicola is home to the remains of St Nicholas (aka Father Christmas), and is an important place of pilgrimage.

Track down trulli in the Valle d'Itria

A hilly landscape of rich red earth planted with olive trees and vines and crisscrossed by drystone walls, the Valle d'Itria between Martina Franca, Locorotondo and Cisternino offers a magical panorama. The region is dotted with *masserie* (farmhouses) and *trulli* (traditional stone-built huts with whitewashed walls and conical roofs; see previous page). Perhaps the best place to see these beehive-like buildings is the town of Alberobello, a UNESCO World Heritage Site with over 1500 *trulli*, the oldest of which date back to the 14th century. Some of the *trullo* here serve as homes; others hold gift shops and the like.

Visit the hilltop villages of central Puglia

With their arches, towers, churches and palaces connected by labyrinths of lanes, the hilltop towns and villages of Puglia's interior are supremely photogenic, with a relaxed, go-slow air that's endlessly beguiling. Dazzling white Ostuni (inset) is the most magnificent example. Other tops spots include Martina Franca, distinguished by its baroque elegance; Cisternino, for its medieval heart and nightlife; Locorotondo, with its circular layout and pitch-roofed houses; and Ceglie Messapica and Carovigno, both with fabulous food scenes.

Along the Adriatic coast

After the cliffs, coves and caves around Polignano a Mare (opposite), the coastline to the southeast softens towards the pretty port of Monopoli, with a host of popular beaches lapped by limpid waters; near Egnazia, you can snorkel above a sunken Roman port (or explore what remains of the site on land). Continuing southeast, rocky areas alternate with long sandy beaches, the most beautiful within the Parco Naturale delle Dune Costiere. The most unspoiled stretch of coast, however, is in the Area Marina Protetta di Torre Guaceto, where the dunes, marshes and crystal-clear waters attract migratory birds, dolphins and turtles.

MORE TIME?

GROTTE DI CASTELLANA Some 40km (25 miles) southeast of Bari, this is Italy's longest cave network. The extraordinary stalactite and stalagmite formations in its 3km-long (1.9-mile) cavern system include the Grotta Bianca (White Grotto), an eerie alabaster cavern that bristles with stiletto-thin stalactites.

MATERA In the neighbouring region of Basilicata, about 70km (43.5 miles) south of Bari, Matera is one of the world's longest continuously inhabited human settlements, its *sassi* (cave dwellings) occupied for some 7000 years. As well as the *sassi*, sights here include the rock-cut, 12th-century Chiesa San Pietro Barisano, and the vast Palombaro Lungo underground cistern.

TRULLI COUNTRY

A *trullo* (the plural is *trulli*) is a unique dwelling found only in the Val d'Itria region of Puglia. Built without mortar from roughly worked limestone, *trulli* are topped with pointed pyramidal roofs of corbelled limestone slabs, often surmounted with a decorative pinnacle that was intended to ward off evil spirits. There are many theories as to the origins of *trulli* design; the most enduring is that the mortarless dry-stone was used as a means of avoiding the tax on buildings imposed by the Kingdom of Naples in the 15th century – a *trullo* could be easily dismantled should its owner get wind that a tax inspection might be taking place.

~ PRACTICALITIES ~

🗎 HOW TO GET THERE

Named after Polish-born Pope John Paul II, Bari's Karol Wojtyła Airport is around 8km (5 miles) northwest of the centre, and is served by international and low-cost airlines from across Europe and the UK.

🏨 WHERE TO STAY

Choose the region's typical accommodations: *trulli* (see box) or *masserie*, vast agricultural properties now often converted to accommodate guests.

📅 EVENTS

Summer is a vibrant time in Puglia, with Ostuni's Festa di Sant'Oronzo (25–27 August), but it's also at its busiest – the beaches are crowded and the most beautiful villages almost inaccessible in the evenings; if possible, visit during the quieter spring or autumn. Staged near Bari from 26 December to the last Tuesday before Lent, the Putignano Carnival is one of the longest and oldest of such events in Europe.

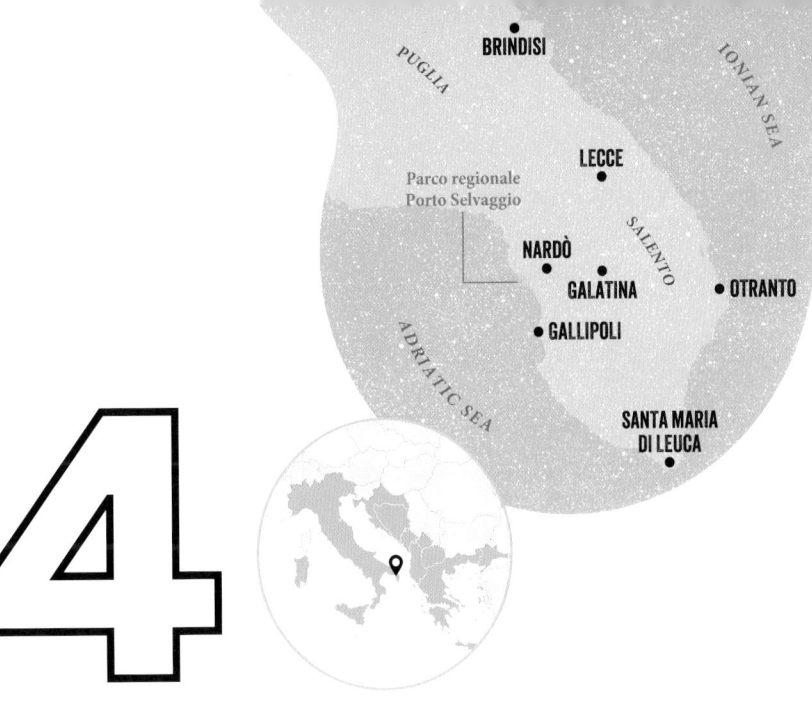

ITALY

24

Baroque beauty & beaches
IN LECCE &
SOUTHERN PUGLIA

'**L**u sule, lu mare e lu ientu' (sun, sea and wind): that's how the Salento region defines itself. Occupying the 'boot-heel' of the Italian peninsula, this is a land bathed to the east by the Adriatic and to the west by the Ionian Sea.** Impoverished and, until recently, relatively isolated, this part of Puglia has a rich history, marked in particular by the Greek presence. On the southeast coast, **Otranto**, like **Gallipoli**, was a major port for trade between the West and East until it was sacked by the Turks in 1480. Easier to defend,

thanks to its inland location, **Lecce** (left) stepped into the breach and became one of the commercial epicentres of the Kingdom of Naples, while the exuberant baroque style that emerged here in the late 16th century spread to all the surrounding towns. Today, **Salento** attracts a flood of tourists in summer for its beaches and coves, its heritage and its ports. But head a little inland and, among the vineyards and olive groves, you'll find peace, quiet and little-visited towns such as **Galatina** and **Nardò**, where local **traditions** like the tarantella dance endure.

Be bedazzled by baroque in Lecce

Lecce is home to a Roman amphitheatre, a fortified castle and some fine Renaissance buildings – but the city's main joy is its exhuberant 17th-century baroque buildings, embellished with a veritable riot of cherubs, animals, plants and gargoyles, finely carved in golden stone. This local style is so distinctive that it's aquired its own name, *barocco leccese* (Lecce Baroque), and the finest example is the Basilica di Santa Croce, whose fever dream of a facade, with its magnificent allegorical carvings, is at its best when illuminated at night.

Port to port, from Otranto to Gallipoli

Photogenic Otranto (inset) was at its peak in the 15th century, when a bloody Turkish incursion signalled its decline. Today, its historic centre retains its thousand-year-old beauty, with its narrow streets, ramparts, castle and splendid 11th-century cathedral, with a fabulous mosaic floor and grisly relics of the Turkish massacre. Gallipoli is a town of two halves, with its modern centre on the mainland and its *centro storico* (old quarter) occupying a fortified island jutting out into the Ionian Sea, its ancient buildings home to boutiques, restaurants and bars. The string of lovely beaches surrounding the town are justifiably popular.

Find frescoes & folklore in Galatina

Galatina is an inland city of elegant baroque palaces, churches and courtyards. The headline sight here is the Basilica di Santa Caterina d'Alessandria, a masterpiece of Puglian Romanesque architecture. Its interior features a pure-white altarpiece set against a frenzy of fabulous 15th-century frescoes in the style of Giotto. Also worth a visit is the Cappella di San Paolo, part of the Palazzo Tondi; the waters of the ancient well here were once used to treat those afflicted with 'tarantism'.

Explore the interior

Head a short way inland of the Salento's beaches to lesser-visited towns such as Alessano, Specchia, Casarano, Galatone, Presicce and Nardò, Lecce's ancient rival. As well as taking in palaces, medieval or baroque churches and peaceful squares, these are places to simply enjoy small-town atmosphere: soak up the pink and ochre hues of faded plasterwork or discover an old-fashioned ice-cream parlour or traditional cantina.

Beach-hop from coast to coast

The Salento's narrow dimensions mean you're never far from the sea – but with so many lovely shores, it can be hard to decide where to settle on the sand for the day. If the wind is coming from the north – the Tramontana – the sandy, shallow beaches of the Ionian Sea (right) will be the calmest; when the Sirocco blows from the southeast, head for the cliffs, coves and caves of the Adriatic (see page 8). If you can't decide, visit Santa María di Leuca, where the two seas meet or, for a taste of the wild, explore the unspoilt Ioanian coastline and pine forests of the Parco Naturale Regionale di Porto Selvaggio.

MORE TIME?

BRINDISI This slow-paced port city offers a lovely waterfront, the 12th-century Tempio di San Giovanni, and the superb frescoes of the Chiesa di Santa Maria del Casale, near the airport.

ABBAZIA DI SANTA MARIA DI CERRATE Out in the countryside 15km (9 miles) north of Lecce, this Romanesque abbey features a fine collection of 13th-century frescoes.

EREMO DI VINCENT A kind of mini Parc Güell in the Salento, the Guagnano home and studio of artist Vincenzo Brunetti is a riot of Gaudí-like mosaic work.

SALENTO'S TARANTELLA

The first descriptions of tarantism in the Salento date from the 11th century, when it was believed that the bite of a local 'tarantula' (actually a species of wolf spider) caused a kind of convulsive hysteria. To rid themselves of the poison, the bitten drank water from the well of the Cappella di San Paolo in Galatina, reputedly blessed by St Paul, and danced the tarantella to the frenzied rhythm of the tambourine and violin, until the effects of the venom wore off. Today, the tarantella or *pizzica* dance is an important part of the region's cultural heritage. The touring La Notte della Taranta festival attracts thousands to Salento in August; the organisers stage regular dance performances too.

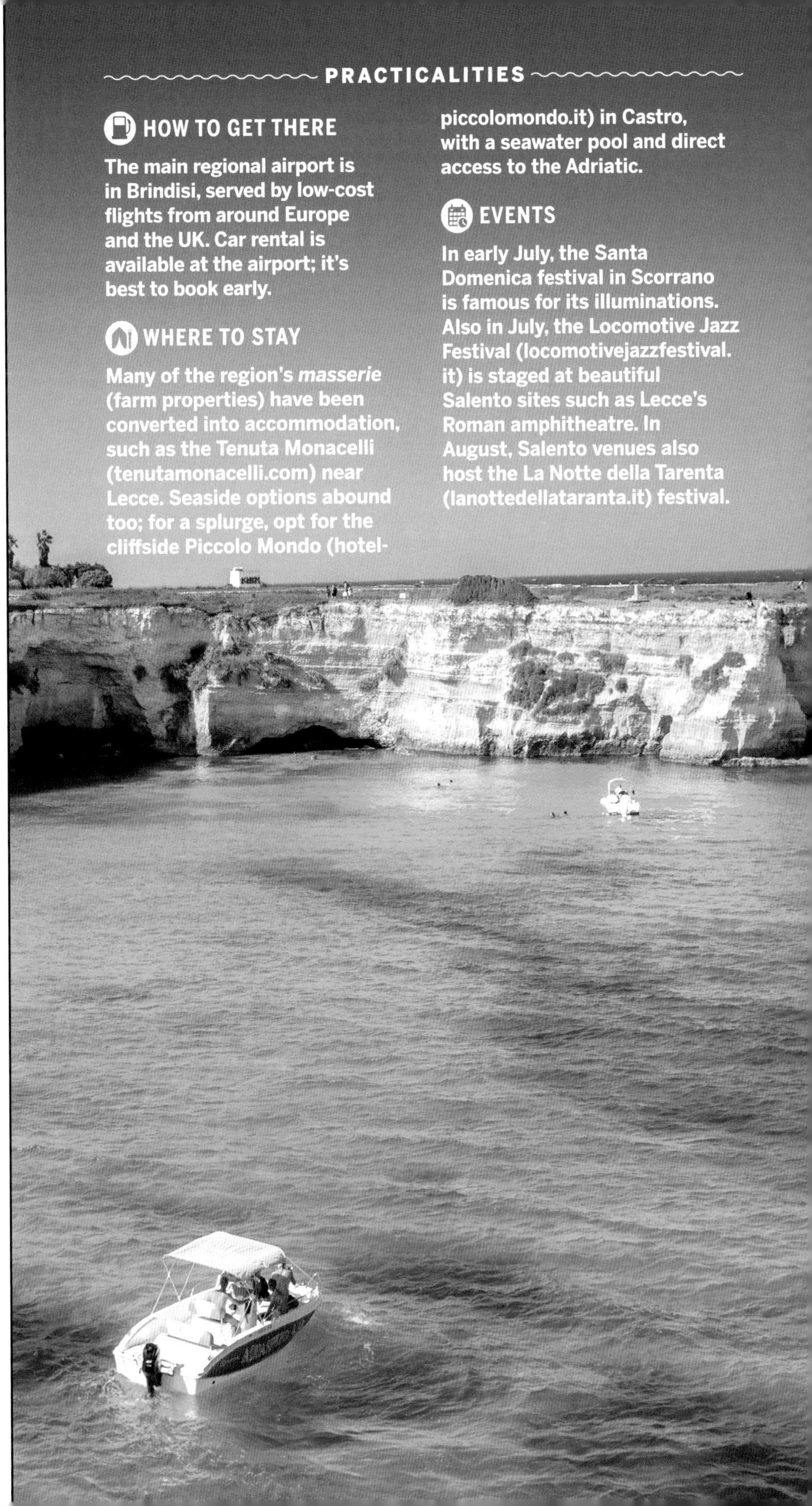

TAORMINA

Etna

IONIAN SEA

VILLA ROMAINE DU CASALE · CATANIA ·

· AGRIGENTO

CALTAGIRONE

SYRACUSE

· NOTO

MODICA

ITALY

Around the coast
IN EASTERN SICILY

The island crossroads of the Mediterranean, Sicily's storied history, beautiful beaches and knockout cuisine have long exerted a powerful appeal. Away from the multicultural marvels of the capital, Palermo, the island's east and southeast coasts deliver a wealth of wonders. In just a few days, you can climb **Mt Etna**, Europe's largest active volcano; enjoy an opera facing the sea in the ancient Teatro Greco of elegant **Taormina**; dive in pellucid waters near neighbouring **Isola Bella**; cruise past the caves and black lava rocks of the **Riviera dei Ciclopi** (Coast of the Cyclops); and feast your eyes (and fill your belly) at the fish market in **Catania**. Heading south, reconnect with **Syracuse's** (left) glorious Greek past, then watch flamingos and herons in the salt marshes of the **Riserva di Vendicari**, and swim in the turquoise waters of its wild beaches before enjoying a cooling granita in **Noto** or a slab of traditional chocolate in **Modica**. Devastated by an earthquake in 1693, Noto and Modica are among the eight towns – including **Catania**, **Ragusa** (see page 109) and **Scicli** – in southeastern Sicily listed as UNESCO World Heritage Sites for their phoenix-like rise from the ashes, adorned with exuberant baroque architecture.

Ascend active Etna

Protected by the Parco dell'Etna and encompassing snowcapped peaks, lunar lava deserts, forests, vineyards and 21 towns, Mt Etna (inset, seen from Taormina's Teatro Greco) is one of the world's most active volcanoes, with eruptions occuring at its four craters and on the flanks. The most accessible ascent to the summit (at around 3350m/10,990ft, depending on eruptions), via the southern slope, starts at Rifugio Sapienza (1920m/6299ft), from where a cable car and then a 4WD vehicle take you up to 2920m (9580ft). Past here, you can approach the craters on foot, routes dictated by the level of volcanic activity. Climbing with a guide is essential; try Gruppo Guide Etna Nord (guidetnanord.com), Gruppo Guide Alpine Etna Sud (etnaguide.eu) or Etna Experience (etnaexperience.com).

Local living, Sicilian style

To get closer to the soul of Sicily, try staying on a working farm at one of the island's atmospheric agriturismos (agriturismo-sicilia.it), in bucolic surroundings of orchards and pasture lands. Surrender to the local rhythms of life during your stay: a long siesta after lunch, then the *passeggiata* (evening stroll) with an ice-cream in hand. And on this devout island, don't miss religious festivals such as the huge Festa di Sant'Agata in Catania (February); the Festa di Santa Lucia in Syracuse (December); or Easter celebrations in Scicli and Modica.

From the old to the new in Syracuse & Catania

Syracuse was, at its peak, the largest city in the ancient world. Its Parco Archeologico della Neapolis, with its Teatro Greco, is one of Sicily's most beautiful historic sites, while the Città Vecchia (Old Town) on Ortygia island contrasts stone buildings with azure seas, and grandiose baroque squares with the lanes of the Giudecca (Jewish quarter). Chaotic Catania paints a different picture of Sicily, but this student town hums with vitality, its black-and-white baroque buildings built with lava that flowed from Etna in 1669. Behind Piazza del Duomo, raucous La Pescheria, Catania's fish market, is a theatrical daily show.

Find the most beautiful beach

Everyone has a favourite seaside spot, but most agree that the pick of Sicily's beaches are at Isola Bella near Taormina; around Noto (Eloro, San Lorenzo, the wild Riserva di Vendicari shores); and near Agrigento, where the Scala dei Turchi cliffs overlook sandy shores.

Hike off the beaten track

From the town of Ispica, 12km (7.5 miles) southeast of Modica, a trail crosses through the 13km-long (8-mile) Cava d'Ispica gorge, whose caves were used as burial sites in the Neolithic era and as dwellings during the Middle Ages. An old watermill houses the Museo Cavallo d'Ispica, which offers a glimpse of rural Sicilian life in days gone by. Another place to stretch your legs, a wild plateau 40km (25 miles) from Syracuse, is the Necropoli di Pantalica (best explored with a guide), with more than 5000 tombs honeycombed into the limestone cliffs between the 13th and 8th century BCE.

MORE TIME?

VILLA ROMANA DEL CASALE Near the town of Piazza Armerina, this 4th-century Roman villa has astoundingly well-preserved multicoloured floor mosaics.
VALLEY OF THE TEMPLES Just south of Agrigento and encompassing the ruined ancient city of Akragas, this 13-sq-km (5-sq-mile) park is the jewel of Sicily's ancient sites.
CALTAGIRONE With a reputation for its ceramics, Caltagirone is most notable for its Scalinata di Santa Maria del Monte, a monumental flight of steps rising from the Piazza Municipio.

A MYTHICAL VOLCANO

Looming over eastern Sicily, Mt Etna's brooding presence leaves little wonder why it has inspired legends. According to Greek mythology, Etna was the mountain thrown by Zeus over Typhon, a snake-headed monster whose eyes could shoot flames and whose mouth spat out fiery rocks. Etna is also said to hold the forge of Hephaestus, Greek god of fire, while in Homer's *Odyssey*, it's the location of the cave in which the cyclops Polyphemus imprisons Odysseus and his men, only to be tricked into letting them escape; blinded by a stab to his single eye, a furious Polyphemus then bombarded their ship with the rocks that still bristle from the sea at Aci Trezza, near Catania.

~~~~~ PRACTICALITIES ~~~~~

☀ WHEN TO GO

April to June and September to October are the most pleasant months. In July, and especially August, prices soar.

⛽ HOW TO GET THERE

Some 60km (37 miles) north of Syracuse and 66km (41 miles) south of Taormina, Catania's International Airport is served by a large number of airlines, with connections to the UK and many European destinations.

🏠 WHERE TO STAY

There's a huge choice of *agriturismo* accommodation; La Corte del Sole (lacortedelsole. it), in a former *masseria* between Noto and the Riserva di Vendicari, offers cooking classes as well as rooms.

📅 EVENTS

The Festa di Sant'Agata is in full swing in Catania from 3 to 5 February. The pre-Lenten carnival in Acireale (carnevaleacireale.eu) is one of the most vibrant in Sicily. In March or April, Holy Week is particularly colourful in Scicli and Modica. Lovers of culture and the performing arts should visit Syracuse between early May and early June, for its Greek Theatre Festival, while Taormina plays host to numerous cinema, theatre, music and dance events between June and September.

FLUMINIMAGGIORE

Spiaggia del Poetto

Parco Naturale Molentargius Saline

CAGLIARI

CARBONIA

MONTE ARCOSU

Sant' Antioco

PULA

NORA

Costa del Sud

PORTO DI TEULADA

CHIA

Capo Malfatano   Capo Spartivento

ITALY

26

Take a history-rich road trip
IN SOUTHERN SARDINIA

Set in the Mediterranean, Sardinia is a land of character, crisscrossed by coastal and mountain roads linking historic towns and protected reserves. A stopover in the waterside capital, **Cagliari**, is a must. Stroll up to the medieval **Il Castello** cidadel, built on a hill overlooking Cagliari and encircled by ramparts (overleaf). Within the walls, a jigsaw of narrow, high-walled alleys connect grand buildings, such as the honey-coloured, 13th-century Cattedrale di Santa Maria and the four absorbing museums of the Cittadella dei Musei. Then head for the **seafront**: follow the promenade under the arcades before reaching **Poetto Beach**. Lined with bars and restaurants, this superb 7km-long (4-mile) strip of white sand is the ideal place to end the day with your feet in the water. Well rested, you can then set off (with a rental car) to explore the southern part of the island, discovering **ancient remains** at evocative Nora, spotting **wading birds** at a salt-marsh reserve, heading underground into **caves** and a one-time mine, and enjoying a string of **beaches and dreamy coves**.

Drive the Costa del Sud

Your road trip starts along the southern coast, winding past jagged cliffs and sparkling shores along the Strada Panoramica della Costa del Sud (SP 71). The 25km-long (15.5-mile) stretch between Porto di Teulada and Chia is particularly scenic: you'll skirt several coves, some topped with ancient Spanish watchtowers, before reaching Capo Malfatano (pause for a swim en route at Spiaggia di Piscinas) and Cala Tuerredda, known for its turquoise waters. Follow the road on through Porto Campana to the Capo Spartivento Lighthouse, with another swimming stop at the superb Cala Cipolla (opposite), before reaching the seaside resort of Chia.

Range around ruins at Nora

A 40-minute drive from Cagliari (or an hour by bus), the busy coastal resort of Pula is the gateway to the ruins at Nora (nora.beniculturali. unipd.it), 4km (2.5 miles) from the centre at the end of a rocky, narrow isthmus. Once one of Sardinia's most powerful cities, Nora was founded by the Phoenicians in the 8th century BCE; later an important Carthaginian centre, it was the island's Roman capital by the 3rd century CE. Some of the exceptional remains here – a theatre, a temple complex and baths – are still adorned with mosaics; you'll need to book a guided tour to explore them.

Combine birding & biking at Molentargius-Saline

In the far south of Sardinia, just east of Cagliari, the reed-fringed wetlands of the Parco Naturale Regionale Molentargius-Saline (parcomolentargius.it) spread out over some 14 sq km (5.5 sq miles). This protected area of marshes and salt flats is home to a rich ecosystem that attracts a host of wading birds – herons, egrets and flamingos – and numerous migratory species, most of which can be seen in spring or autumn. This site is accessible on foot from central Cagliari, and can also be explored by bike; you can rent electric cycles from the Infopoint Visitor Centre at the main entrance.

Meander around a mine in Carbonia

An hour's drive west of Cagliari, Carbonia recalls its mining past with the enthralling Museo del Carbone (museodelcarbone.it), set within a decommissioned coalmine that was once the largest in Italy. Tours into the mineshafts give a claustrophobic immersion into the difficult working conditions that the miners here endured.

Go underground around Fluminimaggiore

There's more below-the-earth intrigue at the vast, ever-chilly Grotte di Su Mannau (en.sumannau. it), where guided tours through the caverns take in a dazzling array of stalagmites, stalactites and other weird and wonderful rock formations. Nestled between sea and mountains, the nearby village of Fluminimaggiore, another former mining town, is also worth a visit, with a small ethnographic museum. The village is around an hour and 20 minutes by car from Cagliari.

MORE TIME?

SANT'ANTIOCO This sizeable island off Sardinia's southwest coast offers wild landscapes and crystal-clear coves set with pretty beaches. Site of ancient Sulci, Sardina's one-time capital, its eponymous main town is now a pretty fishing port. Sant'Antioco is linked to Sardinia by a causeway and road bridge, and is around an hour and 15 minutes by car from Cagliari.
MONTE ARCOSU Take a nature hike in the lovely WWF nature reserve, home to *cervo sardo* (Sardinian deer) as well as wildcats, wild boar and numerous birds of prey. It's around 20km (12.5 miles) southwest of Cagliari, and is best reached by car.

SARDINIAN CUISINE, FROM LAND & SEA

Rustic but tasty, Sardinian cuisine makes wonderful use of local produce from both land and sea. Highlights include the island version of the classic minestrone (made here with pearl-like *fregula* pasta in addition to fresh vegetables and beans), as well as succulent fish and shellfish (tuna, eel, lobster) or spit-roasted *porceddu* (suckling pig). Pasta specialities include *culurgiònes*, a sort of Sardinian ravioli stuffed with potato, pecorino cheese and mint (photo above), while the most popular bread here is the thin, crispy *carasau* flatbread; locals eat it with *casu marzu*, a sheep-milk pecorino cheese wriggling with live maggots.

PRACTICALITIES

HOW TO GET THERE & GET AROUND

Cagliari Airport has direct flights from around Italy and Europe, as well as the UK. You'll have no trouble renting a car on arrival.

WHERE TO STAY

If you're looking to be captivated by the soul of Cagliari, stay in the Castello Old Town; for breathtaking views of the Mediterranean, opt for the Marina district.

EVENTS

Early May sees Cagliari's Sagra di Sant'Efisio (festadisantefisio.it), a feast dedicated to St Ephysius, with a 1km-long (0.6 mile) procession featuring floats and costumed participants, all accompanied by music.

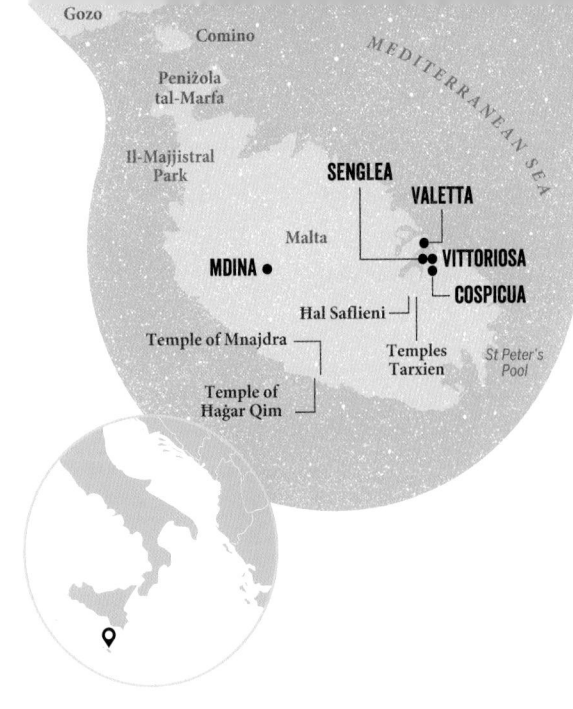

MALTA

From the city to the sea
IN MALTA

With its strategic position to the south of Sicily and in easy sailing distance of North Africa, Malta has had a string of rulers, from Phoenicians to Romans, the Moors to the British – and all have left their mark. The capital, Valletta (left), protected by imposing fortifications, is so jampacked with historic sights that the whole city is a UNESCO World Heritage Site. It was founded by the Knights of St John, whose mighty Co-Cathedral and Grand Master's Palace remain symbols of this ancient order's power. In the interior of the island, the walled city of Mdina is equally atmospheric: an ancient capital, perched high above the sea, where St Paul's Cathedral stands between honey-coloured houses. The main island of an archipelago that also includes Gozo and Comino (see page 118), Malta also hosts some natural gems. Its crystal-clear waters and wrecks make it a divers' paradise, while swimmers seek out sublime coves like St Peter's Pool, a natural lido set among the rocks. There's plenty of hiking, too: in the north of the island, the Marfa Peninsula offers coastal walks through a wetland reserve and comely views of Comino.

Marvel at Malta's megalithic sites

Malta's architectural gems don't all date from the 16th century: the island also has a built history that stretches back to the prehistoric era. The best-preserved of its ancient structures are the mysterious megalithic temples of Ħaġar Qim and Mnajdra, built between 3600 and 3000 BCE and spectacularly situated on coastal cliffs, from where the views are breathtaking. Visitor numbers are limited at the ancient underground necropolis of Ħal Saflieni Hypogeum (book three months in advance); access is easier to the nearby Tarxien Temples, where the monumental stone blocks are decorated with spiral patterns, pitting and animal reliefs.

Hop on a boat for a coastal tour of Malta

Taking to the water is a wonderful way to explore the Maltese coastline, enjoying views of cliffs and hidden coves acessible only from the sea. With dinghy rentals available by the hour from many coastal resorts, you can opt for a short independent excursion; for a longer cruise, hire a boat for the day, paying a supplement for a skipper to let someone else take care of the navigation.

Enjoy nature's bounty

At one time, the stretch of coastline between Golden Bay and Anchor Bay was slated to become a golf course, but thanks to opposition from local environmental groups, it was instead designated as Malta's first national park in 2007. Today, the Park Majjistral (majjistral.org) protects a region of wild sea cliffs, and its network of hiking trails can be followed independently or, to learn more about the flora and fauna, on guided hikes. Snorkelling sessions are also available in the clear waters of Golden Bay, led by specialised eco-oriented guides.

Explore the historic streets of the Three Cities

Facing Valletta across the Grand Harbour, the fortified towns of Senglea (opposite), Cospicua and Vittoriosa are collectively called the Three Cities. The latter, once known as Birgu, is arguably the most interesting, with its 16th-century Fort St Angelo, Inquisitor's Palace and the Malta at War Museum, but all offer a warren of staircases and alleyways, and historic buildings.

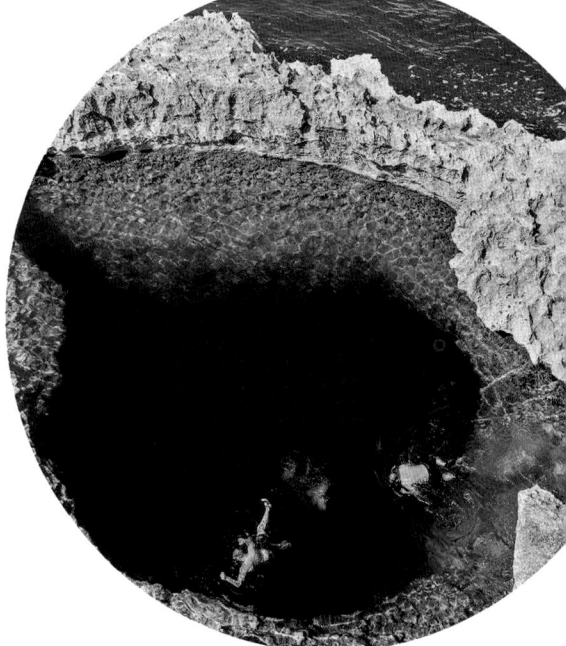

MORE TIME?

COMINO The main reason to visit this small island is to swim in the Blue Lagoon, a truly breathtaking sheltered cove with impossibly turquoise waters glinting over a white-sand seabed. Swim complete, stroll down the coast to the St Mary's Tower, built by the Knights of St John in the 17th century.

SICILY Ferries from Malta reach southern Sicily in just under two hours. From the port of Pozzallo, you can discover Modica, the baroque hill-town of Noto, the charming fishing village of Marzamemi and the splendid beaches of the Riserva di Vendicari, all within a radius of less than 40km (25 miles). Syracuse and its rich historical heritage are just 60km (37 miles) away.

MALTESE MORSELS

Malta has had a variety of occupiers, and its cuisine retains Italian, French, British and Arabic influences. On this Mediterranean island, fish is a local staple, served grilled, in soups and even in pies, but don't miss *stuffat tal-fenek* (rabbit simmered in red wine); or *stuffat tal-bebbux* (stewed snails). Snacks also deserve attention: look out for *ftira*, a flatbread filled with tuna, tomatoes, olives and the like; and *pastizzi* (photo above), flaky pastries filled with ricotta or pea puree; both make a perfect accompaniment to Malta's Cisk beer, best served ice-cold.

~~~~~~ • PRACTICALITIES • ~~~~~~

 HOW TO GET THERE

Malta International Airport in Luqa, just south of Valletta, has direct flights from around Europe and the UK, many with low-cost carriers.

EVENTS

Around Easter, Holy Week is the occasion for large-scale festivities, with spectacular processions island-wide. In October, during the Birgufest, the streets of Vittoriosa are lit up with candles, while period-costume shows and concerts bring the town to life.

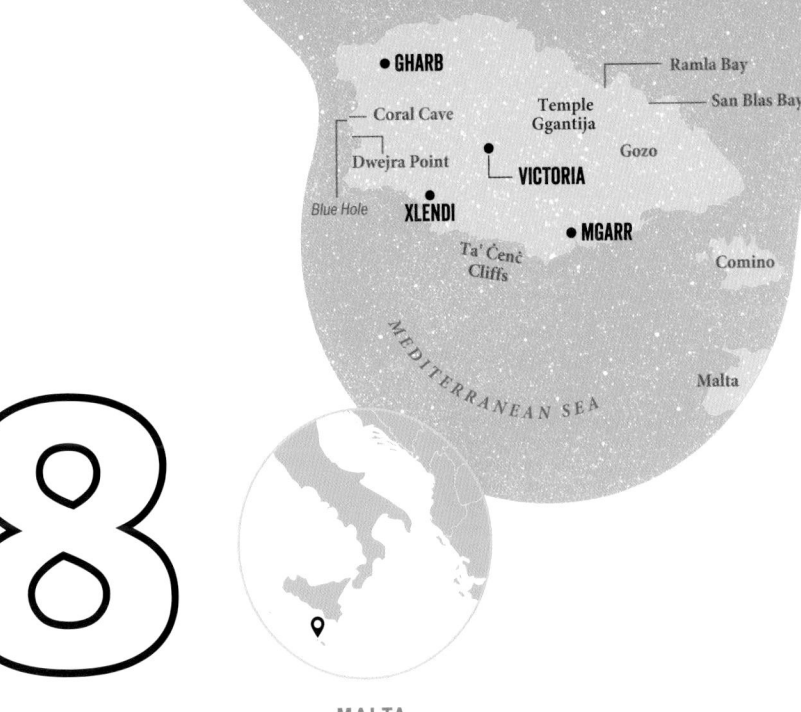

- GHARB
- Coral Cave
- Dwejra Point
- Blue Hole
- XLENDI
- Temple Ggantija
- **VICTORIA**
- Gozo
- Ta' Ċenċ Cliffs
- **MGARR**
- Comino
- Ramla Bay
- San Blas Bay
- Malta

MEDITERRANEAN SEA

MALTA

28

Discover island bliss
IN GOZO & COMINO

Welcome to Gozo, the pretty little pearl of the Maltese archipelago. It lies to the northwest of main island Malta, with its even smaller sister isle, Comino, in between the two.** Given its size, Gozo is easy to explore independently; renting a car or, even better, a **scooter**, gives you the freedom to stop off as the mood takes you (but make advance bookings, especially in the height of summer). Begin in the island's capital, **Victoria** (also known to locals as Rabat), where you'll be seduced by the **Il-Kastell** citadel, with a walkway that offers breathtaking views. Continue on to discover the island's **megalithic sites** – dating back around 5000 years, they are some of the oldest on the archipelago. Laid-back Gozo and even sleepier **Comino** are perfect relaxation destinations, with downtime days spent at gorgeous **beaches**, such as the red-sand **San Blas** and sublime swimming spots like Comino's **Blue Lagoon**. When it's time to get active, head for the many **diving** and **snorkelling sites**, or lace up your hiking shoes and head out on trails like southern Gozo's **Xlendi Walk**, which runs along the **Ta' Ċenċ cliffs** from the port of **Mġarr** (left) to the town of Xlendi.

Explore Gozo's north coast

For beach lovers, the island's north-coast hot-spots are San Blas Bay, a rock-strewn bay of rust-coloured sand; and the turquoise waters of Ramla Bay (opposite). West along the coast, Calypso's Cave offers panoramic views over the bay below, beyond which you'll travel through unspoilt coastline to the Qbajjar Salt Pans, a wild and extraordinary landscape carved into a patchwork of grids. Local families still work the pans during summer, when salt is sold at roadside stalls.

Wonder at wild shores in Gozo's northwest

The northwestern part of the island is home to the super-scenic surrounds of Dwejra Bay, where the wind and the Mediterranean swell have sculpted some of Gozo's most spectacular landscapes. The bay is guarded by the brooding bulk of Fungus Rock, known to Maltese as Il-Ġebla tal-Ġeneral (the General's Rock) in homage to the time when the Knights of St John collected a rare epiphytic plant from its summit, which was believed to have healing properties. Dwejra Bay's Blue Hole, a vertical 10m-wide (33ft), 25m-deep (82ft) chimney running down into the limestone, is a favourite with divers and snorkellers, as are the remains of the Azure Window (see page 116), a natural arch that collapsed in 2017. The scenery here is very end-of-the-world, just as beautiful when seen from the sea on a boat trip.

Take a deep dive or a serene snorkel off Gozo

Gozo is home to a host of excellent snorkelling spots and dive sites. Accessible year-round and suitable for both beginners and advanced divers, key dive sites include Dwejra Bay's Blue Hole (inset) and Coral Cave, as well as Reqqa Point and Wied Il-Għasri, off Gozo's north coast. Off the southeast coast, there's Mġarr ix-Xini and Xatt l-Aħmar, the latter a noted wreck-dive site. Snorkellers have a wealth of choice along the west and north coasts.

Stop over in Comino

This tiny islet between Malta and Gozo is perfect for a lazy day trip, though its key attraction, the marvellous Blue Lagoon, gets busy in high summer; visit in the low season if possible. Regular ferries run between Malta, Gozo and Comino.

Find prehistoric perfection & panoramic views

On the crest of the hill near Xagħra, with soaring views over southern Gozo, Ġgantija is the largest of the Maltese archipelago's megalithic temple sites. Dated to between 3600 and 3000 BCE, the walls of these two structures are over 6m (20ft) high, and together form a total length of 40m (131ft). The well-designed visitor centre displays artefacts discovered during excavations here. To the west, there are more heady views from the Ta'Pinu, a 1920s church on a hilltop near the village of Għarb.

MORE TIME?

MALTA The main island of the archipelago (see page 114) is brimming with diving spots, sunbathing beaches, historical sites to visit and villages to stroll through. Don't miss Mdina, the 'City of Silence', and spend a few days in Valletta or its surrounding districts: the historic Three Cities (Vittoriosa, Senglea, Cospicua) to the east; and, to the west, cosmopolitan Sliema, where Malta's cool crowd come to eat, drink, shop and party.

CLIMBING IN GOZO

Gozo has earned itself a solid reputation among climbers, with some 300 spectacular routes spread over a dozen easily accessible sites. The Dwejra site (above), open to the Mediterranean and to an inland lagoon, has quality rock and magnificent routes, but bear in mind that climbers must avoid disturbing the birds that nest here in spring. Between Xlendi and Munxar, there are over 20 equipped routes in a coastal gorge. Beginners can learn the ropes here, and there are challenging routes for seasoned climbers, too. For more information on the island's well-established climbing scene, contact the Gozo Climbing Association (via Facebook).

🛢 HOW TO GET THERE & GET AROUND

Fly to Malta International Airport near Valletta (see p.114), where you can pick up a rental car (book ahead) or take a direct bus (route X1) to the Ċirkewwa Terminal, departure point for ferries to Gozo and Comino; it's around an hour from the airport by road. The crossing to Gozo takes about 25 minutes.

A number of operators (such as MTS; gozomgarrtouristservice.com) offer scooter rentals.

📅 EVENTS

Gozo stages a host of summer festivals (eventsingozo.com), from village feasts to fireworks displays to the celebrations honouring St Peter and St Paul in the last week of June.

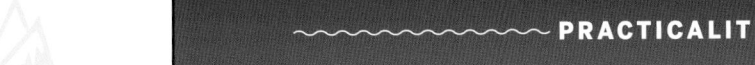

Plitvice Lakes National Park

BOSNIA & HERZEGOVINA

CROATIA

Pag

Paklenica National Park

Ugljan • ZADAR

ADRIATIC SEA

Kornati Archipelago

CROATIA

29

Trace Croatian history

IN ZADAR & NORTHERN DALMATIA

Scenically set on a peninsula jutting out into the Adriatic Sea, the Northern Dalmatian capital of Zadar has a rich history that dates back over 3000 years. Beginning with the Romans, its long line of rulers have bestowed a wealth of wonderful buildings, from a Roman Forum and Venetian fortifications to a series of knockout churches (left). There's plenty of culture too – Croatia's **first university** was established here in the late 14th century, and today, the city's museums cover everything from archaeology to religious art and even illusions. There's also a wonderful alchemy of art and the 'art of living' here: interactive installations sit side-by-side with restaurants and boho bars, creating an original and uplifting atmosphere that's most palpable along the **Riva** waterfront, and in squares such as **Narodni trg**. Zadar's transport links make it a great base for discovering Northern Dalmatia. Lovers of wide-open spaces, hiking and swimming have easy access to **Paklenica and Plitvice Lakes National Parks,** the islands of **Pag and Ugljan**, and the **Kornati Archipelago** (see page 125).

123

Relive the Roman era

It's impossible to overlook the Roman influence in Zadar. This is a city where Roman ruins seem to sprout randomly from the streets, and nowhere is this more evident than in the Old Town, which was built around a Roman Forum, the most notable remains of which include a single intact column and ruined altars dedicated to Jupiter and Medusa. A model of the Forum and a superb 2.5m-high (8.2ft) marble statue of Augustus are on display at the Archaeological Museum (amzd.hr), while the Museum of Ancient Glass (mas-zadar.hr) displays goblets, jars, amulets and Roman urns that offer a fascinating insight into antiquity.

Stroll the stunning Old Town

After the Roman era, Zadar became an important Byzantine capital and later fell under Venetian and Austrian control, and this storied history has left its mark in the beautiful Old Town. Take a walk along its stone-paved streets to discover UNESCO-listed Venetian fortifications and the ornate Land Gate. Zadar's churches offer a perfect illustration of the city's multifaceted history: the circular, Byzantine-style St Donatus (see previous page), dating from the 9th century; the marvellous baroque interior of 17th-century St Simeon's; and St Anastasia's Cathedral, with lovely Old Town views from its bell tower.

Salute the sun on Zadar's waterfront

Zadar's Riva waterfront is the perfect place for a stroll under the palm trees, overlooking the islands of Ugljan and Pašman. It's also the location of two intriguing artworks created by local architect Nikola Bašić in 2005 and 2008. His *Sea Organ*, set within stone stairs that descend into the shore, is a system of pipes and whistles that use the power of wind and wave to create incredible whispers of sound, audible from the steps and while swimming in the sea below. Nearby, Bašić's *Sun Salutation* is a circle of glass panels that collect the sun's rays by day and produce a fabulous light show by night. It'a a hugely popular spot, with tourists and locals alike flocking in to watch the sunset and take in the illuminations.

Hike Northern Dalmatia's national parks

Just an hour's drive northeast of Zadar, in the wooded peaks of the Velebit Range, Paklenica National Park (np-paklenica.hr) is a hiking hotspot. Trails of varying difficulty zigzag through its impressive gorges (keep eyes peeled for eagles, chamois and lynx), while climbers tackle the park's 500-plus routes. Another hour and a half northeast, in the UNESCO-listed Plitvice Lakes National Park (np-plitvicka-jezera.hr), 16 crystalline lakes tumble into each other via a series of waterfalls, with wooden footbridges and pathways snaking around the edges and across the rushing water. It gets very busy, so arrive early.

MORE TIME?

ISLAND OF PAG As well as its rocky, lunar-like landscape and string of Adriatic beaches, Pag is also famous for its Paški Sir cheese, one of Croatia's most popular exports. Pag is linked to the mainland by a bridge, and can be reached by bus from Zadar.
UGLJAN ISLAND Separated from Zadar by a narrow swathe of the Adriatic, and reachable by a 30-minute ferry ride from the city, Ugljan is a perfect getaway, with dreamy coves and pretty villages.
KORNATI ISLANDS Take a day trip from Zadar to this 140-island archipelago (opposite). Partially protected by a national park, its barren, uninhabited isles are ringed with caves, grottoes, rugged cliffs and the deep blue of the Adriatic.

THE ANCIENT GLAGOLITIC ALPHABET

Sharing some similarities with Greek, Hebrew and Armenian, the Glagolitic script is the oldest known Slavic alphabet, created in the 9th century by two monks from Thessalonica, Cyril and Methodius (above). Known as the 'Apostles to the Slavs' for their evangelistic work in the region, they created Glagolitic as a means of transcribing Old Church Slavonic religious texts. The Glagolitic script was later replaced by the Cyrillic alphabet in much of Central Europe and the Balkans, but in Croatia, it was used in liturgical texts until the 18th century. On Cres Island, northwest of Zadar, St Mark's Church holds the 11th-century Valun Tablet, inscribed in both Glagolitic and Latin.

PRACTICALITIES

HOW TO GET THERE

Low-cost carriers operate direct flights to Zadar Airport from all around Europe and the UK. From Zagreb, the Croatian capital, it's around three and a half hours by bus to Zadar.

EVENTS

One of Zadar's biggest summer events is the Full Moon Festival: on the night of the full moon, streetlights are replaced with lanterns and candles, and fresh fish and seafood dishes are sold from street stalls and boats.

CROATIA

30

Island-hopping & hiking
ON THE
DALMATIAN COAST

Overlooked by the rugged Dinaric Alps, Central Dalmatia's coastline **is a scenic stretch of sandy beaches, fishing harbours, coves and offshore islands.** Its string of beautiful pebble **coves**, lapped by the gin-clear Adriatic, are the most obvious draw, and they certainly do draw the crowds. Head inland, however, to find calm and quiet along **mountain hiking** trails and enjoy eye-stretching **coastal views**. As well as its natural attractions, the Dalmatian Coast offers plenty of historical sights, from the ruins of the ancient city of **Salone**, Croatia's most important archaeological site, to the parade of riches in **Split**, dominated by the Roman-era **Diocletian's Palace**, still a living, breathing part of the city where the labyrinthine streets are abuzz with people, bars, shops and restaurants. Beyond the Old Town, head for the sea to swim at **Kašjuni Beach**, then enjoy the shoreside bars and clubs of **Bačvice**. South of Split, beyond the island of **Brač**, **Hvar** (left) is another popular holiday isle, with its sights concentrated in the walled Hvar Town (overleaf). To discover a quieter side of the island, head to the pretty north-coast town of **Stari Grad**, or inland to Hvar's lavender fields.

Go beyond the beach on Brač

The headline locale on the island of Brač – and the poster child for all Croatian beaches – Bol's Zlatni Rat is an impossibly scenic shore, its tongue of smooth white pebbles jutting out into the turquoise sea. It's very popular with swimmers and windsurfers; quieter corners of Brač include the historic centre of Supetar (which also has a decent beach of its own) or the picturesque port of Sumartin. The rest of the island is a glorious melange of cliffs, olive groves, pine forests and vineyards, surrounded by a superb coastline. Various sea links connect Brač to the mainland.

Head to the hills for hikes with heady views

The mountainous landcape of Biokovo Nature Park (biokovo. com) delivers spectacular views of the Makarska Riviera, the islands of Hvar and Brač and, on clear days, across the Adriatic Sea to the coastline of Italy. Numerous rocky trails, some of them demanding, cross this limestone massif to the delight of hikers; you can also take in the views from the glass-walled Skywalk, just off the Biokovo Rd. To reach the park, take the bus from Split to the park entrance in Makarska; journey time is just over an hour.

Enjoy peace & quiet on the island of Vis

This quiet, remote island with its superb beaches has an authentic charm all of its own. It retains something of an air of mystery, having been closed to foreign visitors from 1950 to 1989, when it was used as a Yugoslav military base. Today, people come to enjoy the wilderness, go scuba diving, take a turn around pretty fishing villages such as Komiža and taste the delicious local cuisine. Several companies operate ferries and catamarans between Split and Vis.

Treat yourself to Trogir

Set on a teeny-tiny island, linked by bridges to both the mainland and to the far larger isle of Čiovo, the UNESCO-listed medieval fortified town of Trogir (opposite; visittrogir. hr) is a magnet for visitors. Stroll along cobbled streets to admire the beautiful Romanesque and Renaissance buildings, the most impressive of which is St Lawrence's Cathedral, a three-naved Venetian marvel with lovely views from its bell tower. As dusk sets in, head for the waterfront, where busy bars overlook bobbing yachts in the marina. From Split, buses run to Trogir in around 30 minutes.

MORE TIME?

KAŠTELA Stretching along some 20km (12 miles) of coastline between Split and Trogir, the municipality of Kaštela (kastela-info. hr) is made up of a succession of fortified villages, castles and small port towns. Halfway along the region's coast road, Kaštel Vitturi is the best-preserved of the bastions.
KLIS FORTRESS This imposing fortress (tvrdavaklis.com), whose origins date back to the 2nd century BCE, sits atop a rocky outcrop, and affords an exceptional view of Split and the coastline. The small town below, meanwhile, is renowned for its cuisine; local specialities include lamb roasted over an open fire.

DALMATIAN CUISINE

With its diverse Mediterranean influences, Dalmatian cuisine naturally features plenty of grilled fish and freshly caught seafood, alongside slow-cooked beef simmered with potatoes in a *peka* (cast-iron dish), and seasonal vegetables dressed with olive oil, garlic and aromatic herbs. Standout local specialities include sheep-milk cheeses, while Dalmatian wines are also well worth sampling, from red Plavac Mali to Pošip white, alongside some exceptional Crljenak wines made with an ancient Croatian variety of the Zinfandel grape.

~ PRACTICALITIES ~

HOW TO GET THERE & GET AROUND

Split's International Airport is served by flights from all around Europe and from the UK. From the city, numerous buses and boats connect the various towns in Central Dalmatia.

WHERE TO STAY

In the historic centre and just a few minutes' walk from the beach, Villa Split (villasplitluxury.com) offers smart and contemporary rooms.

EVENTS

In May, the religious feast of St Domnius gives rise to concerts and various events in the streets of Split. The city's Ultra Europe (ultraeurope.com) in July is one of Europe's biggest electronic music festivals.

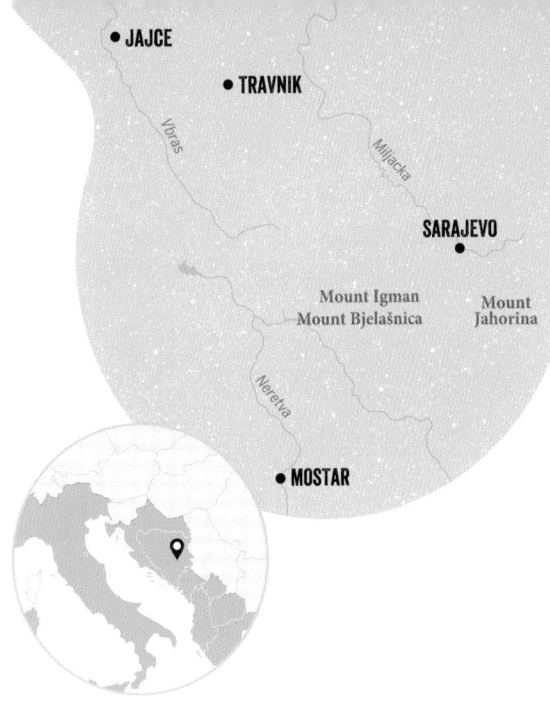

BOSNIA & HERCEGOVINA

Discover diverse history
IN & AROUND SARAJEVO

Despite its beguiling archi-tectural heritage, with mosques and minarets sitting alongside an Ashkenazi Synagogue and Catholic and Orthodox cathedrals, many still associate Sarajevo with two tumultuous events of the 20th century. The assassination of Archduke Franz Ferdinand near the Latin Bridge in 1914, and the 1992–96 Siege of Sarajevo, during the civil war that ripped through the country, have come to define this singular city in the eyes of outsiders. Today, though, the capital of Bosnia & Hercegovina has its eyes firmly fixed on the future, while also acknowledging its troubled past. Sensitively curated displays at the **War Childhood Museum** and the **Galerija 11/07/95** memoria-lise the events of the siege, while gloriously reconstructed buildings such as the **Vijećnica** celebrate the city's rise from the ashes, and sleek new skyscrapers soar above the concrete carbuncles inherited from the communist era. Enjoy a bird's-eye view of the Sarajevo skyline with a ride on the cable car, then explore beyond the city limits, taking a trip to **Mostar** and its symbolic restored bridge or, if you're here in winter, hitting the slopes in the region's **ski resorts**.

From market to mosque in Baščaršija

Whether you're browsing for antiques, haggling over soccer shirts or watching artisans at work, strolling through this atmospheric 15th-century Ottoman quarter is a great way to soak up the soul of Sarajevo. Beyond the bargains, the Baščaršija's cobbled streets lead to some of the city's most famous monuments – the mosques of Gazi Husrev-beg, Ferhadija and Baščaršija; as well as the ornate Sebilj drinking fountain (see previous page) from 1891 and the elegant 1529 Sahat kula (Clock Tower) – and to the city's one-time Jewish quarter.

Ski on Olympic slopes

It may have been somewhat eclipsed by the conflict of the 1990s, but Sarajevo was the venue for the 1984 Winter Olympics. Reachable via a scenic cable car from Sarajevo's Bistrik district, the Olympic bobsled track atop Mt Trebević is long abandoned, but skiing is very much an active pursuit around Sarajevo. Just 30 minutes or so by car from the city, the ski resorts of Jahorina, Bjelašnica and Igman were used during the games, and their runs have a covering of snow until April; they also offer some of cheapest skiing in Europe.

Move on to Mostar

Around two hours by train or bus from Sarajevo, the town of Mostar is home to the swooping arch of the Stari Most (opposite). The name translates as 'Old Bridge', but what you see today is a brilliant reconstruction of the original structure, which was built between 1557 and 1566 on the orders of Suleiman the Magnificent, and destroyed during the civil war. With its pale stone shining in the sunshine once again (and artfully lit by floodlights after dark), Stari Most is a sight to behold; take a seat in one of the surrounding cafes to watch local lads diving from its highest point into the waters of the Neretva below.

Play chess at Trg Oslobodenja

This landscaped square in the centre of Sarajevo, next to the city's expansive Orthodox cathedral, is emblematic in more ways than one: it's notable for having escaped the destruction of the civil war, and also features busts of great Bosnian writers including Ivo Andrić. For many locals, though, Trg Oslobođenja is best-known for the giant chessboard painted onto the paving, where elderly Sarajevans meet daily to engage in spirited strategy battles, with each move analysed and discussed by gatherings of spectators. Anyone is welcome to join in.

MORE TIME?

TRAVNIK This pretty medieval town, once an Ottoman stronghold, is well worth a visit for its 15th-century fortress, colourfully painted mosque and array of Ottoman graves; it was also the birthplace of Nobel Prize-winning Bosnian author Ivo Andrić, whose former home holds a small museum. Travnik is an hour and 40 minutes from Sarajevo by bus.

JAJCE A two-hour taxi ride from Sarajevo, Jajce has a 20m-high (66ft) waterfall (inset) right in the middle of town, as well as a medieval fortress and beautiful churches.

THE REBIRTH OF THE VIJEĆNICA

In 1992, in the midst of the Siege of Sarajevo, one of the buildings targeted by the shelling was the triangular Vijećnica, a beautiful Austro-Hungarian building that, since 1949, had housed the National Library. Staff heroically salvaged some of the collection's most precious pieces, but around two million books, many of them unique, went up in smoke. In 1996, a laborious reconstruction began, funded by the EU and various international donors. Reopened in 2014, with its neo-Moorish striped facade and stained-glass ceiling beautifully restored, the Vijećnica now houses the City Hall and the enthralling Sarajevo 1914–2014 exhibition.

PRACTICALITIES

WHEN TO GO

The climate of Bosnia & Hercegovina combines Mediterranean and continental influences: temperatures can be high in summer and freezing in winter. Unless you're coming here to ski, the best time to visit is from mid-spring to early summer.

HOW TO GET THERE

With direct flights from the UK and European capitals (though not from any French cities), Sarajevo Airport is 12km (7.5 miles) to the southwest of the city, connected to the centre by regular buses.

WHERE TO STAY

The best options in Sarajevo are the *pansions*, some of which are still family-run; top choices include the Hotel Pansion Stari Grad (sarajevohotels.org), in the Old Town, or the Pansion River (sarajevohotels.org), with a lovely location on the banks of the Miljacka River.

CROATIA

Bay of Kotor · **KOTOR**

Lovćen National Park

· **PODGORICA**

Blue Cave

Njegos Mausoleum

Mount Lovćen

MONTENEGRO

Luštica

· **BUDVA**

ALBANIA

SVETI STEFAN

VIRPAZAR

Shkodra Lake

ADRIATIC SEA

ULCINJ ·

MONTENEGRO

32

An Adriatic odyssey

FROM PODGORICA TO KOTOR

With a breathtaking Adriatic coastline and a mountainous hinterland of gorges, azure lakes and peaceful valleys, Montenegro holds a wealth of attractions. Put down your bags for the first day in the pint-sized capital of **Podgorica**. Stroll along the banks of the **Morača River**, past the landmark Millennium Bridge, then head into the centre to take in the city's hotchpotch of Ottoman oddments, Austrian shopfronts, brutalist blocks and shiny new malls, and pop in to the **Museums & Galleries of Podgorica**; displays include artefacts from Doclea, Podgorica's Roman-era antecedent. The next day, hop on the train for the 30-minute journey to **Virpazar** on the shore of **Skadar**, the largest lake in the Balkans. Contemplate its waters from the heights of Virpazar's **Besac Fortress**, built by the Turks in 1478, then take a **cruise** to enjoy the lake's island monasteries, birdlife and floating meadows of water lilies. It's a taster of what's to come along the Adriatic coast, from the beautiful **Bay of Kotor** (left) to **Budva**; while inland, take an overview of the region from the uplands of **Lovćen National Park**.

135

Walk within the walls in Kotor

The country's emblematic poster child, the walled city of Kotor is one of Montenegro's must-see destinations. Stroll in the shadow of its medieval ramparts, through the labyrinthine streets of the Old Town, to admire its museums, churches, cafe-strewn squares and Venetian palaces. Then lose yourself in the breathtaking Bay of Kotor, a snaking arm of the Adriatic Sea, hemmed in by dramatic cliffs and reminiscent of the Norwegian fjords. Kotor town is around an hour an a half by car from Podgorica, or about two hours by bus.

Take to the water around the Luštica Peninsula

The southern shore of the Bay of Kotor is enclosed by the sublime Luštica Peninsula, a place of olive groves and quiet villages like Krtoli, and with a string of unspoilt beaches such as the coves at the fishing villages of Bjelila, Rose, Žanjic or Uvala Veslo, the latter close to the mesmerising Blue Grotto (Plava Špilja). All are accessible by road from Kotor, but many choose to navigate the peninsula from the water, picking up a paddle to kayak the shoreline – take a tour with Adventure Montenegro (adventuremontenegro.com) – or even boarding a semi-submersible with Montenegro Submarines (montenegrosubmarine.me).

Drive the Kotor Serpentine to Lovcen

Between Kotor and Mt Lovćen, the 'black mountain' after which the country is named, the winding Kotor Serpentine (opposite) is one of the country's most beautiful drives, cutting a zigzagging path between the Adriatic and the mountains. Rent a car in Kotor to negotiate the 25 hairpin bends of this heartstopping 17km (10.6-mile) route; your destination is Cetinje, gateway to Lovćen National Park (nparkovi.me/np-lovcen). From here, another mountain road leads to the park's star attraction, the Njegoš Mausoleum. Set atop the 1657m-high (5436ft) Jezerski Vrh, and with an impressive panorama of the mountains and the Bay of Kotor, it's the final resting place of Montenegro's greatest hero, Petar II Petrović Njegoš.

Combine beaches & Old Town charm in Budva

A buzzy seaside resort on the Adriatic that also happens to have a beautiful medieval centre, Budva is just an hour's bus ride from the capital. It attracts hordes of holidaymakers who come to enjoy its magnificent beaches and lively summer-season nightlife, as well as soaking up Old Town charm along the marble-paved streets of the Stari Grad. Stroll around the central square, visit the churches (Orthodox Holy Trinity and Catholic St John the Baptist), and then head for the Citadela which, behind its fortifications, houses an interesting archaeological museum.

MORE TIME?

ULCINJ Popular with visitors from nearby Albania, this small town is surrounded by a large beach (Velika Plaža), while the Salina salt pans and mudflats attract a rich array of birds. It's about an hour and a half by car from Podgorica.
SVETI STEFAN Home to some excellent restaurants, this fortified island village (inset) is linked to the mainland by a narrow causeway and overlooks turquoise waters and pink-sand beaches.

MONTENEGRIN SPECIALITIES

Montenegrin cuisine is a delicious combination of Mediterranean and Balkan gastronomic traditions. Inland, restaurants offer excellent cured meats such as *pršut* (smoked ham), as well as *ispod saca*, slow-cooked lamb, goat or veal roasted on a hearth under a dome-shaped metal lid covered with charcoal. Hearty mountain dishes include *kačamak*, a polenta-based porridge made with potato, cheese and *kajmak* (similar to clotted cream). On the coast, the emphasis is on freshly caught fish and shellfish, grilled in olive oil or cooked up into delicious stews; look out, too, for eel and smoked carp from Lake Skadar.

~ PRACTICALITIES ~

🅿 HOW TO GET THERE & GET AROUND

Podgorica Airport, 11km (7 miles) south of the city, has flights from around Europe and the UK. Most parts of Montenegro are accessible by public transport, but it's easier to rent a car.

🏠 WHERE TO STAY

If you want to feel the pulse of Podgorica, opt for the lively Nova Varoš district, with its bars and small restaurants.

📅 EVENTS

On 7 January, the whole of Montenegro celebrates Orthodox Christmas. In August, Bokeljska Noć (Night of the Mouths) has been staged in Kotor since the 19th century, with fireworks and a sail-past by a fleet of decorated boats.

• ATHENS

Port
of Piraeus

Saronic Gulf

Aegina

Sounion   Kea

PELOPONNESE   Poros

Kithnos

Idra

Spetses

Myrtoan Sea   Serifos

GREECE

Take a culture-rich trip

FROM ATHENS TO AEGINA

The silhouette of the Acropolis impresses on every visit to Athens, whether it's your first or your fiftieth. But while the sacred hill is a must, the Greek capital has preserved many other traces of its ancient history that are equally deserving of your time, from the Agora to the Acropolis Museum. The pleasures of a stay here also include the view from the top of **Lykavittos**, the 'Hill of Wolves', accessible on foot or by funicular; strolls through the lively districts of **Monastiraki** (left) or **Plaka**, with their souvenir and sandal stores and Byzantine churches; and a dip into the nightlife scenes of **Psyrri, Gazi** and **Exarchia**. But when the call of the sea becomes a shout, head to the port of **Piraeus** (see page 141) and set sail for one of the **Saronic Gulf Islands**. Choose attractive **Aegina**, closer to Athens than its sister isles of Spetses or Hydra, but quiet nonetheless. It's home to **ancient sites** such as the Temple of Aphaia, the charming **ports** of Aegina and Perdika, and a string of comely **beaches**. A condensed version of Greek island life awaits you here: settle in at a taverna, order a plate of fried fish, and raise a glass of ouzo to this little piece of paradise.

Discover alternative Athens in Exarchia

Close to Athens' university and the National Archaeological Museum, the Exarchia district offers a different side to the city that's a world away from its ancient remains. Long associated with leftist politics, the countercultural vibe of this 'anarchist district' is best expressed in its street art, with pieces by the likes of INO (ino.net) or Wild Drawing (wdstreetart.com) painted on walls throughout the area, many of them huge in scale. Explore independently or take a guided tour with Alternative Athens (alternativeathens.com).

Enjoy culture & horticulture at the SNFCC

Stray from the city's most touristed areas to visit the Stavros Niarchos Foundation Cultural Center (SNFCC; snfcc.org), southwest of central Athens above Faliro Bay and named after the Greek shipping magnate who funded its construction. Designed by Renzo Piano and opened in 2016, the building is fronted by fountains and shaded by a roof covered with solar panels, beneath which a terrace gives views of the sea and the city. Home to the National Library and the Greek National Opera, it hosts exhibitions, shows and concerts, and is surrounded by a 21-hectare (52-acre) garden. Free shuttles to the SNFCC run from Syntagma.

Sample the Saronic Gulf Islands in Aegina

From the island's busy port town, also called Aegina (inset), bypass the neighbouring Temple of Apollo, its remains dominated by a solitary column, and head instead to the Temple of Aphaia, perched atop a pine-covered hill in the northeast of the island and offering breathtaking views of the Saronic Gulf. Built around 480 BCE, it's said to be one of three temples that, along with the Parthenon and Sounion's Temple of Poseidon, form a 'sacred triangle'. Back towards Aegina Town, move from antiquity to the Byzantine era with a visit to Paleohora. Aegina's capital from the 9th century to the medieval period, it was abandoned in the 1820s, and its buildings – including 30 churches – lie scattered across a remote hillside, linked by a network of paths. It's a special place, made more magical by its relative lack of visitors.

See Aegina Town the traditional way

It might carry a whiff of whimsy kitsch, but taking a ride in one of the colourful horse-drawn carriages that ply their trade along the waterfont in Aegina Town is a lovely and low-impact way to see the town and surrounding coastline, out in the open air and cooled by sea breezes. Drivers point out local sights along the way.

MORE TIME?

POROS From Aegina Town, take a day trip to the Saronic Gulf island of Poros, around an hour and 20 minutes away by ferry, to visit the delightful old centre of Poros Town (Hora) or to embark on hikes in the green hinterland.

CAPE SOUNION The main reason to visit Cape Sounion's diminutive national park is to see the imposing Temple of Poseidon, some 70km (43 miles) south of Athens. Built in 444 BCE, the marble columns of this impressive temple stand on a craggy spur above the sea, and the site affords some seriously splendid views: on a clear day, you can see the islands of Kea, Kythnos and Serifos to the southeast, and Aegina to the west.

AEGINA'S 'GREEN GOLD'

Greece is Europe's leading producer of pistachios, and the nuts grown on Aegina are the cream of the crop. Known to Greeks as *fistikia*, pistachios have been cultivated on the island since the 19th century, and were given PDO (Protected Designation of Origin) status by the EU in 1994. With a delicate and fragrant taste, and a distinctively round shape, Aegina's *koilarati* pistachios flourish in the island's limestone soils, and you'll see them on sale everywhere here. Pick up a pack to take home, or enjoy them in Aegina's restaurants: they're incorporated into sweet treats such as baklava and sprinkled on everything from salads to ice-creams.

PRACTICALITIES

✈ HOW TO GET THERE

Athens International Airport, 33km (20.5 miles) southeast of the centre, is served by flights from the UK and from European and North American cities. Ferries to Aegina, with companies such as Hellenic Seaways (hellenicseaways.gr), depart from the port of Piraeus, which is a 20-minute journey by metro from Monastiraki Station in Athens.

🍴 WHERE TO EAT

Athens' Diporto Agoras (Sokratous 9 & Theatrou. Psyrri) is a tiny taverna in the heart of the Psyrri district, serving unfussy, inexpensive local dishes such as *revithia* (chickpea soup); don't look for the sign — there isn't one. Vegetarians should head for Veganaki (veganaki.gr), near the Acropolis Museum; it serves vegan versions of Greek specialities, including some gluten-free options.

📅 EVENTS

Every year from June to August, the Athens and Epidaurus Festival (aefestival.gr) sees theatre and opera performances around the city, some staged at the ancient Odeon of Herodes Atticus. In September, Aegina celebrates pistachio harvest with the Aegina Fistiki Fest.

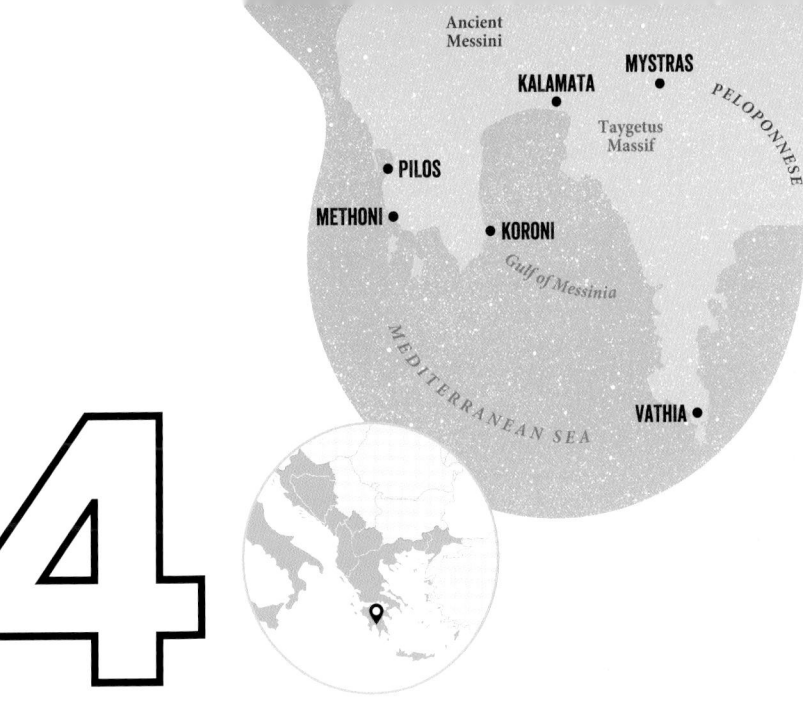

Ancient
Messini

KALAMATA

MYSTRAS

Taygetus
Massif

PELOPONNESE

PILOS

METHONI

KORONI

Gulf of Messinia

MEDITERRANEAN SEA

VATHIA

GREECE

3 4

Take it easy
AROUND THE GULF OF MESSINIA

With a host of ancient remains that bear witness to a fascinating past, this southwest corner of the Peloponnese is also renowned for its delicious olives, sunny climate and magnificent coastline. Ranged around the Gulf of Messinia are some of the most **beautiful beaches in Greece** (such as Voidokilia, left), from long stretches of fine sand to wild coves where you can swim year-round, far from the crowds. Small **fishing ports** are scattered along the shoreline, many guarded by an imposing Venetian-built *kastro* (fort), while inland, **historic sites** such as Mystras or Ancient Messini offer a diverting respite from the resorts. Messinia's main hub is the regional capital, **Kalamata**, a busy port with an enviable location between the calm waters of the **Ionian Sea** and hills planted with olive and fig trees. Many people pass straight through Kalamata, but it's an attractive base from which to explore the region, with a big **produce market** and friendly **cafes and restaurants** on the waterfront and in the Old Town, as well as a host of **museums** devoted to everything from traditional Greek costumes to history and folklore.

143

From Pylos to a palace

As well as featuring a rich historical heritage, best expressed in its imposing Neo Kastro citadel, the town of Pylos, on Messinia's southwest coast, is home to a number of heavenly beaches, including the white-sand Divari and the perfect horseshoe of Voidokilia. After soaking up the sun, head 17km (10.5 miles) north to the ruins of Nestor's Palace. Described in Homer's *Odyssey* as the court of the hero Nestor, this well-preserved Mycenaean complex is crisscrossed by raised walkways; explanatory texts give a good idea of its original dimensions. Pylos is an hour from Kalamata by bus; renting a car is the easiest way to reach the palace.

Visit a Venetian castle at Koroni

Over on the southeast shore of Messinia, and an easy bus journey from Kalamata, Koroni (inset) is a small, peaceful seaside town with a charming marina lined with bars and restaurants, but its main attraction is its Venetian fortress, which has watched over the Messinian coast since the 13th century. From the top of its walls, a magnificent view extends over Koroni and the coast; head beyond the castle to reach the sweep of golden sand at Zaga Beach.

Travel back in time at Ancient Messini

Messinia's drawcards are not just along its coastline. In the midst of the interior, around 40 minutes' drive northeast of Kalamata, the remains of Ancient Messini (opposite) comprise no less than 9km (5.6 miles) of fortifications – among the longest ramparts in the country. They enclose what survives of the one-time Messinian capital, from an impressive amphitheatre (still in use today) to the Sanctuary of Asclepius, the spiritual heart of the ancient city. A small archaeological museum gives information on the site.

Sample fish & seafood

The waters of the Gulf of Messinia are rich fishing grounds. Enjoy their bounty at spots along the Gulf's east coast, en route to Mani. Kardamyli is one of the prettiest resorts, while the cafes of Stoupa come alive on sunny days; the tavernas of neighbouring Agios Nikolaos offer a more intimate dining experience.

Hike the Taÿgetos & marvel at Mystras

With its coniferous forest, streams, viewpoints and marked trails, this mountain range in the Mani region is ideal for hiking. The conical summit of Mt Taÿgetos, often snow-covered, is only accessible in summer. East of the peak, and surrounded by olive and orange trees, the Byzantine town of Mystras is spread over a steep mountainside. This compelling collection of ruins comprises churches, monasteries and palaces, most dating from between 1271 and 1460. From Kalamata, it takes a little over an hour to reach the site by car.

MORE TIME?

METHONI South of Pylos and surrounded by vineyards, with a vast, crumbling Venetian fortress guarding a promontory to the south, this laid-back coastal town is a popular spot. It's particularly pleasant before and after the summer-season crowds depart.
VATHIA Perched in the hills toward the tip of the arid Mani Peninsula, this fortified village is a picturesque place for a wander. Take a walk through narrow streets lined with stone-built houses, some atmospherically ruined, others carefully restored.

KALAMATA OLIVES

Recognisable by their purple-brown colour and generous size, deliciously plump Kalamata olives are renowned the world over, and their ancestral cultivation is the pride of the Greek people. Fruit is often picked by hand, or sometimes with rudimentary machinery. The olives are then cold-pressed to extract the oil, or preserved in brine or olive oil, often flavoured with garlic and herbs. In Sparta (an hour's drive east of Kalamata), get the lowdown on the history, cultivation and production methods of this versatile fruit at the Olive and Greek Olive Oil Museum (piop.gr).

~ PRACTICALITIES ~

🅿 HOW TO GET THERE & GET AROUND

Kalamata Airport has direct flights from around Europe and the UK. Buses operated by KTEL (ktelmessinias.gr) are a great way to get around the region.

🛏 WHERE TO STAY

There's plenty of choice in Kalamata; options along Navarinou Ave enjoy sea views.

📅 EVENTS

The Kalamata Dance Festival (kalamatadancefestival.gr) is a major event staged in Kalamata every July. Since 1940, the Greek national holiday of Ohi Day has been celebrated with parades in Messinia (and throughout the country) on 28 October.

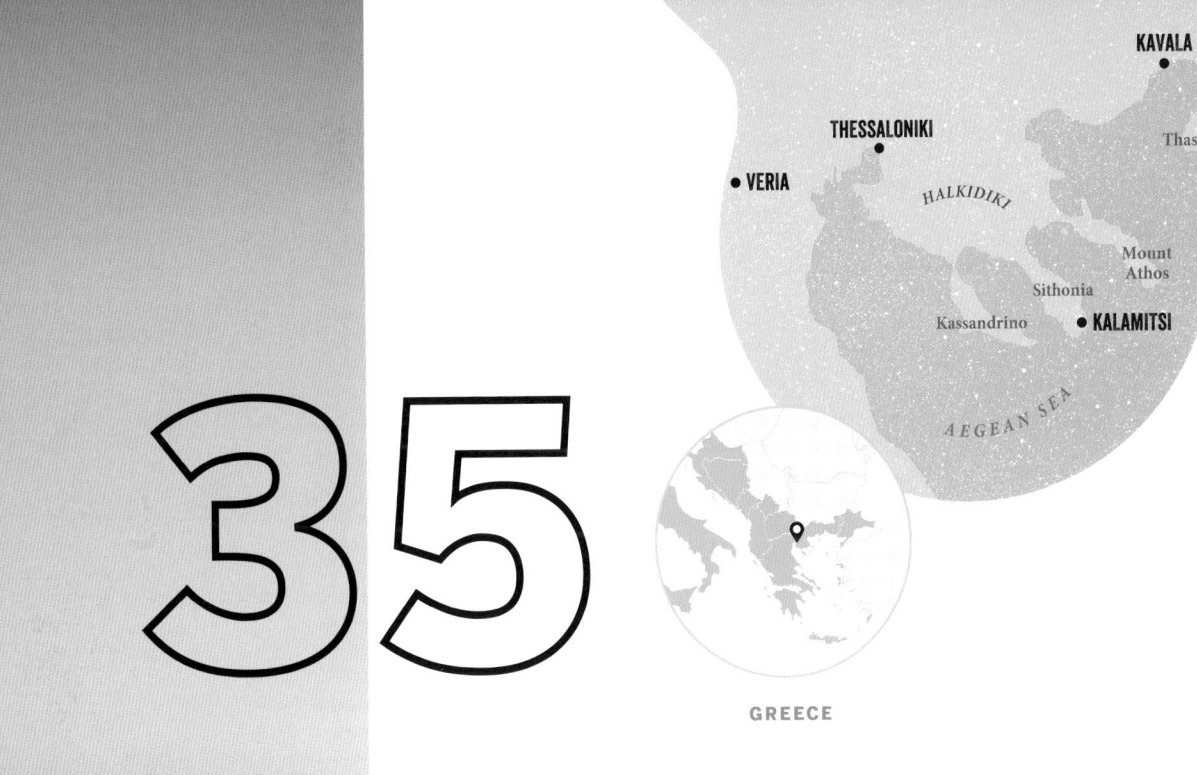

35

Find island adventure
IN THESSALONIKI & HALKIDIKI

Thessaloniki sits on the shores of the Aegean Sea's Thermaic Gulf, not far from the border with North Macedonia. Greece's second-largest city remains relatively unknown to travellers, despite its charms: a beautiful, revitalised **waterfront** overlooked by the **White Tower** (left); and an exceptional architectural heritage. The city's historic draws include the old *kastra* (castle) and Byzantine ramparts; the UNESCO-listed **Monastery of Vlatadon**; the 4th-century Roman remains of the **Rotunda and Arch of Galerius**; and the frescoes of the 5th-century **Panagia** Achiropiitos, one of the oldest Byzantine churches in Greece. Thessaloniki is also considered to be the country's **gastronomic capital**, with a host of tavernas and street-food stalls cooking up memorable meals. There's more to explore southeast of the city in **Halkidiki**, a three-legged peninsula that juts out into the Aegean Sea. The monastic community on the **Mt Athos** 'leg' is best seen from the sea; **Kassandra** and **Sithonia**, with verdant, pine-scented hills and coastlines dotted with beautiful sandy shores, promise **beaches**, **watersports** and **hiking** or **mountain-biking**.

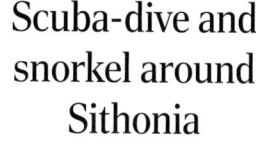

Sample creative cuisine in Thessaloniki

Thessaloniki is home to a vibrant food scene, influenced by Turkish, Jewish and Balkan culinary traditions and making fine use of local produce. It's worth spending some time discovering the city's tavernas, *ouzeries* (serving Greek-style meze) and traditional, family-run *koutoukia*, which often have live music. Menus are heavy on fish and seafood from the Thermaic Gulf (try shrimp *saganaki*, cooked in a feta-laced tomato sauce); vegetables from the fertile hinterland play a starring role, too. You can also enjoy street food treats like souvlaki (grilled chicken or pork skewers), while the famous Modiano Market is replete with produce stalls, shops and cafes.

Discover ancient Macedonia

Around 70km (43 miles) west of Thessaloniki, near Veria, lie the remains of the ancient city of Aigai, first capital of the Kingdom of Macedonia. Showcasing regal resting places from the time of Alexander the Great and his warrior-king father, the Royal Tombs Museum includes the tomb of Philip II, laid to rest in 336 BCE amid silver and gold teasures. Further north, the archaeological site of Pella, with a museum, comprises the ruins of another Macedonian capital, which was also the birthplace of Alexander the Great. Both sites are reachable by bus from Thessaloniki.

See Halkidiki's 'Holy Mountain' from the sea

Home to an Eastern Orthodox monastic community, the Mt Athos 'leg' of Halkidiki holds a series of monasteries built into the cliffside. Women are forbidden to enter this 'monks' republic', but the best way to see them is from the sea. Cruises (inset) circumnavigate the promontory from Ouranoupoli or Ormos Panagias, on the Sithonia Peninsula.

Scuba-dive and snorkel around Sithonia

It's easy to be swept away by the beauty of Halkidiki's middle peninsula, Sithonia (opposite), swathed in olive groves and pine forests, and bordered by sheer cliffs that plunge down to the sparkling sea. Diving, snorkelling and watersports are among the main attractions here. Kalamitsi, at Sithonia's southern tip, is a good place to take to the water.

MORE TIME?

KAVALA Some 150km (93 miles) northeast of Thessaloniki, the busy port city of Kavala has a number of interesting sites, especially in its historic Panagia peninsula, where a Byzantine castle and an Ottoman aqueduct, the legacy of Suleiman the Magnificent, still stand.
THASOS It's not the best-known of the Greek islands, but verdant Thasos, 10km (6 miles) south of Kavala, has plenty of charm, with its olive groves, traditional villages and pretty beaches with crystal-clear waters. The island can be reached by ferry from Kavala in 40 minutes, or Keramoti in an hour and 15 minutes.

JEWISH THESSALONIKI

Thessaloniki's Jewish heritage reaches back 2000 years. Following the 1492 expulsion of Sephardic Jews from Spain during the Inquisition, many settled in Thessaloniki, and the city – then known as Salonika – became home to the largest Jewish community in Greece. Jewish people were in the majority here for several centuries – the city was known as 'Madre de Israel' (Mother of Israel) or the 'Jerusalem of the Balkans' – but the community was devastated during WWII, when many atrocities were committed by German occupying forces. Today, a small Jewish community survives, and the city's Jewish Museum traces their history here.

HOW TO GET THERE & GET AROUND

Located in Thermi, 13km (8 miles) southeast of the city, Thessaloniki Airport has flights from the UK and around Europe, as well as Tel Aviv. For boat trips around Halkidiki's Mt Athos, try Athos Sea Cruises (athos-cruises.gr) or Ormos Travel (ormostravel.com).

WHERE TO STAY

Ano Poli, Thessaloniki's upper town, is the quietest area, provided you don't mind climbing to your accommodation. The waterfront offers beautiful views, but the nights can be noisy.

36

Dip into the Ionian Islands
IN CORFU & PAXI

With cypress-dotted hills and spectacular shore-lines, these alluring island archipelagos have long been visitor favourites. Seven main islands make up the Ionian chain, but visiting just one or two reveals a gorgeous glimpse of what they have to offer. Many head for the brochure-worthy beaches of Kefalonia or Zakynthos, or the fabled shores of Ithaki – but according to Homer, it was in **Corfu** that Odysseus regained his strength after being shipwrecked, and it's easy to appreciate the island's rejuvenating charms. With a cooler climate than mainland Greece and a gorgeously green interior, Corfu also has a rich history. The Venetians, French and British have left architectural evidence of their passage, notably in the old centre of **Corfu Town**, where you can amble along the elegant arcaded **Liston** and visit the remarkable **Palace of St Michael & St George**. **Beaches** such as Paleokastritsa are very busy in season, but venturing inland allows you to escape the crowds. Corfu's **nightlife** is the liveliest in the archipelago; make the most of it before heading off to enjoy the serene charms of nearby **Paxi**.

Visit Venetian forts in Corfu's capital

Strategically located Corfu has been the object of much envy over the centuries. The Venetians took control of what's now Corfu Town (inset) in the 12th century, holding sway on the island until the 17th century while repelling the onslaughts of other invaders, and many of their defensive fortifications have stood the test of time. Of the two citadels framing the Old Town, both of which survived Ottoman sieges, the 15th-century Palaio Frourio, perched on a headland to the east, is huge but only partially accessible, and encompasses a small museum of Byzantine art and the 1840 Church of St George. At the western edge of the Old Town, the ramparts of the 16th-century Neo Frourio (New Fort), offer splendid views.

Saddle up for a trek among the olive groves

Near the village of Ano Korakiana, northwest of Corfu Town, Trailriders (trailriderscorfu.com; booking required) offers horseback rides through beautiful landscapes planted with oaks, olive trees and vines in the foothills of Mt Pantokrator. You can even help look after the horses after the ride. Appropriate outfits (if necessary) and hard hats are provided.

Hike the Corfu Trail

The stellar Corfu Trail crosses the entire island, from Kavos in the south to Agios Spiridon (see previous page) on the north coast, and takes you inland through evocative landscapes – from vineyards and olive groves to pretty isolated villages, gorges and south-coast beaches. The entire 180km (112-mile) route takes around 10 days to complete, but you can do just a few sections. There's further information at the Corfu Trail site (thecorfutrail.com) and via topoGuide (topoguide.gr/Corfu_Trail/Corfu_Trail_en.php).

Cruise along the cliffs of Paxi by boat

The west coast of the tiny Ionian Island of Paxi (often called Paxos) is made up of white-chalk cliffs, resplendent with wave-carved arches and riddled with caves. The best way to enjoy these spectacular shores is a sea trip. Rent a kayak or motorboat in one of Paxi's harbours – Gaios (opposite), Lakka and Loggos – and cruise around the island at your leisure.

MORE TIME?

PARGA This charming town in the mainland region of Epirus can be reached by ferry from Gaios, on the island of Paxi. It's famous for its colourful houses, its beaches and the Venetian castle overlooking it. Some 20km (12 miles) away is the ancient site of the Nekromanteion of Acheron where, according to Homer and Herodotus, consulations took place with an oracle (*nekromanteio*) who channelled dead ancestors for advice.

ANTIPAXOS Just a hop, skip and a jump from Paxi, the smallest of the Ionian Islands is home to some of Greece's most beautiful beaches; top billing goes to the Caribbean-esque Voutoumi.

CORFU SPECIALITIES

Thanks to the island's centuries of Venetian control, Corfu's cuisine has a strong Italian influence. Common speciality dishes include *pastitsada*, minced beef (or even lobster) in a rustic tomato ragu spiced with cinnamon, nutmeg and other aromatics, and served over pasta. In Corfu, sofrito is not the onion-carrot-celery base of many a sauce in Mediterranean cuisine; here, it's a dish of thinly sliced beef in a garlicky white-wine sauce; while *pastitsio tis nonas* is the Greek version of lasagne. The English introduced kumquats to the island in the 19th century, and today, these tart citrus fruits are used to make desserts and other sweet treats, as well as a highly prized liqueur.

~ PRACTICALITIES ~

HOW TO GET THERE

Just south of Corfu Town, the island's airport has flights from across Europe and from the UK. Regular ferries and hydrofoils run between Corfu and Paxi.

WHERE TO STAY

In Corfu, if you want to avoid the seaside resorts, it's best to stay in the northeast of the island, which is much less developed and prettier. Accommodation is limited, so booking ahead is essential.

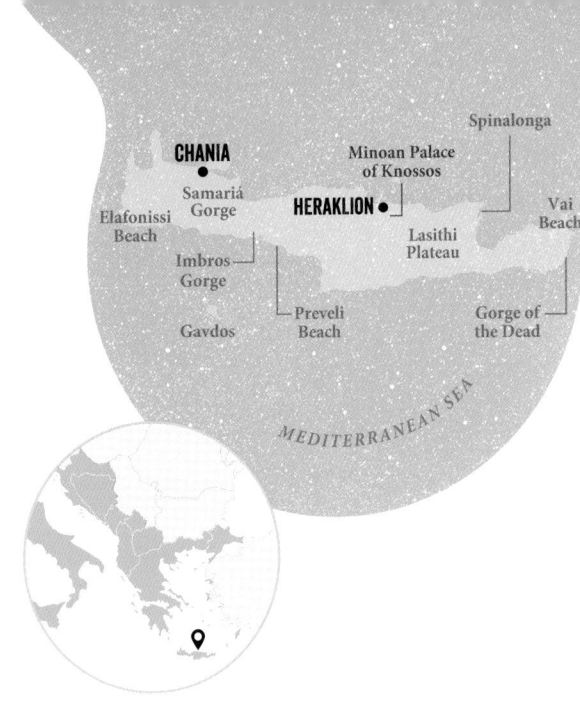

GREECE

37

Combine culture & nature
IN CRETE

The largest of the Hellenic islands, Crete is a condensed version of Greece, and a weekend here offers a tantalising taster of its charms. Underwater caves, shipwrecks and diverse marine life will delight **divers**, while inland, **hikers** can enjoy scenic walks through the island's many gorges. Beach lovers head for the south coast's **Preveli** (with a freshwater strand as well as the sea), the palm-backed **Vai** at Crete's northeast tip or, in the southeast, the delightful **Elafonisi**, with pink-tinged sand and turquoise waters. History buffs won't be disappointed, either. The place where the legendary King

Minos is said to have kept his minotaur, the **Palace of Knossos** (see page 157) was the former capital of the Minoans, whose legacy is preserved in the archaeological museum in the capital, **Iraklio** (Heraklion). The evocative Old Town of **Hania** (Chania; left), with its winding streets and Greek, Ottoman and Venetian architecture, leads to a waterfront promenade lined with pastel houses. Between the two, **Rethymno** is equally attractive, as is the fortified island of **Spinalonga**. And in the interior, venture into the tavernas and *kafeneio* (cafes) of remote villages to enjoy Cretan cooking and warm hospitality.

Check out Cretan farmhouse living

For a hands-on immersion into the traditions of rural Crete, take a trip to one of the island's working farms, many of which have opened up their doors to visitors. You can book in for a few hours or a day (or even overnight – many also offer accommodation); typical activities might include watching olive-oil production, learning how to make local breads and cheeses, or taking a cooking class, as well as pitching in with herb picking and feeding the animals. Recommended Cretan farms include Agreco (agreco.gr), the 'ecotourism village' Enagron (enagron.gr), and the Dalabelos Estate (dalabelos.gr).

Take a hike through gorgeous gorges

Hiking through the many gorges that slice through the Cretan landscape is a must-do for hikers. Most make a beeline for the famous Samaria, but for less-frequented trails, head to the likes of Imbros Gorge (inset), half as long as Samaria at 8km (5 miles), and a two- to three-hour walk from end to end along a scenic one-time mule path. In the east of the island, Zakros Gorge offers a range of lovely walks along a meandering green river (dry in summer); the canyon walls are dotted with Minoan burial sites, earning Zakros its 'Valley of the Dead' nickname. You can walk independently, but guided hikes are also available.

Follow a wine route

Wine has been produced in Crete over four millennia, and this long tradition of winemaking is best explored by taking a tour of the island's wineries, the majority of which are located around Iraklio (winesofcrete.gr). If you have a car (and a designated driver), it's easy to plot a route around the wineries, which offer tastings, tours and a wealth of information on the local grape varieties. Alternatively, take an organised wine tour with Made in Crete (madeincrete.com), including transport, tastings and lunch.

Paddle a sea kayak along the Cretan coast

What could be more exciting than discovering the Cretan coastline from a kayak? Numerous operators rent kayaks with which you can explore the coast independently, and organise guided excursions lasting a few hours or a full day; two-day excurions to discover the coves and cliffs that dot the southern coast are also available.

MORE TIME?

GAVDOS Anendyk Seaways (anendyk.gr) offers summer ferries (around two hours from Hora Sfakion) between Crete and this southernmost of the Greek islands, a wild and unspoilt place with lovely beaches and a pine-and-cedar-swathed interior.
LASITHI PLATEAU Dotted with windmills and overlooked by the peaks of the Dikti Mountains, this fertile plateau in eastern Crete's Lasithi Province is home to the Dikteon Cave where, according to legend, the earth goddess Rhea is said to have given birth to Zeus, safe from the clutches of his cannibalistic father Cronos. The artfully lit interior is a riot of impressive stalactites.

CRETAN RAKI

While ouzo is very popular in other parts of Greece, in Crete it's all about raki. Also known as *tsikoudia*, this fragrant, clear spirit is distilled from *strafylla*, the pulp that remains after grapes are crushed and pressed to make wine. Similar to French marc and Italian grappa (though unlike Turkish rakı, no anise is added here), Cretan raki is a popular aperitif, and you'll often be offered a glass to round off a meal at the island's tavernas. Production begins in October at the island's distilleries, and Cretan villages celebrate the event with tastings. If it's chilly, try *rakomelo*, flavoured with honey and cinnamon and often served warm.

~~~~~~~~~~~~ PRACTICALITIES ~~~~~~~~~~~~

🅿 HOW TO GET THERE

Crete has two international airports, in Hania and Iraklio. Low-cost airlines run to both from European cities and the UK.

🅰 WHERE TO STAY

Inland, especially around Hania and Rethymno, staying on a farm offers an atmospheric alternative to the beachside hotels. Many offer farm-to-table meals, too.

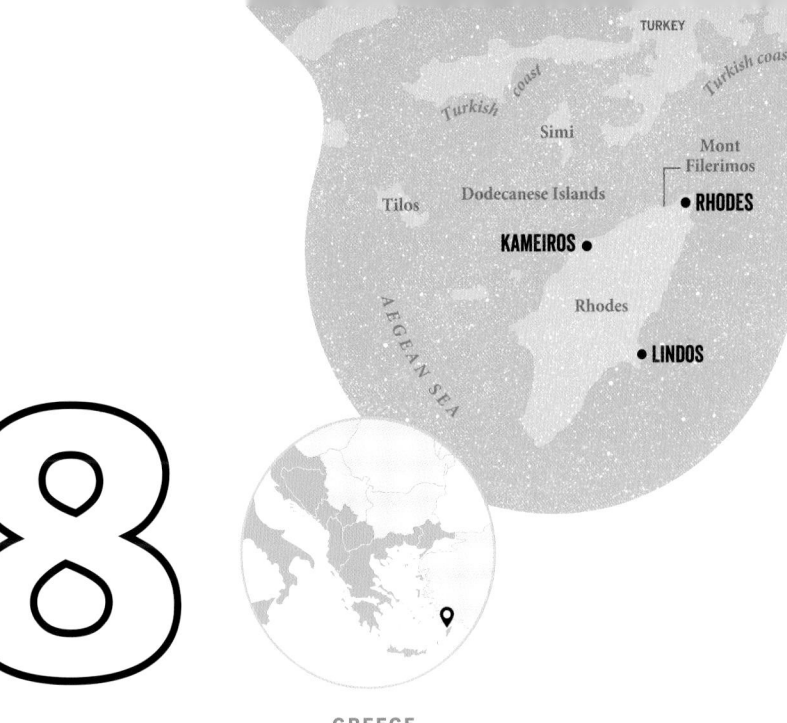

GREECE

38

Discover Dodecanese delights
IN RHODES & SYMI

From an Old Town built by the Knights Hospitaller to breathtaking coastlines and a string of secluded coves, Rhodes and its little sister Symi offer a promising programme for a long weekend. Sitting pretty in the southeastern Aegean, these neighbouring islands offer a contrasting set of delights. Strolling through Rhodes' Old Town is like walking through a textbook of Byzantine, Ottoman and Italian architecture. To the south, the view from the **Acropolis of Lindos** (see page 161) rewards the effort of climbing to its hilltop perch; the whitewashed town below, with its superb beaches, is best enjoyed when the high-season crowds have departed. Once you've had your fill of history on the island of the Knights of St John, board a ferry (journey time is about an hour) to the **island of Symi** (left), which offers a relaxed respite from Rhodes' busy resorts. Here, the surprisingly colourful neoclassical buildings in the **port of Gialos**, a legacy of Italian colonisation, rival the charm of the island's numerous unspoilt coves, many only accessible from the sea. Take a swim, enjoy local cuisine at a shoreside taverna, then explore the roads and trails that crisscross this arid, mountainous and relatively undeveloped island.

Wander the Knights' Quarter in Rhodes Town

Rhodes' capital has a modern centre and a marvellous medieval Old Town (inset), stronghold of the Knights of St John in the 14th and 15th centuries. Stroll along the meticulously restored Street of the Knights, visit the castle-like Palace of the Grand Master and head for the fantastic Archaeological Museum. Set in the Knights' former hospital, a sun-kissed ensemble of weathered stone with beautiful manicured gardens, it displays a wealth of ancient treasures unearthed in Rhodes, such as an exquisite marble statue of Aphrodite from the 1st century BCE.

Take a break from the beach at Rhodes' ancient sites

There's much to discover in the countryside away from Rhodes' resorts. Hire a car or scooter and head 12km (7.5 miles) southwest of Rhodes Town to the hilltop site of Ancient Ialysos, conquered by successive invaders and with a tangle of Doric, Byzantine and medieval remains. Within the restored 15th-century Filerimos Monastery, a paved Way of the Cross climbs through the shade of pine and cypress trees. Southwest, Ancient Kamiros was founded in the 10th century BCE, and the remains here – baths, temples, private homes and public squares – are remarkably intact, set in a natural amphitheatre overlooking the sea.

Kayak to Symi's secluded coves

Many of Symi's beaches are not accessible from the land. Some can be reached by boat from the main port, Gialos, but seeing them by way of paddle-power offers a more intimate means of transport. Several operators offer guided kayak tours to discover little-visted crystal-clear coves, where you can enjoy snorkelling and swimming away from the crowds.

Tan in the company of goats

Humans aren't the only ones to appreciate the charms of Symi's Marathounda Beach. This peaceful, sheltered pebble cove is frequented by the goats that live on this side of the island, which wander at will between the deckchairs, doing their best to grab a free lunch from picnicking visitors. You don't have to share your sandwiches, however, as there's a shoreside taverna serving up delicious local specialities such as Symi shrimps. Marathounda can be reached by boat or by road, the latter a little bumpy for scooters.

MORE TIME?

DIVING Visibility is excellent in the waters offshore of Rhodes. Several diving centres offer courses (PADI certification in two or three days), and wreck and cave dives for the more experienced.
TILOS If you have the opportunity to extend your stay in the Dodecanese, consider visiting the island of Tilos. Two hours by ferry from Rhodes (and an hour and a half from Symi), this is a relatively undeveloped island, with quiet beaches and lovely hiking in the undulating interior laced with footpaths.

SYMI'S SPONGES

Step off the ferry to Symi in Gialos and it won't be long before you encounter artful displays of plump natural sponges, piled up outside souvenir shops all over town. The island's sponge-diving tradition stretches back to Ancient Greece, and the industry here peaked in the 19th century, when the trade in sponges was a major source of revenue. Islanders collected them by freediving down to the seabed, often suffering decompression sickness for their troubles. The industry waned following Symi's Italian occupation in the early 20th century, but sponges are still collected here today – with the aid of scuba gear, of course.

PRACTICALITIES

🅿 HOW TO GET THERE

Served by direct flights from many European cities as well as the UK, Rhodes Airport is one of the busiest in Greece. Dodekanisos Seaways (12ne.gr) offers at least one daily crossing to Symi.

🅽 WHERE TO STAY

For a room with a sea view in Rhodes, the New Town has just the right amount of modern buildings along the beaches. The options in the Old Town, however, have more cachet.

ⓘ GOOD TO KNOW

Symi is only a few kilometres from the coast of Türkiye. Even if your smartphone tariff covers Europe, it's best to to deactivate mobile data when not using Wi-Fi, as you might be billed for non-EU usage.

39

BLACK SEA

İSTANBUL ●

Princes Island
BÜYÜKADA ●

SEA OF MARMARA

TÜRKIYE

From Europe to Asia
IN İSTANBUL

The only city in the world that straddles two continents, İstanbul is a place of compelling contrasts, where incessant traffic and buzzing markets are juxtaposed with peaceful tea gardens and resplendent mosques. And with centuries of **historic remains** scattered amid its modern streets, İstanbul is a museum unto itself. Spending just a weekend here will barely scratch the surface, but you can get a fine flavour of İstanbul in a few short days. Kick off with headline sights such as **Topkapı Palace**, the lavish former home of the Ottoman sultans, replete with brilliantly coloured tiles and gleaming marble, and designated a museum in its entirety. But beyond its big-ticket destinations, İstanbul is a place to simply enjoy the whirlwind of its daily life, from the crowds in its centuries-old markets to the back-and-forth of boats ferrying passengers between its **European and Asian shores**. It can be overwhelming and exciting in equal measure – so take time to sit back and enjoy quieter pleasures, such as the fantastic cuisine, from *köfte* meatballs and meze to fresh-caught fish. Savour teas and Turkish-style coffees along with sweet treats like baklava or the very best *lokum* (Turkish delight) you will ever taste.

Marvel at İstanbul's mosques

Among İstanbul's 3000-odd mosques, there are three that you absolutely must not miss. An unsurpassed masterpiece of Byzantine art, the Aya Sofya was consecrated as the Hagia Sophia church in 537 CE and transformed into a mosque nine centuries later; it became a museum in 1935, and was reconverted into a working mosque in 2020. With its cascading domes and multiple minarets, its immediate neighbour, the Blue Mosque is, if possible, even more stunning. Head to the bazaar district to take in the third of the trio: the Süleymaniye Mosque, perched on one of İstanbul's seven hills and providing a landmark for the entire city.

Dive in to the city's bargain bazaars

İstanbul is a feast for the senses, and nowhere is this more evident than in the city's marvellous markets. The vibrant colours of the Spice Bazaar (opposite), near the Eminönü waterfront, are a firework display for the eyes – and the *lokum* (Turkish delight) is a temptation for your palate. Head for Beyoğlu's Fish Market to take in colourful displays of fresh produce as well as meat and fish, or haggle for bargains at the city's vast, chaotic and fascinating Grand Bazaar.

Soak up the city's hammams

Visiting one of the city's venerable hammams is an essential activity in İstanbul; cover yourself with a *pestemal* (bath sheet) before entering the *hararet* (steam room), where you can be washed, scrubbed and massaged. Head to the breathtaking 16th-century surrounds of the Kılıç Ali Paşa Hamam (kilicalipasahamami.com), or the lavish Cağaloğlu Hamamı (cagalogluhamami.com.tr).

Cross the Bosphorus

Hop on a ferry or cross one of the three bridges that span the Bosphorus Strait, the wide waterway that bisects the city and also serves as its main artery, linking the Sea of Marmara to the Black Sea. Overlooking the water are a series of grand mansions known as *yali* (inset), built on the banks of the Bosphorous by the well-to-do since the 18th century. But even these are eclipsed by the waterside palaces of Dolmabahçe, the last residence of the sultans; and Beylerbeyi, with its marble bathing pavilions (one for the men, one for the harem).

MORE TIME?

ASIAN SHORE Take a ferry to spend a day on the city's Asian Shore, browsing the Kadıköy Market in the morning, and devoting the afternoon at the splendid imperial mosques of Üsküdar.
PRINCES' ISLANDS Discover a slice of old İstanbul by boarding a ferry to Büyükada, the largest of the nine Princes' Islands. Located 20km (12 miles) southeast of the city on the Sea of Marmara, and with motorised vehicles prohibited, it's a hugely popular escape for city-dwellers in the summer (go in the off-season if you can).

TIME FOR TEA

Keyif is the Turkish art of relaxation with intent, and there's no better place to get a sense of what these moments of idle pleasure consist of than İstanbul's çay *bahçesi* (tea gardens), where the city's residents settle in for long sessions of drinking tea, smoking hookah, chatting and playing games. The waterfront çay *bahçesi* are some of İstanbul's most atmospheric: try Moda Aile Çay Bahçesi in Kadıköy, with its view of the Sea of Marmara and the minarets of Old İstanbul; or Dolmabahçe Çay Bahçesi at the Dolmabahçe Palace.

Malatya Pazarı

ÜRÜN ADI:

ZEREŞK ÜZÜMÜ

YTL

35 TL

475

PRACTICALITIES

WHEN TO GO

April to May and September to October are the best time to visit İstanbul, without the excessive heat of summer or the biting cold of winter; these are also the periods with the most festivals.

HOW TO GET THERE

İstanbul New International Airport has flights from around Europe and the rest of the world, and is connected to the centre by metro trains.

WHERE TO STAY

İstanbul's districts are cities in themselves, with extremely varied accommodation options and prices; however, the bulk of the options are in Sultanahmet and Beyoğlu.

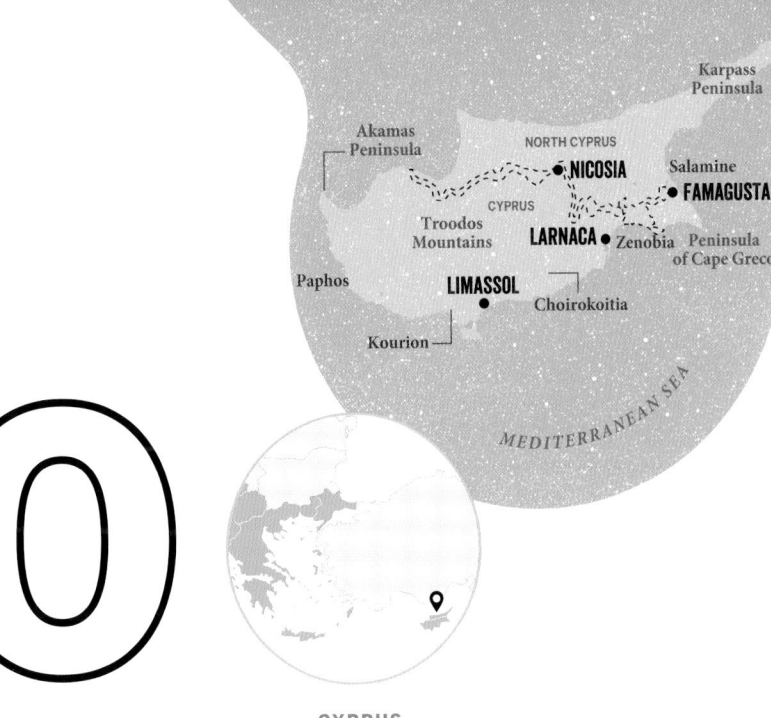

CYPRUS

Discover the diverse
IN CYPRUS

Despite its relatively modest dimensions, Cyprus has an incredibly rich variety of attractions and a compelling blend of Greek (Orthodox) and Turkish (Muslim) cultures. Since 1974, this Mediterranean island – whose closest neighbours are Türkiye, Lebanon and Syria – has been split in two by the UN-controlled Green Line between the Greek-Cypriot Republic of Cyprus to the south and the Turkish Republic of Northern Cyprus. In the capital, this line separates Greek **Nicosia** (Lefkosia; left) from Turkish **Lefkoşa**, but it's easy to hop between both sides to enjoy museums, ancient buildings and lively cafes. Away from the city, Cyprus' beautiful beaches beckon, most famous of which is **Petra tou Romiou**, site of the fabled **Aphrodite's Rock**. Less frequented shores include the protected **Lara Beach** on the Akamas Peninsula, a nesting ground for **green turtles**; while in the south lie the ever-popular beaches around **Larnaka**, **Lemesos (Limassol)** and **Cape Greco**. But be sure to venture **inland** to discover fabulously frescoed Byzantine churches, hilltop villages and a marvellous crop of monasteries, as well as several diverting ancient sites, from neolithic villages to Roman remains.

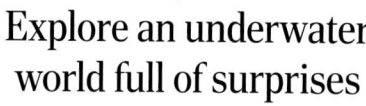

Discover ancient Cyprus

Cyprus holds several ancient sites, of which the oldest is hillside Choirokoitia, dating from around 7000 BCE; the implements and utensils found in and around its cylindrical stone and mud dwellings have given valuable insight into neolithic culture. Founded in the neolithic era and later a Mycenaean settlement, the spectacular city of Ancient Kourion (opposite) also holds an early Christian basilica, and its Roman remains include an amphitheatre that's still used to stage operas. The great statues and porticoes of the ancient city-kingdom of Salamis give an idea of its former splendour, while the Pafos Archaeological Site, with its Roman theatre and agora, is best-known for its intricate mosaics based on ancient Greek myths.

Track down the hidden treasures of the Troödos

Home to the 1952m-high (6404ft) Mt Olympus (not to be confused with the fabled Greek peak of the same name), the Troödos Mountains are a magnet for hikers, with miles of marked trails in the Troödos National Forest Park. Bird-watchers will particularly appreciate the Kalidonia Waterfalls Trail, where they might spot nightingales and Cyprus and Sardinian warblers. The Troödos are also home to a smattering of Byzantine churches adorned with colourful frescoes, some of them UNESCO World Heritage Sites.

Explore an underwater world full of surprises

Cyprus' crystal-clear waters are home to a rich array of marine life, including the green turtles (inset) that lay eggs on the island's beaches, as well as a number of excellent dive sites, from underwater caves to wonderful wreck dives. Among the latter, the remains of the *Zenobia*, a 200m-long (656ft) cargo ship grounded off Larnaka, is ranked among the world's top five wreck-dive sites. It's easy to sign up for courses and hire equipment at the island's diving centres.

Enjoy wind-powered watersports

With consistent winds breezing around the coastline year-round, Cyprus is well-known as a top spot for windsurfing and kitesurfing, with conditions suitable for both beginners and aficionados. Experienced windsurfers will be happy off Lady's Mile Beach (actually 7km/4 miles long) on the southwest coast or Morfou Bay in the northwest, while beginners head for Lanarka's Mackenzy Beach or Pissouri Bay, between Lemesos (Limassol) and Pafos on the southwest coast.

MORE TIME?

WINE VILLAGES With its sun-drenched, south-facing slopes home to numerous vineyards, the Odomos region in the southwest of the island is the centre of Cyprus' winemaking industry. Take the time to visit the region's *krasochoria* (traditional winegrowing villages) and taste the local products, including Commandaria, a sweet fortified wine made in Cyprus since 800 BCE.
FAMAGUSTA AND THE KARPAS PENINSULA Explore the old walled town of Famagusta (Gazimağusa), then head into this wild peninsula on the eastern tip of the island, with its snoozy villages and superb deserted white-sand beaches.

DISCOVER THE DELIGHTS OF A TURKISH BATH

The Hamam Omerye (hamamomerye.com) is a bubble of well-being and luxury in the heart of the Old City of Nicosia (Lefkosia). These beautifully renovated 16th-century Turkish baths offer top-of-the-range services (scrubs, massages, body treatments) in an enchanting setting; book ahead. The Büyük Hamam (or Grand Hammam), over the Green Line in North Nicosia (Lefkoşa), is another historic 16th-century bathhouse; it's currently undergoing renovation, but it's worth asking around to see if it has reopened.

PRACTICALITIES

☼ WHEN TO GO

Cyprus has an average 340 days of sunshine a year, so there's never a bad time to visit, but trips in the shoulder season (May to June and September to October) offer fewer crowds and perfect weather for hiking.

⛽ HOW TO GET THERE

The Republic of Cyprus has two international airports, in Paphos and Larnaka, with flights from around the UK and Europe. Ercan International Airport in the Turkish Republic of Northern Cyprus has flights from Türkiye and the UK. If renting a car, bear in mind that driving is on the left-hand side of the road throughout the island.

⌂ WHERE TO STAY

Nightlife lovers will prefer Agia Napa. Agrotourism (see agrotourism.com.cy) is on the rise, with activities such as cookery classes and horse-riding on alongside accommodation.

📅 EVENTS

On Whit Monday, coastal towns such as Larnaka and Limassol celebrate Kataklysmos, which evokes the biblical great flood with live music, markets and water fights on the beach.

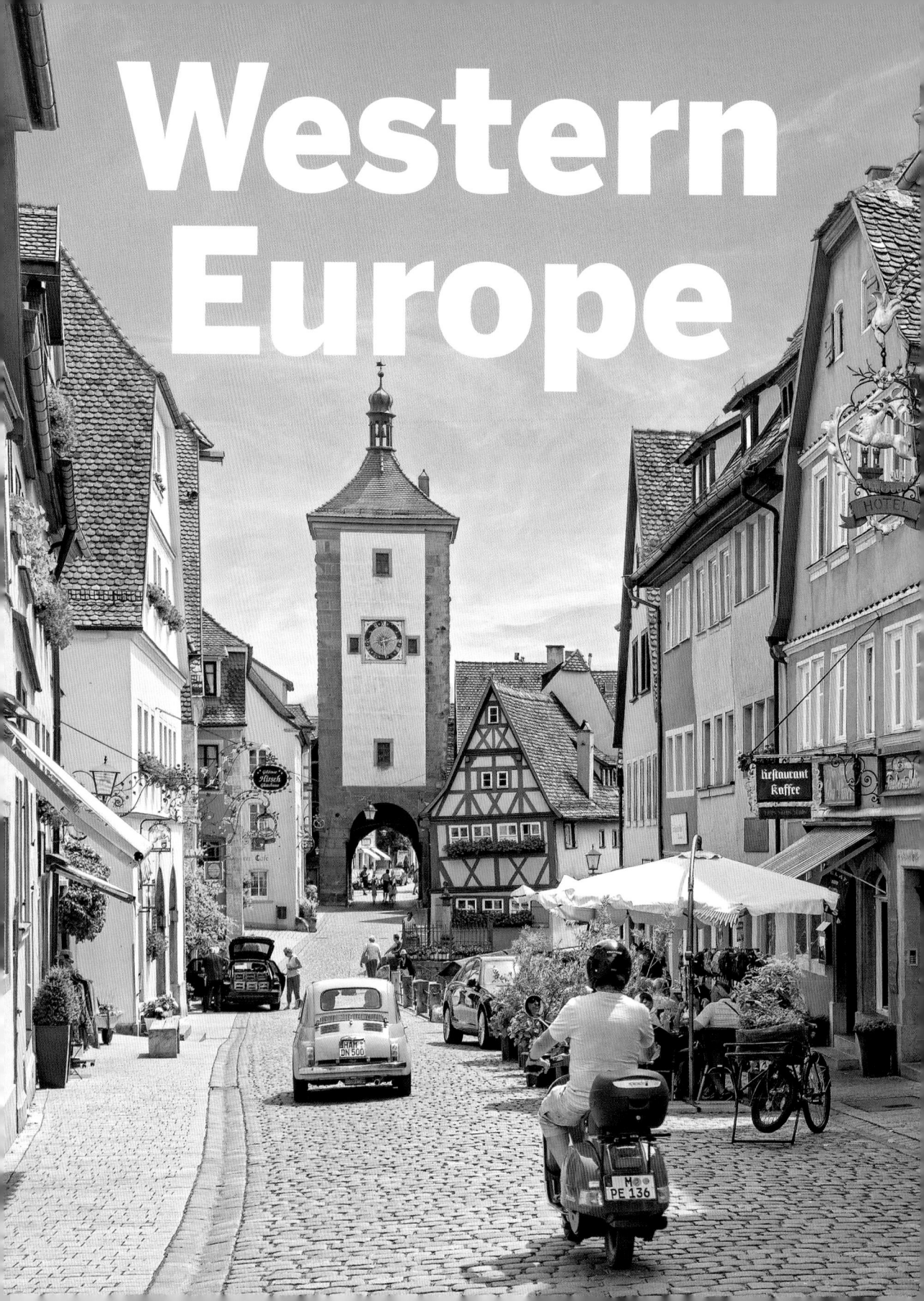

Western Europe

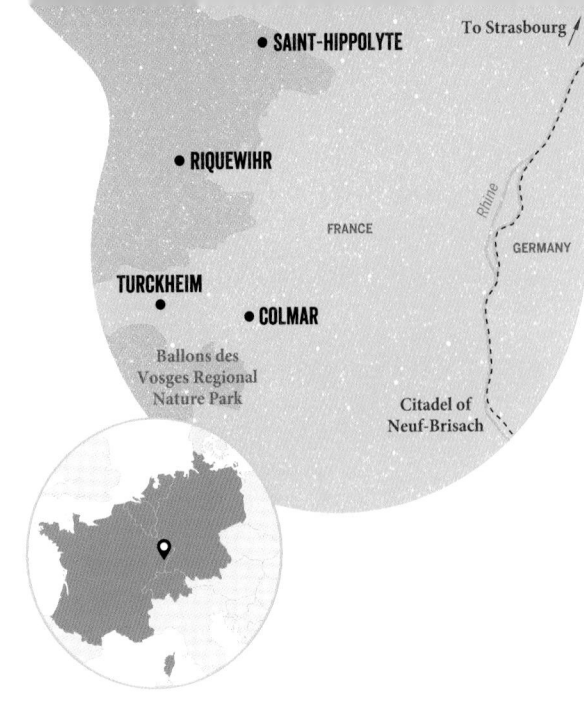

SAINT-HIPPOLYTE

To Strasbourg

RIQUEWIHR

FRANCE

Rhine

GERMANY

TURCKHEIM

COLMAR

Ballons des
Vosges Regional
Nature Park

Citadel of
Neuf-Brisach

FRANCE

41

Explore the Alsace
IN COLMAR
& AROUND

The third-largest city in the Alsace, Colmar is home to an exceptional architectural heritage and an equally fine clutch of restaurants. It's hard to resist the charm of its streets and squares, lined with brightly coloured half-timbered buildings (left) that look plucked from the pages of a medieval folktale. Take in the stained-glass and 15th-century triptych in the **Église des Dominicains**, and the polychrome mosaic roof of the **Collegiate Church of St-Martin**, then explore the **Musée Bartholdi**, an homage to the sculptor who created the Statue of Liberty. Colmar is also the 'capital' of the **Route des Vins d'Alsace**, one of the country's most alluring **wine routes**; the cellars are open for tastings (make room in your luggage for the inevitable souvenirs), while vineyard tours reveal the secrets of this unique terroir. Scattered along the route, the **villages of the Alsace** (alsace-essentielle.fr) rival each other in charm, bristling with castles and bell towers and guarding a culture that's part French, part German and 100% Alsatian.

Marvel at the Issenheim Altarpiece

In the heart of Colmar, a former Dominican convent – snazzily revamped by architects Herzog & de Meuron – serves as the setting for the Musée d'Unterlinden (musee-unterlinden.com). The collection runs from medieval statuary to paintings by Monet, Picasso and Renoir, and there are diverting temporary exhibits, but star attraction is the exceptional Issenheim Altarpiece. Painted in the late 16th century, the polyptych realistically depicts New Testament scenes, and has been hailed as one of the most profound works of faith ever created.

Dine in a winstub

The *winstub* is to Alsatians what the bistro is to Parisians: a cultural treasure trove and a convivial meeting place. In Saint-Hippolyte, the Hupsa Pfannala (hupsapfannala.com) is housed in a handsome half-timbered house in the heart of the village. Visitors and locals alike come here to feast on typical Alsatian dishes: snails, *bouchée à la reine* (chicken vol-au-vents), *baeckeoffe* (a mutton and pork casserole), beer-braised knuckle of pork and, above all, the house speciality, Hupsa Pfannala: potatoes sautéed with bacon and onions, slathered in Alsatian cheese and baked in the oven.

Patrol the streets of Turckheim by night

In Turckheim (turckheim.com), a typical Alsace village just west of Colmar, old traditions are kept alive. During the 13th century, this town of half-timbered houses was vulnerable to fire, and each evening a night-watcher made their way through the alleyways, reminding residents to extinguish fires and candles before going to bed. The tradition is revived every evening in summer to the delight of visitors, with a costumed watcher relating local history: it's kitschy but fun.

Walk or cycle a wine trail

Vineyards and charming landscapes often go hand in hand, as demonstrated by the picturesque 170km-long (106-mile) Route des Vins d'Alsace (opposite; routedesvins.alsace), which passes through some 120 winegrowing villages and clocks up about 720 wineries, many open for tours and tastings. Don't try to visit them all; instead, walk or cycle around a few from charming historic villages, such as Riquewihr.

Ponder the past in Bergheim & Rouffach

Housed in a 16th-century building in the medieval centre of Bergheim (ville-bergheim.fr), the Maison des Sorcières (Witches' House) is a fascinating little museum that recounts the story of the witch trials held in the village between 1582 and 1683, and sheds light on the prejudices and superstitions of the time. In Rouffach, the Tour des Sorcières (Witch Tower) dates from the 13th and 14th centuries and was formerly used to imprison women thought to be witches.

MORE TIME?

VALLÉE DE MUNSTER This is one of the gateways to the Vosges Mountains, where the switchback Rte des Crêtes offers a succession of sublime panoramas. With accommodation, guides and specialist stores, Munster is a perfect base for hikers.
MASSIF DU HOHNECK Along the Rte des Crêtes, this mountain paradise is a magnet for hikers and mountain-bikers, with a network of trails in the Parc Naturel Régional des Ballons des Vosges winding through peaks and pastures.

THE CITADEL OF NEUF-BRISACH

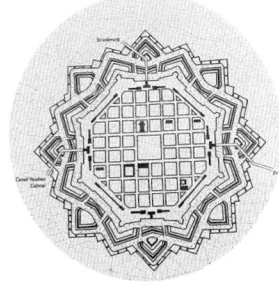

Known as the 'Citadel of the Sun King', the fortified town of Neuf-Brisach was founded by Louis XIV in 1697, as a means of strengthening French defences and preventing the area from falling to the Habsburgs. Shaped like an eight-pointed star and built with pink Vosges sandstone, Neuf-Brisach is enclosed by 17km (10.6 miles) of well-preserved perimeter walls. The town is considered the most accomplished work of renowned military architect Sébastien Le Prestre de Vauban, and is one of the 12 Vauban fortifications at the western, northern and eastern borders of France that are listed by UNESCO as World Heritage Sites.

~~ PRACTICALITIES ~~

🚃 HOW TO GET THERE

The closest airport to Colmar is Strasbourg-Entzheim, some 10km (6 miles) southwest of the city; from central Strasbourg, TER 200 train runs to Colmar in 30 minutes. Direct TGV trains also run to Colmar from Paris' Gare de l'Est; journey time is around two and a half hours.

🏨 WHERE TO STAY

Colmar is home to several fine places to stay in historic surroundings: try the Maison des Têtes (www.maisondestetes. com), named after the 106 grotesque heads and masks that adorn its facade. Less expensive but equally charming is the Villa Élyane (www.villa-elyane.com), with three comfortable rooms and two suites.

📅 EVENTS

With its Christmas market, Colmar is enchanting during the festive season when the twinkling lights give the city a fairy-tale air. In April, a huge market of designers and producers takes over the town centre to celebrate spring. During the busy grape harvest (from late August to late October), local vineyards offer visitors the chance of pitching in with the grape-picking. The regional tourist board (visit. alsace/en) has more details.

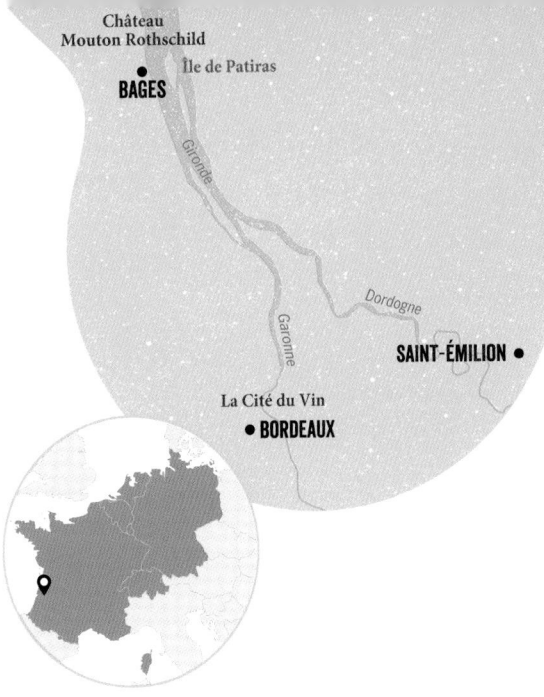

Château
Mouton Rothschild
Île de Patiras
BAGES •

Gironde

Dordogne

Garonne

SAINT-ÉMILION •

La Cité du Vin
• **BORDEAUX**

FRANCE

42

Take a viticultural tour of the
GIRONDE, IN &
AROUND BORDEAUX

T he Bordeaux wine region
is one of the oldest in
the world, and has been
heralded as one of the most
prestigious since antiquity.
UNESCO-listed for its outstanding
architecture, the city of Bordeaux is
the **world's wine capital**, and the
viticultural exhibits at the unique
Cité du Vin set the tone. While the
superb buildings in Bordeaux's
centre retain the grandiose imprint
of the age of enlightenment, it's
the city's cultural mix that makes it
such a vibrant and beguiling place.
There's much more to discover
about the fascinating world of wine
in the wider **Bordeaux region**.
From the **Médoc Wine Route**
to the vineyards of **Graves** and
the **Sauternais**, via the Blayais,
St-Émilion (and its medieval city;
left) or Entre-deux-Mers, there
are **six major wine routes**. In
the **Médoc**, prestigious estates
line the D2, the mythical **Route
des Châteaux**: 80km (50 miles)
between **Margaux**, **St-Julien** and
St-Estèphe, via **Pauillac**. But the
region also lends itself to hiking
through the marshlands, fishing
in rural lakes, or taking it easy in
an open-air Bordeaux *guinguette*
(cafe) on the banks of the Gironde.

Visit Pauillac's wonderful 'wine village'

In the heart of the Pauillac vineyards, the Médoc's viticultural traditions take centre stage at the Village de Bages. This aged winegrowing hamlet lay abandoned for many years, but in the early 2000s, it was completely restored by Jean-Michel Cazes, owner of the prestigious Château Lynch-Bages here (jmcazes.com). It's now a tourist-oriented 'wine village', with cellar tours and a shop selling locally produced specialities, as well as fine food and wine at the Café Lavinal bistro on the main square.

Find fine wine & exemplary art at Château Mouton Rothschild

In Pauillac, and with its vineyards spreading back from the Gironde Estuary, Mouton Rothschild (chateau-mouton-rothschild.com) is one of the most prestigious châteaux in the Bordeaux region. Designed in 1926 by architect Charles Siclis, its 100m-long (328ft) Great Barrel Hall can hold up to 1000 oak casks. In an older cellar, the Museum of Wine in Art displays everything from silverware to tapestries, and the labels created to adorn each vintage of this legendary wine since 1945; the roster of artists runs from Chagall, Picasso and Dalí to Andy Warhol, Keith Haring, Jeff Koons, Anish Kapoor and Peter Doig.

Cycle or stroll the Bordeaux waterfront

Overlooked by gorgeous blonde-stone buildings, the banks of the Garonne are lined with car-free quays that are best explored on foot or by bike. Starting from the Pont de Pierre (opposite) on the left bank, a 4.5km (2.8-mile) promenade follows the curve of the river to the north, passing the Porte de Bourgogne, the Porte Cailhau, the Place de la Bourse and the watery reflections of the Miroir d'Eau, a striking symbol of the city's renewal. Beyond the Esplanades des Quinconces, the Sunday morning market in the Chartrons district is a perfect place to sample local oysters. Past the skatepark, cross over the Pont Jacques Chaban-Delmas, Europe's highest lift bridge; on your way back south along the right bank, stop off at Hangar Darwin, with arts spaces, restaurants and a skatepark in a former military barracks.

Enter the temple of wine

In the heart of Bordeaux on the banks of the Garonne, the Cité du Vin (inset) is set in a contemporary building resembling a wine decanter. Dedicated to the culture of wine, its exhibits offer a sensory, thematic approach, covering everything from grape varieties, harvesting and the winemaking process to celebrated winemakers, industry trends, and wine and the divine. The tour ends with a glass of wine at the Belvédère, with 360-degree views over the city.

MORE TIME?

ÎLE DE PATIRAS From Pauillac, cruises (including lunch) with La Compagnie Des 2 Rives (croisieres-les2rives.com) head out to this vine-swathed islet in the Gironde Estuary; you'll climb the 122 steps to a lighthouse overlooking the Médoc vineyards and estuary.
ST-ÉMILION This beautiful village (saint-emilion-tourisme.com) is known both for its world-class wines and for its marvellous medieval centre, surrounded by its precious UNESCO-listed vineyards. The steep, narrow streets lead to the Cloître des Cordeliers (now home to a winery), and the Église Monolithe, a subterranean church topped by the Clocher de l'Église bell tower.

LES CANNELÉS

Bordeaux might be lauded for its wines, but the city is also justly proud of its *cannelé* (or *canelé* with a single 'n' for purists). A staple of Bordeaux gastronomy, these small caramelised cakes, crunchy on the outside and soft within, are flavoured with vanilla and rum, and are traditionally baked in fluted copper moulds. The simple recipe is thought to have been created by nuns of the Couvent des Annonciades in the heart of Bordeaux, who made *cannelé* with spilled flour and sugar that they collected from split sacks unloaded at the city's port. Pick up these sweet treats, prepared according to traditional methods, at branches of La Toque Cuivrée (la-toque-cuivree.fr).

PRACTICALITIES

HOW TO GET THERE

Bordeaux is reachable by direct TGV trains from Paris in just over two hours, and has good rail links with other French cities. Bordeaux Airport, 12km (7.5 miles) west of the city and connected to the centre by tram, has flights from around Europe and the UK. The Bordeaux region is also well served by buses and TER trains.

WHERE TO STAY & EAT

In the centre of Bordeaux, Mama Shelter (mamashelter.com) is a safe bet, with its minimalist, whimsical design. The famous Marché des Capucins (Tuesday–Sunday; marchedescapucins.com) is home to a number of typical bistros.

EVENTS

In June, Bordeaux celebrates wine with its Fête Le Vin (bordeaux-fete-le-vin.com), with dozens of tasting booths lining the quays and entertainment in the evenings, while tall ships moor up at the Port de la Lune. At the beginning of April, in the Médoc, dozens of winegrowers open the doors of their cellars and châteaux for the Portes Ouvertes weekend (portesouvertesenmedoc.com).

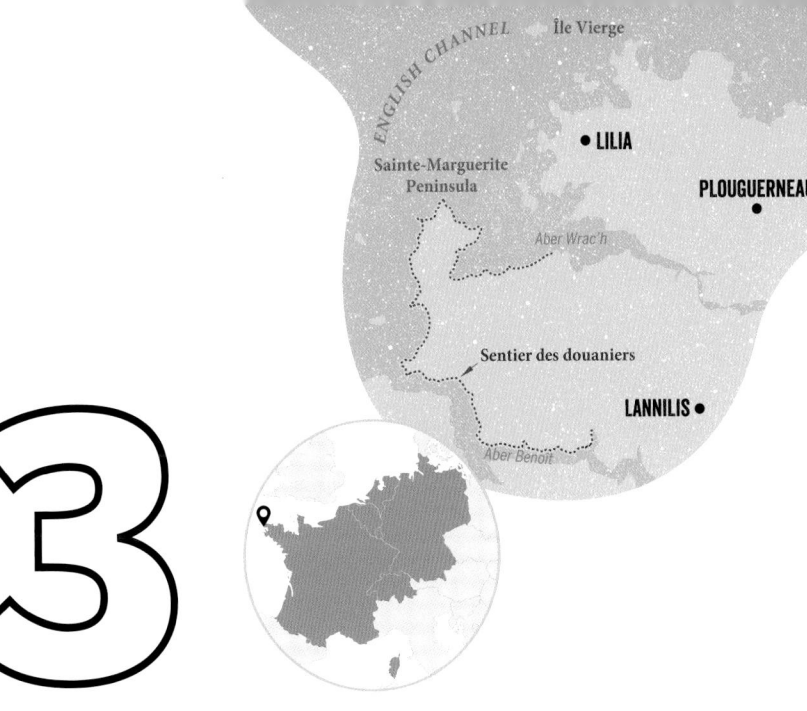

43

Between land & sea
IN FINISTÈRE

Known here as *abers*, the deep tidal inlets that cut into the coastline of Finistère, this most westerly pocket of Brittany, are protected by an army of islands and reefs; while at low tide, the vast mudflats provide an important habitat for birds. The coastline, meanwhile, is home to a string of quiet fishing villages where the local people have long made their living from the sea, gathering seaweed and harvesting **oysters**, the star attraction of Finistère cuisine. Finistère has several *abers*, from the southerly **Aber Ildut**, facing the Iroise Sea, as well as the Élorn and Aulne estuaries near the port of Brest, but **Aber Benoît** and **Aber Wrac'h** are the deepest; they're also the most bucolic and wild. To find out more about their riches, head for **museums** such as the Ecomusée des Goémoniers et de l'Algue (Seaweed Museum) in **Plouguerneau**; and the Maison des Abers, a small interpretation centre in **Saint-Pabu**, which also organises nature outings. The busy port of Aber Wrac'h, as well as **Lilia** and its seafront settlement in the commune of Plouguerneau, both make excellent bases.

Explore the Aber archipelago

The largest of Finistère's tidal inlets, the waters of Aber Wrac'h are sprinkled with tiny islands such as Cézon, Wrac'h and Stagadon, mere specks of sand, shingle and low-lying trees that are best visited by way of guided kayak excursions offered by the Landéda Sailing Centre (cvl-aberwrach.fr), in the mainland port of Aber Wrac'h. Closest isle to the mainland is tiny Cézon (also reachable on foot at low tide), with a ruined fort designed by Vauban in 1694 to command the entrance to the *aber*, as well as WWII blockhouses. Sailing excursions in the *aber* and day trips to Île Vierge are also available.

Take a coastal hike around Landéda

From the port of Aber Wrac'h, you can take in the changing tidal landscapes of the *abers* by hiking a marked circular trail around the coastline of the Landéda commune. The 23km (14-mile) route takes around six hours on foot and loops around Ste-Marguerite Peninsula, with its wild dunes and sumptuous sea views, and runs along the north shore of Aber Benoît. The local tourist board (abers-tourisme.com) has more information on each stage and a downloadable route map; click on 'Rand'Abers 2'.

Admire the view from the Île Vierge Lighthouse

At 82.5m (271ft) high, this formidable tower is Europe's highest stone lighthouse (opposite), standing sentinel over the *abers* and surrounding islands and marking the entrance to Aber Wrac'h. To enjoy the view from the top, you'll need to climb a total of 397 steps, admiring the interior walls clad in pretty opaline tiles (inset). To get there, board a motorboat at the tip of Castel Ac'h, in Lilia (vedettes-des-abers.com).

Have a drink by the sea at Hoalen in Lilia

Opposite the Île Vierge lighthouse, in Lilia-Plouguerneau, a comely former boathouse is home to the Ocean Store, the original boutique of Breton clothing brand Hoalen (hoalen.com). As well as the clothing store, the building is also a great spot for a coffee, a beer or a glass of wine at the Homard Noir Pub, with a lovely outdoor terrace overlooking the water.

MORE TIME?

MENEHAM
Some 15km (9 miles) northeast along the coast from Lilia-Plouguerneau, this 19th-century fishers' hamlet is a pleasant place for a coastal stroll. Carefully restored, its stocky stone buildings sit sheltered from the winds among giant rock outcrops (see page 180).
BASILIQUE NOTRE-DAME DU FOLGOËT This splendid church, around 15km (9 miles) east of Lannilis, is a riot of flamboyant Gothic art, with lovely stained-glass windows within.
LANDERNEAU Head 30km (19 miles) southeast of Plouguerneau to wander the Old Town and its Pont de Rohan, a medieval bridge that holds a row of corbelled houses.

ABERS OYSTERS

Introduced to Lannilis by French industrialist Édouard Delamare-Deboutteville at the end of the 19th century, *huîtres* (oysters) thrive in the waters of Finistère's *abers*, where plankton-rich seawater melds with fresh river water, itself loaded with nutrients. Today, oyster farming know-how is shared by a dozen companies divided between the Benoît and Wrac'h *abers* – Aber Benoît's Prat-ar-Coum (prat-ar-coum.fr) has been in business since 1898 – and the bivalves they produce are renowned across France.

~~~~~~ PRACTICALITIES ~~~~~~

HOW TO GET THERE

The Finistère capital of Brest is just under four hours from Paris by train, with Saint-Pabu, Lannilis and Lilia-Plouguerneau lying some 30km (19 miles) north. The KorriGo website (korrigo.bzh) is a useful tool for working out public-transport connections. Brest also has an airport, some 10km (6 miles) northeast of the city, with flights from around France, as well as Greece, Spain, Italy and Ireland.

WHERE TO EAT

For Abers oysters, try the Maison Legris oyster bar (huitres-legris. com), on the seafront in Lilia, or the family-run Prat-ar-Coum restaurant on the banks of Aber Benoît. You can also pick up an oyster or seafood platter at the Viviers Bretons market in Plouguerneau, and take your picnic to the beach.

EVENTS

The Horizons Open Sea Festival (horizons-opensea.fr), staged in June in the port of Aber Wrac'h, offers everything from live music, workshops and children's events to DJ nights.

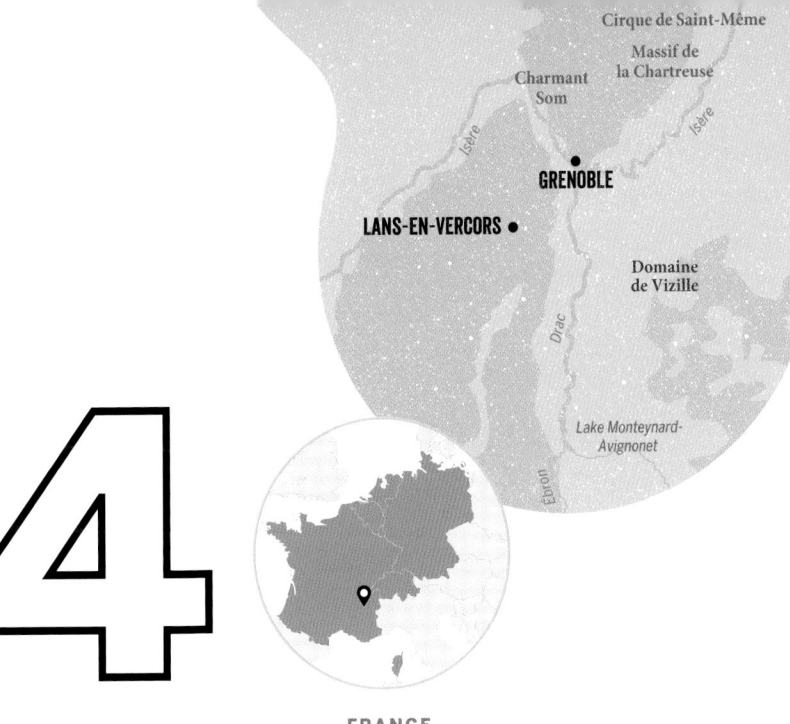

Cirque de Saint-Même

Massif de
la Chartreuse

Charmant
Som

Isère

Isère

GRENOBLE

LANS-EN-VERCORS

Domaine
de Vizille

Drac

Lake Monteynard-
Avignonet

Ebron

FRANCE

44

Up into the Alps
AROUND GRENOBLE

'**A**t the end of every street, there's a mountain' – so said the 19th-century novelist Stendhal of his native Grenoble, and it's a deserved description of this peak-haloed city. Just 110km (68.4 miles) from Lyon, 140km (87 miles) from the Italian border and the same distance from Geneva, the **largest city in the French Alps** is the gateway to a series of **massifs** whose names – Chartreuse, Belledonne, Vercors, Trièves, Oisans – are music to the ears of **skiing** enthusiasts, while the **hiking** trails that lace the surrounding mountain landscapes keep visitors flocking year-round. The dynamic **former capital of the ancien regime** province of **Dauphiné** has plenty of charm, its 19th-century Haussmann-style blocks blending handsomely with more modern buildings, many a legacy of the 1968 Winter Olympics. The largely pedestrianised **Old Town** is fringed by the **Isère River**, over which the spherical pods of the **cable car** (left) glide to the hilltop **Fort de la Bastille**. Add a crop of stellar museums and sound sustainable credentials and you have the perfect destination for an alluring Alpine weekend.

Take in a mountain panorama

Up in the heights of the Lans-en-Vercors, within the Parc Naturel Régional du Vercors (opposite), those with a head for heights can take in a mountain panorama from the aptly named Vertige des Cimes (Vertigo of the Peaks) lookout. At an altitude of 1715m (5627ft), this metal platform juts out from the mountainside and delivers breathtaking views of Grenoble and the surrounding mountains, with snowcapped Mont Blanc in the background. It's accessible via an easy hike in summer (see rando.parc-du-vercors.fr for route details), and in winter by the lifts of the Vercors ski resort.

Visit the Musée de Grenoble

Housed in a modern building near the banks of the Isère, the Musée de Grenoble (museedegrenoble. fr) was one of the first museums in France to open its doors to modern art, and though its collection spans everything from an antiquities wing with statuettes from ancient Egypt and Greece, alongside European art from the Renaissance onwards, the main highlight are its contemporary works by 20th-century luminaries such as Bonnard, Ernst, Léger, Magritte, Miró, Modigliani and Soutine.

Climb to the Bastille

Grenoble's fortress (bastille-grenoble.fr) was built in the early 19th century to defend the city against incursions by the Duchy of Savoy. Its hilltop position, perched 263m (863ft) above the city, delivers gorgeous views: head to the Belvédère Vauban to take in the loopng course of the Isère, the ruler-straight Cours Jean-Jaurès and the surrounding mountains, with Mont Blanc in the distance. The Bastille is reachable by the téléphérique cable-car, with equally arresting views on the way up.

Amble the meadows of Charmant Som

In the heart of the Chartreuse lies one of the most beautiful massifs on the outskirts of Grenoble. The summit of Charmant Som rises to a modest 1867m (6125ft), and its gentle flanks are home to one of the Isère department's last Alpine pastures, where cheese is still made in situ. In summer, its sheep-grazed slopes are a popular destination for hikers.

Cross swinging bridges over a brilliant blue lake

Sandwiched between the peaks of Écrins National Park on one side and the cliffs of Vercors Regional Park to the other, the Lac de Monteynard-Avignonet is best-known for its two Himalayan bridges (inset), which swing over the lake's startlingly bright turquoise waters. Though they wobble thrillingly as you cross, the steel structures of the 220m-long (722ft) Drac and 180m-long (590ft) Ebron bridges are perfectly secure, with anti-sway cables and protective grids. Cross them both as part of the four-hour 'classic' hiking route, which includes a short boat trip; visit the website (lac-monteynard.com) for details.

MORE TIME?

DOMAINE DE VIZILLE Just south of Grenoble, this elegant 17th-century château houses a museum dedicated to the French Revolution (musees.isere.fr), and is surrounded by an immense park, with formal gardens and an ornamental lake.
CIRQUE DE SAINT-MÊME In the heart of the Parc Naturel Régional de Chartreuse, on the outskirts of Saint-Pierre-d'Entremont, the Cirque de Saint-Même is home to four gushing mountain waterfalls. A signposted loop route takes in the three lower cascades; pack a picnic and take a paddle in the chilly waters after your walk. There's a fee for the car park in high season.

LA GRANDE CHARTREUSE

North of Grenoble, the Chartreuse massif is inextricably linked with the religious order of the same name. In 1084, six Carthusian monks chose this isolated spot as the setting for the ascetic life they wished to lead. Cloistered behind high walls, the immense complex is home to some 30 monks today, whose existence is based on solitude, silence and the production of their eponymous bright-green herbal liqueur, which still serves as their main source of income. The monastery is closed to the public, but you can visit the nearby Musée de la Grande Chartreuse (musee-grande-chartreuse.fr) in Saint-Pierre-de-Chartreuse to learn more about the monastic order and their famous tipple.

PRACTICALITIES

☼ WHEN TO GO

Grenoble and the surrounding region can be visited in all seasons. The mountain climate of the Alps is characterised by warm, sunny summers (perfect for hikers) and cold, snowy winters (synonymous with skiing).

🚆 HOW TO GET THERE

Grenoble station is well served by SNCF trains. Allow around three hours from Paris for direct trains. Linked to Grenoble by shuttle buses, Alpes-Isère Airport is 40km (25 miles) northwest of the city, and is served by flights from European capitals and several destinations in the UK.

⛺ WHERE TO STAY & EAT

In Grenoble, the 1924 Hôtel (1924hotel.com) has a central location and slick 1930s-inspired decor. Good choices around the city include Hôtel Beau Site (beausitehotel.fr) in Saint-Pierre-de-Chartreuse; Hôtel du Col de l'Arc (hotelcoldelarc.com) in Lans-en-Vercors; and Au Gai Soleil du Mont Aiguille (hotelgaisoleil.com), which is near Chichilianne.

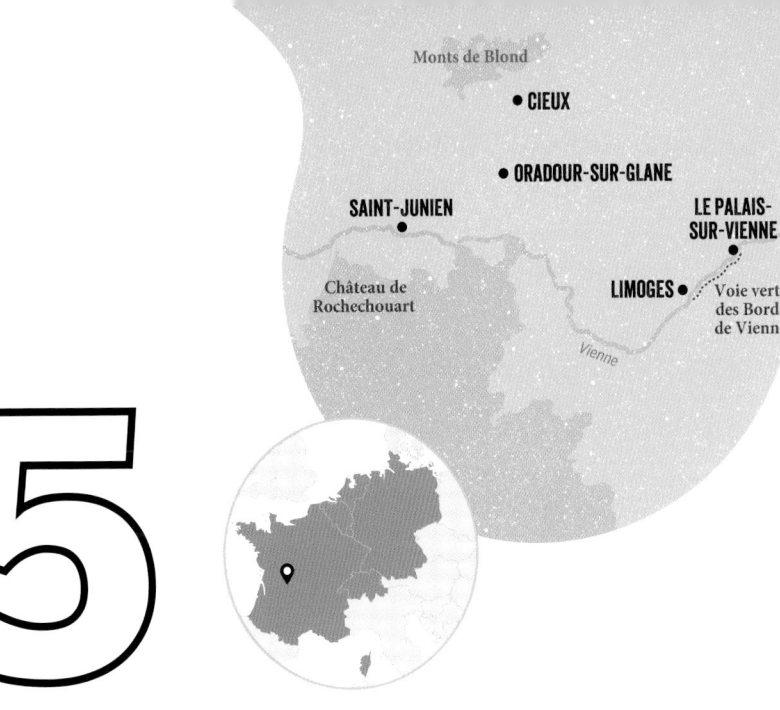

Monts de Blond

● CIEUX

● ORADOUR-SUR-GLANE

SAINT-JUNIEN
●

LE PALAIS-
SUR-VIENNE
●

Château de
Rochechouart

LIMOGES ●   Voie verte
des Bords
de Vienne

Vienne

FRANCE

45

Lounge in the Limousin
AROUND LIMOGES

Although the name Limoges is associated mostly with porcelain, it's also known as a *ville d'art et d'histoire* (city of art and history), with numerous listed monuments and beautiful half-timbered houses. These riches combine with an industrial past that boosted the development of the **former capital of the Limousin region** in the 20th century. Today, Limoges and the area around it are increasingly popular with visitors looking for green tourism adventures and cultural cachet. The French

'capital of the arts of fire, porcelain, enamel and stained glass' is an ideal destination for a **weekend in the countryside** while enjoying the **attractions of a big city**. For an idea of the heritage here beyond Limoges itself, detour to **Saint-Léonard-de-Noblat** (left), where in addition to medieval remains the town showcases **industrial and craft activities**, some of which, such as leather and porcelain work, are still going strong. And for some ancient history in mountainous surrounds, seek out the Monts de Blond and their collection of prehistoric sites.

Contemporary art in a Gothic château

Atop its rocky promontory 40km (25 miles) west of Limoges, Château de Rochechouart houses the Musée d'Art Contemporain de la Haute-Vienne (musee-rochechouart.com). This remarkable 16th-century castle has exhibition spaces displaying works by Raoul Hausmann, co-founder of the Dada movement, Ettore Sottsass and performance artist Robert Filliou. The château has also preserved two rooms of Renaissance frescoes, meaning it offers a perfect blend of Gothic architecture and art.

Discover the capital of porcelain

Founded by the Romans over 2000 years ago, Limoges (limoges-tourisme.com) is built around two historic centres: the upper town, formerly the viscount's castle district; and the ancient episcopal city, focused on St Étienne Cathedral. Located on the Vienne River, the city is home to several protected historic monuments and, for over ten years now, has also been developing a number of contemporary art spaces. Don't miss a visit to the Adrien Dubouché national ceramics museum.

Preserving the past at Oradour-sur-Glane

On 10 June 1944, a unit of the Waffen-SS Das Reich rounded up the villagers in the square of Oradour-sur-Glane (oradour.org), northwest of Limoges, under the pretext of an identity check. In one afternoon, 643 people were massacred and the village was burnt to the ground. To preserve the memory of this tragedy, the village has been left as it was, and is a poignant place to recall the horrors of WWII.

Learn the legends of the Monts de Blond

Foothills of France's Massif Central, the Monts de Blond (tourisme-hautlimousin.com) rise 515m (1690ft) and stretch for some 10km (6 miles) northwest of Limoges. Created by erosion, the granite terrain lends the landscape an aura of mystery. Starting from the village of Cieux, the Circuit des Mégalithes (11km/7 miles) allows you to discover menhirs (standing stones) and dolmens (portal tombs), such as the Rocher des Fées and the Ceinturat, constructed by the region's ancient inhabitants and listed as historic monuments.

MORE TIME?

SAINT-JUNIEN Saint-Junien has specialised in the leather industry since the 9th century, making the city the French home of luxury gloves. Ganterie Agnelle (agnelle.com), founded in 1937, remains one of the few manufacturers to export worldwide.

VOIE VERTE Between Limoges and Le Palais-sur-Vienne, the Voie verte des Bords de Vienne is a foot- and bike-path following the course of the river, alternating fantastic views of Limoges' historic centre with an immersion into nature. At the aquatic centre in Le Palais-sur-Vienne you can rent a canoe to take you down the Vienne back to Limoges.

THE ROCHECHOUART METEORITE

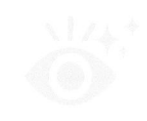

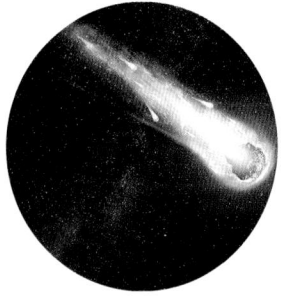

The town of Rochechouart was built in the impact crater of a giant meteorite which, over 200 million years ago, wiped out all forms of life within a 500km (310 mile) radius. Although erosion over the years means few traces remain of this catastrophic event, evidence of the impact can be seen in the rocks it created, which have been used in the construction of buildings in the Rochechouart area.

PRACTICALITIES

HOW TO GET THERE

Limoges train station (pictured) is three hours, 15 minutes from Paris and two hours, 30 minutes from Bordeaux. The city's airport welcomes international flights from budget airlines.

WHERE TO STAY

Le Poudrier (le-poudrier.com) offers guest rooms, a treehouse and a houseboat in an idyllic spot on the banks of the Vienne, northeast of Limoges city centre. In summer, don't miss the Saint-Léonard-de-Noblat farmers' market.

EVENTS

Every May in Limoges, tens of thousands of people attend the Cavalcade de Printemps, a parade of colourful floats and brass bands.

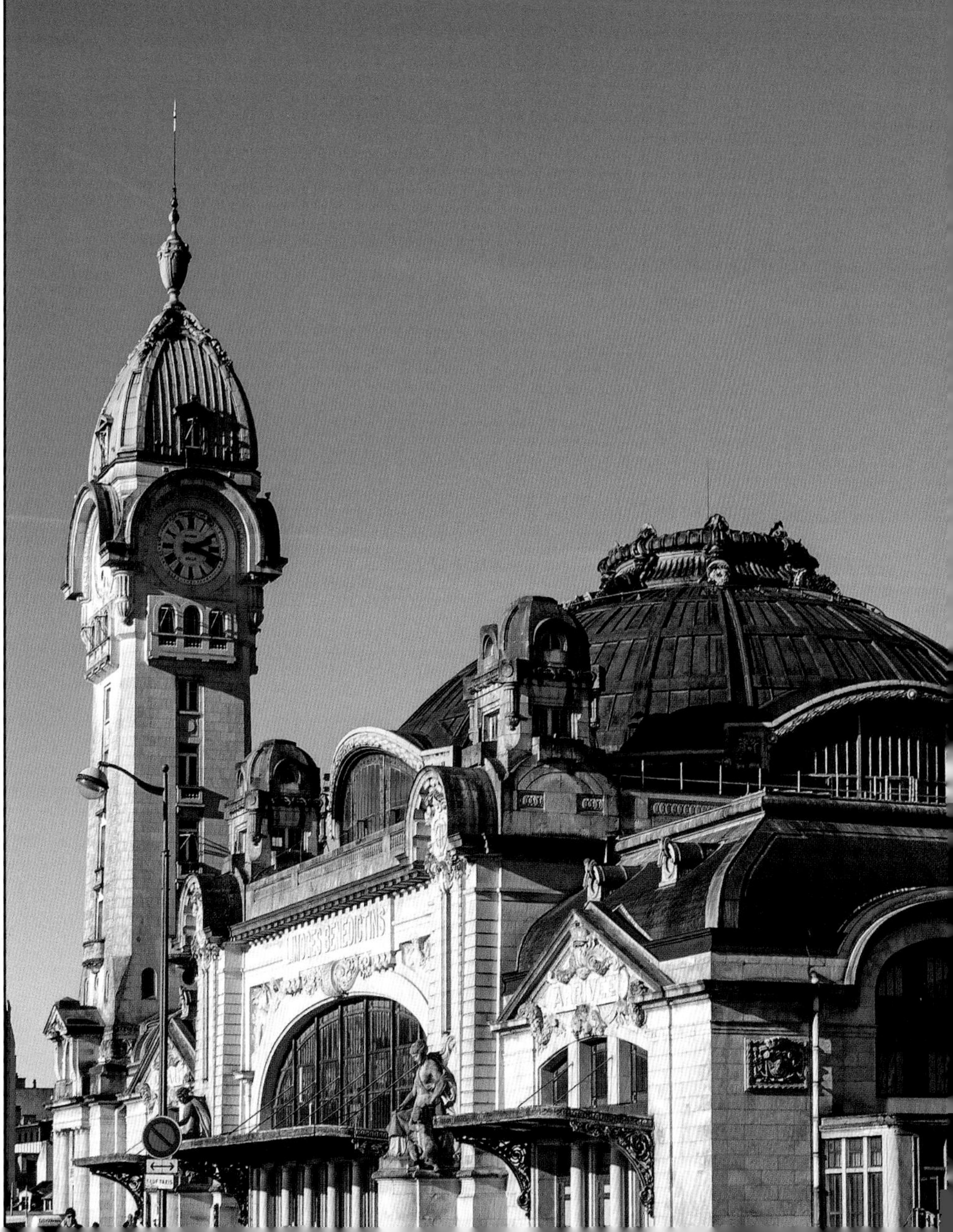

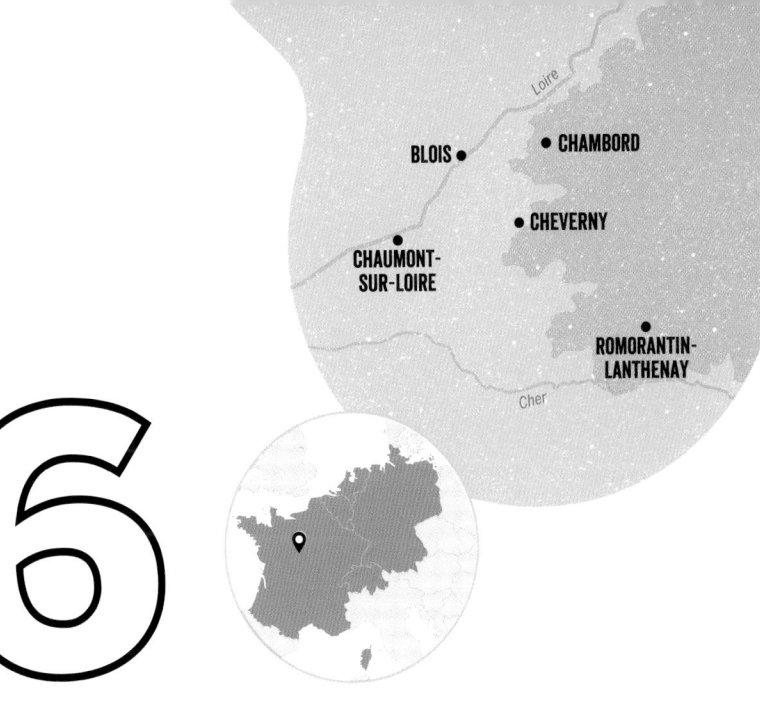

FRANCE

46

Beyond the châteaux
IN THE LOIRE VALLEY

For an unforgettable royal stay in the Loire Valley, drop your bags off in **Blois.** The capital of the Loir-et-Cher *département* sits nicely in the middle of this region of fabulous castles, and in summer, shuttle buses provide quick and easy access to three of the most famous châteaux: Cheverny, Chaumont and Chambord. Alternatively, rent or bring your own bike and cycle through this land loved by French monarchs. Around Blois' own castle (overleaf; chateaude-blois.fr), long a preferred residence of the royal court, the town's historic centre mixes medieval houses and Renaissance buildings (see page 195). Take a stroll through the **Évêché Botanic Garden**, whose terrace overlooks the Loire. Then, to find out more about this noble river and its wildlife while enjoying another beautiful view, head to the **Observatoire Loire** (observatoire-loire.fr), a multipurpose venue that has exhibitions and educational outings by boat or bike. You can hire a **canoe-kayak** in Blois (loire-kayak.com) for a trip on the water, stopping off on one of the river's islands. Or for a unique perspective over this storied land, book a balloon flight and gaze down on the home of kings.

The many attractions of Cheverny

Cheverny, 15km (9 miles) southeast of Blois, provides plenty of reasons to visit. First and foremost is its beautiful 17th-century château (chateau-cheverny.fr), built of local Bourré stone and inspiration for Captain Haddock's Marlinspike Hall in the *Tintin* stories. Also making a visit worthwhile are the 12th-century church of St Etienne with its caquetoire (conversation chair) and the nearby Renaissance château de Troussay (chateaudetroussay.com), the smallest in the Loire Valley, set in a wonderful English-style park. And finally, what better way to round off a trip than with some local wine at Maison des vins de Cheverny (maisondesvinsdecheverny.fr).

Escape to Chambord

In addition to a Renaissance château with stunning architectural features (double staircase, sculpted vaults, panoramic terraces), Chambord (chambord.org) is also a park listed as a World Heritage Site by UNESCO: an expanse of forests, meadows and moors, inhabited by deer, boar and wildcats. Pick your preferred means of transport – on foot, by bike or electric cart – and enjoy.

Take a break in nature

Southeast of Blois is Sologne, an immense forested area, populated by game and dotted with ponds, red-brick villages and luxurious manor houses – ideal for unplugging from the world. To understand the uniqueness of this landscape, visit the Musée de Sologne (museedesologne.com) in Romorantin-Lanthenay, or the Maison des Étangs (maison-des-etangs.fr). To get out and explore the area, join one of the nature trips organised by Sologne Nature Environnement (sologne-nature. org) or the Domaine national de Chambord (chambord.org), visiting sections normally closed to the public.

Enjoy the charms of Chaumont-sur-Loire

To visit Chaumont-sur-Loire (domaine-chaumont.fr) is to enjoy an exceptional château with a postcard view of the Loire Valley (see previous page). It's also a chance to explore the town's gardens – in the spotlight from late April to early November during the popular International Garden Festival – and to admire the works of contemporary art within the castle's grounds. And don't forget the surrounding countryside and its gourmet delights and natural attractions.

MORE TIME?

BOAT TRIP ON THE LOIRE
Embark at the port of Chaumont-sur-Loire for a traditional boat trip on the river with a team of enthusiasts (milliere-raboton.net). Or set sail from Saint-Dyé-sur-Loire, with Les Marins du port de Chambord (marins-port-chambord.fr).
BALLOONING OVER THE LOIRE Fancy a unique perspective over the Loire Valley and its châteaux? A number of providers – such as Balloon Revolution (balloonrevolution.com), based in Amboise – offer hot-air balloon flights above the magical region around Chambord, Amboise and Chenonceaux.

THE TEMPLARS OF ARVILLE

In the far north of Loir-et-Cher is one of France's oldest Knights Templar establishments, the Commanderie d'Arville (commanderie-arville. com). Texts mention this place as far back as the first half of the 12th century, not long after the Order of the Temple was founded in 1118. Knights were trained here prior to their departure on crusades to the Holy Land. Today, the former stables house an instructive centre covering the history of the order, its involvement with the Crusades and European politics at the time, and its eventual dissolution after the arrest of all the Templars in France in 1307, on the orders of King Philip IV.

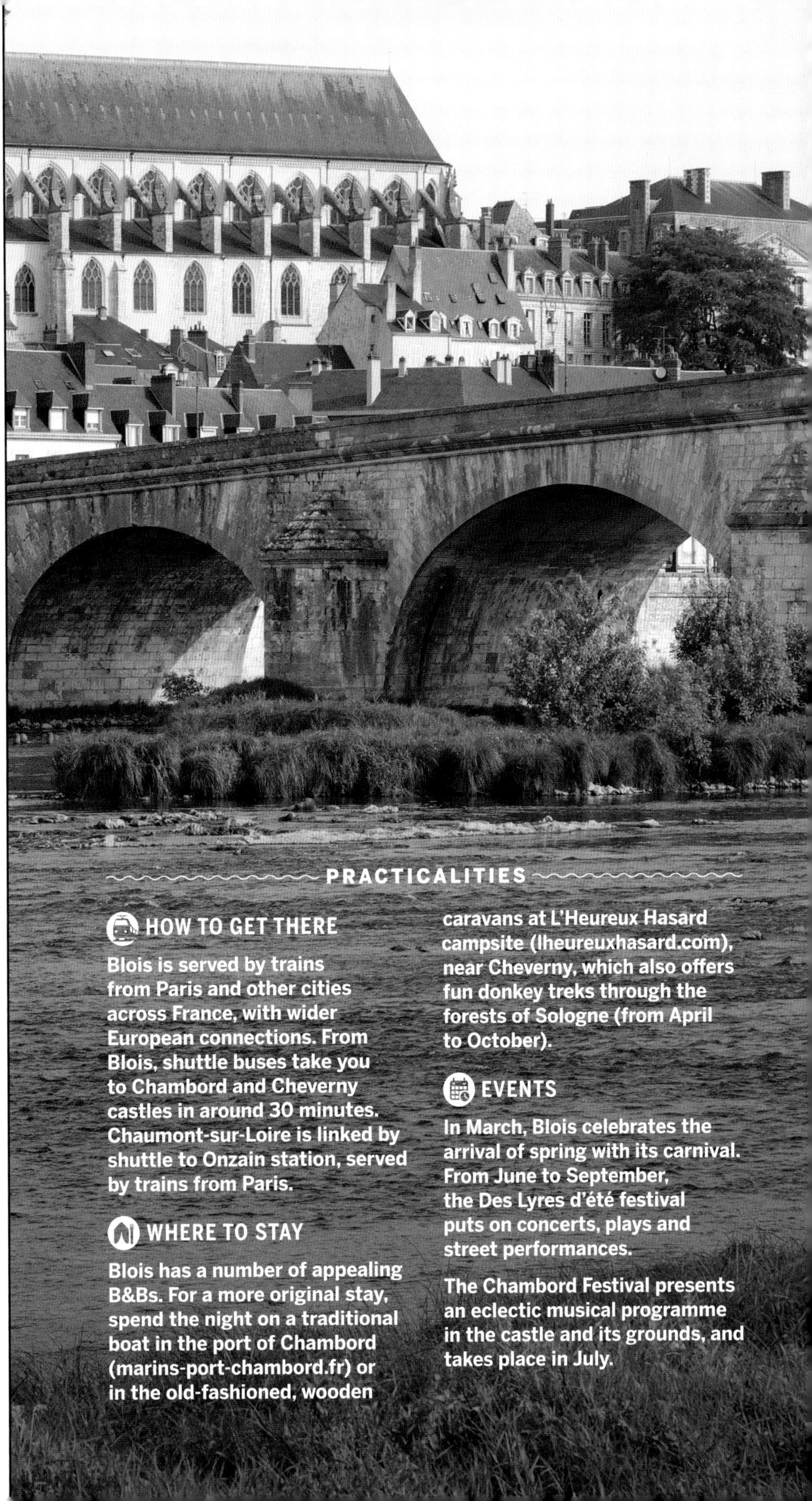

～～ PRACTICALITIES ～～

HOW TO GET THERE

Blois is served by trains from Paris and other cities across France, with wider European connections. From Blois, shuttle buses take you to Chambord and Cheverny castles in around 30 minutes. Chaumont-sur-Loire is linked by shuttle to Onzain station, served by trains from Paris.

WHERE TO STAY

Blois has a number of appealing B&Bs. For a more original stay, spend the night on a traditional boat in the port of Chambord (marins-port-chambord.fr) or in the old-fashioned, wooden caravans at L'Heureux Hasard campsite (lheureuxhasard.com), near Cheverny, which also offers fun donkey treks through the forests of Sologne (from April to October).

EVENTS

In March, Blois celebrates the arrival of spring with its carnival. From June to September, the Des Lyres d'été festival puts on concerts, plays and street performances.

The Chambord Festival presents an eclectic musical programme in the castle and its grounds, and takes place in July.

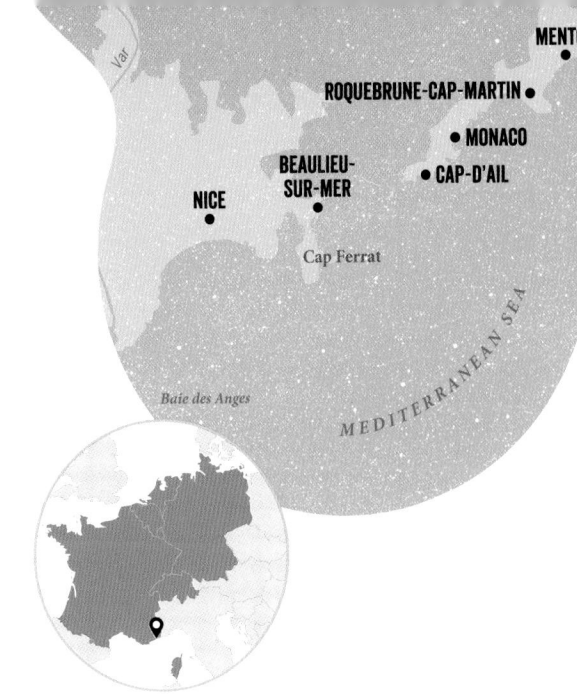

MENTON

ROQUEBRUNE-CAP-MARTIN

MONACO

BEAULIEU-SUR-MER

CAP-D'AIL

NICE

Cap Ferrat

Baie des Anges

MEDITERRANEAN SEA

47

FRANCE

Find Côte d'Azur chic

IN NICE & THE FRENCH RIVIERA

Renowned for its sunny climate, sandy beaches, colourful buildings and chic residents, Nice, capital of the Côte d'Azur, also shines with a diverse mix of museums, architecture and gastronomy. Listed as a UNESCO World Heritage Site in 2021, 'Nissa la Bella' is a corner of France that holds many delights for visitors. Stroll the legendary **Promenade des Anglais**, lined with palm trees and refined buildings; climb up **castle hill** for a view of Nice's rooftops and the Bay of Angels; explore the pretty alleys of the Italianate **Old Town** (left); and visit its **art museums**, palaces and baroque churches. Feeling hungry? Sample some of the city's **culinary specialities** on the terrace of a **Michelin-starred restaurant** or take a tasty world tour in the food halls of the **Gare du Sud**. Finally, extend your stay in style with some time spent on the Riviera: the rugged coastline, stretching to the Italian border, plunges into an azure sea and is punctuated by **seaside resorts**, each more chic than the last. You can even check another country off your list with a trip to Monaco, trying your luck at the casino.

Discover Nissart culture

Nissart culture has a long history defined by its links to both France and Italy. To find out more, head for Vieux Nice, the old district where traces of the city's Italian past can be found. Wander the narrow streets and look up to discover the handsome, multicoloured facades that are so typically Nice but feel a bit Italian. Take in the cathedral of St Réparate, the Palais Lascaris, and the lively markets and cafe terraces of the Cours Saleya. Try *socca* (thin pancakes), *pissaladière* (pizza-like tart) and other local snacks at Chez Thérésa (theresa-nice.com) on the Cours, or at Chez Pipo (chezpipo.fr) in the port district.

Scale the heights of Cimiez

High on a hill above the city, the Cimiez neighbourhood is home to elegant villas, 19th-century hotels, two major art museums devoted to the works of Matisse and Chagall, and ancient remains that repay a visit. Originally a Roman stronghold, Cimiez is now a chic residential district. In the 1890s, Queen Victoria regularly wintered at the Régina, a monumental palace converted into apartments, where Matisse lived 50 years later – it can still be admired (from the outside) today.

Visit Mamac

The Musée d'Art Moderne et d'Art Contemporain (mamac-nice.org) exhibits a major collection of works by the Nice School of artists. Explore the world of Yves Klein, Niki de Saint Phalle, Ben Vautier and Martial Raysse. You'll also find pop-art classics and contemporary pieces, all housed in a stunning Modernist building. The panoramic view of the city from the roof terrace isn't bad, either.

Along the Côte d'Azur

Take a boat trip from Port Lympia along the Côte d'Azur's gorgeous coastline, or travel by car or train to discover coast-hugging resorts revelling in beauty and breathtaking panoramas. Head to Beaulieu-sur-Mer or Cap-d'Ail to lounge on sandy beaches, to Roquebrune-Cap-Martin to meander the narrow streets of the old village up to the castle, or to Menton (inset) to visit botanical gardens and baroque churches.

MORE TIME?

VILLA EPHRUSSI DE ROTHSCHILD An architectural wonder built in the early 20th century, this pink-fronted palace (villa-ephrussi.com) overlooks Cap Ferrat, 9km (5.6 miles) east of Nice, and houses some 5000 works of art. The park's nine themed gardens offer a world tour of plant species.
MONACO OCEANOGRAPHIC MUSEUM Photos, specimens and old equipment invite visitors to discover the history of underwater exploration in one of the most iconic buildings of 'the Rock' (Monaco's nickname). Its aquarium (musee.oceano.org) is one of the largest in Europe.

PAN BAGNAT

Originally a dish for the poor in the 19th century, *pan bagnat* is a quintessential Côte d'Azur sandwich that is characterised by the round shape of its dough. The name literally means 'bathed bread' and any self-respecting *pan bagnat* must be doused with a good amount of olive oil. The filling is usually a sandwich version of the famous Niçoise salad: tuna, hard-boiled eggs, anchovies, spring onion, black olives. The best places to try it? Lou Balico (loubalico. com) opposite Mamac, Kiosque Tintin next to the Marché de la Libération, or La Gratta in the port district. Bon appétit!

~ PRACTICALITIES ~

🚆 HOW TO GET THERE

Nice-Ville Station is served by trains from Paris (six hours), Lyon (four hours, 30 minutes), Marseille (two hours, 40 minutes). The airport sees arrivals from across Europe.

🏨 WHERE TO STAY & EAT

Hôtel Amour (hotelamournice. fr) and the Windsor (hotelwindsornice.com) have stylish decor and are conveniently located.

Top places for dining include L'Uzine, serving Mediterranean dishes (luzine-restaurant.com); Olive & Artichaut (oliveartichaut. com), for traditional cuisine; and Peixes for its fish ceviche (peixes.fr).

📅 EVENTS

Key events include the Nice Carnival at the end of February (nicecarnaval.com) and the Nice Jazz Festival in July (nicejazzfestival.fr).

The Fête du Citron in Menton in February (fete-du-citron. com) celebrates all things lemon-related, while the Monaco Formula 1 Grand Prix in May is all about the fast cars.

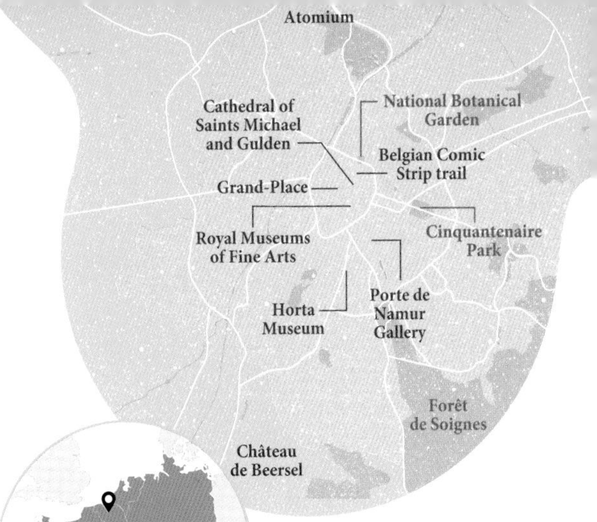

48

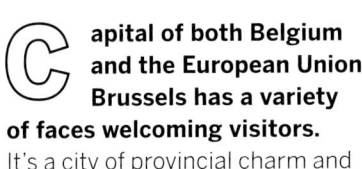

BELGIUM

Soak up every side of
BRUSSELS

Capital of both Belgium and the European Union, Brussels has a variety of faces welcoming visitors. It's a city of provincial charm and international importance, where pleasant surprises are guaranteed and the senses are always stimulated. Draw yourself away from the awe-inspiring **Grand Place** (left) and visit the **Cathedral of Sts Michael and Gudula**, follow the paths of the **Cinquantenaire Park** and the **botanical garden**, get acquainted with **Art Nouveau at the Horta Museum** and with the paintings of the Old Masters at the **Royal Museums of Fine Arts**. The quirky is also part of Brussels' complexion, seen in the **Manneken Pis**, the **Comic Book Trail** featuring almost 50 **murals**; and the **Atomium**, a curious reproduction of an oversized iron crystal molecule, built in 1958. Neighbourhoods away from the centre but well worth exploring include Matongé, where Brussels' African community provide a contrast with the rest of the city; and more traditional Les Marolles. And don't forget to indulge in the time-honoured tradition of enjoying a beer in an **estaminet**.

Stand in awe in the Grand Place

Prepare for visual overload as you enter the Grand Place, the immense square lined with magnificent buildings that tell the story of a prosperous history. The Gothic, 15th-century city hall and a dozen or so elaborate merchant guildhalls form a unique architectural ensemble at the heart of Brussels. Among the most spectacular are the House of the Bakers (at no. 1); the House of the Dukes of Brabant, whose facade features a fine array of busts; and the Swan (at no. 9), which was home to the butchers' guild – then a workers' cafe which counted Karl Marx among its customers.

A passion for comics

The Comic Arts Museum (opposite; cbbd.be) houses a rich collection of works by national cartoon creators, the pioneers of contemporary comics, in a glorious Art Nouveau building dating from 1906. In the upstairs galleries, accessed via a glass-lit vestibule adorned with a statue of Tintin, visitors can learn about the heroes of Belgian comics from the 1920s to the 1960s, including Tintin himself (Hergé), Gaston Lagaffe (Franquin), Blake and Mortimer (Jacobs) and the Smurfs (Peyo). Several city streets feature street art dedicated to the comic strip too.

Ponder the plants at the National Botanical Garden

Located north of the city, the National Botanical Garden (inset) is a welcome oasis of rolling lawns, lakes, arboretums, a moated castle and greenhouses, filled with over 18,000 plant species from every corner of the globe. It's an ideal place to unwind, read, picnic or peruse the tropical collections – the orchids and water lilies are the most prized plants here.

A taste of Africa

The neighbourhood of Matongé is the hub of Brussels' African community and offers a shopping experience like no other in the city. In the 1950s, Congolese students made this area southeast of the centre home and have been joined in the years since by people from many other countries. Travel from Europe to Africa by starting at Porte de Namur station, roaming shops selling everything from bright wax-print fabrics to extra hot chillies, stopping to enjoy a meal at one of the area's restaurants, and visiting the art galleries.

MORE TIME?

FORÊT DE SOIGNES An appealing patch of nature in the Brussels region, this forest (foret-de-soignes.be), surrounded by picturesque villages, is a cathedral of vegetation that's ideal for walks and bike rides.
BEERSEL CASTLE Some 10km (6 miles) south of the city, you can explore this moat-wrapped medieval fortress in a bucolic setting (visitbeersel.be/Kasteel-Beersel).

LES MAROLLES

It's in Brussels' Les Marolles district that you'll find the city's authentic spirit, a cheeky sense of humour and a sense of fun. The neighbourhood today has a diverse demographic, with old Marolliens who speak Brusseleir (a Brabant dialect), immigrant populations and hipsters creating a buzzing atmosphere. It's a delicious, unusual side to the capital and Sunday is the best day to experience it – start at the flea market in Place du Jeu-de-Balle, before moving on to Rue des Renards to visit antique shops and art galleries, and then have a lazy lunch in a traditional restaurant.

PRACTICALITIES

HOW TO GET THERE

Brussels is well connected by plane, train and road to destinations across Europe and further afield.

WHERE TO STAY

The city has a wide choice of accommodation, from youth hostels to luxury hotels. Offering good value for money in a prime location right next to the Grand Place, Hotel Hubert (hotelhubert-brussels.be) welcomes guests with a warm, vintage design.

EVENTS

For three weeks in May, the Kunsten Festival des Arts (kfda.be) presents a selection of recent theatre, dance, film and visual arts from around the world.

49

Wander through Wallonia
IN LIÈGE & THE HAUTES FAGNES

If Liège, capital of Wallonia, puts you in a good mood, with its tasty beers and waffles, gourmet restaurants and architectural curiosities, the surrounding countryside does an equally great job of keeping that smile on your face. Start with the jewels of Liège's heritage: **St Paul's Cathedral**; **the Church of St-Jacques**; and the **Collegiate Church of St Barthélemy** (overleaf) with a baptismal font, dating from 1118, that's one of the most illustrious **works of Mosan art** in the world. Amble through the streets, lose yourself in the flower-filled cul-de-sacs of the

Hors-Château district and admire the 17th- and 18th-century houses. To learn more about the city, visit the **Cité Miroir** cultural centre (citemiroir.be). Nearby towns to add to the itinerary include **Spa**, one of Europe's first thermal spas; and **Stavelot**, with an abbey once home to the Stavelot-Malmédy prince-abbots. If castles are a must, there are a few that reward a visit nearby. Finally, breathe in the fresh air of the **Hautes Fagnes Nature Park** (left; botrange.be). Among its marked trails, the Grande Ronde des Fagnes (9km/5.6 miles) is one of the best for seeing what the park has to offer.

Climb the 374 steps of Montagne de Bueren

Not really a mountain (but tell your lungs that after you've walked up its 374 steps), the Montagne de Bueren staircase connects two of Liège's neighbourhoods and repays the effort with expansive city views; you can catch your breath on the way up, pausing at the landings and benches. Originally, this structure was used to defend the town – it linked the citadel barracks directly to the town centre in the event of an invasion. Today, it ranks among 'the most extreme staircases in the world' according to the *Huffington Post*.

Go underground at the Blegny mine

Put on a jacket and hard hat and descend into the bowels of the earth, to depths of up to 60m (197ft), to discover the former mine at Blegny (blegnymine.be), located between Liège and Maastricht. Find out more about the work of the miners, coal extraction and processing. Blegny is one of only four authentic coal mines in Europe with galleries that are still accessible, and was recognised as a UNESCO World Heritage Site in 2012.

Admire Val-Dieu Abbey

After visiting this still-active Cistercian monastery (opposite; abbaye-du-val-dieu.be), founded in 1216 northeast of Liège and producing an excellent beer that can be sampled in its cafe, walk through the 19th-century park that's listed as a historic monument. Follow the life trail, admire the trees, river, pond and bridges, and look out for the Bible quotes in four languages.

Visit the Val Saint Lambert Crystal Glassworks

Located in a castle in Seraing, the Val Saint Lambert Cystal Glassworks (val-saint-lambert.com) is a museum covering the know-how and history of pure crystal. Discover vases, jewellery, lighting and other decorative objects, take part in a glassblowing demonstration, and applaud the work of the cutters and engravers. Guided visits available. From Liège, it's a 20-minute drive or a 30-minute train ride.

Get high at Signal de Botrange

Located in the Hautes Fagnes, at an altitude of 694m (2277ft), Signal de Botrange is the highest point in Belgium (and indeed the three Benelux countries). Put on warm clothes – the mountains can be chilly and wet – take binoculars to observe the wildlife, and then head for the Mont Rigi area above Malmedy, a former leather-tanning centre near Liège, from where several trails start. The 5km-long (3-mile) Fagne de la Poleûr is fully signposted and accessible to all.

MORE TIME?

CASTLE-HOPPING Don't miss Waimes' Reinhardstein Castle, Modave's namesake castle, Waroux Castle in Ans, or Chokier Castle in Flémalle.
ÎLE AUX CORSAIRES Situated between the Ourthe River and the Ourthe Canal, this former industrial site is now home to exceptional flora (calamine pansy, swollen campion). Its name is said to derive from the pirate games children used to play here.
BEHIND THE SCENES AT SPA-FRANCORCHAMPS Visit the pits, the press room, the announcer's booths and the legendary podium on which the world's greatest drivers celebrate at this world-renowned F1 circuit (spa-francorchamps.be).

THE CWARMÊ DE MALMEDY

Part of the intangible heritage of the Wallonia-Brussels Federation, the Cwarmê de Malmedy is one of Belgium's most popular carnivals. For four days up to midnight on Shrove Tuesday (Mardi Gras), processions of masked and costumed characters parade through the streets. This moment of popular celebration was recently the subject of a thriller novel, combining suspense and Belgian humour: *Malmedy, les masques et la mort*, by Patrice Hainaut – a book you'll find at the Malmundarium, the local history museum, and in the town's bookshops.

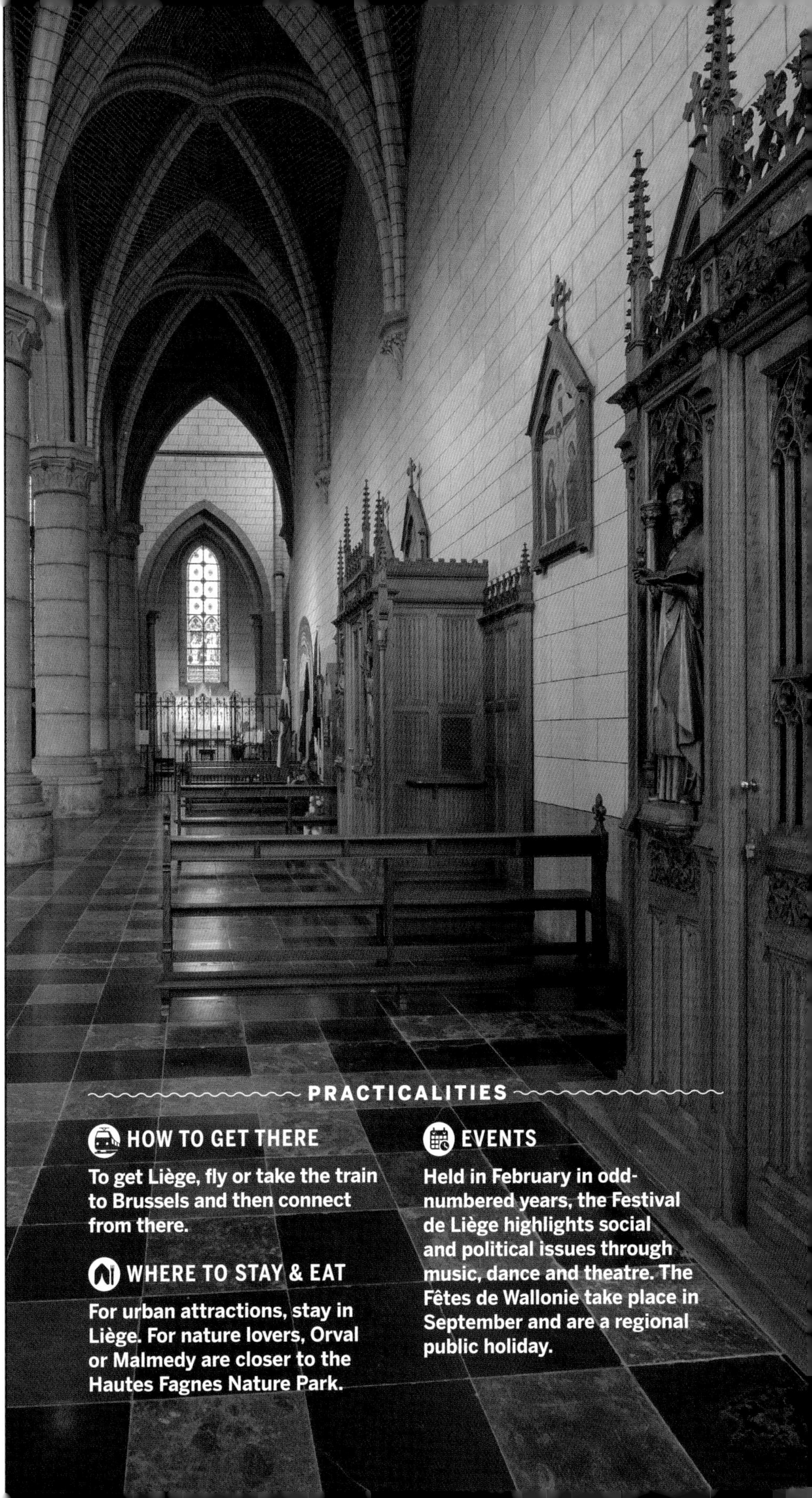

~~~~~~ **PRACTICALITIES** ~~~~~~

🚆 HOW TO GET THERE

To get Liège, fly or take the train to Brussels and then connect from there.

🏠 WHERE TO STAY & EAT

For urban attractions, stay in Liège. For nature lovers, Orval or Malmedy are closer to the Hautes Fagnes Nature Park.

📅 EVENTS

Held in February in odd-numbered years, the Festival de Liège highlights social and political issues through music, dance and theatre. The Fêtes de Wallonie take place in September and are a regional public holiday.

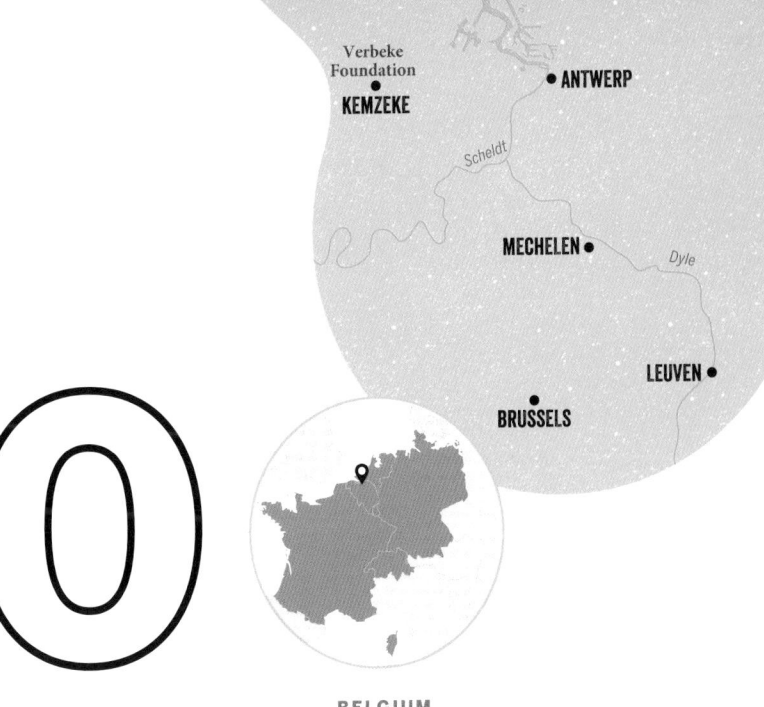

BELGIUM

50

A taste of Flanders
BETWEEN ANTWERP & MECHELEN

In Antwerp, Flanders' biggest urban centre, you'll find a captivating combination of art and fashion. In this city of Rubens there's the opportunity to find beauty in all its forms, whether at the Museum Plantin-Moretus, with its priceless early printed manuscripts; or in Notre-Dame Cathedral, with its artistic treasures. Antwerp is also home to contemporary collections such as the MAS (mas.be), the 'Museum on the River' in the lively Eilandje district. This 62m-high (203ft) tower offers an awesome view of the docks, the Scheldt River and the city from its terrace. From the Saint-André district all the way to the trendy Zuid neighbourhood, fashion-conscious visitors can scour designer boutiques and luxury warehouses, before visiting the Musée de la Mode (momu. be), which holds the world's largest collection of Belgian fashion. After enjoying these urban pleasures, give in to the charms of much quieter Mechelen, on the banks of the Dyle River. With its handsome canals, amazing architecture, artistic heritage and famous beer, this small city makes a big impact.

Subterranean Antwerp

In the Middle Ages, Antwerp was crisscrossed by a network of canals, streams and moats, but over the centuries these waterways, known as the Ruien (deruien. be) were vaulted and gradually disappeared underground. They're now open to the public and visitors have two options to see them: a group tour with a guide who tells interesting anecdotes; or an individual visit, still accompanied by a guide but with an interactive tablet detailing the stories. Boots and paper overalls are supplied. You can also take a boat tour, which is fun but short (10 minutes) and you only see a small part of the network.

Seek out Rubens

The works of Flemish painter Peter Paul Rubens (1577–1640) are everywhere in Antwerp, where he spent much of his life and where he died. From the house where he lived (rubenshuis. be) to his works in the Royal Museum of Fine Arts (KMSKA; kmska.be) and from St James' Church (sintjacobantwerpen. be) to the Cathedral of Our Lady (dekathedraal.be), existing fans and newcomers to Rubens' genius will find plenty to delight and educate them from this great Flemish painter.

Two-wheel sightseeing on the Architectuurroute

An original way to explore Antwerp's built heritage is to set off on the Architectuurroute, a bike trail that starts from Antwerp's main square and takes in the city's landmark buildings and some unsung highlights. The full route is 30km (19 miles) but there's also a shorter version (16km/10 miles). Look out along the way for the Steen fortress and museum; the MAS gallery (inset) and the new Port Authority building; as well as the *Kerkschip*, a German supply ship converted into a church; the Belle Époque district of Zurenborg, and the only house built by Le Corbusier in Belgium.

Meet little-known Mechelen

Reason enough to visit Mechelen (opposite) would be to see the magnificent, Gothic, UNESCO-listed St Rombout Cathedral; its 15th-century tower rises 97m (318ft) above the town. But Mechelen has much more to offer: a splendid town square; ancient buildings, including beguinages (lay religious communities for women); and canals to meander along. And don't forget to stop by the Het Anker brewery and sample one of its famous beers.

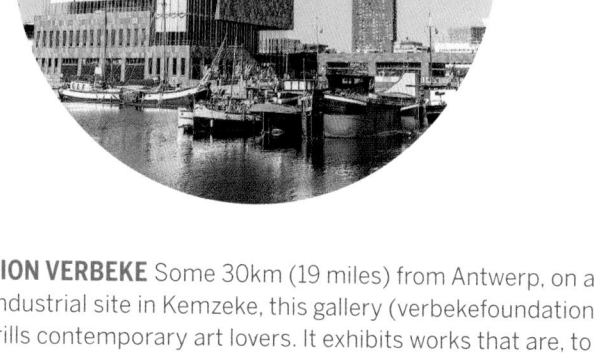

MORE TIME?

FONDATION VERBEKE Some 30km (19 miles) from Antwerp, on a former industrial site in Kemzeke, this gallery (verbekefoundation. com) thrills contemporary art lovers. It exhibits works that are, to say the least, unusual, such as the CasAnus, a piece in the shape of a colon that is also a hotel you can sleep in.

LEUVEN Visitors flock to Leuven (Louvain in French) above all for its flamboyant Gothic town hall, then for its 13th-century Grand Béguinage (a UNESCO World Heritage Site) and to stroll the paths of the botanical garden, created in the 18th century. The city is 50km (31 miles) from Antwerp and 25km (15.5 miles) from Mechelen.

THE PORT OF ANTWERP

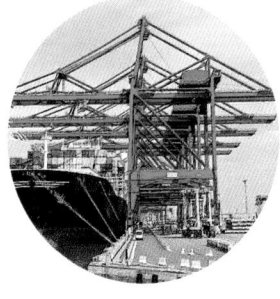

The port of Antwerp, on the Scheldt estuary, is one of the world's largest shipping hubs. A three-hour excursion aboard the *Flandria* (flandria.nu) allows you to fully appreciate the facilities, which extend right up to the Dutch border. The port's expansion in the 1960s meant that seven villages had to be razed to the ground, but the hamlet of Lillo remains, within the confines of a former military fort. You can visit its small museum and enjoy a drink on the terrace of one of its two cafes.

PRACTICALITIES

HOW TO GET THERE

Antwerp is easily reached by train and plane from various destinations across Europe. Brussels is just over an hour away by frequent rail services.

WHERE TO EAT

For a gourmet lunch in quaint surroundings, head for Het Gebaar (hetgebaar.be) at the entrance to Antwerp's Botanical Gardens, where famous Belgian chef Roger van Damme has taken up residence.

EVENTS

From June to the end of August, the Summer of Antwerp (Zomer van Antwerpen; zva.be) presents a rich programme of circus and street-theatre performances, film screenings and concerts. Events are often free. Every year in July, the world's biggest electro music festival, Tomorrowland (tomorrowland.com), is held in Boom, 16km (10 miles) south of Antwerp, for two weeks.

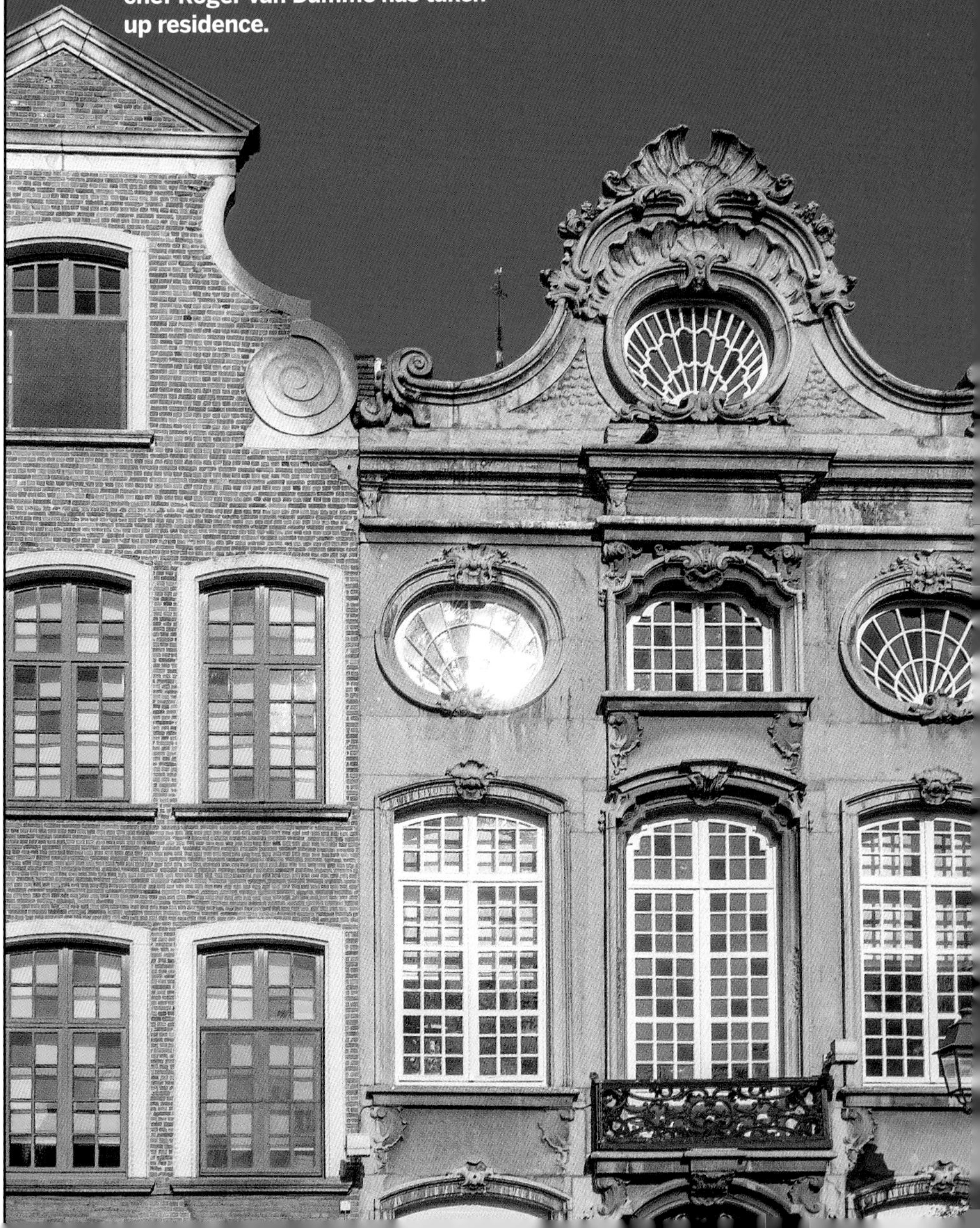

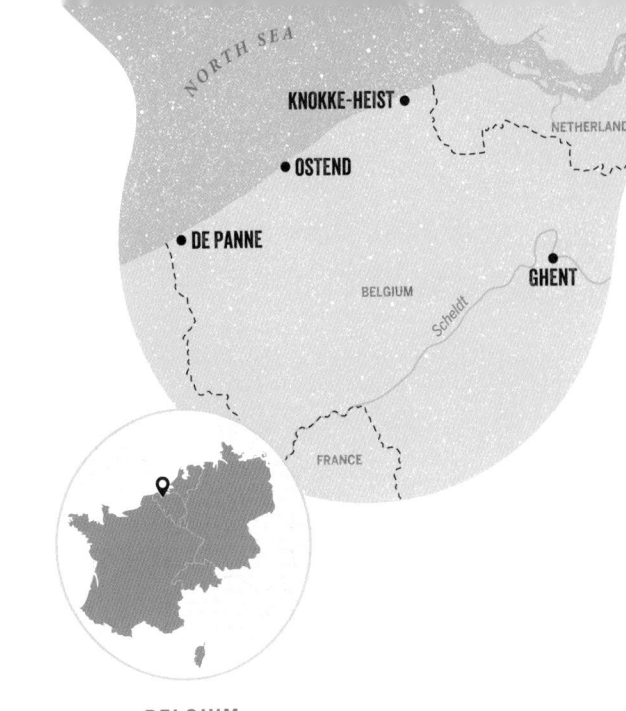

NORTH SEA

KNOKKE-HEIST •

• OSTEND

NETHERLANDS

• DE PANNE

BELGIUM

GHENT

Scheldt

FRANCE

BELGIUM

51

See a different side to Flanders
IN GHENT

I t would be a mistake to think of Ghent as just the little sister of much-loved (and touristy) Bruges. It's not. Ghent, once a flourishing city-state and a key port in the Middle Ages, promises a unique, colourful experience on a weekend break. The historic town centre is the perfect place to start your exploration: **St Bavo's Cathedral**, **the cloth market** and **the town hall** can be reached on foot, by bike or by tram. A trip to the city should also include the **university district** with the **MSK** (Museum of Fine Arts; mskgent.be) and the **botanical garden** to the south. A must for soaking up Ghent's atmosphere is the **Lys River**, best explored on **foot** along the quays or by **boat** (left), bobbing on the water. Take time to admire the city's architectural highlights as well, some of which date back to the 12th century, and hear the fascinating stories behind them, including that of the magnificent Marriott Hotel, whose golden swans are a clue to its past life as a brothel. Round off a stay with a walk up the **Graslei** (grass quay), where ships once offloaded their cargoes of grain, before choosing a terrace to **enjoy a waffle and a local beer** or tucking into some fine dining in a former factory.

213

Take an audio-guide tour of the Castle of the Counts

The residence of the Counts of Flanders (historischehuizen.stad. gent/en/castle-counts) is wrapped in the arms of the Lys River to the north of the historic centre and is a must-see, evoking the history of the valiant knights who left their mark on the city. The audio guide, voiced by the famous Flemish actor Wouter Deprez, is a highlight – try not to laugh as you listen to some of the rather sordid anecdotes.

Get lost following street artists

Well hidden between two busy streets, Werregarenstraat (inset) – renamed Graffitistraatje or 'graffiti alley' – offers a constantly changing canvas for street artists, who add colour to Flemish bricks and bring soldiers and ballerinas face-to-face in their pieces. Other examples of their art can be found all over the city; and walking around, looking for them, is a good way to explore. To help you find them, download the map of works to find on visit.gent.be.

Fine dining in a former factory

Like Ghent itself, the modern Pakhuis brewery (pakhuis.be) combines history and modernity. Housed in a large former warehouse in the heart of the Old Town since 1991, it offers a menu of well-mastered Franco-Belgian classics and finely crafted vegetarian options, all set against a backdrop of wrought-iron beams supporting a huge glass roof – a proud tribute to its industrial past.

Take in the sights from the belfry

Like almost all towns in Belgium, Ghent features a magnificent belfry, symbolising municipal power and the wealth of the merchant guilds. This one is right next to the cloth market. With a head for heights and comfy shoes, climb to the top of this 14th-century building, listed as a UNESCO World Heritage Site, reaching 91m (299ft) above the city. Catch your breath as you admire the bells and the famous dragon, symbol of the town, whose history is recounted on the 1st floor.

MORE TIME?

SEASIDE A 40-minute train ride from Ghent takes you to the Belgian coast and Ostend. Despite its long, beautiful sandy beach, this resort has lost some of its 19th-century lustre, when it was home to the local bourgeoisie. But it's located on the Belgian coast's tramline, the longest in the world, making it the ideal jumping-off point for coastal escapades. With 67 stops, the tram runs from De Panne, near the French border, to Knokke-Heist, just before the Netherlands, providing over two hours of travel with a view of the North Sea and its immense beaches (opposite). For more information, visit dekusttram.be.

DELICIOUS CUBERDONS

The origins of the *cuberdon*, a sweet that is a source of national pride, are somewhat obscure. Some say it was born in the dispensary of a pharmacist in Ghent, while others attribute its creation to a clergy member from the Bruges region (so, not so far away). Whatever its history, this raspberry-flavoured purple cone is a favourite with Belgians and visitors alike, and can be found around Ghent, including at the market stalls on the historic Groentenmarkt. Enjoy it on the spot – its thin, crunchy outer layer and runny core make it impossible to export.

PRACTICALITIES

HOW TO GET THERE

Eurostar trains serve Brussels-Midi Station, from where it's a 30-minute connection to Gent-Sint-Pieters Station. Flights connect major cities with Brussels International and Brussels-Charleroi airports. Buses also run from Brussels to Ghent.

GOOD TO KNOW

Ghent, in particular the historic centre, is particularly geared towards pedestrians and cyclists. The city has introduced a Low Emission Zone (LEZ) that regulates vehicle access (the most polluting cars are banned). If you are travelling to Ghent with your own vehicle, you must register it in advance at: lez.stad.gent/en/flows/controleertoegang.

WHERE TO EAT

Along with Pakhuis (see previous page), find time for Maison Elza. Eggs Benedict, bagels and afternoon tea are all on the menu at this restaurant, done out in kitsch decor and just a stone's throw from the Castle of the Counts. Bonus point: you can watch the boats go by on the Lys from the small terrace, as if suspended above the water.

To Waterland,
the port of Monnickendam
& Marken Peninsula

NSDM-werf

AMSTERDAM-
NOORD

To Haarlem

Westergasfabriek

Buiksloterweg
port

Negen Straatjes

Go off the beaten track
IN AMSTERDAM

Amsterdam is home to
an abundance of sights
appealing to every
traveller – and that can be
a problem, with overtourism
in this relatively small city
an increasing issue.** Lovers of
history and architecture will rightly
delight in the UNESCO-listed **canal
belt**, the **gabled houses of the
Golden Age** and the poignant
Anne Frank Museum. Art buffs
will obviously make a beeline to
the **Rijksmuseum**, the **Van Gogh
Museum**, the **Stedelijk Museum**
and the science-focused **NEMO**
(left). Fans of experiences forbidden elsewhere will head for the
city's **coffee shops**. But beyond

Rembrandt, romantic canals and
recreational cannabis, there's
a place floating deftly between
cutting-edge design and **maritime traditions**, less touristy but
very much alive, where off the main
visitor trails are new neighbourhoods providing breathing space
and exciting opportunities. In
recent years, this Amsterdam has
found its most powerful expression
on the other side of the Ij River,
where the city's **hippest district**
now rubs shoulders with the bucolic landscapes of **Waterland**. But it
can also be found in the centre, in
the culture of the **brown cafes** and
the inventiveness of the **galleries**
and hidden **boutiques**.

Across the water to Amsterdam-Noord

Just over the Ij from the centre of the city, Amsterdam-Noord is an open-air laboratory for architectural and alternative experiments – at the NDSM-werf ferry port you'll be greeted by a dismantled atomic submarine and find the country's largest artists' squat in the former shipyard. Don't miss the fabulous Noorderlicht Café, housed in a greenhouse on the water's edge here. At the Buiksloterweg port, the EYE (you'll understand its name when you see it) is the architecturally audacious Dutch cinema museum, while the neighbouring tower, formerly Shell's headquarters, has become A'DAM Lookout – from its 22nd-floor roof terrace, you'll have the most incredible view across Amsterdam.

Shopping in the Negen Straatjes

There's no shortage of opportunities for shopping in Amsterdam, but no district presents as many attractive and original options in a beautiful setting as the Negen Straatjes (de9straatjes.nl). These nine little streets – between the Prinsengracht and the Singel, and crossed by the Keizersgracht and the Herengracht – are lined with clothing and hyper-specialised shops (glasses, toothbrushes, art books), all worth a look.

A taste of 'jenever' in a brown cafe

Bruine cafés (brown cafes) owe their name to the tobacco stains left on their walls over the years by the Amsterdammers who frequented them. Even today, they retain a loyal, regular clientele. Enjoy a beer or, better still, a glass of *jenever* (gin-like spirit) at one of the small candlelit tables, and experience *gezelligheid* (conviviality) the Dutch way. There are more than a thousand brown cafes in Amsterdam, and some of the highly recommended include 't Smalle (t-smalle.nl), near Westermarkt; and De Kat in de Wijngaert (dekatindewijngaert.nl), in the Jordaan. Many organise regular jazz jam sessions.

Explore Waterland by bike

Just 9km (5.6 miles) north of Amsterdam, Waterland spreads out its lush green fields and water-filled furrows, observed on high by local herons. It's a journey taking you back several centuries through a rural landscape, and is great for cycling. Board the free Buiksloterwegveer ferry (behind Centraal Station) and cross the Ij. From the dock, discover the picturesque port of Monnickendam (inset), and the Marken Peninsula (opposite), which has kept its fishing-village atmosphere.

MORE TIME?

WESTERGASFABRIEK Just off the western edge of the Jordaan neighbourhood, this former industrial complex houses a host of bars, restaurants, a Sunday market and even a cinema in its Neo-Renaissance buildings.

HAARLEM Just a 15-minute train ride from Amsterdam, Haarlem is a classic Dutch town of charming cobblestone streets, historic buildings, interesting museums and friendly cafes, all livened up by a vibrant student population.

KING'S DAY

The Netherlands is probably the only country in the world with a national holiday that changes according to the birthday of the current sovereign. Until the abdication of Queen Beatrix in 2013, *Koninginnedag* (Queen's Day) was celebrated on 30 April, but since the coronation of her son, Willem-Alexander, *Koningsdag* (King's Day) has been celebrated on 27 April, his birthday. The whole country is decked out in orange – the colour of the House of Orange-Nassau, reigning since the 19th century – and awaits the king's appearance at Amsterdam's Royal Palace. A carnival atmosphere and flea market add to the fun. To visit the city on this date, book very far in advance.

WHEN TO GO

Rain is possible, even likely, during any season in Amsterdam. The rain/sun balance is most favourable from Easter to September, but this is also peak tourist season. In July and August, many businesses are closed.

HOW TO GET THERE

Amsterdam Centraal is the main station for national and international trains, including Eurostar. If you're coming by plane, Schiphol Airport, 18km (11 miles) from Amsterdam, has direct flights to just about everywhere and is connected to the city by regular trains.

EVENTS

In January, for Tulip Day, the Dam (the city's main square) is decked out with 200,000 flowers. Amsterdam organises two popular Fashion Weeks (amsterdamfashionweek.nl) in February and September. The first weekend in August is Gay Pride (pride.amsterdam), celebrated on the canals, and in mid-August, the Grachtenfestival (grachtenfestival.nl) puts on classical concerts.

THE HAGUE

DELFT

GOUDA

ROTTERDAM

Rotterdam
Zuid

KINDERDIJK

NETHERLANDS

53

Admire the architecture
IN ROTTERDAM

Amsterdam is a wonderful place to visit, but a
victim of its own popu-
larity, so head to Rotterdam
instead, Europe's leading port,
for a quieter, architecturally
awesome escape. Arriving at the
station, close to the centre, means
you can **explore the city** on foot.
Start with a taste of local gastronomy at the **Markthal** (central
market), found in a remarkable
modern building. Nearby, visit the
Overblaak housing estate, with
its astonishing yellow, 45-degree-
tilted cube houses built between
1970 and 1980. Striking landmarks
such as the **Van Nelle Fabriek**,
a UNESCO-listed 'ideal factory'
from the 1930s and a classic of
Dutch modernism; or the **Huis
Sonneveld**, characteristic of
Dutch functionalism, await you
elsewhere. From prewar beauties
to current masterpieces, it's an
open-air gallery dedicated to architecture and design that's worth
strolling through. Then jump on a
waterbus, train or bike to enjoy the
famous **windmills of Kinderdijk**,
the art and history of **Den Haag
(The Hague)**, the celebrated
pottery of **Delft** and the fabulous
cheese of **Gouda**.

Inviting southern neighbourhoods

Once you've checked off the central highlights, head for Rotterdam Zuid, the city's southern district, across the famous red Willemsbrug bridge or its neighbour the Erasmusbrug, nicknamed the 'swan' – photographers will appreciate the view both day and night. The Katendrecht industrial peninsula was once home to the city's red-light district, and is now home to a series of elegant buildings.

Have a break in a historic building

Take a water taxi from the centre of Rotterdam to Wilhelminapier and seek out the Hotel New York. You're standing in front of the Holland America Line company building. Many ships set sail for the USA (in particular New York – hence its name) from the docks just in front of this building, now a national monument. The company's HQ moved to Seattle in the 1970s and this building was converted into a hotel-restaurant some 20 years later. Book a room for the night, or enjoy dinner in cool, historic surroundings.

Spend the day in Den Haag

It's easy to reach Den Haag by train from Rotterdam – in just 30 minutes, you're in the political centre of the Netherlands. After a delicious brunch at Walter Benedict (try the scrambled eggs with truffles), walk through the royal city, crossing its central square, passing its shopping arcades, admiring its preserved historic buildings and, above all, enjoying masterpieces of the Dutch Golden Age, such as Vermeer's *Girl with a Pearl Earring*, exhibited in the Mauritshuis.

Good times in Gouda

The small town of Gouda, which gave its name to the famous cheese produced here since 1668, is also just a 30-minute train ride from Rotterdam. Amble along its canals, look up at its historic facades and reach the central square where the Stadhuis, the red-shuttered town hall, stands. Not far away is the Goudse Waag (goudsewaag.nl), the museum where you can enjoy a tasting of the celebrated local speciality.

Pedal to Kinderdijk

The 19 historic windmills of Kinderdijk run alongside a canal (inset) that joins the New Meuse River whose reeds and endemic species invite you to take a stroll. All the windmills are still in operation, and some are even inhabited. Others offer a glimpse into the lives of the millers and their families who lived there until just a few decades ago. It's a classic image of the Netherlands, and the UNESCO site makes for an exciting visit, just 25km (15.5 miles) from Rotterdam by bicycle. Coming by pedal power gives you the chance to cruise along the canal, stopping wherever you please. Tired? Put your two-wheeler on the waterbus (fast ferry running from May to October) for the trip back to the city.

MORE TIME?

DELFT Renowned for its blue-and-white pottery, this town played a prominent role in the Dutch Golden Age, not least because of one of its illustrious inhabitants, the painter Johannes Vermeer. Your to-do list should include a visit to the Delft factory, a walk along the canals and a visit to the remarkable town hall.

PEDAL POWER

Fiets (bicycles) are the means of transport for which the Netherlands is famous, and bikes are available for visitors to rent in Rotterdam. A dense network of cycle paths crisscrosses the city and its surroundings. One 28km (17-mile) route follows the north and south banks of the New Meuse (downloadable map at rotterdam.nl/nieuwe-maasparcours). Other options include Roaming Rotterdam, which focuses on the city's iconic architecture and landmarks (10km/6 miles), and Rondje Katendrecht (15km/9 miles), which follows the quays and crosses the ports of Rijnhaven and Maashaven. Pick up maps from the tourist office. Rental shops and bike-share stations abound.

PRACTICALITIES

HOW TO GET THERE

Rotterdam Centraal Station is well connected by rail to other Dutch and European destinations. Flights land at Rotterdam-The-Hague Airport; a bus takes visitors into the city. Amsterdam's Schiphol Airport is just 30 minutes away by train and has many more connections.

GOOD TO KNOW

Where does the pulse of lively Rotterdam beat fastest? In Witte de Withstraat. Located south of the city centre, this is the coolest street in town, with inspiring boutiques, art galleries, trendy bars and fine dining.

LUXEMBOURG

54

Be surprised by
LUXEMBOURG

The first thing that comes to mind for many people when they hear the name 'Grand Duchy of Luxembourg' is probably finance and European Union institutions. All true, and yet Luxembourg City, squeezed between Belgium, France and Germany, is one of the continent's most unusual and underrated capitals. Combining the remains of **a fortress** with **modern architecture** and **contemporary art** on a rocky spur, the first impression the city makes is one of pleasant surprise. In the ravines where the Pétrusse and Alzette rivers flow, interspersed with waterfalls, lined with colourful houses and vegetable gardens, sometimes with meadows and ancient abbeys, is a much more village-like place, where **nature** is always present. The city's contrasts are striking, even in the languages spoken – over 67% of its inhabitants are foreigners, comprising **165 different nationalities**. Leaving the capital behind, visit the **Eisch and Moselle valleys**, the former with its castles and the latter with its wine; or the **red earth of the Minett region**, whose hilly landscapes are dotted with forests and vineyards, villages and forts.

Take on the fortress city

A World Heritage Site, the remains of the fortress (gates, bastions, redoubts and casemates) of the city of Luxembourg, and its old quarters enclosed within the ramparts, are fascinating to explore. A guided tour of the Bock casemates carved out of the rock, the Vauban Circuit (following in the footsteps of the eponymous French military engineer) and the UNESCO walking and cycling tour of the Old Town (see previous page) and fortifications (luxembourg-city. com) all tempt you to take part in a city-wide treasure hunt, with breathtaking views along the way.

Enjoy the art & architecture of Kirchberg

The Red Bridge leads from the city centre to the Kirchberg Plateau, a futuristic world where daring buildings designed by visionary architects are constantly springing up. This is where European institutions and banks are based. Hop on a bike and discover the iconic architecture (European Investment Bank, Court of Justice of the European Union, Deutsche Bank, the Philharmonie Luxembourg) and sculptures by famous artists (*The Chair* by Magdalena Jetelová, *Bird Cage* by Su-Mei Tse, *Exchange* by Richard Serra). Then immerse yourself in the luminous Contemprary Art Museum, designed by IM Pei.

Search for castles

To the north of the capital are a host of castles. The lovely Eisch Valley has seven of them, across 24km (15 miles). But the most interesting are to be found in the Luxembourg Ardennes. The most romantic of these? Vianden Castle (opposite; 11th–14th century) and its medieval town. The most unexpected? Clervaux Castle, in the north of the duchy, which has a beautiful and moving collection of photographs, *The Family of Man*. A series of 503 images – by the likes of Robert Capa, Henri Cartier-Bresson, Dorothea Lange and Robert Doisneau – was compiled in 1955 by Edward Steichen of New York's MoMA and cover the range of human experience: life, death, love, work and friendship.

Explore the Grand Duchy by bike & on foot

In addition to a dense network of cyclepaths (600km/373 miles), Luxembourg has a formidable array of marked trails for discovering its regions on foot. The Mullerthal Trail takes you through the forests, streams and rock formations of the country's Little Switzerland. Éislek Pied offers a great choice of local walks in the Ardennes. And the Escapardenne Eislek Trail crosses a wide variety of landscapes between Belgium and Luxembourg. More suggestions can be found on luxembourg.public.lu.

MORE TIME?

MOSELLE VALLEY Hillsides planted with vineyards, picturesque villages, famous vintages, a few museums and nature reserves (Haff Réimech; A Wiewesch) – Luxembourg's Moselle Valley (inset) offers a delightful rural day trip.

MINETT Thanks to its iron-rich red soil (*minett*), the south of the country was responsible for the Grand Duchy's industrial boom from the 19th century onwards. Today, reinvention is in full swing, with mines converted into nature reserves, blast furnace tours and the iron metropolis of Esch-sur-Alzette, European Capital of Culture in 2022, attracting a new kind of tourism.

A EUROPEAN CAPITAL

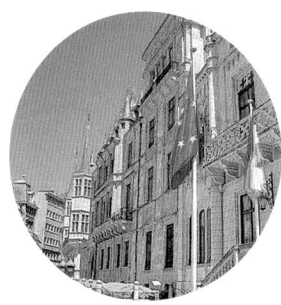

In 963, Sigfried, Count of the Ardennes, built a fortress on the steep outcrop of Bock. Over the centuries, this exceptional strategic position made it one of Europe's largest fortified cities. Passing through the hands of the Burgundians, Habsburgs, Spanish, France's Louis XIV and then the Prussians, the site was constantly upgraded and reinforced – until it was dismantled in 1867 and Luxembourg, now a neutral country, opened up to the world and enjoyed rapid industrial growth. In 1952, it became home to various European institutions, and today Luxembourg City is, alongside Brussels and Strasbourg, the third capital of the European Union.

PRACTICALITIES

HOW TO GET THERE & AROUND

TGV trains connect Paris to Luxembourg in two hours, 15 minutes via Metz. From Brussels, allow around three hours.

Public transport (bus, tram, train) is free throughout the Grand Duchy. Luxembourg City has the vel'OH! bike-share scheme (30 minutes free). Two lifts (free; bicycles accepted) link the upper and lower towns. The panoramic lift between Pfaffenthal and the upper town offers a fantastic view of the Alzette Valley.

WHERE TO STAY

Book a room at the charming Les Jardins d'Anaïs (jardinsdanais.lu) hotel in the heart of the central Clausen district. Or, a short walk away, there's the pleasant youth hostel (youthhostels.lu) on the banks of the Alzette River.

EVENTS

In summer, the country's many castles often host festivals, including the Knights' Festival in Vianden.

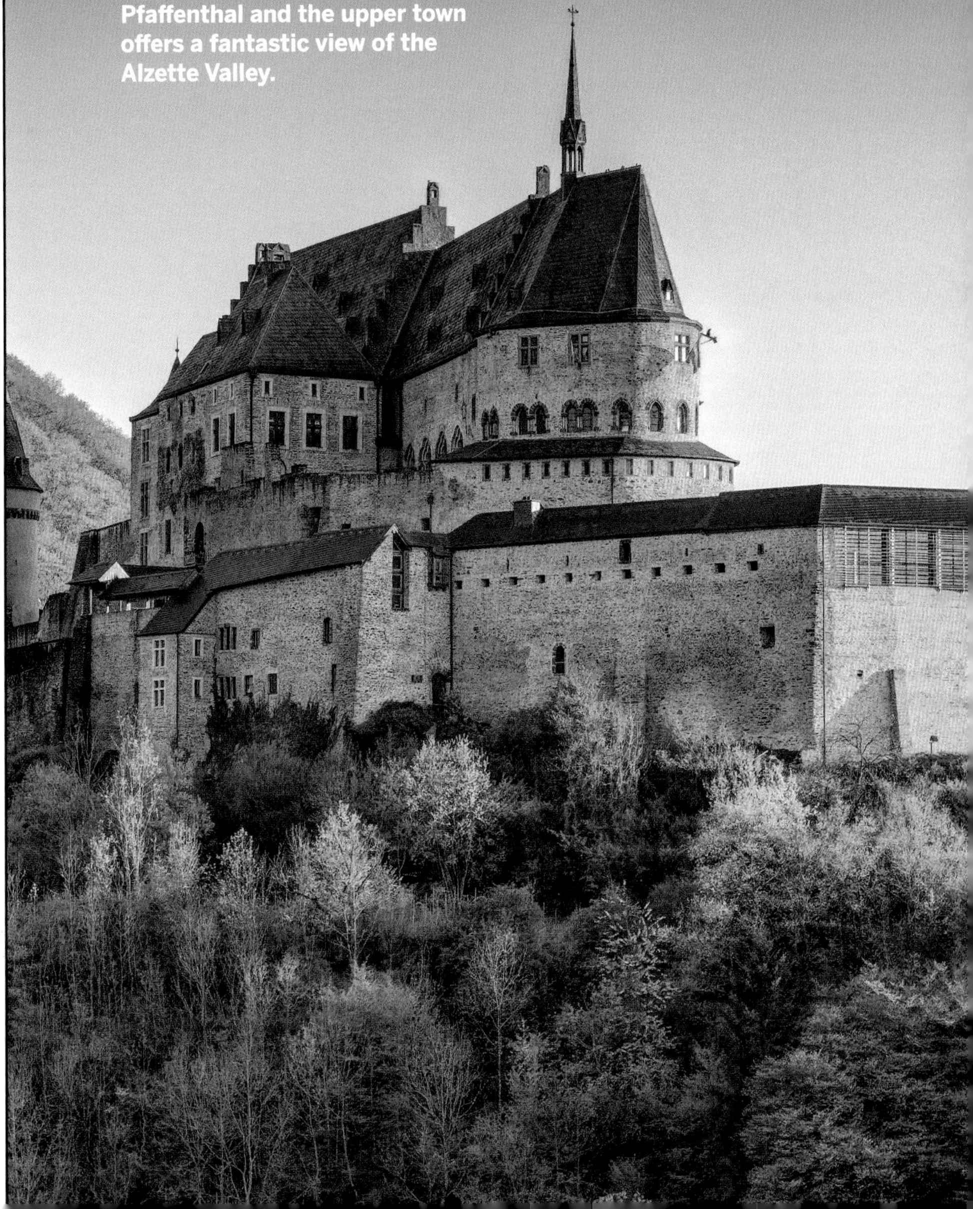

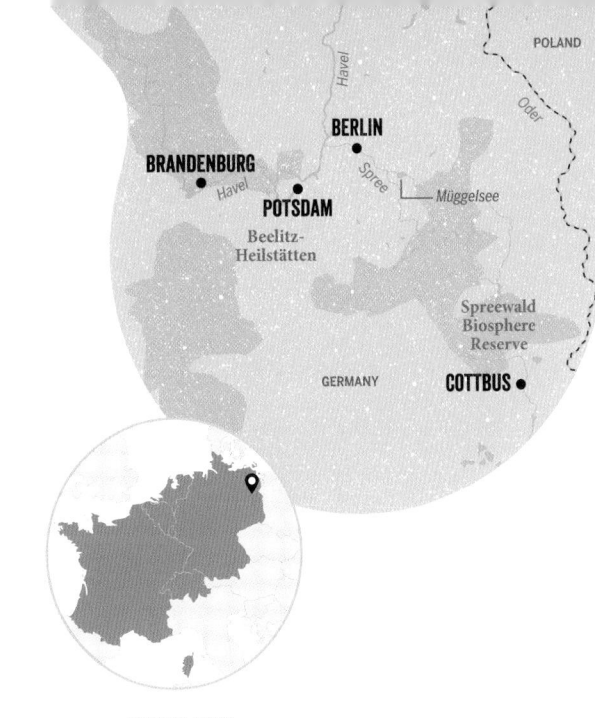

55

Combine art & nature
IN BERLIN

Berlin's historic monuments and museums and its unbridled nightlife can easily easily fill a weekend. Charlottenburg Palace, the Reichstag, the Brandenburg Gate and the Holocaust Memorial are just some of the jewels in the German capital's **rich historical crown**. **Museumsinsel** (Museum Island) is dedicated to art and history, with prestigious collections displayed at the Pergamon Museum, the Altes Museum and the Neues Museum. But art can be found everywhere here, as demonstrated by the **East Side Gallery**, a section of the Berlin Wall covered in paintings. In this city once split in two, torn between the Western and Soviet worlds, reunification has been celebrated since 1990 in an eating, drinking and partying scene that runs from *Biergarten* to techno clubs. But if you prefer urban pleasures in moderation, and also have more rural interests, Berlin is an equally ideal destination. The city is home to **vast green spaces**, such as the wonderful Tiergarten, and is gateway to the natural attractions of Beelitz Forest and the Spreewald.

Walk through the canopy in Beelitz Forest

At the end of the 19th century, Berliners suffering from tuberculosis were treated in a sanatorium built in Beelitz Forest, about 50km (31 miles) southwest of the capital. Today, it's a striking spot, with its ruined buildings scattered among the trees; so impressive that it features in several music videos and films (including *The Pianist*). Part of the complex is being restored, but you can still visit some of the ghostly buildings and the tunnels connecting them. A walkway runs through the treetops (inset), offering an unusual aerial experience 23m (75ft) above the ground.

Explore the watery world of the Spreewald

Just 90km (56 miles) from Berlin lies a natural gem listed as a UNESCO World Heritage Site: the Spree Forest Biosphere Reserve (opposite). This network of navigable canals stretches for 276km (171 miles) and can be discovered using a variety of watercraft (rowing boat, kayak and so on). Back on land, a lovely walk along the water's edge is a chance to discover flora and fauna as rich and varied as their habitats – you might even be lucky enough to come across rare species, such as black storks, otters or toads.

Admire princely eccentricity at Branitz Palace

Prince Von Pückler-Muskau (1785–1871) was a garden enthusiast, and it was in Branitz, today a neighbourhood of Cottbus, 130km (81 miles) southeast of Berlin, that he created his masterpiece. This aristocratic landscape gardener gave free rein to his imagination here and created, on a barren site, an exceptional English garden embellished not only with sculptures, but also with lakes and waterways that can be explored by gondola. The highlight of the estate are two vegetation-covered earth pyramids, the larger of which forms an artificial island and contains the remains of the prince and his wife.

Take a tour of Potsdam by boat

Potsdam, a World Heritage-listed combination of mansions and gardens, is well worth a visit and is just 30–45 minutes from Berlin by public transport. Located on the Havel River, its main attractions are the palace and park of Sanssouci, the pride of Prussia's King Frederick II (aka the Great), but there are many other wonders that can be enjoyed on a romantic boat trip on the river – see schifffahrt-in-potsdam.de

MORE TIME?

MÜGGELSEE The largest lake in the Berlin region, 20km (12 miles) south of the capital, is a popular summer beach destination. Here you can rent boats or go hiking in the surrounding forest when the weather isn't mild enough for swimming, or visit the engine room of the Museum im Alten Wasserwerk, a former waterworks.
BRANDENBURG-AN-DER-HAVEL This medieval town, crisscrossed by canals, and home to the first Margraves (rulers) of Brandenburg, contains a number of interesting sights in its historic core, including the 12th-century Cathedral of St Peter and St Paul.

MAUERPARK

This park in the Prenzlauer Berg neighbourhood was once nicknamed the 'death strip', as it separated East and West Berlin – a section of the Wall can still be seen here, covered in graffiti. Now a green space, Mauerpark is where locals and visitors like to meet up for some outdoor fun, especially on Sundays. Activities on offer include a large, friendly flea market, barbecues and, weather permitting, games of pétanque and basketball, plus open-air karaoke. It's a welcoming space where everyone's invited to join in.

~ PRACTICALITIES ~

HOW TO GET THERE

Since 2020, Berlin has had a new international airport, Berlin Brandenburg Airport, served by airlines from around the world. Arriving by rail is also an option – trains, including night trains, run to the capital from multiple destinations, including Amsterdam, Brussels and Paris.

WHERE TO EAT

On Sundays, the courtyard of the Kulturbrauerei (kulturbrauerei.de), a red-brick former brewery from the 19th century transformed into a huge cultural centre, hosts Street Food auf Achse. Dozens of food trucks and other stalls offer specialities from across the globe. There's a *Biergarten* too, and it's not unusual to hear live musicians. In winter, the courtyard is covered, and a fire keeps visitors warm.

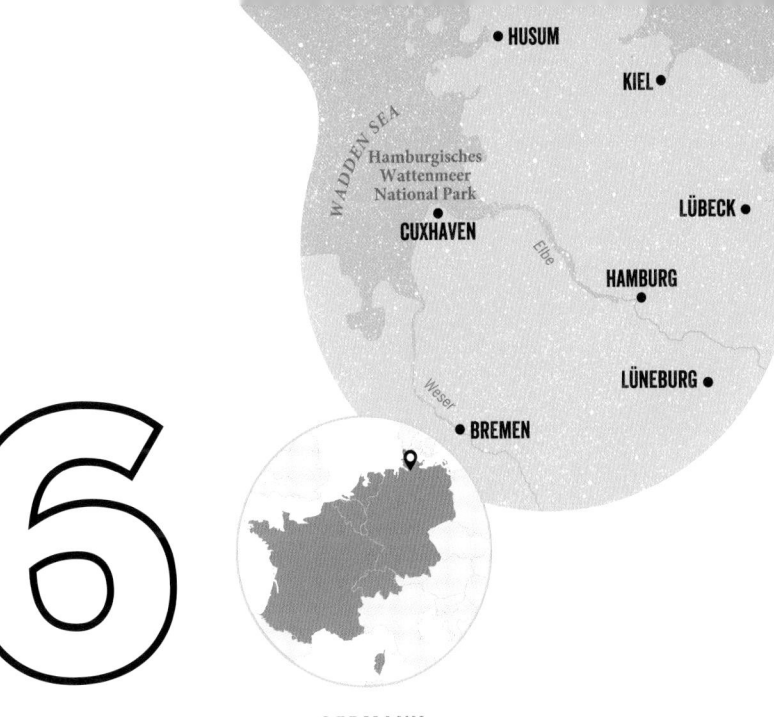

GERMANY

56

Recharge your batteries
IN HAMBURG & ON THE ELBE RIVER

Peaceful villages, shimmering lakes, lush pastures and scattered forests – the vast Elbe estuary, which flows into the Wadden Sea near Hamburg, is a veritable patchwork of landscapes. This region of northern Germany offers **outdoor activities** to enjoy in fine weather (cycling, walking, wildlife watching) but is not overrun by visitors. The country's second-largest conurbation, **Hamburg** owes its prosperity to the sea and to centuries of maritime trade. Straddling the Elbe River and crossed by canals, it's a dynamic city that features **innovative architecture**, such as the Elbphilharmonie (see page 235), alongside traditional buildings, like the Neo-Renaissance town hall with its clock tower. The city's **rich cultural offerings** add to its appeal, and include the Museum of Arts and Crafts and the International Maritime Museum. On Saturday evenings, a renowned electro-punk scene keeps night owls happy, while on Sunday mornings, the fish market attracts gourmets. Close to Hamburg, many smaller towns and cities provide an extra taste of this engaging region.

Cycle along the Elbe

A superb cyclepath (elbe-cycle-route.com) stretches along the Elbe River for 1300km (808 miles), providing the perfect opportunity to hop on a bike in Hamburg and pedal to the Wadden Sea without having to worry about steep gradients or traffic. On the right bank, you'll follow the river's green verges, while on the left bank, you'll cross several nature reserves where grazing cattle might be your only company.

Visit the saltworks town of Lüneburg

Lüneburg (see previous page) is a medieval city within a 30-minute train ride of Hamburg. It's a picturesque Hanseatic town, built on a human scale, where romantic lanes and handsome squares lined with red-brick and half-timbered buildings exude a welcoming atmosphere. A highlight of any visit is the Salt Museum, where you can learn more about the fascinating 1000-year history of Lüneburg's saltworks and the 'white gold' that made the town rich and powerful.

Take a trip to Lübeck

Just 45 minutes by train from Hamburg, Lübeck, nicknamed Queen of the Hanseatic League, is packed with historic treasures. The many exceptional sights to visit in this ancient port include the Holstentor (inset), the city's gateway with its cylindrical towers; the Old Town built on an island in the Trave River; medieval churches; tiny houses built in backyards; and the town hall, one of the most beautiful in the country.

Observe the fauna of the Wadden Sea

The Wadden Sea coastline is a precious haven of biodiversity. For bird-watching in this national park (nationalpark-wattenmeer.de) of mudflats, wet meadows and sandy beaches, head for the fishing port of Cuxhaven, where the birdlife flourishes and an attractive waterfront makes for a pleasant stroll. You can also head to the town of Husum, another ideal base for witnessing impressive avian antics, along with the chance to catch a glimpse of seals.

MORE TIME?

BREMEN A superb Hanseatic city on the banks of the Weser River, Bremen is home to a beautifully preserved historic centre and an impressive cathedral with medieval crypts. It's around an hour by train from Hamburg.

KIEL This city on the Baltic coast is popular with watersports enthusiasts. The world's biggest sailing event, Kiel Week, attracts three million visitors every year.

SCHWERIN A landmark in this town, known as the 'city of seven lakes', is the enchanting Schwerin Castle (mv-schloesser.de), a former ducal residence where the Mecklenburg-Vorpommern parliament now sits.

THE HAMBURGER

The history of this world-famous dish dates back to the 12th century when the Tatars (Turco-Mongol horsemen) placed pieces of beef under their saddles to tenderise them. The technique was exported to Russia and Germany in the 17th century via sailors, and soon 'Hamburg-style steak' – salted, often smoked and accompanied by onions – became seen as an ideal food for long sea crossings. In the mid-19th century, Germans migrating to the US took the recipe with them, where it evolved into the bun-and-burger combination we know today.

HOW TO GET THERE

Hamburg Airport is linked to the city via the S1 S-Bahn line, taking around 25 minutes. The city is well connected to other German and international destinations by road and rail too – the main train station is in the centre of town.

WHERE TO STAY

At the retro-style Henri Hotel (henri-hotels.com) you'll enjoy modern comforts in the heart of the Altstadt (the Old Town).

EVENTS

Hamburg is a city with plenty going on. Each May, Hafengeburtstag is the main event of the year – a three-day celebration of the port's birthday, with beer and live music. At the end of July/beginning of August, it's the turn of the major Gay Pride event (hamburg-pride.de) to liven up the streets of the city, particularly in the Sankt Georg district. Later in August, around a hundred international musicians rock Wilhelmsburg (msdockville.de/festival), on the south bank of the Elbe. Finally, in December, numerous Christmas markets brighten up the winter gloom.

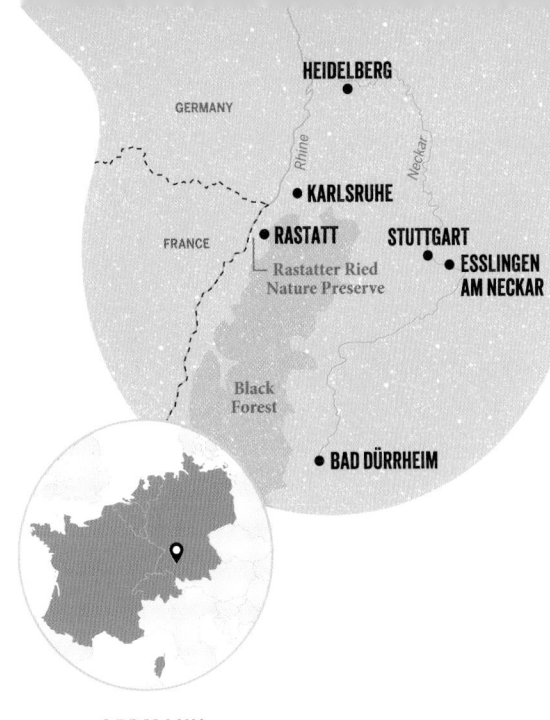

GERMANY

57

Go from medieval to Mercedes
IN BADEN-WÜRTTEMBERG

O n foot, by bike or by kayak, it's easy to get out and experience the **wide-open spaces of Baden-Württemberg.** Filled with vast forests – including the famous **Black Forest** – tempting vineyards and green meadows, and just a stone's throw from the banks of the Rhine, this region of southwest Germany, bordering France and Switzerland, has an irresistible appeal. Its rolling countryside is dotted with traditional villages and splendid castles, testimony to a brilliant medieval golden age. Numerous **spas** attract visitors coming to sample the benefits of the mineral waters on offer. State capital **Stuttgart** has many attractions as well, including the **State Gallery** (staatsgalerie.de) and the **Kunstmuseum** (kunst-museum-stuttgart.de), which can keep art lovers in raptures for days. Motorheads won't want to miss the collections on display at the **Mercedes and Porsche museums**. And everyone can happily indulge in a shopping spree, a filling meal of *Maul-taschen* dumplings and a wild night out in one of the city's cool bars or clubs.

Ride the Radel-Thon

The Radel-Thon (radelthon.info) is a long (83km/51.6 miles) cycling loop surrounding Stuttgart that passes through verdant vineyards and magnificent forests, and skirts a number of lakes and castles. Along the bucolic, well-marked route are numerous possible starting and finishing points served by buses and trains from central Stuttgart.

Kayak in Esslingen

In Esslingen am Neckar (see previous page), the scenic Neckar Canal lends itself perfectly to a half-day's kayaking. After gliding beside the green banks of this tranquil waterway, continue your visit in the colourful streets of Esslingen's beautiful medieval heart, then relax in the renowned Merkel'sches baths, close to the town centre. Esslingen is only 10 minutes by train from Stuttgart.

Visit Karlsruhe

Karlsruhe's majestic castle is often described as Germany's Versailles. Climb its tower for a great view of the city's fan-shaped streets below, where a lively downtown is brimming with cultural venues, cafes and restaurants, whose terraces are packed on sunny days. Allow one hour by train from Stuttgart.

Explore the Rastatter Rheinaue Nature Reserve

On the banks of the Rhine, opposite the Sauer Delta in France, the Rastatter Rheinaue Nature Reserve is a place of peace where you can observe wild animals, including numerous migratory birds. This wonderful forest has numerous trails, easily accessible by bike from Rastatt, one hour by train from Stuttgart.

Hike in the Black Forest

Beginning just southwest of Stuttgart, the Black Forest unfolds its patchwork of landscapes (opposite), made up of spruce forests, vineyards, streams and waterfalls. No fewer than 24,000km (14,913 miles) of signposted hiking trails let you take a deep breath of fresh air while taking in the views, whether on foot, by bike – or even on skis in winter.

MORE TIME?

HEIDELBERG With a dominating castle towering over its Old Town, this historic city (inset) is the epitome of German Romanticism and a top destination for a cultural getaway. From Stuttgart, it's about 45 minutes by train.

BAD DÜRRHEIM At the start of the Black Forest, these wonderful thermal baths leave visitors with soothed bodies and unforgettable memories. In this temple of relaxation, you can relax in the salt grotto, sauna and saltwater pool. Bad Dürrheim is one hour, 15 minutes' drive from Stuttgart.

MAULTASCHEN

A speciality of the region, traditional *Maultaschen* are as delicious as they are comforting. The recipe involves large dumplings stuffed with a wide variety of meats (although vegetarian *Maultaschen* are also available today), then folded into a rectangular shape. They are eaten boiled with potato salad, grilled with onions and eggs, or in soup with a meat-based broth.

PRACTICALITIES

HOW TO GET THERE

Direct trains link Stuttgart to major German cities along with international destinations, including Paris. Alternatively, Stuttgart Airport has European-wide connections, including London, Istanbul and Rome.

WHERE TO STAY

The historic centre of Stuttgart-Mitte is the most appealing place to stay. Centrally located, it brings together the city's main points of interest, such as the old castle and the opera house.

EVENTS

In April–May, Stuttgart Spring Festival (stuttgarter-fruehlingsfest.de) is akin to a beer festival accompanied by a wealth of traditional markets. In September–October, Cannstatter Volksfest (cannstatter-volksfest.de) turns the city into a giant funfair, with four-million visitors enjoying the rides and giant beer tents. December's Christmas market sees huge crowds milling around its festive stalls.

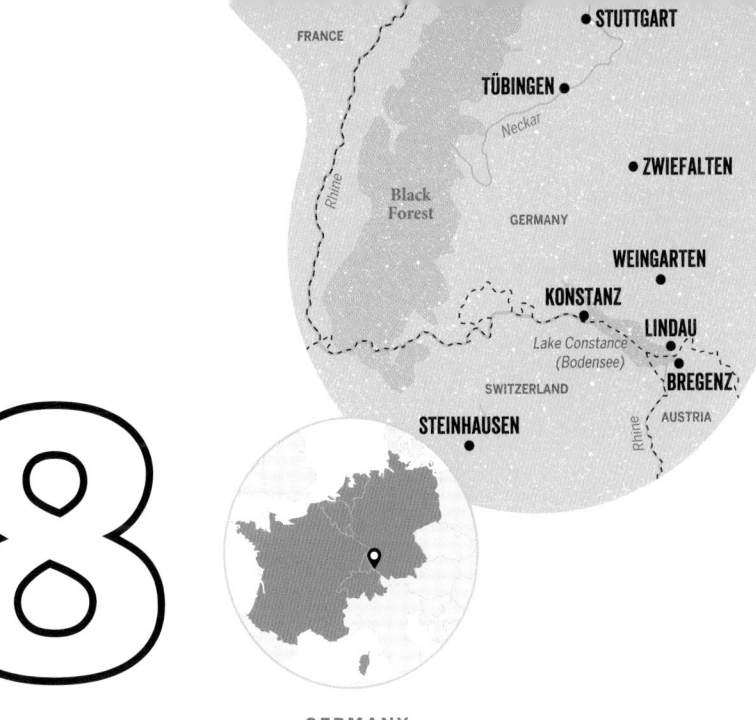

GERMANY

58

Take the scenic route
FROM STUTTGART TO LAKE CONSTANCE

Straddling the borders **of Germany, Austria and Switzerland, Lake Constance (Bodensee in German) is easily accessible via a number of fast motorways – but taking a slower, more picturesque route, stopping off at delightful towns and historic buildings along the way, is a more pleasurable alternative.** As soon as you leave starting point Stuttgart, you'll find yourself surrounded by vine-covered hills. First stop, the small town of Tübingen lives to the rhythm of its university, one of the oldest in Europe. The Old Town, crowned by a turreted castle and overlooking the Neckar River, a tributary of the Rhine that can be paddled along, is captivating, as is its *Biergarten*, buzzing with students. Heading south to Friedrichshafen, you'll cross the hills of the **Swabian Jura Mountains** and find three magnificent baroque religious buildings along the way: **Zwiefalten Abbey** combines delicate colours with exuberant sculpture and stucco; more modest **Steinhausen Church** charms with its angels and animals decor; while impressive **Weingarten Abbey** is the largest baroque church in the country.

Dream among the flowers of Mainau

Nicknamed 'Flower Island', Mainau (mainau.de) is a wonderful green oasis sitting in the waters of Lake Constance. It's home to a surprising variety of flowers and trees, thanks to a mild, almost Mediterranean climate, and can be visited year-round. The gardens were laid out in the 18th century by the Grand Dukes of Baden around a sumptuous baroque castle, and today draw visitors with their thousands of tulips, roses, dahlias and more blooms.

Explore Lake Constance by boat & bike

If Lake Constance isn't beautiful enough on its own, it's also surrounded by quaint villages, historic abbeys, dramatic castles and enticing beaches, all set against a backdrop of meadows, orchards, marshes and Alpine foothills. Boating and biking are two of the best ways to explore it. The Constance–Meersburg ferry allows you to cross from one shore to the other, bicycles are easy to hire, and a well-marked cyclepath (bodensee-radweg.com) circumnavigates the whole lake, covering 273km (170 miles).

Dive into the story of Konstanz

Adjacent to the Swiss border and cut through by the Rhine, the city of Konstanz has a lively atmosphere, thanks to its university, port and tourism. Its development in the Middle Ages was down to a booming cloth trade and the town's religious importance – in 1414–1418, it hosted the council that re-established the unity of the Catholic Church after the Papal Schism between Rome and Avignon. Twisting alleys crowd around the 11th-century cathedral. The former warehouse of the Konzilgebäude (1388), where the conclave that elected Pope Martin V met in 1417, is now used as a concert hall.

Pick your favourite lake view

In the southeast of Lake Constance, the small island town of Lindau combines a beautiful Old Town, a cute harbour with two lighthouses (one dating from the 13th century), a picture-postcard setting and views of the Alps. For a change of perspective, take the boat to the Austrian shore and Bregenz, from where you can ride a cable car to the top of Pfänder (1064m/3491ft) and enjoy another breathtaking view of the lake – weather permitting.

MORE TIME?

AROUND THE LAKE The best of Lake Constance can be experienced in just two days, but with more time, you can also visit the reconstructed Neolithic lakeside village of Unteruhldingen, the monastic island of Reichenau, the baroque church of Birnau (inset), Salem Monastery and Palace, the Old Town of Meersburg and much more.

MORE BAROQUE If you've developed a taste for the baroque on this trip, complete your education with a visit to Ulm Minster and Ottobeuren Abbey on the way back to Stuttgart.

THEATRES OF THE SACRED

The baroque style, with its curves and colonnades, plays on perspective, sculpted angels, swirling cherubs and sweeping curtain effects, transformed churches of the 17th and 18th centuries into theatres of the sacred. After the Council of Trent (1545–63), the church went to great lengths to win over the faithful, and the baroque style triumphed in Upper Swabia, between Ulm and Lake Constance. One of the finest examples in the area is the abbey in Zwiefalten, and the Oberschwäbische Barockstraße (Upper Swabian Baroque Road), marked by cherubs is a great way to discover many other examples of this flamboyant architecture.

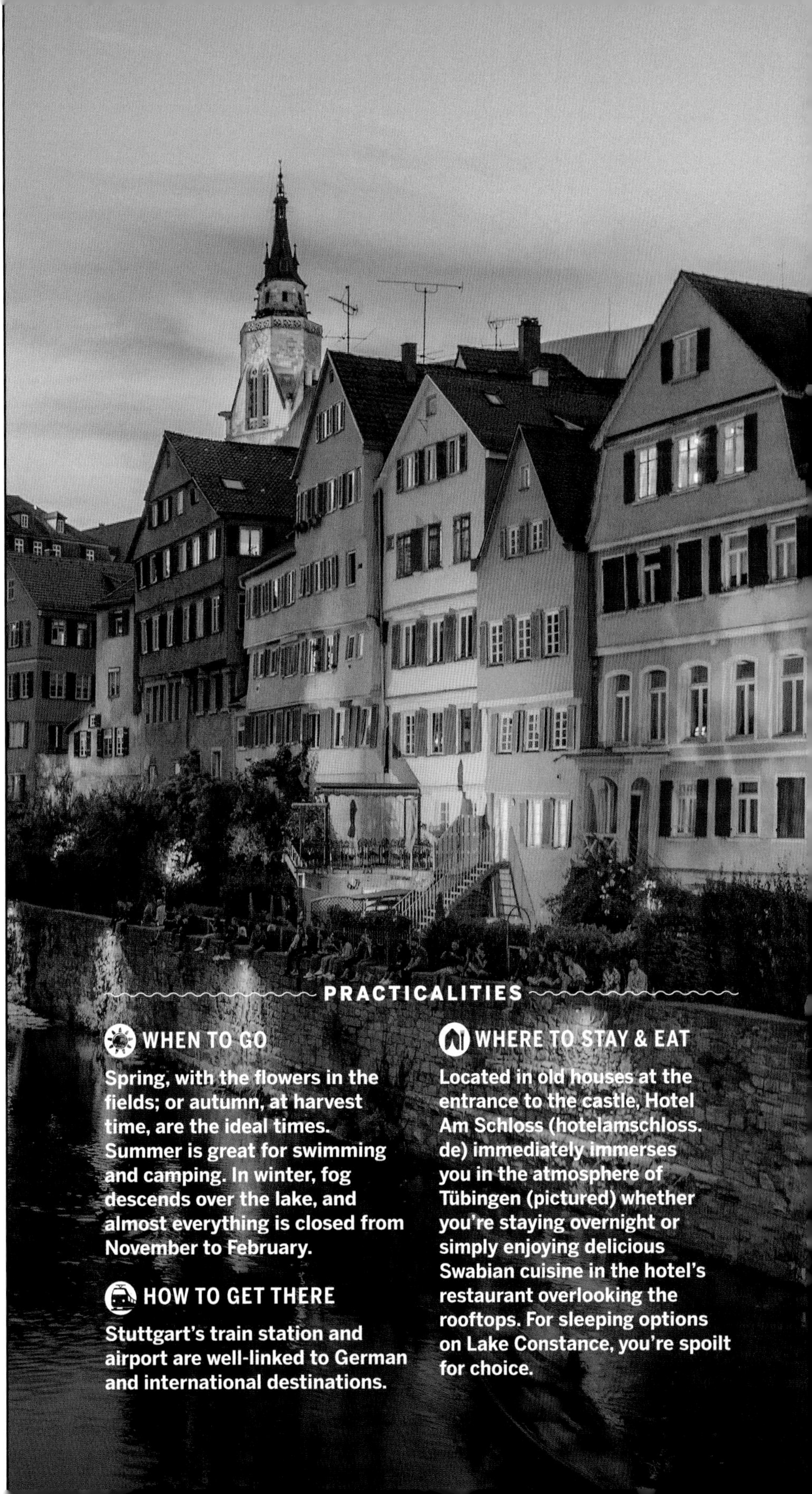

PRACTICALITIES

WHEN TO GO

Spring, with the flowers in the fields; or autumn, at harvest time, are the ideal times. Summer is great for swimming and camping. In winter, fog descends over the lake, and almost everything is closed from November to February.

HOW TO GET THERE

Stuttgart's train station and airport are well-linked to German and international destinations.

WHERE TO STAY & EAT

Located in old houses at the entrance to the castle, Hotel Am Schloss (hotelamschloss. de) immediately immerses you in the atmosphere of Tübingen (pictured) whether you're staying overnight or simply enjoying delicious Swabian cuisine in the hotel's restaurant overlooking the rooftops. For sleeping options on Lake Constance, you're spoilt for choice.

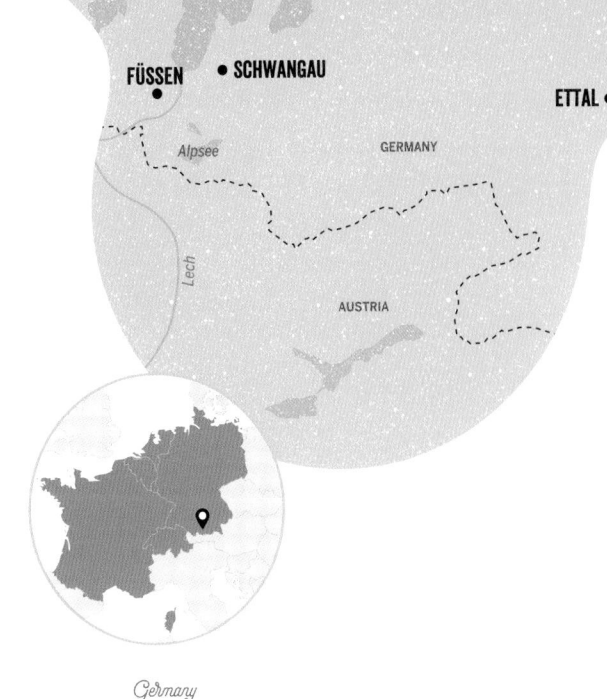

FÜSSEN • SCHWANGAU
ETTAL •
GERMANY
Alpsee
Lech
AUSTRIA

Germany

59

In the footsteps of the 'Mad King'
IN BAVARIA

A romantic and whimsical monarch if ever there was one, Ludwig II of Bavaria, nicknamed 'the Mad King' for his penchant for daydreaming and extravagance, left an indelible fairy-tale imprint on the Alps in his home region. His admiration for German composer Wagner led to a fascination with music and festivities in general, but it was in art history and architecture that he left his greatest legacy. The sumptuous castles he had built at great expense are today the **icons of southern Germany**. The most famous is undoubtedly astounding **Neuschwanstein** (left), with every detail overseen by Ludwig. It's little wonder that this is the country's most-visited attraction and is said to have inspired Walt Disney. Its neighbour, **Hohenschwangau**, is where the monarch spent his holidays and where he first met Wagner. To the east, **Linderhof** was modelled on Versailles and is the smallest but most opulent. Between castle-hopping, take in Bavaria's natural wonders – or, time it right, and join the party at Munich's annual Oktoberfest, visiting the state capital's plentiful sights between beers.

German mythology at Hohenschwangau Castle

Maximilian II of Bavaria, father of Ludwig II, had Hohenschwangau (hohenschwangau.de/schloss-hohenschwangau) built from 1832 to 1836 for use as a summer hunting and summer residence. The castle remained Ludwig II's summer residence when he became king, until his death in 1886. Neogothic in style, its four corner towers and crenellated walls give it a medieval appearance. The swan, beloved bird of Wagnerian hero Lohengrin, is a recurring theme in the 90 frescoes on display inside – Ludwig was obsessed with this character from the opera of the same name.

Walk through a fairy tale at Neuschwanstein

You can't get more fairy-tale-like than the building that was Walt Disney's model for the castle in *Sleeping Beauty* – Neuschwanstein (neuschwanstein.de). Perched on a rocky outcrop amid wooded peaks and often cloaked in strands of mist, this romantic, medieval-style castle was designed by Ludwig II himself and owes its design to the operatic works of Wagner. The highlight of the visit is the Singers' Hall, where sublime gilding and frescoes depict scenes from *Tannhäuser*.

Explore the highlights of the House of Wittelsbach

Just south of Hohenschwangau Castle, on the east bank of the Alpsee (opposite), the fascinating Museum of the Bavarian Kings (hohenschwangau.de/museum-der-bayerischen-koenige) looks back at the history of the first local dynasty, the Wittelsbachs. You can admire Ludwig II's famous blue-and-gold dress, and the view of the lake and the Alps is fantastic.

Stroll through historic Füssen

Set against the gentle hills of Bavaria's Allgäu region, Füssen (inset) seduces visitors with its medieval streets, baroque churches and Gothic fortifications. The inner courtyard of the Hohes Schloss, a marvellous late-Gothic castle and former retreat of the bishops of Augsburg, is a true masterpiece of trompe-l'œil architecture.

Visit Germany's Versailles at Linderhof

Set on a hilltop and surrounded by formal gardens and fountains, Linderhof (schlosslinderhof.de) is a tribute to the Sun King and was largely inspired by Versailles. Completed in 1878, it's the most lavish of the castles inhabited by Ludwig II, with a bedroom lit by a crystal chandelier, an artificial waterfall, a Moorish pavilion and a Venus grotto inspired by Wagner's *Tannhäuser* opera.

MORE TIME?

MUNICH Bavaria's metropolis is a city of contrasts, allowing visitors to admire Old Masters at the Pinakothek and then the latest cars at the BMW Museum, all in the same day.

LECHWEG Starting in Füssen, this 125km (78-mile) long hiking trail (lechweg.com) follows the Lech tributary of the Danube through wild alpine landscapes, ending in the Austrian Tyrol.

OKTOBERFEST

Every year, up to seven million visitors come to the Theresienwiese, a wide open space in Munich, to celebrate Oktoberfest. This beer-focused event dates back to 1810, when Ludwig I married Therese of Saxe-Hildburghausen. For just over a fortnight from mid-September onwards, Weissbier and other lagers flow like water. When it comes to what to wear, there's no question – traditional Bavarian costumes are the order of the day and can be rented for the occasion (lederhosen for men; dirndl for women), and polka dancing is de rigueur.

PRACTICALITIES

HOW TO GET THERE

Füssen railway station is the closest to the castles; from Munich, the journey takes one hour. Hohenschwangau's bus station also serves Neuschwanstein. Many tour operators offer day trips from Munich.

GOOD TO KNOW

Access to Neuschwanstein and Hohenschwangau castles is only possible with a guided tour (in English or German). Come as early as 8am to get tickets for the day or, better still, book online. The two castles are only 30 to 40 minutes' walk apart.

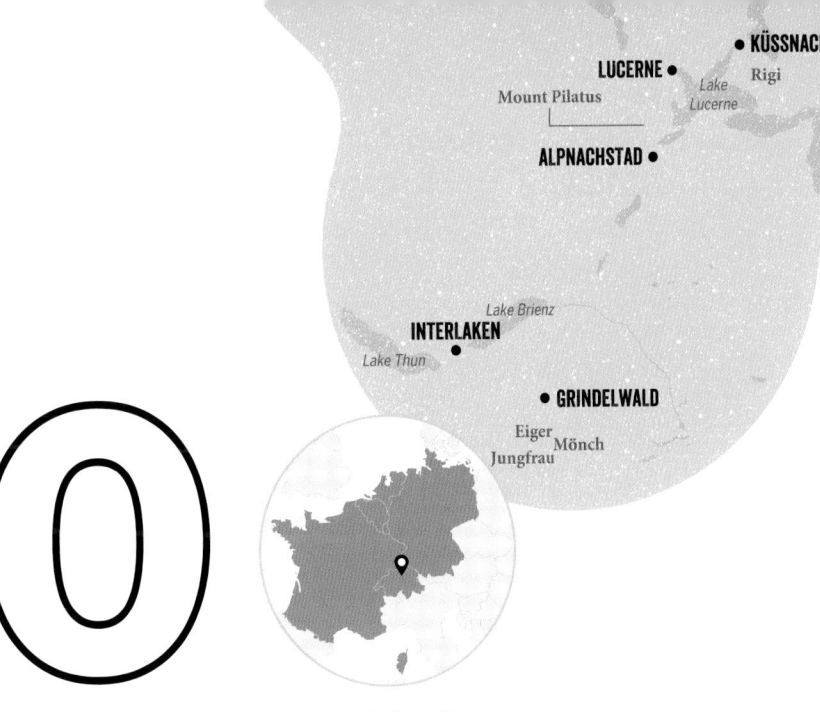

60

SWITZERLAND

Find romance
IN LUCERNE

A medieval Old Town with wonderful architecture, a cobalt-blue lake and a setting consisting of mythical mountains such as Pilatus and Rigi – the lakeside city of Lucerne has good looks aplenty and is arguably the most romantic of Swiss towns. Browse the art and antique on central Haldenstrasse, or the thrift and souvenir shops of Löwenstrasse. Pause at the superb **Kapellbrücke** (Chapel Bridge, left), considered to be the oldest covered bridge in Europe, and climb the ramparts for a view across the rooftops.

Lucerne is also the jumping-off point for incredible **rail escapades** and paddleboat rides on the namesake lake. In the 19th century, Goethe, Queen Victoria and Wagner flocked here – the latter now has a museum in his name, notable for its collection of early musical instruments. And if the buildings, history and location aren't enough to tempt you to spend a weekend here, the town comes alive with a three-part **music festival** spread across the year: sacred music in spring; symphonic music in summer; and keyboard music in autumn.

249

Wander the charming Old Town

Any visit to Lucerne should begin with hearing the creaks of the ancient Kapellbrücke. This venerable covered wooden bridge dates to the 14th century and features an original octagonal water tower and a painted ceiling that tells the story of the town. Downstream, a second wooden bridge, the Spreuerbrücke, is famous for its *Danse Macabre* (Dance of Death) paintings, depicted in 60 triangular panels. For a panoramic view, head up the medieval ramparts, where you can gaze out over the rooftops, lake and mountains.

Summit Mt Pilatus by cogwheel train

Don't miss experiencing one of Switzerland's most beautiful excursions – a trip up Mt Pilatus (opposite; pilatus.ch) on the world's steepest cog railway. In around 30 minutes from the village of Alpnachstad, and after no fewer than three 48% gradients, you reach the top of 'the broken mountain', so named for its bumpy appearance. At an altitude of 2132m (6995ft), the view takes in some 73 Alpine peaks and glittering Lake Lucerne below.

Attend a concert at the Lucerne Festival

If you're keen to visit Lucerne for its music festivals (lucernefestival.ch) spread out over the year, make sure to book well in advance. This popular, world-renowned series of concerts brings music lovers and performers to the city from around the world.

Visit Küssnacht by bike

From Lucerne, cyclepaths take you along the lake and through charming villages. Head northeast for about 15km (9 miles) and prepare to fall in love with gorgeous Küssnacht, where you can learn more about national hero William Tell (hohlegasse.ch), and ride along a sunken path that's like something out of a fantasy movie.

Take a dip in Lake Lucerne

The crystal-clear waters and sandy beaches of Lake Lucerne (lakelucerne.ch) are perfect for swimming and relaxation when the weather's fine. To get to know this glacial lake without getting wet though, opt for a cruise on one of the elegant steamboats that sail its waters.

MORE TIME?

INTERLAKEN Lakes Thun and Brienz, magnificent bodies of turquoise water, greet you on your arrival in Switzerland's outdoor sports capital, Interlaken. Nearby, you can reach Europe's highest train station, Jungfraujoch (3454m/11,332ft), enjoying one of the most beautiful rail excursions in the world on the way.
GRINDELWALD Rising above the pretty resort of Grindelwald, the Eiger (ogre), the Mönch (monk) and the Jungfrau (maiden) are three mythical peaks that promise thrills for mountaineers and unforgettable views for hikers.

TRAINSPOTTING

Since the invention of the railways, Switzerland's landscapes have proved to be an extraordinary playground for engineers looking for a challenge – and an unmissable draw for trainspotting enthusiasts, enjoying a hobby that can often become an obsession. The Swiss inclination for trains consists of a passion for the history of the lines, their technical characteristics and records they break. The first sign you might have come down with the trainspotting bug yourself is falling in love with the collections of Lucerne's brilliant Swiss Museum of Transport. It could be the start of a lifelong romance.

~~~~~~ **PRACTICALITIES** ~~~~~~

🚆 HOW TO GET THERE & AROUND

Lucerne is a three-hour train ride from Geneva, an airport with plenty of international connections. Once there, the Tell-Pass (tell-pass.ch), sold at the Lucerne tourist office, allows unlimited travel in the Lucerne region by train, bus, boat and cable car.

📅 EVENTS

In February, the Lucerne Carnival is in full swing, the largest event in the city's calendar. Parades and over-the-top festivities provide a great opportunity to party with the locals.

61

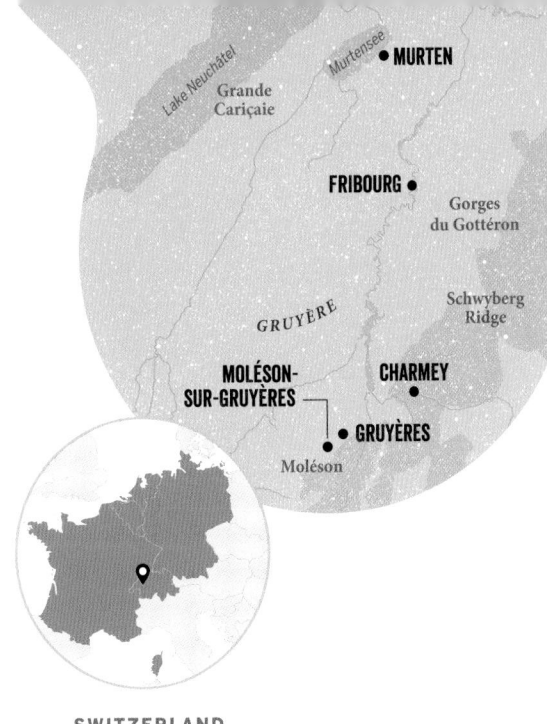

Marvel at the medieval
IN FRIBOURG

I n the Middle Ages, a 2km (1.2-mile) wall protected the Swiss city of Fribourg. Today, you can relive its fascinating history by admiring the well-preserved remains of that wall, plus Gothic buildings dating to the 15th century (more than 200 of them), a cathedral dedicated to St Nicholas (the view from its tower is splendid) and 11 medieval fountains scattered throughout the city. Lose yourself in the narrow streets and soak up the lively atmosphere before taking a break in one of the many cafes or searching for souvenirs in one of the pretty boutiques. Then take the old funicular up **Moléson** mountain and enjoy the expansive panorama. Looking for alfresco adventures? Hike between lakes and mountains on the **Schwyberg Ridge**, and discover the Fribourg Pre-Alps with their authentic alpine chalets. To recover, head to the thermal waters of **Les Bains de la Gruyère**, a spa with indoor and outdoor pools. See Gruyère cheese made at a local dairy and then enjoy its complex flavour while replenishing expended calories with that most traditional of Swiss dishes, fondue.

Say 'cheese' in Gruyères

Situated at the foot of the Pre-Alps, medieval Gruyères (see page 252) is an inviting place to visit. Wander through the pedestrian centre, visit the castle (chateau-gruyeres.ch), a huge fortress looming above the town, and discover the artisanal production of Gruyère PDO cheese at the Maison du Gruyère – you can sample the famous cheese either at the factory or in one of the many restaurants in town.

Learn how Swiss cheese is made

Around 5km (3 miles) southwest of Gruyères, a 17th-century dairy (moleson.ch/fabrication-du-fromage) makes the region's namesake cheese the old, time-honoured way. In summer, visitors are invited to watch the process every day at 10am. The dairy also sells what it makes, while its restaurant serves fondue, hearty vegetable soup and other typical mountain dishes. Those with stamina can set out on the 'cheese dairy path' (7km/4 miles), through the lush green pastures, leading from the Pringy dairy to the Moléson dairy (opposite), passing mountain chalets where cheese is still made along the way.

Commemorate a Swiss victory in Murten

Charming fortified Murten (inset), located on the shores of the lake of the same name, was the scene of one of Switzerland's greatest battles in which the Swiss defeated the troops of the Duke of Burgundy, Charles the Bold. The victory was recorded in a famous saying well known to Swiss schoolchildren: 'Charles the Bold lost his wealth in Grandson, his courage in Murten and his life in Nancy'. Explore the city walls, then discover Murten Castle. In the Old Town, take in the beautiful stone houses and the Bern Gate with its famous clock (which has to be wound every 24 hours for it to work), before heading to the lake for a walk along its shores.

Fill up on nature at La Grande Cariçaie

La Grande Cariçaie (grande-caricaie.ch), west of Fribourg, is a vast, protected marshland covering eight nature reserves that are home to a quarter of Switzerland's flora and fauna (around 800 plant and 10,000 animal species). Numerous signposted trails are available to explore on foot or by bike. Keep your eyes peeled for red kites, great egrets, and snipe with their beaks in the marsh.

MORE TIME?

GORGES DU GOTTÉRON From the Old Town of Fribourg, follow a circular trail through forest, past brooks and under imposing sandstone cliffs along the Gottéron Valley.
VULLY The country's smallest winegrowing region nestles at the foot of Mt Vully (vully.ch), on the shores of Lake Murten. The area has around 152 hectares (376 acres) of Pinot Noir and Chasselas vines, shared by around 20 winemakers who produce about 80,000 bottles a year.

FRIBOURG FONDUE

Unlike other types of fondue (including its neighbour, the Savoyard fondue), the Fribourg fondue is made exclusively with Vacherin Fribourgeois PDO cheese. Using a traditional Swiss recipe, this cheese is very smooth and creamy and is eaten with bread and/or potatoes. Another local speciality is the *fondue moitié-moitié* (half-and-half), made with 50% Swiss Gruyère and 50% Vacherin Fribourgeois. You can enjoy them in (almost) any restaurant in the region.

~ PRACTICALITIES ~

🚆 HOW TO GET THERE

Fribourg has train connections to plenty of destinations in the rest of Switzerland, plus France, Germany, Austria and Italy.

🏕 WHERE TO STAY & EAT

The canton of Fribourg has restaurants to suit all tastes – and cheese lovers, especially. For accommodation, the options are equally varied: eco-hotels, B&Bs and traditional hotels.

📅 EVENTS

In July, don't miss the Les Georges festival (lesgeorges.ch), featuring Swiss and international artists. As for the Suisse Fondue Festival (suissefonduefestival.ch) in November, it's a celebration of Fribourg gastronomy that turophiles (cheese-lovers) will want to make a note of in their diaries.

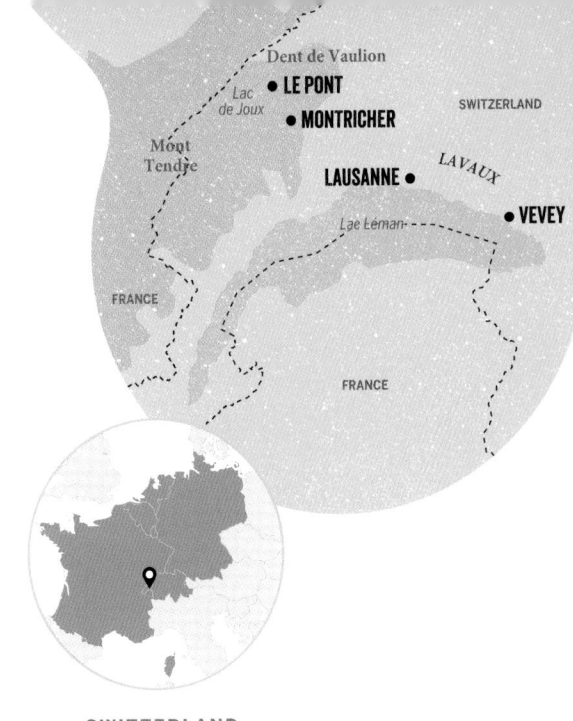

62

Contemplate panoramic views
AROUND LAUSANNE

An inland sea snuggled between the Jura and Alpine mountain ranges, Lake Geneva has an unrivalled natural setting. This blue expanse of water, which stretches along the border of France and Switzerland, has a singular charm. Its shores are dotted with some delightful **medieval towns**, such as Vevey (with its Charlie Chaplin connections) and **ancient castles** including Château de Chillon. The surrounding area is home to a **tapestry of landscapes**, from terraced vineyards at Lavaux (left) to high-altitude peaks like Mt Tendre, vast forested areas

and pastoral valleys. Handsome **Lausanne** is an ideal base from which to explore all this natural and constructed beauty, and before you set off to conquer the waves and the peaks, devote a day to visiting the city itself. The capital of the canton of Vaud, Lausanne is built on a gently rising slope and shows off a strong **architectural heritage** in streets brimming with historic buildings. But, above all, it's the dynamic cultural scene – the Béjart Ballet company is world famous – and slow pace of life that make this such an endearing destination.

Drink in the vineyards of Lavaux

Let yourself be wowed by the tiered vineyards of the Lavaux region, one of Switzerland's most beautiful destinations and a UNESCO World Heritage Site. Covered in terraces overlooking Lake Geneva (inset), and divided up by picturesque stone walls, these cultivated lands form a poetic landscape that easily wins visitors over. Before heading home, enjoy a winetasting session, particularly of Chasselas or Pinot Noir. Lavaux is 30 minutes by car or one hour by train from Lausanne.

Cruise Lake Geneva

At the Lausanne-Ouchy landing stage, take your place on a steamboat from the Belle Époque fleet (cgn.ch) for an unforgettable cruise on the calm waters of Lake Geneva. Numerous themed excursions offer dazzling views across the water to the mountains bordering the lake, as well as gourmet experiences, such as the 'Festival de fondues' excursion that will delight fans of melted cheese.

Scale the heights of the Dent de Vaulion

Rising above beautiful Lac de Joux (myvalleedejoux.ch) stands a mountain that is an icon of the region – the Dent de Vaulion. To marvel at the 360-degree panorama offered by its 1482m (4862ft) peak, start your hike from the village of Le Pont and follow the signposts through forests and pastures inhabited by chamois. It's easy to reach the mountain's viewpoint from where you can survey eight lakes and the imposing Mont-Blanc massif. Le Pont is a 45-minute drive or one-hour train ride from Lausanne.

Visit Chaplin's World in Vevey

Just 20km (12.5 miles) from Lausanne, the medieval town of Vevey sits between Lake Geneva and vine-covered hillsides and is well worth a visit. In addition to a handsome historic core of cobbled streets and elegant, colourful facades, the town is home to Chaplin's World (chaplinsworld. com). This fascinating museum is dedicated to the artist, and offers an interactive visit with plenty of Chaplin memorabilia, all located in a tranquil wooded park. From Lausanne, it's a 15-minute train ride to Vevey.

MORE TIME?

MT TENDRE The highest point in the Swiss Jura, Mt Tendre (1679m/5509ft) offers wonderful views of Lake Geneva, the Alps and Risoux Forest. It can be reached via the Jura Crest Trail, a five-hour walk through idyllic scenery, or by road via the village of Montricher.

CHÂTEAU DE CHILLON Particularly photogenic, 1,000-year-old Chillon Castle (opposite; chillon.ch) is strategically located on a rocky, oval-shaped island in Lake Geneva. Period furniture and frescoes fill the towers and halls, and the place is so fairy-tale-like you half expect Sleeping Beauty to make an appearance.

LAKE GENEVA PERCH

Lake Geneva is home to many species of fish, but it's perch that has become a famous local speciality. Cooked in the meunière style (floured, then pan-fried with a knob of butter and parsley), and accompanied by steamed potatoes, they are served in many of the region's restaurants, and are a safe bet when you're not sure what to order. Enjoying a meal of perch in fine weather on a sunny terrace by the water is a classic Lake Geneva experience.

PRACTICALITIES

HOW TO GET THERE & AROUND

Lausanne is easy to reach by train from elsewhere in Switzerland and from many international departure points. The local public-transport network is admirably well-developed, easily connecting most destinations.

WHERE TO STAY

In the centre of Lausanne, the elegant Hotel de la Paix (hoteldelapaix.net) is the perfect place to enjoy an exceptional view of the city and Lake Geneva.

EVENTS

The Lausanne Lumières festival (lausannelumieres.ch) returns every year at the end of December, illuminating the facades of the city's most famous buildings. Around the same time, Bô Noël (bo-noel.ch) brings a festive feel to the streets of the centre with its Christmas markets.

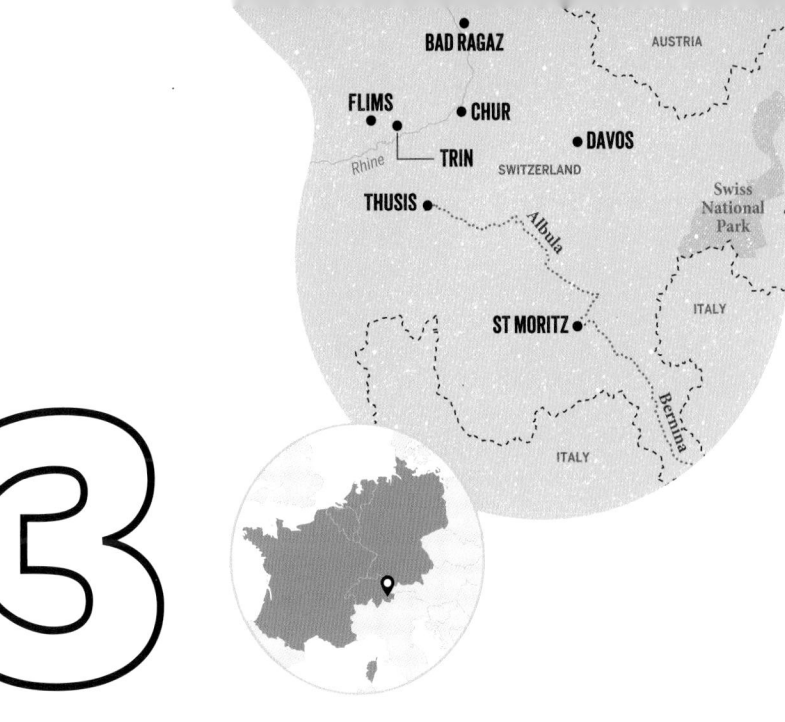

63

Ride the rails
IN GRAUBÜNDEN

I f you're looking for Heidi's Switzerland, the canton of Graubünden is where the fictional character lived out her adventures. The country's largest canton is also one of its least populated, and the only one where you'll hear **Romansh**, the country's fourth official language, spoken regularly. Here, more than anywhere else in Switzerland, nature has remained untouched, protected by the very **first national park in the Alps**. To marvel at the breathtaking scenery and the mind-boggling feats of Swiss engineering, take the train, specifically the Rhaetian Railway, which provides services in the region. Buying a ticket for a train ride in Graubünden might mean travelling the **steepest line in the Alps**, taking a journey across a spiralling viaduct (overleaf) or stopping off at snow-covered stations at altitudes over 2000m (6562ft). All expeditions start in **Chur**, the canton's pretty little capital and Switzerland's oldest city, inhabited for 3000 years, but it's to St Moritz and Davos that winter sports enthusiasts will want to head, for top skiing and lively apres-ski scenes.

Connect with ancient Alpine nature

Hiking in the Swiss National Park (nationalpark.ch) takes you back in time to 1914 when this, the very first national park established in the Alps, was created. It's an enormous wilderness, full of endemic flora and fauna and only disturbed by a few roads used by postal buses, which drop you off at the start of grand hikes through an astonishing variety of environments. Be prepared for animal encounters, as marmots, chamois and eagles are almost guaranteed to make an appearance.

Take the most beautiful train ride in the Alps

Make yourself comfortable on the *Glacier Express* (glacierexpress.ch) and let gasp-inducing landscapes of glaciers and lakes and gravity-defying engineering provide the show through the carriages' extra-large windows. Across 291 bridges and through 91 tunnels, the *Glacier Express* glides past a roll call of Swiss natural splendour between the upmarket resorts of St Moritz and Zermatt.

Switzerland's Grand Canyon

In the Rhine Gorge the famous river has carved out a vertiginous, 400m-deep (1312ft) path through white rocks. There are several hikes that will give you a good view of this masterpiece of nature created by an ancient glacier – the most complete takes three hours, 30 minutes, and starts at the tiny town of Trin.

Ski in St Moritz

Alpine tourism was born in stylish St Moritz in 1864. Fame has not changed the place much – the population is still barely 5000 – but it remains the international epicentre of winter sports, with activities including the Snow Polo World Cup (on a frozen lake, see right), international bobsleighing, White Turf horse racing and, of course, skiing. And when you've had your fill of outdoor fun, the town has probably the world's largest concentration of luxury boutiques for a spot of shopping in its attractive centre.

MORE TIME?

DAVOS The crème de la crème of global capitalism gathers in Davos every year – meaning it's easy to forget that this town also offers adventurous skiing for all in a beautiful location.
BAD RAGAZ The 37°C (99°F) waters near this small town in northern Graubünden have been attracting spa visitors since the 16th century. For therapeutic bathing, visit the Tamina thermal baths (resortragaz.ch), while Pfäfers Abbey and the nearby caves are well worth a visit while keeping dry.

DO YOU SPEAK ROMANSH?

Switzerland has four official languages: German (spoken by the majority), French, Italian and Romansh – the latter used by just 0.8% of the population, or 60,000 people, almost exclusively in Graubünden canton. This Romance language is related to Ladin and Friulian, both of which are still spoken in Northern Italy. Over the past few decades, German has become the majority language in Graubünden, but you'll still hear Romansh used in the Engadin Valley, as well as in the Albula and Surselva regions – and in the automatic train announcements.

PRACTICALITIES

✦ WHEN TO GO

If you want to ski in St Moritz or Davos, the season runs from mid-December to Easter. Hiking trails in the Swiss National Park and the Rhine Gorge are open from June to October. Thanks to Swiss engineering, the trainlines are open year-round.

🚆 HOW TO GET THERE & AROUND

Chur is two hours by train from Zürich (regular services), itself connected to plenty of international destinations. Note that the direct trains to Chur pass through Zürich Airport too. The Graubünden Pass is an economical option if you want to make the most of the canton's rail and bus network.

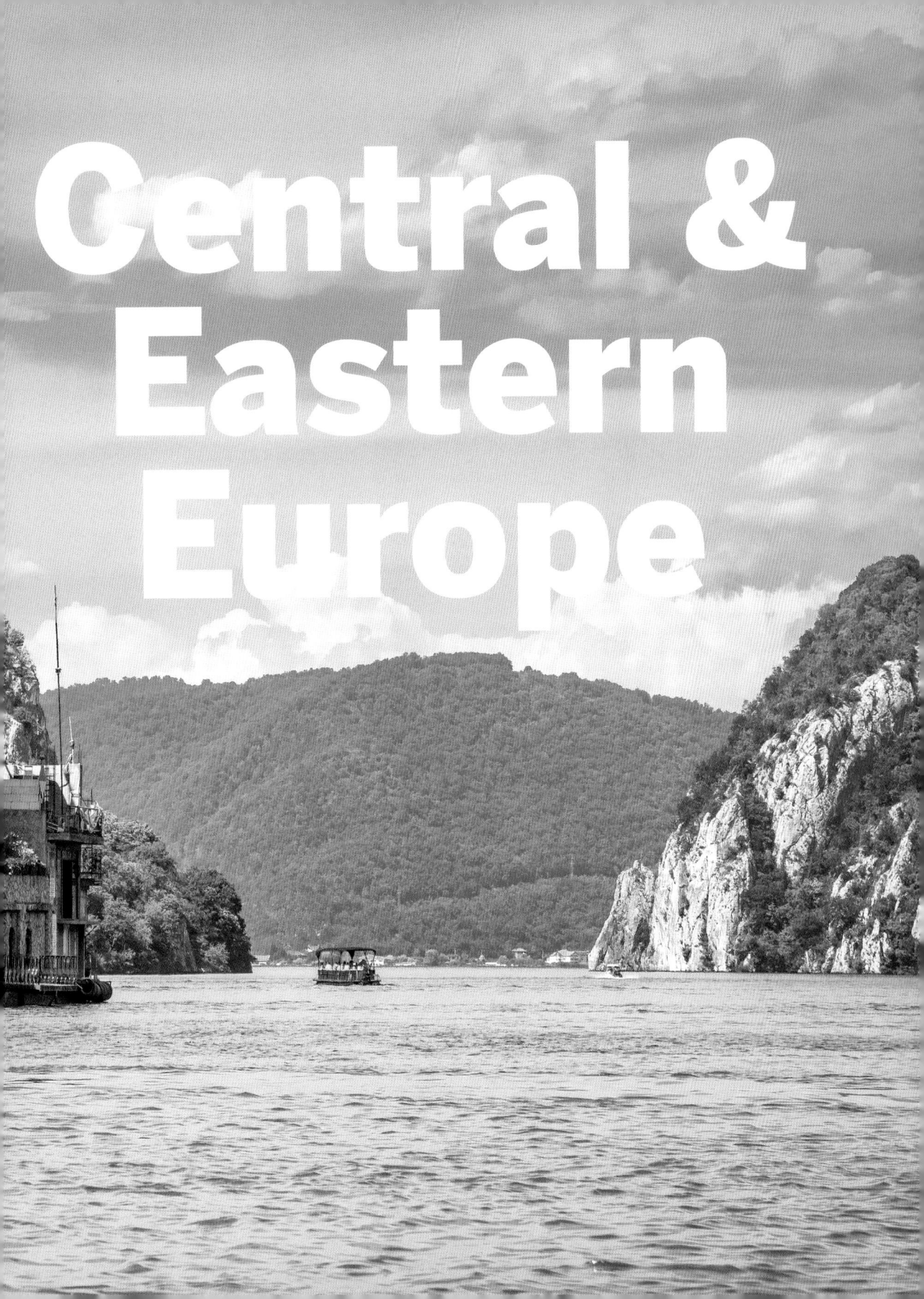

Central & Eastern Europe

WARSAW
OLD TOWN

Market Square

Barbican

Royal
Castle

Palace of Culture
and Science

Vistula

To Łódź

ŚRÓDMIEŚCIE

Ghetto Wall
remains

Lazienki
Park

To Wilanów

POLAND

64

Be moved by the past
IN WARSAW

Like a phoenix, Warsaw has always risen again from whatever history has **thrown at it.** By the end of WWII, the once prosperous Polish capital was a ruin, and the ancient centre had to be completely rebuilt. The result is a wonder of reconstruction that allows visitors to **rediscover centuries of history along its streets**. Behind thick ramparts sits the **Old Town** (overleaf). Pass the red walls of the **Barbican**, then continue to beautiful **Market Square**, lined with tall houses and watched over by Syrenka (the Mermaid, left, emblem of the city). On the square, the **Museum of Warsaw** deftly traces the city's history. Further on, **St John's Cathedral** was 90% destroyed in 1944 but, now restored, is another symbol of resurgence, while the **Royal Castle**, with its period furniture and works of art, and the **Church of St Anne** are just a stone's throw away. Get to the **Śródmieście district** via the magnificent **Saxon Garden**. On Próżna St, stand in front of the **remains of the Warsaw Ghetto**. Finally, climb to the 30th floor of the **Palace of Culture and Science**, 'donated' by Stalin during the Soviet era, for a panoramic view of this resilient city.

Honour Jewish Warsaw

Of Poland's 3.3 million Jews before WWII, only around 380,000 were still alive in 1945. In a splendid contemporary building, the POLIN Museum brings the story of Poland's Jews to life by tracing a thousand years of history of the country's Jewish community. Various displays illustrate successive waves of immigration, pogroms and the horrors of WWII. The closer you get to the section devoted to the Holocaust, the darker and more confined the space becomes, until you end up in the ghetto itself.

Take a history lesson at the Warsaw Rising Museum

This necessary museum covers the Warsaw Uprising against the German occupiers between 1 August and 2 October 1944. Although heroic, the uprising was doomed to failure because it lacked any outside support. Photos, videos, 3D films of the city in ruins, sound recordings, eyewitness accounts, reconstructed sewers and a bunker provide a gripping and immersive experience, worth an extended visit. In the basement, an exhibition presents the uprising as experienced by the Germans.

Be king or queen for the day in Wilanów

Spend a baroque afternoon in Wilanów, Warsaw's most beautiful palace (opposite), 10km (6 miles) south of the city centre. Built in 1677 for King John III Sobieski, the palace is a riot of Rococo decor and historic furniture. After exploring the interior, stroll through the park surrounding it. In winter, thousands of multicolored LEDs in the Royal Garden of Light show give it a fairy-tale air.

Listen to a Chopin tune

Frédéric Chopin (1810–49) is a celebrated figure in the history of Polish music. Visit the museum dedicated to him, then pay your respects in Holy Cross Church, where his heart, preserved in cognac, rests. Finish with a piano recital organised by Best Chopin Concerts (chopinconcerts.pl) or Time For Chopin (timeforchopin.eu).

Take a break in Łazienki Park

This peaceful city park is dotted with museums and palaces and has peacocks strutting their stuff in its verdant gardens. Highlights include the neoclassical palace on the island in the middle of the lake, the Japanese garden, the sculptures in the Orangery and the small semi-circular Myślewicki Palace.

MORE TIME?

NEON MUSEUM The only colourful feature of Communist Warsaw were the neon signs on the facades of several buildings, now saved and displayed in this museum.

ŁÓDŹ The 'Manchester of Poland' (so-called because of its textile industries) is now a creative, post-industrial metropolis, brightened up by street-art murals and renowned for its nightlife.

PŁOCK Sitting on a cliff overlooking the Vistula River, Płock has a pretty historic centre and the Mazovian Museum with a formidable collection of Art Nouveau items.

MARIE SKŁODOWSKA

Better known by her married name Marie Curie, Marie Skłodowska (1867–1934) was a figurehead of modern physics born in Warsaw. Her birthplace has been transformed into a small museum detailing the life and work of the scientist who laid the foundations for radiography, nuclear physics and cancer radiotherapy. Winner of the Nobel Prize in Physics in 1903 and the Nobel Prize in Chemistry in 1911, Marie Curie was not only the first woman to win this distinction, but also the only person in history to have been awarded in two fields.

PRACTICALITIES

HOW TO GET THERE

Direct flights to Warsaw depart from many European destinations. Several bus and train connections also link the capital to cities across the continent.

WHERE TO STAY & EAT

Close to the historic centre, Motel One Warsaw Chopin (motel-one.com) offers contemporary design and excellent value for money. Or opt for the bright rooms of Lull Hostel (lullhostel.pl), a youth hostel in trendy Praga. Looking for a good meal? Book a table at Gospoda Kwiaty Polskie (gospodakwiatypolskie.com), Bibenda (bibenda.pl) or Bez Gwiazdek (bezgwiazdek.eu).

EVENTS

In October, the Warsaw Film Festival (wff.pl) will delight cinephiles. In winter, Christmas markets are held from the end of November, and open-air skating rinks operate from December to March.

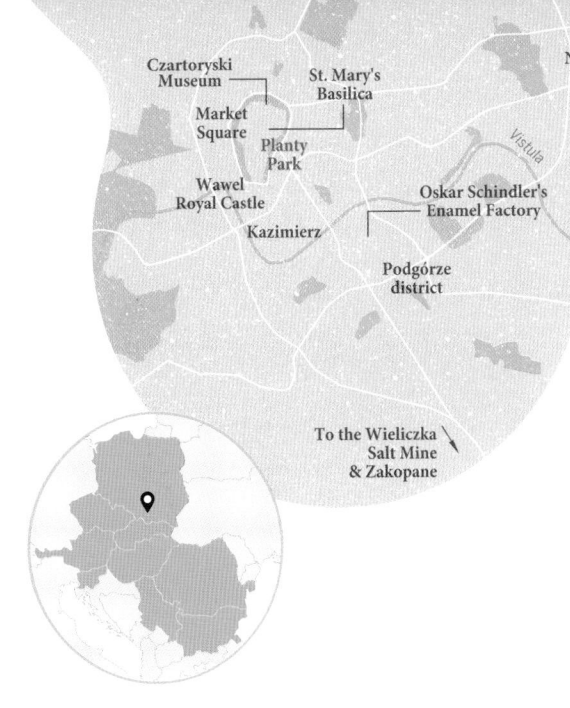

Czartoryski
Museum

St. Mary's
Basilica

Market
Square

Planty
Park

Wawel
Royal Castle

Oskar Schindler's
Enamel Factory

Kazimierz

Vistula

To
Nowa
Huta

Podgórze
district

To the Wieliczka
Salt Mine
& Zakopane

65

POLAND

Walk through a history book
IN KRAKÓW

The story of Kraków is a book of light and shadow, where the glorious Middle Ages and Renaissance chapters contrast with the darker pages written in the 20th century.** Witness Kraków's golden age, when the city was the capital of Poland, in the huge **Market Square** (Rynek), with its arcaded cloth market, town hall tower and domed Church of St Adalbert. Next door, **St Mary's Basilica** has two bell towers of intriguingly unequal height. Overlooking the **Vistula River**, **Wawel Royal Castle** (left) houses a museum, divided into five sections, which recalls the opulence of the former kingdom – if you're short on time, prioritise the Royal Apartments and the Exhibition of Oriental Art. The 1939 invasion of Poland by Nazi Germany put an end to Kraków's heyday. A ghetto for the city's Jews was created in the **Podgórze district** and the castle was totally destroyed, while 60km (37 miles) away, more than a million people were killed in **Auschwitz-Birkenau concentration camp**. Guided tours (auschwitz.org) bring home the scale of the tragedy that took place there. Round off your visit by crossing the Vistula to stroll the wide avenues of **Nowa Huta**, a working-class suburb that was the model of social realism during the Communist era.

Jewish history in Kazimierz

South of Kraków's Old Town, the Jewish quarter of Kazimierz (opposite) is brimming with flea markets and cafes. Take a walk through the streets and discover the baroque interior of the Temple Synagogue or the painted ceiling of the Remuh Synagogue. Wander the paths of the 'new' Jewish cemetery between moss-grown graves before buying a *zapiekanka* (a sandwich filled with cheese and vegetables) on Nowy Square. In the evening, mingle with locals in neighbourhood bars like Eszeweria and Propaganda.

Into the mines of Wieliczka

Just 12km (7.5 miles) from Kraków, the Wieliczka Salt Mine (inset) hides an unreal spectacle within its walls. Open since the Middle Ages, the mine includes over 300km (186 miles) of tunnels. Venture down to a depth of 135m (443ft) to gaze at chambers and chandeliers sculpted from salt, underground lakes rippling to the tunes of Chopin, and a series of chapels – the Chapel of St Kinga, 54m (177ft) long and 12m (39ft) high, is made entirely of salt from floor to ceiling, and from the altar to the candelabra. Book a visit at wieliczka-saltmine.com.

Stroll through Planty Park

Surrounding the Old Town where the city's ramparts once stood is Planty Park, an excellent place for a walk around the historic city. Visit the surviving remains of the defences: St Florian's Gate and the Barbican, a medieval fortress.

Visit the original Schindler factory

Oskar Schindler was a Nazi businessman who ended up saving 1200 Jews from the death camps by putting them on a list of essential workers for his enamel factory in Kraków. Made world-famous by Spielberg's film *Schindler's List*, you can learn more about the story at the former factory that now houses an immersive exhibition dedicated to the life of the ghetto's inhabitants during the Nazi occupation of Kraków. The reconstruction of Oskar's office and the ghetto's streets, the soundtrack and archive images create a moving experience.

Admire masterpieces

In the heart of the historic centre, the Princes Czartoryski Museum (mnk.pl/branch/the-princes-czartoryski-museum) holds a rich collection of art and artefacts, including several masterpieces by European painters. Here you can admire Rembrandt's *Landscape with the Good Samaritan*, a *Madonna and Child* by Catena, and works by Brueghel the Younger and Cranach.

MORE TIME?

ZAKOPANE Located at the foot of the Tatra Mountains, Zakopane is a popular mountain resort for skiers and hikers. In the 19th century, its beautiful houses and traditional wooden churches attracted numerous Polish and European artists to holiday here. A funicular in the town takes you to the top of Gubałówka mountain (1120m/3675ft) in just a few minutes, from where the views are spectacular.

COOKING PIEROGIES If you're a fan of these delicious traditional Polish dumplings, sign up for a cooking class and learn how to make them yourself. You'll find more information at the Kraków tourist office.

THE KRAKÓW DRAGON

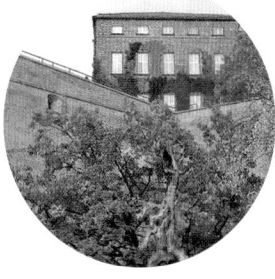

Legend has it that in the Middle Ages a terrible dragon terrorised Kraków. Numerous knights tried in vain to defeat it, before a simple cobbler managed to kill the beast by trickery. After stuffing a calfskin with sulphur, he left the bait in front of the dragon's lair. The voracious monster fell for the trick, burnt its his throat devouring the calfskin, and drank so much water from the Vistula River to soothe the burns from the sulphur that it died. As a reminder, a sculpture of the dragon, spitting fire every five minutes, has been placed in a cave beneath the castle hill.

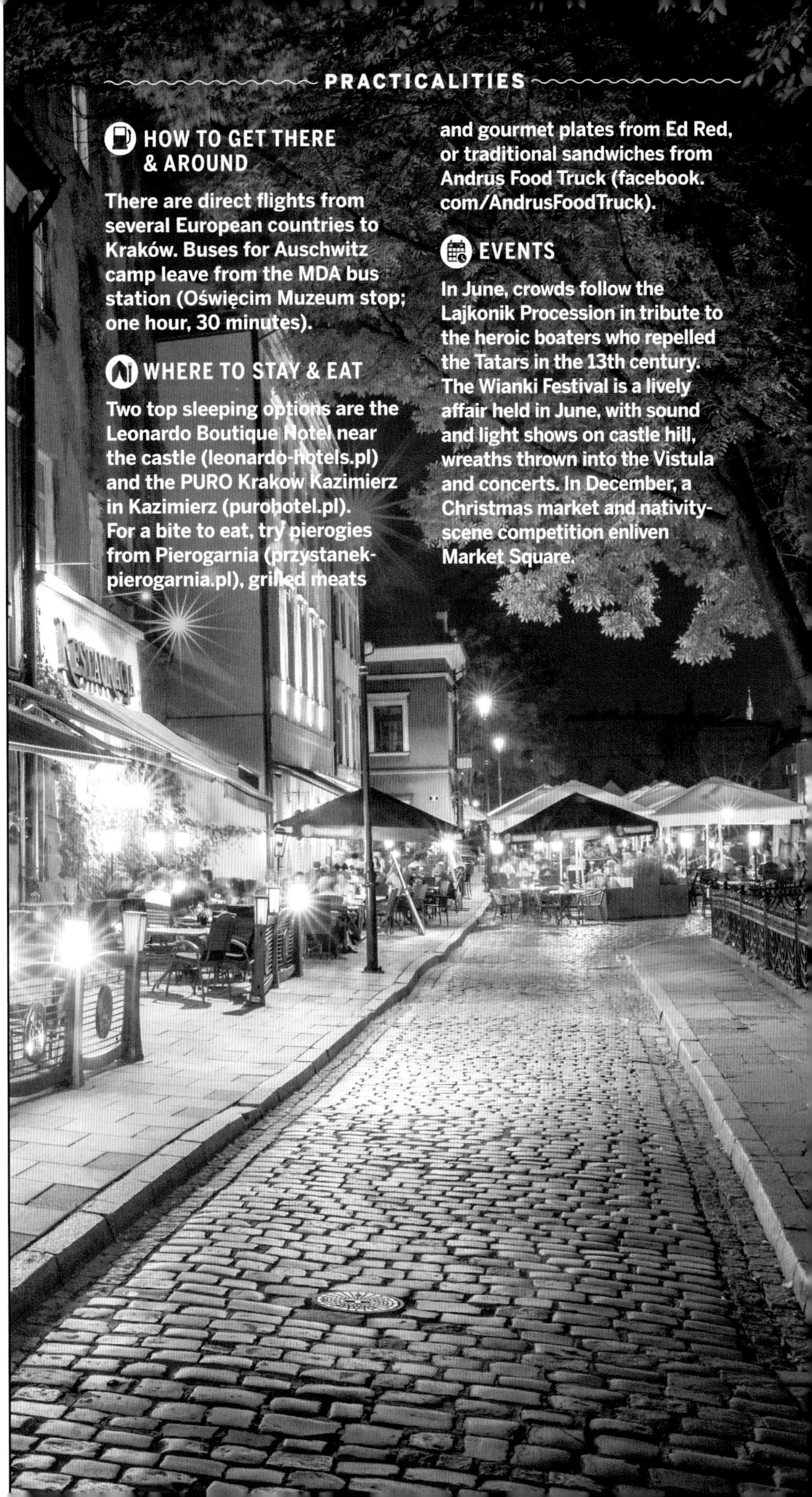

PRACTICALITIES

HOW TO GET THERE & AROUND

There are direct flights from several European countries to Kraków. Buses for Auschwitz camp leave from the MDA bus station (Oświęcim Muzeum stop; one hour, 30 minutes).

WHERE TO STAY & EAT

Two top sleeping options are the Leonardo Boutique Hotel near the castle (leonardo-hotels.pl) and the PURO Krakow Kazimierz in Kazimierz (purohotel.pl). For a bite to eat, try pierogies from Pierogarnia (przystanek-pierogarnia.pl), grilled meats and gourmet plates from Ed Red, or traditional sandwiches from Andrus Food Truck (facebook.com/AndrusFoodTruck).

EVENTS

In June, crowds follow the Lajkonik Procession in tribute to the heroic boaters who repelled the Tatars in the 13th century. The Wianki Festival is a lively affair held in June, with sound and light shows on castle hill, wreaths thrown into the Vistula and concerts. In December, a Christmas market and nativity-scene competition enliven Market Square.

HOLESOVICE / To Kutná Hora

Štvanice

Vltava

Kampa —

Jalta Hotel

Dětský — — Štvanice

Rotunda of
Saint-Martin

To Český
Krumlov

Vyšehrad
Citadel

CZECHIA

Uncover another side of
PRAGUE

Take a step off the tourist trail in the Czech capital and discover the favourite spots, cool neighbourhoods, secret corners and oases of calm beloved by Praguers. Begin by swapping Prague Castle for quieter **Vyšehrad Citadel, the city's spiritual home for a thousand years**. Perched on a hill above the city and the Vltava River, the site attracts locals who come here for weekend walks. To join them, take the metro to Vyšehrad then head up **Pevnosti St**, lined with ancient gates. Don't miss the 11th-century **Rotunda of St Martin**, a stroll along the **ramparts** and through the **park**, and a visit to the basilica to see the **Art Nouveau** paintings on its walls. The adjoining cemetery is the final resting place of painter Alfons Mucha. Take the stairs down to the **banks of the Vltava** to admire the Cubist houses on Libušina St and Rašínovo Quay, and then head off to delve deeper into the lesser-known sides of this **free-spirited**, **cosmopolitan city** on an atypical itinerary. The islands sprinkled in the river offer a mix of attractions, from jazz clubs to swimming pools. Holešovice is where global eating options and underground bars draw the hipster community, while away from the centre is 'Little Hanoi': focus of Prague's booming Vietnamese population.

Taste Vietnam in 'Little Hanoi'

Vietnamese form the third-largest foreign community in the Czech Republic and seemingly run every grocery store in Prague. For a trip to Vietnam without leaving Europe, buy a metro ticket (line C to Kačerov) followed by a bus ticket (bus 113 to Sídliště Písnice) and you'll reach 'Little Hanoi', a shopping and restaurant area in the south of the city. There are many wholesale and retail stalls and a multitude of canteens where you can try pho (soup), *bò bún* (beef and rice noodles) or *bánh cuốn* (delicate stuffed rice pancakes). It's all a far cry from traditional Czech food – for something more traditional, you can grab a delicious *trdelník* (spit cake, inset) from a street vendor here too.

Relive communist paranoia in a bunker

The Soviet era left Prague with a thousand, often invisible, fallout shelters. Who would suspect that the Jalta Hotel (hoteljalta.com) has a bunker in its basement that can accommodate 150 people? In the event of an attack, it was intended to shelter Communist dignitaries, and the hotel was built solely to conceal it. Guided tours include the infirmary with its operating table, the arsenal, and a listening room once used by the secret police to spy on hotel guests.

The Vltava islands

Overlooked by tourists but very popular with Praguers, the dozen or so islands along the Vltava repay a visit. Each has its own appeal, from pedal-boating on Žofín to listening to jazz at Dětský's top club. With its pretty square, 17th-century houses and modern-art museum, Kampa (opposite) is undoubtedly the most romantic. A little further afield, large Štvanice offers a swimming pool in the Vltava on its eastern side, and venues including a theatre, a beer garden and an electro club to the west.

Mingle with the cool set in Holešovice

In this former industrial suburb, hipsters have replaced workers; and foundries, breweries and slaughterhouses have been transformed into art galleries, restaurants and bars. Don't miss the wooden Airship Gulliver, stranded on the roof of the excellent DOX museum (dox.cz), dedicated to contemporary art. Or Vnitroblock (vnitroblock.cz), a hybrid venue combining a cultural space, a bookshop, a cafe and a concept store, nestled in a huge brick factory.

MORE TIME?

KUTNÁ HORA This UNESCO-listed town, 70km (43 miles) from Prague, was once one of the richest in Bohemia, thanks to its silver mines – marvellous churches and a castle bear witness to this affluent past. But there's also a chilling ossuary. In 1348, with the onset of the Black Death, 30,000 people were buried in the cemetery here, then, a few centuries later, the bones were transformed into chandeliers, coats of arms, crosses, candlesticks and more. Goosebumps guaranteed.

ČESKÝ KRUMLOV Encircled by the Vlatva, this medieval village charms visitors with its colourful houses and cobbled, flower-filled lanes. It's three hours by bus from Prague.

PROVOCATIVE ART

For over 30 years, visual artist David Černý has been shaking up the Prague art scene by taking over the city's corners. In Žižkov, the *Miminka* (Babies), disquieting faceless figures, climb the TV tower or crawl through the courtyard of the Kampa Museum. A four-legged Trabant takes a walk past the German embassy. In the Lucerna Arcade, an improbable equestrian statue of King Wenceslas hangs from the ceiling. In Národní Třída, the mirrors of a giant sculpture of Franz Kafka's head constantly reshape the writer's face to evoke his book *The Metamorphosis*, while Sigmund Freud holds on to a beam on the corner of na Perštýně and Husova streets. See more at davidcerny.cz.

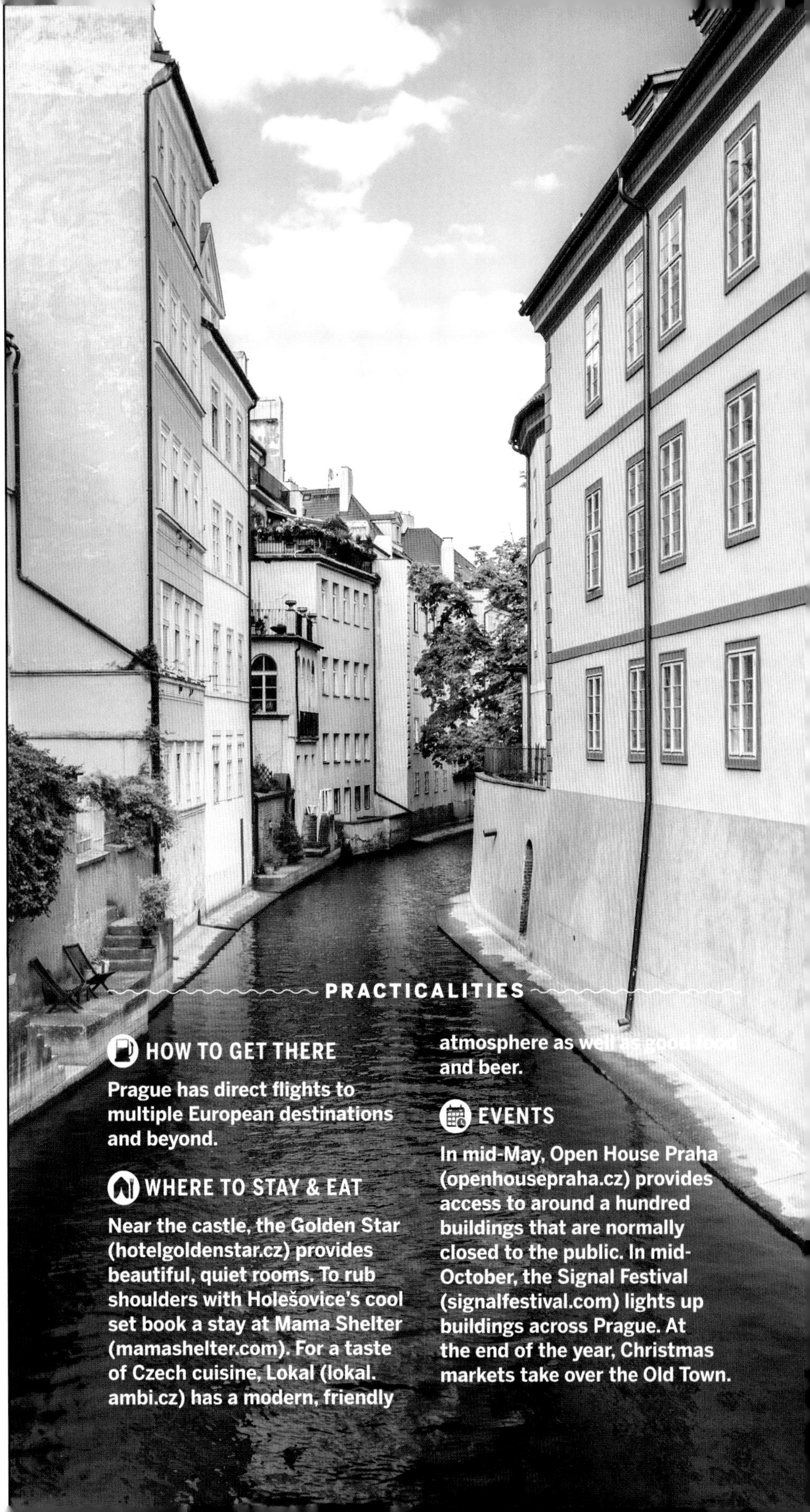

PRACTICALITIES

📱 HOW TO GET THERE

Prague has direct flights to multiple European destinations and beyond.

🏠 WHERE TO STAY & EAT

Near the castle, the Golden Star (hotelgoldenstar.cz) provides beautiful, quiet rooms. To rub shoulders with Holešovice's cool set book a stay at Mama Shelter (mamashelter.com). For a taste of Czech cuisine, Lokal (lokal. ambi.cz) has a modern, friendly atmosphere as well as good food and beer.

📅 EVENTS

In mid-May, Open House Praha (openhousepraha.cz) provides access to around a hundred buildings that are normally closed to the public. In mid-October, the Signal Festival (signalfestival.com) lights up buildings across Prague. At the end of the year, Christmas markets take over the Old Town.

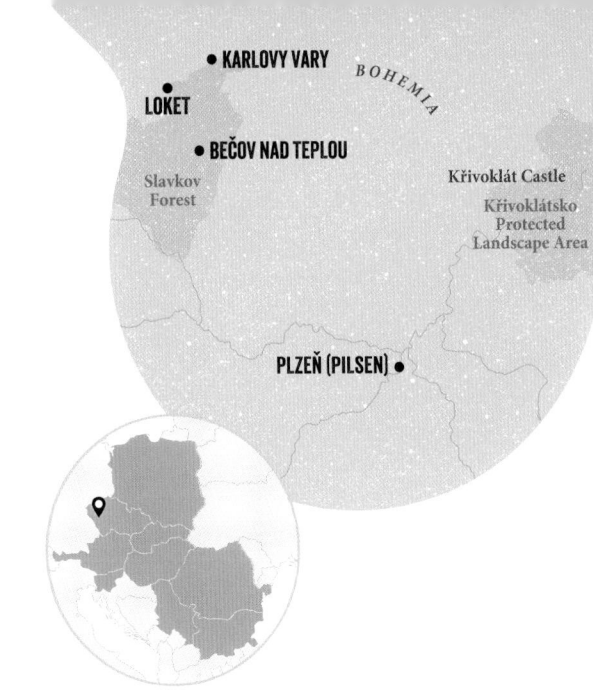

67

Find relaxation & beer
IN PLZEŇ & BOHEMIA

West of Prague lie the green hills and forests of Bohemia, a bucolic region of adorable towns, imposing castles and unspoiled countryside. Start in **Plzeň (Pilsen)**, famous for its medieval centre and brewing tradition. Head for the **Square of the Republic** to inspect the pastel facades and the **St Bartholomew Cathedral** (left), with its 103m-high (338ft) bell tower offering the best views of the city. Don't miss the Moorish-style **Great Synagogue** too, before letting the scents of malt and hops emanating from the **Pilsner Urquell brewery** guide you to the birthplace of the famous Pilsner (Pils), created here in 1842. A guided tour (prazdrojvisit.cz) reveals the mysteries of brewing, knowledge that the **Brewery Museum** can help you delve deeper into. Next door, an **underground network** leads into a maze of 11km (7 miles) of cellars and galleries, dug out as early as the 14th century to brew beer and defend the locals. For post-sightseeing relaxation, visit **Spa Purkmistr** (purkmistr.cz) which provides a range of hop-based treatments, including beer baths, scrubs and massages. You'll be in great shape the next day for a **hike in the Slavkov Forest** or an excursion to **Křivoklát Castle**.

Discover the designs of Adolf Loos

'Ornamentation is a crime that only serves to mask design flaws': so said the famous Austrian architect Adolf Loos, precursor of the Modernist movement, who designed the interiors of several apartments in Plzeň in the 1920s and 1930s. An ode to simplicity, Brummel House is distinguished by its built-in furniture and functional layout. In the Kraus family apartment, panelled walls rub shoulders with dark green marble, the living room ceiling is adorned with mahogany slabs, and the opposing mirrored walls in the dining room give the impression of infinite space. Guided tours can be booked at adolfloosplzen.cz.

Follow in royal footsteps in Karlovy Vary

The atmosphere in Karlovy Vary (inset) still evokes the elegance and prestige of the spa towns of the belle époque. Russian tsars, Habsburg emperors and many other crowned heads stayed here, as did great artists and thinkers of the time. Like them, you can stroll through the parks and under the arcades before sitting down on a terrace to drink sulphurous thermal water from a porcelain cup. Then relax at the Carlsbad Plaza Castle Spa (carlsbad-plaza.com), which has a modernised spa and underground pool.

Walk on the wild side in Slavkov Forest

For a real nature bath, head for Slavkov Forest, a huge green paradise with a succession of wooded mountains, meadows and peat bogs. Virtually uninhabited, this protected natural area is a biosphere reserve where numerous hiking trails can take you further into its wild terrain. Let yourself be captivated by the song of countless birds or surprised by the sudden appearance of a deer. Informal capital of the region, Bečov nad Teplou, is worth a visit for its castle, a mix of Gothic and Renaissance buildings.

Walk the ramparts of Křivoklát Castle

Lost in the middle of a dense, game-filled forest, Křivoklát Castle (opposite) was a favourite of many Czech rulers. Built in the 13th century, this former royal residence provides an insight into the medieval life of the Bohemian kings. Be dazzled by the Gothic architecture of the chapel and royal hall, admire the library's 52,000 books, shiver in the torture room or patrol the ramparts and enjoy the view from the top of the watchtower.

MORE TIME?

LOKET Tucked in a bend of the Ohře River, this almost island town is far from the hustle and bustle of Prague and offers a peaceful contrast to the capital. Discover its pretty square and Gothic castle before browsing the porcelain that's made in the town's renowned factory.

PILSNER BEER

Plzeň's brewing tradition dates back to the Middle Ages, but it was only in 1842 that the town's burghers decided to improve the mediocre quality of local beers by creating the first modern brewery – Pilsner Urquell, the birthplace of Pilsner lager. Saaz hops, malt and the city's very soft water were the ingredients for success, but it was the low fermentation (10–15°C/50–59°F) used by Josef Groll and the filtering that made Pilsner famous. The type of light, clear lager produced here is particularly refreshing, and provided a model for making lager later adopted by Heineken, 1664 and Budweiser.

PRACTICALITIES

🚉 HOW TO GET THERE

Fly or get the train to Prague (Europe-wide connections) and then take a train from Prague Central Station to Plzeň (or rent a car).

🏕 WHERE TO STAY & EAT

In Plzeň, one of the city's best hotels is the Art Deco-style Continental (hotelcontinental. cz). In Karlovy Vary, opt for the Hotel Romance (hotelromance. cz), which has a spa. When it comes to eating out, Czech specialities can be tried at Lokál Pod Divadlem (lokal-poddivadlem.ambi.cz) or U Mansfelda (umansfelda.cz). To sample the local brews, your best bet is the Měšťanská Beseda Pub (mestanskabeseda.cz).

🗓 EVENTS

In March, don't miss the installations at BLIK BLIK (blikblik.cz), the local festival of lights. Pilsner Fest kicks off the first weekend of October – expect free-flowing beer and live music.

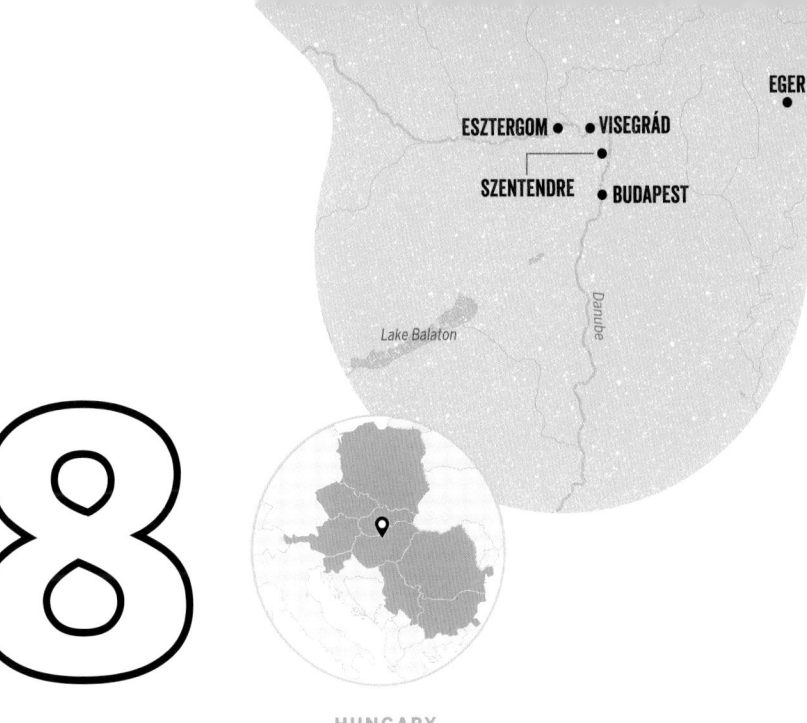

68

Fall in love with
BUDAPEST &
THE DANUBE

The Hungarian capital, Budapest, spreads out on both sides of the Danube, a river that is spanned by several bridges, the most famous and oldest of which is the Chain Bridge. To the west, the Buda Hills are capped by iconic Buda Castle. To the east, the lively streets of Pest have pretty cafes and majestic Andrássy út boulevard. Architectural wonders (parliament building, left) line both banks, from baroque and neoclassical buildings to Art Nouveau treasures. And there's no shortage of interesting sites in the Jewish Quarter, from vast Klauzál tér square to the restored ghetto wall. Seeing Budapest from the Danube only accentuates the city's beauty. There are a multitude of boat tours to choose from, and even a short, no-frills outing is enough to capture the romance of this place. Budapest is a party town too, one of Central European best cities for nightlife. Bars and restaurants buzz with energy and give visitors the chance to taste Hungarian food and wine. Close enough to the capital for easy day trips are places like historic Esztergom, with a massive basilica that rises above the Danube; and Lake Balaton, an inland sea hugely popular with Hungarians.

Dive into Budapest

'Taking the waters' is part of everyday life in Budapest and the rest of Hungary, thanks to hundreds of mineral-rich hot springs . The capital is home to numerous baths, and it would be a crime to stay here without enjoying at least one. The justly popular Széchenyi Baths (inset) are mixed, well-maintained and have large outdoor pools that are a delight to splash around in – the water is maintained at a steady 40°C (104°F). Equally worthwile are the spectacular, Art Nouveau Gellért Baths, famous for their colonnaded indoor pool.

Revel in romkocsmák

A great night out in Budapest has to involve *romkocsmák*, literally 'ruin bars': venues set up in abandoned buildings and their courtyards, and furnished with salvaged decor. An underground avant-garde spirit reigns – people were happily drinking spritz cocktails here long before they became fashionable everywhere else. Perhaps you'll discover the next cool cocktail to dethrone it – unless you're tempted by *pálinka*, Hungarian traditional brandy.

Escape to the Danube Bend

If a short jaunt on the Danube in Budapest leaves you hungry for more, why not embark on a day trip to the Danube Bend, north of the capital, probably the prettiest stretch of the river. Stop off in towns along the way, such as Esztergom, with its green-domed basilica (the country's largest church); Visegrád, dominated by an imposing hilltop fortress; and Szentendre, which is full of quaint cobbled streets.

A night at the opera

When he had the opera house built (1875–84), Emperor Franz Joseph wanted it to rival that of Vienna and Paris. Needless to say, he pulled out all the stops, and this Neo-Renaissance building, richly decorated in a baroque style, impresses with its opulence, which is even more evident after a recently completed restoration project. You can visit the building, but the best way to enjoy its splendour is to spend an evening taking in a ballet or opera in the stunning auditorium.

MORE TIME?

EGER This baroque town is one hour, 45 minutes by car or two hours by train from Budapest, and rewards the journey with a 12th-century castle and famous wines in the Valley of the Beautiful Woman (on the outskirts, accessible by minibus), where rock-cut cellars host tastings.

LAKE BALATON In this landlocked country, Balaton (opposite) is considered an 'inland sea'. Balatonfüred, on the north shore, is only 90 minutes by car from Budapest and offers beautiful walks and all kinds of water-based activities in an exclusive resort atmosphere.

ART NOUVEAU

The Art Nouveau movement (late 19th–early 20th centuries), and especially its Viennese variant, the Secession style, is everywhere in Budapest. Sinuous lines, asymmetrical shapes and rich ornamentation, such as coloured ceramics and glassware, characterise this aesthetic, clearly visible at the Franz Liszt Academy of Music and the Gellért Hotel. Among other major examples are works by Ödön Lehner (1845–1914), nicknamed the 'Hungarian Gaudí'. He designed the Royal Postal Savings Bank, the Museum of Applied Arts, and the Institute of Geology.

🅿 HOW TO GET THERE

Many airlines serve Budapest Airport from cities across Europe, North America and Asia.

🅰 WHERE TO EAT

The capital is home to several markets, where it's great fun to mingle with the locals, do a little shopping and sample local specialities at great prices. Head for Vásárcsarnok, Hungary's largest covered market (dating from 1897) to stock up on cured meats, honey and paprika, or the Szimpla Kert Sunday farmers' market, a famous 'ruin bar'.

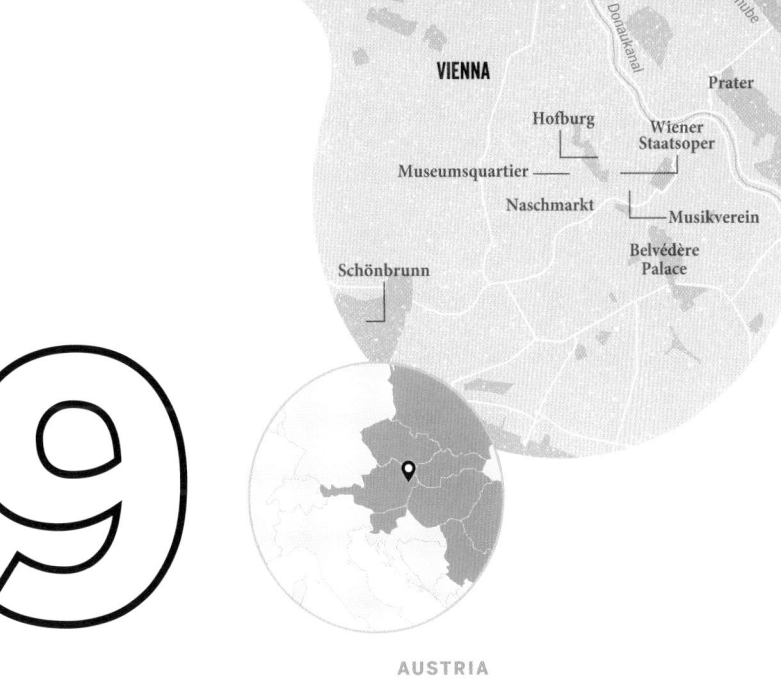

AUSTRIA

69

Explore Mitteleuropa
IN VIENNA

Think of Vienna, and you might think of Empress Sissi, artist Gustav Klimt, composer Johann Strauss and indulgent cakes in elegant cafes. But Vienna has more to offer than stereotypes. If the Austrian capital seems disproportionately large for the size of the country, it's because for centuries it was the centre of the most powerful empire in Central Europe, bringing together very different cultures and languages (Czech, Hungarian, Bosnian). Today, Vienna is more than ever a **melting pot**; its **food**, **lifestyle** and **culture** are now nourished by Turkish, Balkan and even French influences. The German spoken here is so soft it sounds almost Italian; the wine sipped here comes from the urban vineyards surrounding the city; and the cuisine eaten here covers everything from schnitzel to goulash. The Viennese know how to enjoy life, whether cycling along the **Danube**, going to a concert or exhibition, or winding down in **Heurigen** (wine taverns) and **Beisln** (rustic inns). Join them for breakfast in a *Kaffeehaus* and learn why the word '*viennoiserie*' is used to describe the world's tastiest pastries.

Immerse yourself in the baroque

Baroque architecture and garden lovers are in for a treat in Vienna. The former Habsburg capital is home to three magnificent imperial palaces: the Hofburg, a former medieval fortress that over the centuries became a refined palace with numerous outbuildings and is now dedicated to Empress Sissi (sisimuseum-hofburg.at); the Belvedere Palace (see previous page; belvedere.at), home to several major art collections and a glorious park; and Schönbrunn (schoenbrunn.at), an Austrian Versailles, built in the 18th century for Emperor Joseph. The latter's park includes a labyrinth and the world's oldest zoo still in operation.

Spend the evening at the opera

Concerts featuring Johann Strauss' *Blue Danube* are almost guaranteed to be heard around every corner. But there's more on offer in Vienna, a city that celebrates classical music in all its diversity, every evening, with the world's greatest artists. Treat yourself to the latest audacious staging of a great opera at the Wiener Staatsoper (opposite; wiener-staatsoper.at) or an inspired interpretation of a famous work at the Musikverein (inset; musikverein.at).

Taste the product of Viennese vines in a Heuriger

Vienna contains the world's largest urban vineyard, and it's in a Heuriger that you'll find the resulting wines in all their joyous varieties. These taverns – originally dedicated just to tasting Grüner Veltliner – have become popular places where hearty food and Viennese zither music accompany the drinking. Those in the centre are quite touristy, but the Heurigen in the village of Grinzing, 20 minutes from Vienna and surrounded by vineyards, have retained plenty of charm.

Say hello to neighbouring Bratislava

Just 60km (37 miles) from Vienna and linked by the Danube, Slovakia's pretty capital, Bratislava, offers an enjoyable excursion across the border. Dominated by its dazzling white castle, it can be visited in a day, and has cultural dynamism alongside historical interest.

Have some fun at the Prater

North of Vienna, a city within a city awaits – the Prater. One of the world's oldest fairgrounds, it has 250 attractions and captivates Viennese and international visitors year-round. Among its highlights is the Giant Ferris Wheel (wienerriesenrad.com), which has been running for 130 years – re-enact famous scenes from *The Third Man* and *The Living Daylights*, which were filmed here, and enjoy the panoramic view over the city.

MORE TIME?

NASCHMARKT Vienna's premier farmers' market (naschmarkt-vienna.com) is a lively place where you'll be spoilt for choice, wandering between mouthwatering food stands, inviting cafes and Saturday's *Flohmarkt* (flea market) stallholders.

MUSEUMSQUARTIER The former imperial stables rub shoulders with contemporary buildings to form this exceptional museum district (mqw.at), bringing together the greatest Austrian collections of the 20th and 21st centuries.

THE THIRD MAN IN VIENNA

Voted best British film of the 20th century by the British Film Institute in 1999, *The Third Man* (Carol Reed, 1949) was shot in postwar Vienna. Graham Greene's dark, melancholy script finds a counterpoint in the zither music of Anton Karas, whom the director met at a *Heuriger* near the Prater. The Giant Ferris Wheel at the Prater provides the setting for a memorable scene. Inseparable from Vienna, the film is shown three times a week at the BurgKino (burgkino. at), and guided tours (drittemanntour. at) take place in the sewers, where Orson Welles' character tries to escape.

~ PRACTICALITIES ~

🖥 HOW TO GET THERE

Vienna International Airport has flights to and from destinations across Europe and further afield. The city's main train station has connections to several European cities, including sleeper services.

🏨 WHERE TO STAY

The Hotel Sacher (sacher.com), located opposite the Opera House and close to famous Café Mozart, is legendary if pricey. Alternatively, book a room at one of the city's excellent guesthouses, such as Pension Kraml (pension-kraml. hotelsinvienna.org).

📅 EVENTS

Vienna is very popular during the festive season, as well as in the January–February ball season. Many events take place in summer – Donauinselfest is the top music offering. Early autumn is marked by the grape harvest and sees the start of the cultural season.

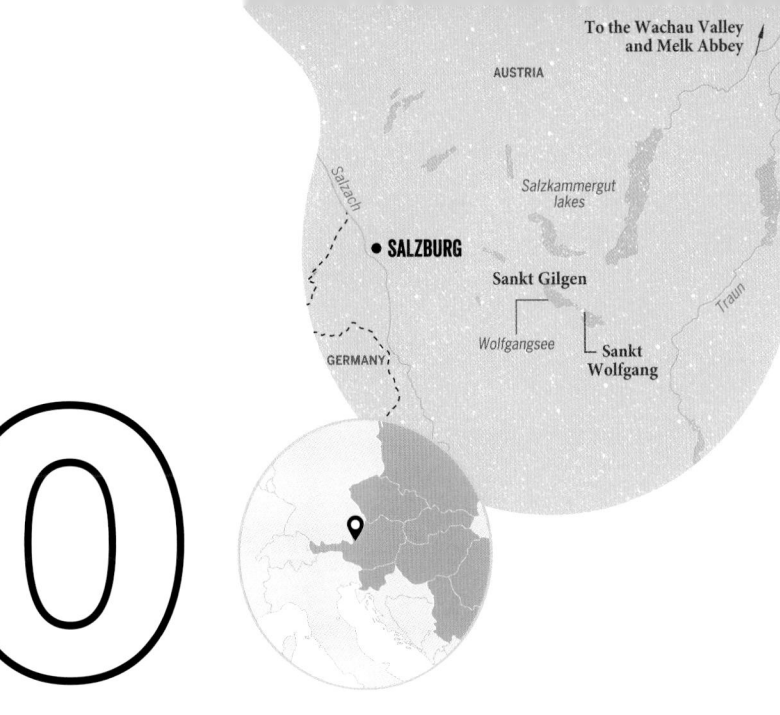

To the Wachau Valley
and Melk Abbey

AUSTRIA

Salzach

Salzkammergut
lakes

● SALZBURG

Sankt Gilgen

Wolfgangsee

Traun

Sankt
Wolfgang

GERMANY

AUSTRIA

70

Follow in musical footsteps

IN SALZBURG & WOLFGANGSEE

While Vienna is Austria's capital, Salzburg is where the country's cultural and artistic pulse beats. The city where Mozart was born in 1756 pays homage to its celebrated son in several monuments and one of the world's most renowned classical music festivals. Salzburg is also where, from the 13th century onwards, the ruling prince-archbishops built splendid edifices, leaving a wonderful architectural heritage to be discovered in the pedestrianised Old Town and its surrounding hills. From splashing fountains to squares lined with handsome houses, from lush gardens to majestic bell towers and domes, there's no doubt you'll fall in love with the baroque style that gives the city such a distinct character. Just as easy to fall for are the many sweet treats the city is known for. Then set course for the beautiful Wolfgangsee Lake. Like Salzburg, it appeared in *The Sound of Music*, and is just the spot for a relaxing overnight stay, offering swimming with mountain views and leisurely bike rides.

Up to the Hohensalzburg Fortress

For a great panorama of the city, head up to Salzburg's fortress, the Hohensalzburg (see previous page), on the summit of the Festungsberg. This is one of the best-preserved castles in Europe, with original rooms untouched since 1501 and a museum featuring a wide range of medieval torture instruments. The highlight of the visit is the particularly striking Golden Room, with its ceiling recreating a starry sky.

Listen out for The Sound of Music

The five-time Oscar-winning musical was filmed in Salzburg and the nearby Salzkammergut lakes, including Wolfgangsee. Follow your own tour in search of instantly recognisable locations: Mirabellgarten and its sculptures, the setting for 'Do-Re-Mi'; Maria's home at the Benedictine convent of Nonnberg; and the gazebo where lovers sing 'Sixteen going on Seventeen' in Hellbrunn Park.

Find fresh air around the Wolfgangsee

Just 30km (19 miles) from Salzburg, this lake is home to two charming resorts: Sankt Wolfgang and Sankt Gilgen. Visit the latter to see the Mozart House – which actually pays tribute to his sister Maria Anna, herself a talented composer. A bike tour of the lake, swimming in its clear waters and summiting the Schafberg (1783m/5850ft) on the SchafbergBahn (opposite), a cog railway dating back to 1893, should be top of your itinerary.

Pay tribute to Mozart in his hometown

In the heart of Salzburg, the house where Mozart was born on 27 January 1756 is a place of pilgrimage for music fans. Now a museum, the Mozarts Geburtshaus (mozarteum.at) at 9 Getreidegasse, still contains the instruments he played on – his violin and clavichord. The larger Tanzmeisterhaus (House of the Dance Master), on Makartplatz, is where the whole family moved when Wolfgang Amadeus was 17 years old; it holds one of the composer's pianofortes. Round off your homage by attending a concert in the Mirabell Palace's Golden Hall (mozart.co.at).

Admire the ceilings of Salzburg Cathedral

Capped by a dome and symmetrical spires, the city's cathedral (inset) is an outstanding example of baroque art – it was actually the first to inaugurate this style north of the Alps – and is also where Mozart was baptised. In the nave, the stuccowork is wonderful and the sumptuous ceiling frescoes depicting the Passion of Christ are worth a crick in the neck.

MORE TIME?

SAIL THE BLUE DANUBE IN THE WACHAU VALLEY This peaceful, romantic valley between Melk and Krems an der Donau is a UNESCO World Heritage Site, thanks to its countryside and culture. It owes its beauty to the Danube, medieval villages, clifftop castles and vineyards, and is a great place for some slow travel by boat or along the bike path. Don't miss the Benedictine Abbey of Melk, a baroque beauty adorned with angels, gilding and frescoes, with an incredible library and an ornate marble hall. Trains run to Melk from Salzburg in under three hours.

SWEET-TOOTH HEAVEN

You can't beat Salzburg if you have a sweet tooth. Try a *Nockerl*, a famous sweet soufflé made with 'snow-covered' eggs representing the Salzburg mountains, or a *Mozartkugel*, a bite-size mouthful of chocolate, pistachio, marzipan and praline. And wherever you are in Austria, enjoy delicious apple strudel in puff pastry.

HOW TO GET THERE

Salzburg Airport is 20 minutes from the city centre and has flights to a few international destinations. Sankt Gilgen is 50 minutes from Salzburg by postbus, with departures every hour. Allow an extra 50 minutes to reach Sankt Wolfgang. Boats run between the two villages in high season.

EVENTS

In July and August, the Salzburg Festival (salzburgerfestspiele. at) delights classical music aficionados with a rich programme of concerts and operas. Tickets should be booked months in advance.

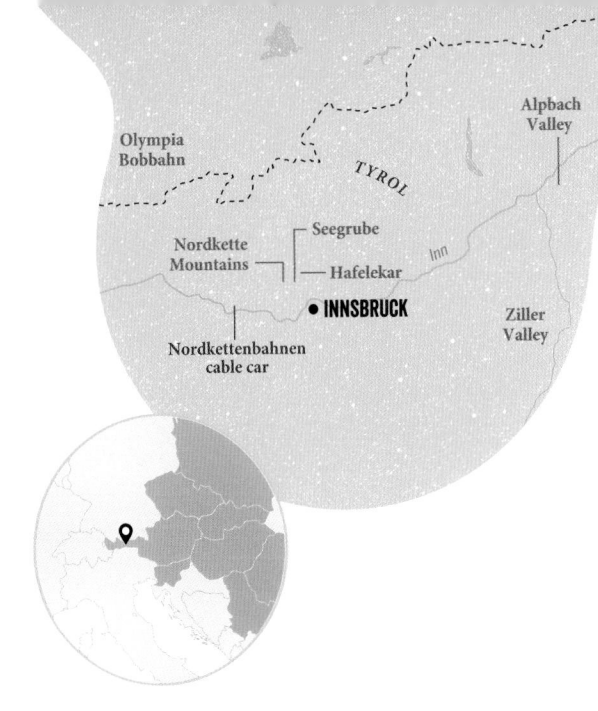

Olympia
Bobbahn

Alpbach
Valley

TYROL

Nordkette
Mountains

Seegrube

Hafelekar

Inn

● INNSBRUCK

Ziller
Valley

Nordkettenbahnen
cable car

AUSTRIA

71

Take a deep breath
IN INNSBRUCK
& TYROL

Innsbruck is a great ambassador for the Tyrol, a region of mighty mountains, pretty villages and folk traditions. The town itself became the ducal seat of the Habsburgs in 1420 and enjoyed its peak during the reign of Emperor Maximilian (1493–1519). In addition to the Goldenes Dachl (Golden Roof), a Gothic wonder nestling in the medieval part of town, numerous palaces and monuments still bear witness to the days of imperial splendour, presenting Innsbruck's past in a fabulous parade of buildings watched over by Alpine summits. Because mountains are never far away and because Innsbruck hosted both the 1964 and the 1976 Winter Olympics, the town also features an impressive sports infrastructure and a couple of hands-on attractions. Just a few minutes from the centre, the rocky peaks and lush pastures of the Nordkette mountain range (left) are the playground of hikers, via ferrata enthusiasts, skiers and mountain bikers – a healthy dose of outdoor excitement guaranteed. And for even more spectacular nature, the Ziller and Alpbachtal valleys are among the most beautiful in the area.

Along Maria-Theresien-Strasse & around

In this shopping street lined with welcoming cafes and restaurants, the mix of baroque facades against a backdrop of awe-inspiring mountains is magical. Check out St Anne's Column, St George's Chapel and the Triumphal Arch, then head for Herzog-Friedrich-Strasse for a close-up view of the Golden Roof. Decorated with sublime murals and covered with 2657 gilded copper tiles, this is the crown jewel of Innsbruck's architecture. A stone's throw away, the bell tower offers a 360-degree view of the city's rooftops and surrounding peaks.

Relive Habsburg times

Start a Habsburg tour in the rococo apartments of the Imperial Palace, home of the former ruling dynasty from 1460, then head to Innsbruck's Gothic gem, the Court Church. It houses the mausoleum of Emperor Maximilian, sculpted in marble and guarded by 28 impressive bronze statues. On a hill southeast of town, Ambras Castle, a Renaissance palace, is also worth a visit, especially for its Habsburg portrait gallery with paintings by Titian, Velázquez and Van Dyck.

Soar up the Nordkettenbahnen

The Nordkette is the mountain range just north of Innsbruck and a fabulous place for outdoor fun, with a host of downhill mountain bike and hiking trails and two via ferrata routes. In just eight minutes from the city centre, a futuristic cable car takes you 860m (2822ft) up to the Hungerburg stop. To go even higher into the kingdom of the ibex, the line continues to Seegrube at 1905m (6250ft) and Hafelekar at 2256m (7402ft).

Ride the Olympia Bobbahn

Fan of the movie *Cool Runnings*? Then this experience is not to be missed. Take on the role of bobsleigh champion and hurtle down the Olympia Bobbahn, the track built for the 1976 Winter Olympics. Famous for its dozen or so bends and speeds of over 100km/h (62mph), it also includes a frightening 800m (2625ft) descent. For the full experience, a professional pilot can accompany you. Or for a less pulse-raising option, enjoy the view from the Bergisel Ski Jump (inset), a few minutes from downtown Innsbruck.

MORE TIME? **OUTDOOR ACTIVITIES IN THE TYROL** Accessible by train from Innsbruck in just 90 minutes, the Ziller Valley is an eden for downhill mountain bikers and rafters looking for thrills on the Ziller River. The more secluded Alpbachtal Valley offers excellent hiking opportunities for all levels.

ALMABTRIEB: A TRANSHUMANCE FESTIVAL

From mid-September onwards, some 3200 cowherds and shepherds bring their livestock down from the mountain pastures to the barns where they spend the winter – an event known as the *Almabtrieb*. This transhumance gives rise to some 50 festivals, culminating on the first Saturday in October when, to the sound of the alphorn, the cows parade in magnificent headdresses made of Alpine roses, pine branches or silver thistles and crosses. Music, food and traditional costumes also play an integral part in the celebrations.

🚋 HOW TO GET THERE & AROUND

Innsbruck airport is 3.5km (2 miles) from the centre and is connected by bus. The railway station is served by trains from across Austria and neighbouring countries too.

From Innsbruck, you can reach the Ziller Valley by train in 90 minutes. The valley is served by a private railway, the Zillertalbahn (zillertalbahn.at), which runs the 32km (20 miles) from Jenbach to Mayrhofen. A *Dampfzug* (steam train) is also in operation.

72

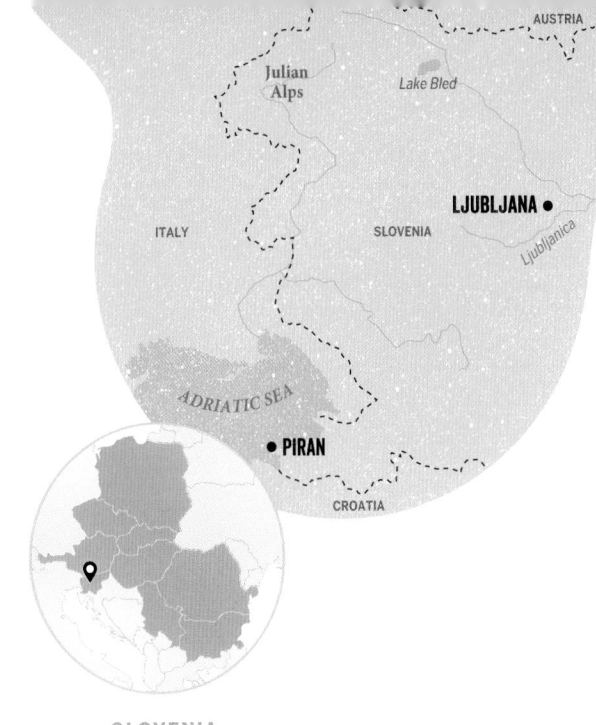

SLOVENIA

Big things in small packages
IN LJUBLJANA

Ljubljana, the capital of Slovenia, is appealingly lively and beautiful – and small. Crossed by the Ljubljanica River, which gives it a rural atmosphere, the city offers some excellent reasons to visit. An exceptional architectural heritage combines medieval vestiges with **flamboyant baroque buildings** and an **innovative early 20th-century aesthetic** – between 1920 and 1950, Jože Plečnik adorned the capital with elegant bridges, government buildings, pyramids and lampposts. Ljubljana is also one of the most eco-friendly cities in the world – it was named **European Green Capital** in 2016 – and is compact enough for easy exploration by bike or on foot. Some 50,000 students create a buzzy vibe and share the wealth of **museums**, **restaurants** and **bars** with visitors. The city feels like a mix of Italian dolce vita with a Balkan accent. And if you have time to go beyond the Slovenian capital, you can explore the rest of the country. Although small, Slovenia has some stunning scenery to offer, with the Julian Alps, the Škocjan Caves and the Adriatic Sea all providing the perfect excuse to venture out – two standout options for day trips are Lake Bled and Venice-lookalike Piran.

Climb up to the castle

Whether on foot or by funicular from Vodnikov trg square, heading to castle hill, aka Grajska Planota, 375m (1230ft) above the capital, is an experience not to be missed. Sitting at the summit, Ljubljana Castle (ljubljanskigrad.si) dominates the city with its robust architecture, dating mainly from the 16th century. To access the rampart walk and enjoy a view of the Old Town, climb (via a double-headed iron staircase) to the 19th-century watchtower in the southwest of the castle's courtyard.

See the works of an inspired architect

The Ljubljana you visit today owes much of its charm and beauty to Jože Plečnik (1872–1957), one of the precursors of postmodernism. Born when Slovenia was under Austro-Hungarian rule, the architect studied with Otto Wagner in Vienna, then endowed his hometown with buildings inspired by the Viennese Secession and Orientalism: the Triple Bridge; the Central Market; and his most celebrated building, the National and University Library (nuk.uni-lj.si), which has a large reading room open to non-students every Saturday afternoon.

Meander along the Ljubljanica River

A walk along the banks of the river that runs through the heart of Ljubljana is a must on any visit; entirely pedestrianised and bike-friendly, the riverside paths are an invitation to enjoy the emerald green of the water. Make a gastronomic pause at the Central Market (inset) to the north, or take a journey through the city's history at Novi Trg to the south, which in the Middle Ages was a fortified fishing village. And don't even try to resist the temptation of the cafes that transform the riverbanks into one long outdoor terrace in summer.

Time travel in Stare Mesto

From Prešernov Trg (a square named after Slovenia's greatest poet), you can reach Ljubljana's Stare Mesto (Old Town) via the Triple Bridge, a historical work of art dating back to 1842 and extended between 1929 and 1932 with two pedestrian footbridges designed by Jože Plečnik. Once across the river, the Old Town spreads out around three adjoining squares: Mestni Trg (Town Square); Stari Trg (Old Square); and Gornji Trg (Upper Square). Together they hold a rich mix of medieval gabled houses and baroque buildings.

MORE TIME?

BLED A short (less than an hour) train ride separates the capital from one of Slovenia's most beautiful spots, Lake Bled (opposite). A medieval, cliff-clinging castle stands guard over the water here, and in the middle of the lake, a small island is home to a delightful church, easily visited by boat
PIRAN Three hours by bus from Ljubljana, Piran was ruled by Venice for five centuries, and today is one of the best-preserved Venetian ports on the Adriatic. It's also a great place to enjoy fresh fish and a stroll through picturesque lanes.

SLOVENIAN BRANDY

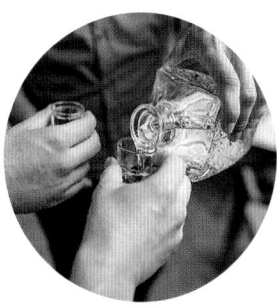

The Balkans are renowned for their strong, fruity brandies, and Slovenia is no exception – you can enjoy *žganje* distilled from a variety of fruits, including *borovnica* (wild blueberry), *slivovka* (plum) and *češnjevec* (cherry). Among the best though is *Pleterska Hruška*, created from pears by the monks of the Pleterje Monastery in the southeast of the country. If brandy doesn't appeal, don't worry: Slovenia is now full of excellent craft breweries too.

PRACTICALITIES

HOW TO GET THERE

Many major European cities have direct flights to Ljubljana: the airport is about 30 minutes from the centre. There are also direct trains from Austria, Germany, Hungary and Serbia.

WHERE TO STAY & EAT

For a glamorous sleeping option, choose the Vander Urbani Resort (vanderhotel.com), which brings together four beautifully restored 17th-century buildings in the middle of the Old Town.

Ljubljana's culinary scene is booming. If you're here between mid-March and mid-December, head to the Central Market for the Open Kitchen (odprtakuhna.si), an event held every Friday from 10am to 10pm when local chefs cook up their specialities.

EVENTS

The Ljubljana Festival (ljubljanafestival.si) takes place in July and August, with concerts, opera, theatre and dance, mainly in the open air.

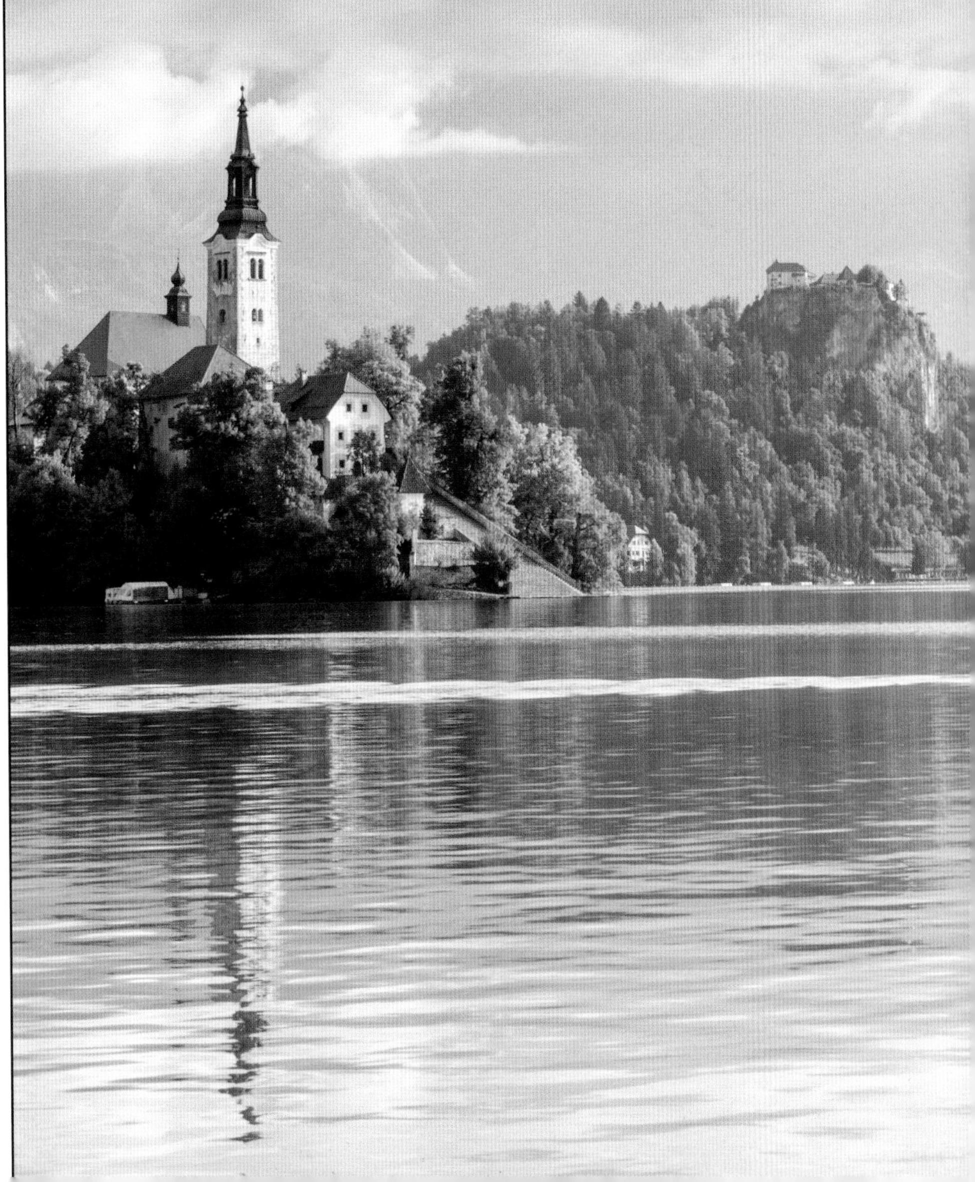

73

ROMANIA

Take a tour of Transylvania
IN CLUJ-NAPOCA

The north of Transylvania in Romania possesses a remarkable collection of natural and cultural riches. Hiking trails crisscross the Carpathian Mountains, magnificent churches and castles lie scattered in forested valleys, and it's straightforward to move from university towns and cities of elegant architecture, such as Sibiu, Bistrița, Sighișoara or Brașov, to remote villages with wooden churches and the occasional rousing tunes of local folk music. The country's second-largest city, Cluj-Napoca, is here too, and contains wonderful Gothic and baroque buildings. Its Old Town, a maze of ancient streets filled with contemporary art galleries and flower-filled gardens, lends it an undeniable appeal. But Cluj-Napoca is also firmly rooted in the 21st century. This student city with its large Hungarian community – the population speaks both Romanian and Hungarian – offers a nightlife scene teeming with busy venues and excellent restaurants. Nearby, a host of towns offer further interesting insights into the region's history, culture and landscapes.

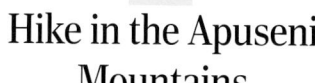

Discover Romulus Vuia Park

On the outskirts of Cluj-Napoca, 5km (3 miles) from the city centre, Romulus Vuia is an open-air ethnographic museum (muzeul-etnografic.ro) featuring superb reconstructions of traditional wooden houses, farms and churches from a multitude of regions – making it the ideal way to discover rural Romania without driving miles. Among many standout buildings, don't miss Cizer Church; its interior is entirely covered with frescoes painted on wood. The park also hosts numerous cultural events, including a permanent exhibition on Transylvanian folk culture from the 18th to the 20th centuries.

Explore Turda & around

South of Cluj-Napoca, Turda is famous for its salt mine (salinaturda.eu), 900m (0.6 miles) of spectacular underground corridors (inset). After a tour of the mine, head into the Cheile Turzii gorge, a natural reserve with abundant fauna, especially birds and butterflies. You can hike through the impressive canyon with limestone walls that measure 300m (984ft) in height, creating a haven of coolness. The gorge is a 30-minute bus ride from Turda, itself 40 minutes by *maxitaxi* from Cluj-Napoca.

Hike in the Apuseni Mountains

Lace up your hiking boots for a day trip to the majestic Apuseni Mountains (parcapuseni.ro). Lined with numerous hiking trails, this massif is a mosaic of landscapes combining karst formations, sinkholes, caves and waterfalls. To get there from Cluj-Napoca, start from Răchițele, a village surrounded by pastures, old farmhouses and pine forests. Allow an hour by bus from Cluj-Napoca to Huedin, then 20 minutes by minibus from Huedin to Răchițele.

Visit Bánffy Castle

The remote village of Bonțida, 30km (19 miles) northeast of Cluj-Napoca, is home to the ancient stones of Bánffy Castle (banffycastle.ro), built in the 17th century. This remarkable building (opposite) was once home to an aristocratic family who lived in this luxurious palace. Today, although damaged by time, the castle is still an enchanting place to visit, easily reached on an hour's bus ride from Cluj-Napoca.

MORE TIME?

SIBIU With its Art Nouveau buildings and prestigious houses, this medieval pearl of Transylvania has an alluring elegance mixed with a bohemian feel, underlined by its many works by street artists. Sibiu is two hours, 15 minutes by car from Cluj-Napoca.
BISTRIȚA Cafe-filled cobbled streets, marvellous Renaissance buildings, colourful houses and whitewashed churches make Bistrița a particularly picturesque town. This peaceful place also provides access to the Bârgău Valley, Dracula's lair in the novel of the same name. The town is two hours by car from Cluj-Napoca.

DRACULA

The Dracula legend is based on Bram Stoker's 1897 book of the same name, which portrays an immortal vampire with a thirst for blood. Inspired by Vlad III, the former prince of Wallachia also known as the Impaler, the novel was a great success and has enjoyed lasting appeal. Near Brașov in Transylvania, Bran Castle (see page 302) became associated with the brutal Vlad III, and consequently with Dracula. Today, the castle attracts visitors from all over the world, while the vampire character Stoker created continues to intrigue and terrify.

Bran Castle (see page 302)

~~~~~~~~ **PRACTICALITIES** ~~~~~~~~

🅿️ HOW TO GET THERE

Cluj-Napoca Airport has international connections, including Paris, Munich Barcelona and Istanbul.

🏕️ WHERE TO STAY

In the heart of the Old Town, the Fullton Hotel (fulltoncentral.ro) has rooms done out with clean, modern decor.

📅 EVENTS

The Transylvania International Film Festival (tiff.ro) is a major event in Cluj-Napoca. Every year in June, movie buffs from around the world come together to celebrate the world of cinema. In early August, electronic music takes centre stage at the Untold Festival (untold.com), a massive, fun gathering.

SOFIA

BOYANA • • VRANA
 • LAKE PANCHAREVO

MOUNT VITOSHA •

• RILA

BULGARIA

74

Learn about Balkan history
IN SOFIA

Surrounded by mountains in the heart of the Balkans, Sofia's strategic location made it a focus for invasion over the centuries, resulting in a mix of civilisations bringing their cultural influences, creating the city we see today. In the Bulgarian capital's centre, St George's Rotunda Church sums up this eventful history. Built in the 4th century on the site of Roman baths, it's been used as a Catholic church, a mosque and an Orthodox church. The nearby remains of a Roman amphitheatre recall the time when Sofia was a popular holiday resort for emperors, while the Banya Bashi Mosque is a reminder of Ottoman rule. Elsewhere, Aleksander Nevski Cathedral, with its green and gold bulbs; St Nicholas' Church and its constellation of gold-leaf mosaics; and the flamboyantly styled National Theatre stem from the Tsarist era. More austere, the buildings of the Largo were constructed in the Stalinist style favoured by the Soviets. The final piece of the history puzzle is the National Palace of Culture, a Neosocialist behemoth that required more steel than the Eiffel Tower.

Life in Soviet times

To see what daily life was like for a Bulgarian family in the 1980s, visit the Red Flat museum (redflatsofia.com). Equipped with an audio guide, you can walk from room to room in this time-warp apartment where objects and anecdotes help you better understand the way locals lived at the end of the communist era. Open drawers, leaf through photo albums, try on clothes – make yourself at home. Tickets can be purchased next door at the Gifted Urban Art & Culture Hub.

Wander the city's parks

Leafy trees, dappled paths and the scent of roses and wisteria – Sofia's parks are a delight. Discover the statues of the Royal Garden, which borders the National Gallery. Mingle with the chessplayers in the Municipal Garden, opposite the Ivan Vazov National Theatre (see previous page). At the foot of the old thermal baths, relax in front of the flowerbeds and let the sound of the fountains relax you. Then finish your tour in Borisova Gradina Park, a favourite of Sofians.

Fresh air on Mt Vitosha

Often capped by snow, Mt Vitosha towers 2290m (7513ft) above Sofia. In just an hour you can leave behind the hustle and bustle of the capital and find yourself in the mountains, surrounded by fir trees. The ski resort of Aleko here is the starting point for a lovely hike to Cherni Vrah peak, where a sublime view of the city is your reward (two-hour round trip). To get there, get off at Vitosha metro station and take bus 66 or a cab to the Simeonovo cable car in Sofia's southern suburbs.

Peruse the treasures of Boyana

A 25-minute cab ride from the centre of Sofia, Boyana Church contains some of the finest remains of medieval art in Eastern Europe. The wall frescoes here are masterpieces of Byzantine pictorial art; the expressive features and harmonious proportions hinting at the later Italian Renaissance. Just north, the National Museum of History (sofiahistorymuseum.bg) is a must for more historical insights, with its solid gold Thracian collection and the Rogozen Treasure: 20kg of silver coins dating from the 5th to 4th centuries BCE.

MORE TIME?

LAKE PANCHAREVO This lake, 16km (10 miles) from the capital, is a popular resort for Sofians who can enjoy a wide range of watersports here. Take the metro from Serdika to Tsarigradsko Shose, then the 1K bus to Banyata Pancharevo.
RILA The Rila Mountains, 120km (75 miles) south of Sofia, are home to a stunning namesake monastery (inset), decorated with sublime wood paintings. While here, take the opportunity to hike into the mountains and discover the Seven Rila Lakes, the result of glacial erosion.

BULGARIAN YOGHURT

What's the secret of ever-popular Bulgarian yoghurt? At the beginning of the 20th century, studies were carried out to explain the exceptional longevity, for the time, of the Bulgarian people. The result of the studies showed a link between long life and the high consumption of local yoghurt. Bulgarian Stamen Grigorov unlocked the secret of this magical dairy product – Lactobacillus Bulgaricus, a bacterium that enables fermentation and, as a probiotic, acts on the intestinal flora by slowing down the decay that causes ageing.

~ PRACTICALITIES ~

🅿 HOW TO GET THERE

Low-cost, direct flights connect many European cities with Sofia.

🏨 WHERE TO STAY & EAT

Avoid the many slightly old-fashioned options and book the nicely decorated and very central R34 Boutique Hotel (r34-boutique-hotel.hotels-sofia.net) or opt for the quieter setting of the Rosslyn Central Park (centralparkhotel.bg), which is situated opposite the National Palace of Culture.

The traditional food served at the Hadjidragan tavern (izbite.com) will leave you with fond memories, as will the dishes at Cosmos (cosmosbg.com) and the tapas at CAVA (facebook.com/CavaWineTapas). At Made in Blue (facebook.com/madeinbluesofia) you can enjoy your meal inside surrounded by quirky decor or outside on the pretty terrace.

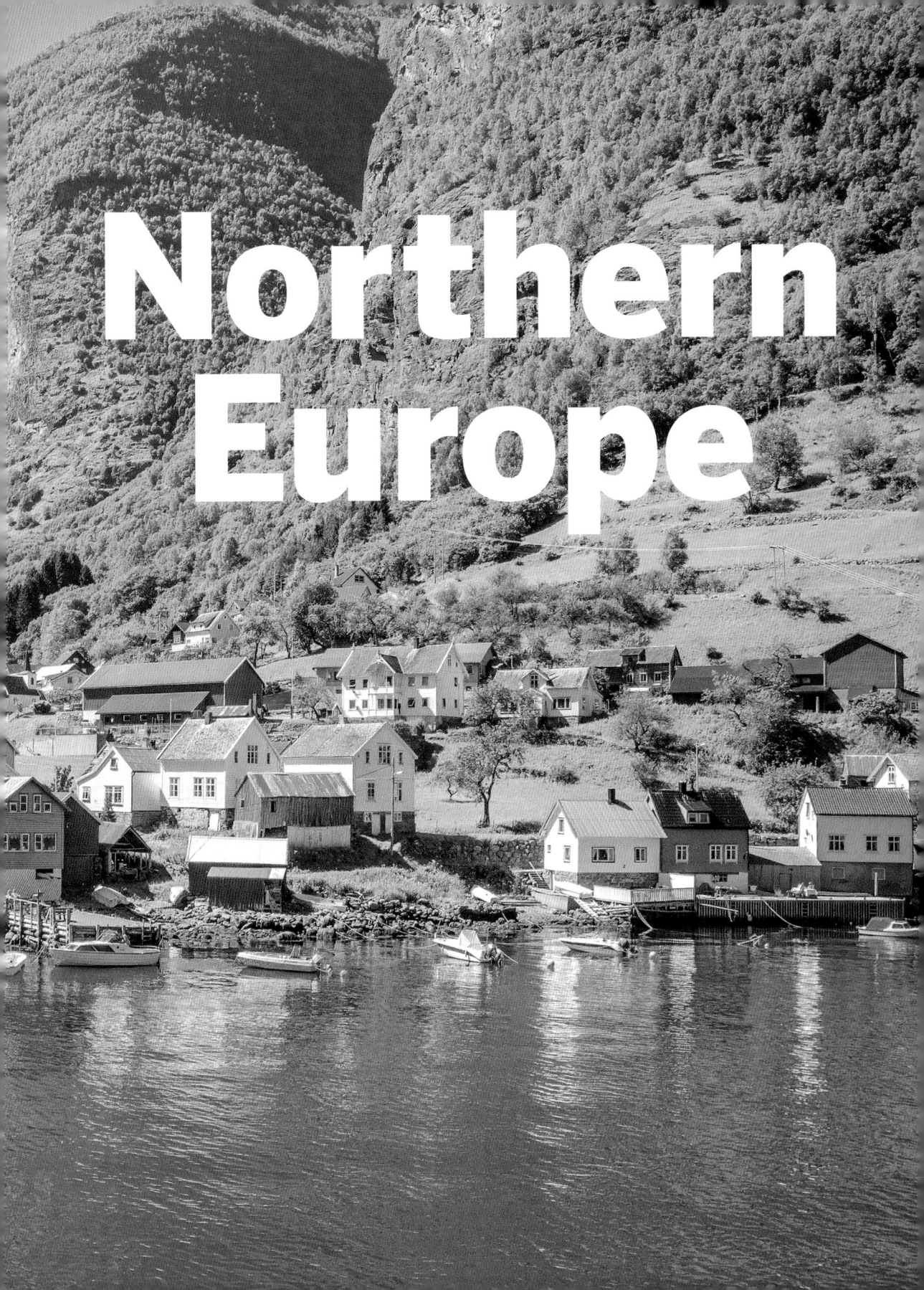

Northern Europe

75

Browse the cool neighbourhoods of SOUTH LONDON

Venture south of the Thames and you find some of London's trendiest, most dynamic and multicultural neighbourhoods. Little known to tourists, these treelined former Victorian suburbs have managed to retain a village-like feel and a welcoming community spirit. The railways reached everywhere in this part of the city, and their once practical but unattractive arches are now home to breweries, bars, restaurants and excellent shops visited by the cool crowd from all across the British capital. You can revel in the multicultural vibe of Brixton, with its many markets (left), African textile stores and world cuisine. Make time to tour the artist studios, rooftop terraces, eclectic shops and unusual bars of Peckham. For a taste of the countryside without leaving the capital, enjoy the almost rural atmosphere of Dulwich and its elegant park, cafes, independent boutiques and excellent art galleries. Then sample the best of London's craft beers in the markets and backstreets of Bermondsey.

Immerse yourself in Brixton's African & Caribbean culture

Start with a little history of the UK's African and Caribbean populations at the Black Cultural Archives (blackculturalarchives.org). Then it's on to Brixton Village Market (see previous page; brixtonvillage. com) for a gastronomic tour of the world in a covered arcade, where over 130 retailers offer an enticing mix of restaurants, cafes, cocktail bars (inset), grocers and stalls of all kinds. Continue your market shopping along Electric Avenue and then browse the boutiques, bars and street-food options of Pop Brixton (popbrixton.org), housed in shipping containers.

Barhop Bermondsey's microbreweries

Embark on a tour of the bars and microbreweries tucked beneath Victorian railway viaducts in Bermondsey, on the banks of the Thames. The Bermondsey Beer Mile (bermondsey-beer-mile. co.uk) features around 30 craft-beer establishments along a 2km (1.2-mile) stretch, including the Barrel Project (thebarrelproject. co.uk) and Kernel Brewery (thekernelbrewery.com). Soak up that beer with food from Maltby Street Market (maltby.st), then fill up on culture at the White Cube Gallery (whitecube.com) and the Fashion and Textile Museum (fashiontextilemuseum.org).

Going off the beaten track in multicultural Peckham

With its multitude of railway-arch and rooftop bars, cultural spaces and clubs, Peckham is one of London's coolest neighbourhoods. The action revolves around Rye Lane, packed with trendy places to have a drink or party. Don't miss the Bussey Building (copelandpark. com), a former factory that now houses a theatre, bars and yoga studios, as well as an open-air cinema (rooftopfilmclub.com) and a vinyl store that transforms into a concert hall in the evening. Another must-see venue is Peckham Levels (peckhamlevels.org), a former car park where food trucks, bars, workshops, exhibitions, a club and lots of other local initiatives can be found across several floors.

Enjoy village life in Dulwich

Stroll through this leafy, peaceful corner of London and you'll discover Dulwich Park, one of London's most picturesque, as well as outdoor cafes, traditional pubs, one-of-a-kind boutiques and one of Britain's oldest public art museums. Designed by architect Sir John Soane and opened in 1817, the Dulwich Picture Gallery (dulwichpicturegallery.org.uk) houses a remarkable collection of British portraits, as well as works by the great European Masters of the 17th and 18th centuries. Lovers of street art will appreciate the graffiti inspired by these more traditional paintings found throughout the neighbourhood (dulwichoutdoor gallery.co.uk).

MORE TIME?

BATTERSEA POWER STATION Abandoned for decades, the legendary Battersea Power Station (batterseapowerstation.co.uk) has finally opened to the public after years of redevelopment. This historic and iconic South London building is now home to stores, restaurants, bars and much more.
TELEGRAPH HILL London has many marvellous viewpoints, but there's one in the south of the city that few visitors know about and that locals love – take in the city-spanning panorama from Telegraph Hill in Lewisham.

WORLD CUISINES

The neighbourhoods of South London are teeming with restaurants, grocery shops, cafes and multi-ethnic food stalls. From Nigerian cafes to Ghanaian restaurants, from Afghan stores to Caribbean cuisine, treat your taste buds to delicious dishes that rarely appear on menus elsewhere. A few places to try include: Tiwa N Tiwa for unpretentious Nigerian cuisine, Kudu (kuducollective.com) for refined South African dishes, and Persepolis (foratasteofpersia. co.uk) for vegan Iranian specialties, all in Peckham; or Fish, Wings & Tings for Caribbean classics in Brixton.

~ **PRACTICALITIES** ~

HOW TO GET THERE & AROUND

From Central London, the Victoria, Northern and Jubilee tube lines, as well as the London Overground and some local trains, serve several stations in the southern neighbourhoods. Brixton and Bermondsey are the most accessible. Once there, it's easy to get around on foot, by bus or by bike.

WHERE TO STAY

Although there is a choice of Airbnb accommodation (at better prices than in the centre), hotels are rarer in South London. The Victoria Inn (victoriainnpeckham. com) in Peckham and The Half Moon (halfmoonhernehill.co.uk), in Herne Hill, near Brixton, offer beautiful designer rooms.

EVENTS

Excellent music festivals take place in South London, including in Brixton, Peckham, Clapham and Crystal Palace. Highlights include Cross the Tracks (xthetracks.com) in May, Mighty Hoopla (mightyhoopla.com) and the Lambeth Country Show (lambethcountryshow.co.uk) in June, and South Facing Festival (southfacingfestival.com) in July and August. Check out the Brixton Academy programme (academymusicgroup.com/ o2academybrixton) for concerts year-round.

76

ENGLAND

Have some seaside fun
IN BRIGHTON

Renowned for its long pebble beach, colourful boutiques and quirky British charm, London's favourite seaside resort, Brighton, offers a fun-filled getaway just one hour south of the capital. This city on the Channel coast in the county of East Sussex has made the most of its setting and has enjoyed a shifting assortment of visitors over the last 250 years, going from a small fishing village to a renowned health resort in the 18th century, and from a middle-class retreat in the 19th century to a hugely popular tourist destination in the 20th and 21st. For a seagull's view of the city, Channel and hills of the South Downs, ascend the Brighton i360 observation tower. Watch the sun set over the beach, then dive into a nightlife that's as lively as it is friendly – start with a pint in a traditional pub and finish by showing off your best moves on a dance floor. Finally, round out your south-coast sojourn with some further exploration on side trips along the Channel and inland, travelling between scenic fishing villages, quaint towns and famous white-chalk cliffs.

Shop in the colourful Lanes

The historic heart of Brighton is The Lanes neighbourhood, home to independent boutiques, old-fashioned pubs and winding streets and alleys. A northern, more bohemian extension of The Lanes, North Laine is packed with unusual eating options, thrift shops and tattoo parlours. If you're a fan of retro fashion, check out Snoopers Paradise (snoopersparadise.co.uk): two floors of bric-a-brac, antiques and bargains up for grabs.

Discover the unusual history of the Royal Pavilion

A visit to the Royal Pavilion (inset) is a visit to a unique palace finished in 1823 for King George IV in an Anglo-Indo-Arabic-Chinese style. A bewildering mix of architecture, with minarets, domes and opulent interiors, it just about works and shows George's no-expense-spared approach to design. The collection at the Brighton Museum & Art Gallery (brightonmuseums.org.uk) opposite is equally eclectic.

A pint in a traditional pub

Brighton isn't short of lively places to have a drink or party the night away, but if there's one British experience not to be missed, it's ordering a pint in a centuries-old pub full of charm and history. One of the city's best is The Bath Arms (batharms.pub), open since 1864. If you prefer a more modern venue, The Walrus (thewalrusbrighton.com) is an excellent choice loved by locals, with quirky decor and subdued lighting.

Back to childhood at Brighton Palace Pier

Enjoy a lunch of fish and chips on the beach or indulge in mouth-watering dishes at Shelter Hall food market (shelterhall.co.uk) on the seafront before sampling the many delights of Brighton's famous Palace Pier (see previous page; brightonpier.co.uk). Arcade games, funfair rides, candy stalls and bars are all on offer along its 525m (1722ft), hovering above the water since 1899.

Walk along the White Cliffs

There's nothing like an invigorating stroll to clear the head after a night out, so follow the superb coastline of the Seven Sisters (opposite), a country park bordered by white-chalk cliffs between Brighton and Eastbourne, and shake off those cobwebs. Hiking trails, magnificent views and a variety of wildlife make this an ideal destination for outdoor enthusiasts.

MORE TIME?

LEWES Pretty Lewes is a small medieval town with quaint streets and a castle worth visiting. It's easily accessible from Brighton, just a 15-minute train ride away.

ARUNDEL Perched on a hill in its eponymous town west of Brighton, ancient Arundel Castle (arundelcastle.org) is one of the oldest and most beautiful in Britain, dating back to 1067. Take in the wonderful views over the surrounding countryside and be sure to visit its appealing gardens.

TEEN SPIRITS

In the 1960s, two subcultures and rival gangs, the 'rockers' and the 'mods', repeatedly clashed on Brighton Beach; memorable brawls that made international headlines, as rebellious British youth tried to forge identities based on musical choices and dress codes: rock'n'roll and biker looks for some, modern jazz and tailored outfits for others. Today, the city retains a rebellious streak, but these days it's more bohemian, avant-garde and open-minded.

PRACTICALITIES

🚆 HOW TO GET THERE

Trains from Central London reach Brighton in around an hour. Direct trains from Gatwick Airport take just 30 minutes. Once there, the city is small enough to easily get around on foot.

🏨 WHERE TO STAY & EAT

Artist Residence (artistresidence.co.uk) and My Brighton (myhotels.com) are conveniently located and among the city's coolest sleeping options.

Don't leave without trying the fish and chips at English's (englishs.co.uk), a local institution; the Sunday roast at the traditional Lion & Lobster pub (thelionandlobster.co.uk); or the Indian cuisine at the Chilli Pickle (thechillipickle.com).

📅 EVENTS

The Brighton Festival (brightonfestival.org) is the highlight of the year, bringing together a multitude of arts, from music to theatre to literature for three weeks in May. Brighton Pride (brighton-pride. org), one of the UK's biggest, takes place in August.

To the Cotswolds

OXFORD

WATFORD

LONDON

Thames

South Downs

ENGLAND

Make a literary odyssey
TO OXFORD

O ne hour by train from London is the city of Oxford and its eponymous university. One of the oldest universities in the world, it is said to have been founded in 1096. Over the centuries, its renowned colleges, such as Christ Church, Magdalen and Trinity have seen thousands of students pass through, including Sir Thomas More (a close adviser to Henry VIII), poet and playwright Oscar Wilde, and politicians Margaret Thatcher, Tony Blair and Bill Clinton. Author JRR Tolkien even taught there. The city revolves around its multiple colleges, but does have other attractions too. The Pitt Rivers Museum (prm.ox.ac.uk) will win over anyone with an interest in anthropology, while the Ashmolean Museum (ashmolean.org) brings together works from Antiquity to the Renaissance. Two other highlights are the Bodleian Library, one of the oldest university libraries on the planet, and the Radcliffe Camera, probably the most photographed monument in town. And when it comes to literary heritage, Oxford is second to none – many writers have found inspiration in its handsome streets.

Wave your wizard's wand

The colleges of Oxford University influenced JK Rowling, author of one of the world's greatest book series following the exploits of Harry Potter. Visit Christ Church (chch.ox.ac.uk) for a tour of the Great Hall (see previous page), inspiration for the dining room in Hogwarts, the wizarding school Harry attends. The long tables, the portraits on the walls, the teachers' table were all replicated in the movies. To get there, take the same staircase the actors used in the films. Other Harry Potter locations in Oxford include the Bodleian Library's Divinity School (visit.bodleian.ox.ac.uk), used as backdrops for the Hogwarts library and infirmary.

Along the Thames

The Thames that flows through Oxford is a very different river to the one found in London. It's much narrower, more peaceful and even has a different, Oxford-unique name, the Isis. For a saunter along its banks, walk down Poplar Walk opposite the entrance to Christ Church College, then join Meadow Walk. In summer, bring a picnic to enjoy with a view of the city; in autumn, the changing colours of the trees add to the charm of the experience.

Follow in Lewis Carroll's footsteps

Christchurch's Great Hall also had a real-life famous diner in the form of writer Lewis Carroll who was a teacher at the college. One of the stained-glass windows in the room references the author and his best-known work, *Alice's Adventures in Wonderland*. Carroll (born Charles Dodgson) was very close to the dean and his three daughters, Edith, Alice and Lorina Liddell. One day, during a boat trip on the nearby Thames, he invented the story in which Alice is the heroine, and which still enthrals generations of readers today. You can immerse yourself in this world at Alice's Shop (inset), a grocery store from Carroll's time that's now a souvenir shop.

Move between literary worlds

Less well known than Lewis Carroll and JK Rowling, Philip Pullman, a former Oxford student at Exeter College, is famous for the *His Dark Materials* trilogy in which a tragic love story plays out across a multiverse of different worlds. Key locations in the books are fictional Jordan College, home to main character Lyra (in the TV adaptation of the books, New College stood in for it) and Oxford Botanic Garden.

MORE TIME?

HARRY POTTER STUDIOS To complete your introduction to wizarding, visit Harry Potter Studios (wbstudiotour.co.uk) in Watford, north of London.
THE COTSWOLDS The bucolic idyll that is the Costwolds is just 30km (19 miles) from Oxford. It's impossible not to fall in love with the region's rolling landscape dotted with impossibly cute villages, all grouped together in England's second-largest protected area (after the Lake District).

AFTERNOON TEA

In Oxford, as in many other places in the UK, the tradition of taking afternoon tea is alive and well. While strolling along High St, take a tasty break at the Grand Café (thegrandcafe. co.uk). Behind its sky-blue neoclassical facade you'll find some of the world's best scones, accompanied by a delicious English tea (there's plenty to choose from) to wash them down with. Even more chic, the Randolph Hotel (graduatehotels. com/oxford-uk) also offers afternoon tea in a refined setting, serving up sweet and savoury delicacies and the obligatory tea.

HOW TO GET THERE

Trains to Oxford run frequently throughout the day from London's Paddington and Marylebone stations, taking approximately one hour. If flying into London Heathrow, you can reach Oxford by direct bus (80 minutes).

WHERE TO EAT

For breakfast, head to the Oxford Brunch Bar (oxfordbrunchbar. co.uk), where cosy decor and a gourmet menu (try the porridge) come with reasonable prices. For dinner, opt for the Turf Tavern. This 12th-century pub is a little hidden away, but if you manage to find it, you'll be treated to a pint of local ale and traditional pub food in a historic setting.

Lake District

IRISH SEA

WORSLEY

LIVERPOOL • • MANCHESTER

Peak District

• CHESTER

PORTMEIRION   WALES

Snowdonia National Park   ENGLAND

ENGLAND

78

Find inspiration

IN NORTHWEST ENGLAND

Welcome to the northwest of England, a land of industry and brick cities steeped in history. And as soon as you move away from the urban areas, you'll find it's a rural land too – full of fields and hills and dotted with lakes and peaceful villages. Start your adventure in **Manchester** (left) with a stroll along the **canals**, which give an idea of the scale of the city's former textile production, then take refuge from the likely rain in one of the city's museums or pull up a chair in a cosy pub. Next, head for **Liverpool** (one hour by train)

for a musical tour in the footsteps of the Beatles. Explore the Cavern Quarter and learn everything about the Fab Four at the **Beatles Museum**, followed by some music at the **Cavern Club**, where the famous quartet made their debut back in the early '60s. A reminder of Liverpool's former role as an important port at the mouth of the Mersey can be found in **Albert Dock** (see page 327), where old warehouses have been converted into pubs and museums. And then, city life enjoyed, make time for some outdoor escapades in the nearby countryside.

Hike in the Peak District

Just outside Manchester, the Peak District National Park (inset; peakdistrict.gov.uk) has spectacular landscapes that draw hikers from across the country. Its rocky escarpments wind their way through a string of limestone valleys, gorges, caves, lakes and wild moors, a parade of natural features that can be much less crowded than other national parks. Just one hour by train from Manchester, Buxton, a handsome town in its own right, is the gateway to the Peak District.

Marvel at the Maritime Museum

In one of the world's former largest ports, in the heart of the legendary Liverpool Docks stands the huge Maritime Museum (liverpoolmuseums.org.uk/maritime-museum). In addition to evoking the city's fascinating maritime past, the museum's four floors do an engrossing job of covering the hopes and dreams of the millions of migrants who set sail from the city to try their luck in the US, Canada and Australia, and of covering Liverpool's role in the transatlantic slave trade.

Wander the picturesque streets of Worsley

The pretty small town of Worsley can be visited on foot along a 5km (3-mile) circuit that follows the banks of the Bridgewater Canal. Walk past numerous barges moored on the water, follow the route through a maze of half-timbered, mock Tudor houses and round off the trip with a visit to the recently opened RHS Garden Bridgewater. Worsley has excellent public-transport connections with Manchester, 9km (5.6 miles) away.

Fall in love with medieval Chester

One of Britain's most important Roman strongholds, Chester has preserved a wealth of historical remains from over the centuries. Among them are the red sandstone walls, originally built in Roman times and stretching for 3km (2 miles). The city is also home to a Benedictine abbey turned cathedral, as well as the iconic Rows, whose Victorian buildings now contain independent shops. To reach this charming city, allow one hour by bus from Manchester or Liverpool.

MORE TIME?

LAKE DISTRICT This national park (lakedistrict.gov.uk), one of the most beautiful in Britain, is covered with glacial lakes, green hills and rugged mountains, including England's highest, Scafell Pike.
SNOWDONIA Another national park worth a visit, Snowdonia (aka Eryri National Park; snowdonia.gov.wales) lies in northwest Wales. Its mountainous terrain is riddled with rivers, lakes and attractive villages, including Portmeirion and its unusual architecture.

THE FAB FOUR

Originally from Liverpool, the famous Beatles left an indelible mark on the city where they had their first successes. John Lennon, Paul McCartney, Ringo Starr and George Harrison experienced a meteoric rise to fame in the 1960s, leaving their mark on rock history with classic like 'Hey Jude' and 'Let It Be'. Two of the four band members may no longer be with us, but the Fab Four legend continues to draw music-loving travellers to the city where museums and music venues recall the heady days of Beatlemania.

PRACTICALITIES

HOW TO GET THERE

Manchester Airport has global connections. The city's main train stations have services from across the UK, as does Liverpool.

WHERE TO STAY

To be in the thick of the action in Manchester, find accommodation in the streets around the cathedral, Piccadilly Gardens or the canal.

EVENTS

Among the many events that liven up the streets of Manchester and Liverpool are the former's Parklife (parklife. uk.com), the country's largest contemporary music festival; and the latter's International Music Festival (limfestival. com) in July, a hugely popular music gathering featuring the biggest stars in pop, reggae, rock and soul.

79

ENGLAND

A tale of two cities
IN BRISTOL & BATH

For a weekend of contrasts, spend time in two of southwest England's most popular destinations. For British creativity at its best, start in the old port and current cool hot-spot that is Bristol. Street art, concerts, museums – the cultural life here has much to offer. Explore the marina and visit **SS Great Britain** (ssgreatbritain.org). This was the largest passenger steamship in the world when it was built in the mid-19th century and carried passengers all the way to Australia. Nearby, **M Shed** covers the history of Bristol and its people. Just outside the city centre, enjoy a meal at one of Cargo's street-food locations (wappingwharf.co.uk/cargo), housed in shipping containers. For a complete change of scene (and century), with a dash of Jane Austen thrown in for good measure, visit genteel Bath, just 21km (13 miles) east. Its **Pulteney Bridge** (left), beautiful gardens and grand architecture will transport you back two centuries, and the canal offers some lovely walks and bike rides along its banks. Take tea at the Pump Room and live your best *Bridgerton* life.

Finding Banksy

Bristol's undisputed celebrity is Banksy. The street artist's identity is unknown but they were born in Bristol and their politically charged, anti-establishment works can be found in many of their hometown's neighbourhoods. One of the most famous is *The Girl with the Pierced Eardrum*, inspired by Vermeer's *The Girl with the Pearl* Earring, hidden in an alleyway by the marina. Go in search of their works by exploring the city using the map sold by the tourist office, or book a place on a Bristol Street Art Tour.

Bathe like the Romans

As the name suggests, Bath is known for its thermal baths, built by the Romans around 70 CE. The historic sight is well preserved and well worth a visit to (pun intended) soak up the atmosphere and sample the spring water at the end. It's not possible to swim here anymore though, so to enjoy the city's naturally heated waters, head to Thermae Spa Bath (thermaebathspa.com). The rooftop pool offers views across the city's rooftops, best contemplated at sunset.

Follow in Jane Austen's footsteps

It's impossible to ignore the life and work of the famous author of *Pride and Prejudice* (among many other novels) on a visit to Bath. The Jane Austen Museum (janeausten.co.uk), in the centre of the city, retraces the years she spent here and explores her vision of the society of the time. Discover interactive displays, maps of her former homes and letters from the writer, before biting into a traditional 19th-century snack in the museum's tearoom.

Escape to Clifton

After admiring the impressive Clifton Suspension Bridge (opposite) spanning the River Avon, Victorian facades, boutiques and cafes await you in this chic neighbourhood to the west of Bristol – the terrace of Primrose Café (primrosecafe.co.uk) is a top choice for brunch or a homemade pastry. The elegant domain of Bristol's wealthy 19th-century merchants, Clifton has retained a village atmosphere that's very different from the rest of the city.

MORE TIME?

STONEHENGE There's something mesmerising about stone circles, and Britain's most famous, Stonehenge (inset), can be visited on a day trip from Bristol or Bath. These mysterious monoliths on Salisbury Plain have fascinated pilgrims and the curious for over 5000 years, and seeing them at sunrise or sunset makes the experience even more magical. Book your tickets several months in advance, as the number of visitors is limited. To get there by public transport, take the train to Salisbury, then a bus to Stonehenge.

A ROYAL CRESCENT

It's definitely worth wandering northwest of Bath's city centre to admire the gorgeous architecture of the Circus and, just beyond, the magnificent Royal Crescent. The Georgian houses that make up this elegant block are built in an arc and border a huge park. It's easy to imagine what life was like for aristocrats strolling here in the late 18th and early 19th centuries – a life captured in the hit TV series *Bridgerton*, which was partly filmed here. If you'd like to learn more about Georgian Bath, push open the door of number one – the house has been converted into a museum and has some great insights into the period.

 HOW TO GET THERE

Trains to both Bath and Bristol run from London's Paddington Station (one hour, 20 minutes and one hour, 45 minutes, respectively). There are frequent trains between the two cities.

WHERE TO EAT

On Abbey Green, a small square behind Bath Abbey, try a delicious Bath bun in the tearoom that bears the sweet treat's name – the recipe for this local pastry dates back to the 18th century. Don't forget the traditional cup of tea to accompany it.

Alderney

FRANCE

DIÉLETTE ●

Guernsey
Herm
●
SAINT-PIERRE-
PORT

BARNEVILLE-
CARTERET

Sark

ENGLISH CHANNEL

To Granville

Écréhou

● TRINITY

Jersey

BRITISH ISLES

Take it easy

IN THE CHANNEL ISLANDS

Jersey, Guernsey, Alderney, Sark and Herm make
up the Channel Islands,
**a self-governing archipelago
that's British but sits just a few
miles from the French coast.**
Though all the islands feel a world
away from traffic and urban stress,
the two largest still offer plenty
of traveller appeal: **Jersey** has
a population of almost 100,000
and lots of good shopping, pubs
and historic sites; **Guernsey**,
second biggest, has miles of
coastline alternating between
beaches and cliffs, an unspoiled
interior and centuries-old ports.

To escape civilisation, head to the
smaller islands, and to escape
cars completely, visit Herm (left)
and Sark where the only transport allowed is tractors, bikes,
horses – and your own two legs.
All the islands offer energising
walks along the **English Channel**,
stop-offs in rocky coves, swimming breaks in bays carpeted with
golden sand – and the chance to
hear local dialects that stem from
medieval Norman French. Which-
ever island you pick, a relaxed
atmosphere with as much or as
little activity as you fancy will
tempt you to extend your stay.

333

Nature at its best in Jersey & Les Écréhous

Known as the Isle of Flowers, the largest Channel Island, Jersey (inset), is particularly resplendent in late spring when the blooms are out. It's best explored by bike, cycling through charming villages past delightful cottages, or on foot, following a hike on its steep cliffs. A small, uninhabited archipelago located 11km (6.8 miles) northeast of Jersey, Les Écréhous is made up of rocks and reefs, ideal for those who love deserted landscapes. Grey seals and dolphins frequent the area and can be spotted on a RIB ride to the islands.

Follow Victor Hugo & go into exile in Guernsey

Guernsey, the Green Island, has a lot to offer in terms of pretty harbours, enticing beaches, English-style gardens, old castles, maritime fortifications and trails through postcard-perfect countryside. Above Saint Peter Port, the island's adorably cute capital, visit Hauteville House, the home-museum where French author Victor Hugo spent the last 15 years of his 19-year exile and where he wrote *Les Misérables*.

Laze on the beaches of Herm, Sark & Alderney

On a sunny day, the fine sandy beaches of these islands, lapped by turquoise waves, seem to mimic the Caribbean. On Herm and Sark (opposite), cars are forbidden, meaning you can expect absolute peace and quiet. On Alderney, you can take the only railway in the Channel Islands in carriages once used on the London Underground.

Drive around Jersey in a classic car

Jaguar or Aston Martin? Or maybe the MG V8 roadster? In Trinity Parish, Jersey Classic Car Hire (jerseyclassichire.com) rents out iconic vehicles dating from the early 1930s to the mid-1970s for you to cruise around the island in. For a longer trip, the same company also offers 1960s Volkswagen Kombis.

MORE TIME?

NORMANDY COAST The D-Day beaches on the Normandy coast are endless ribbons of sand bordered by wild dunes. The Vélomaritime allows you to discover them by bike, stopping at the legendary Sword, Juno and Gold beaches along the way. And if you'd like to learn about WWII, head for the Caen Memorial Museum (memorial-caen.com). Ferries run from Jersey and Guernsey to ports in Normandy.

FISHING ON FOOT

The tides in the English Channel can be impressive, leaving the seascape looking like the lunar surface at low tide and like a sparkling blue bay at high tide. In Jersey, at low tide, the island almost doubles in size, and that's the time to get out the nets to go hunting on foot for crabs, razorclams and abalone. Be sure to check tide times and take a guide with you if you're just starting out.

~~~ PRACTICALITIES ~~~

HOW TO GET THERE & AROUND

Jersey, Guernsey and Alderney have airports, but only the first two have international connections as well as domestic flights. Ferries operate from UK and French ports with several a day in high season (reduced schedule in winter) and also run between the islands themselves, meaning visiting a few or all of the islands is possible on a single trip.

81

WALES

Visit the past & the future
IN CARDIFF

Wedged between an ancient fortress and an ultramodern waterfront, the capital of Wales has one foot in the past and the other firmly in the 21st century. After seeing a decline from the 1950s, the world's former leading coal port has since reinvented itself and now presents visitors with a number of architectural innovations on its bay (left), including the Senedd (the Welsh National Assembly; overleaf) and the superb Wales Millennium Centre, the country's leading arts venue. Another iconic structure is the Millennium Stadium, which looks like a spaceship and hosts rugby matches – the game is a veritable religion in this part of the world. Modern and dynamic, Cardiff is also a city of shops, bars and restaurants, but its past is not hard to find too. At the southern end of Bute Park, the favourite green space for locals with the River Taff flowing through it, is Cardiff Castle (see page 339; cardiffcastle.com): a fascinating combination of Roman remains, Norman castle and extravagant neogothic features added in the 19th century, all perfectly capturing the essence of this old but new city.

Spot extinct species at the National Museum

In addition to an impressive collection of paintings, including 19th-century masters (Monet, Renoir, Van Gogh), Cardiff's National Museum (museum.wales/cardiff) has a zoology department with 1800 animals, including 10 specimens of extinct species, such as the thylacine, the dodo, the moa, the great auk, the passenger pigeon and the huia. Most impressive are the complete skeleton of a mammoth and that of a whale washed up on the Welsh coast.

Visit a fairy-tale castle

On a wooded hill above the village of Tongwynlais on the northern edge of Cardiff, Castell Coch is a fine example of Victorian era neogothic architecture. Using the 11th-century remains of a previous fortress as a base, architect William Burges built this fairy-tale fantasy for the 3rd Marquess of Bute, the richest man in the world at the time.

Feasting at Riverside Market

Every Sunday from 10am, the embankment alongside the Taff and opposite the rugby stadium is taken over by the stalls of Riverside Market. Vendors sell everything from cheeses, sourdough and jams to vegetables, charcuterie and pastries. Create your own picnic and enjoy it on the chairs along the river.

A glimpse of the Iron Ring

A quick train ride north of Cardiff gets you to huge Caerphilly Castle, a 13th-century fortress that served as a model for the castles of the Iron Ring, the series of forts built in North Wales by English King Edward I (1272–1307) to secure English control there. If Caerphilly piques your interest, head north to indulge your castle curiosity in Harlech, Conwy, Caernarfon and Beaumaris.

Boarding a floating bus

From Bute Park, two waterbuses (bute-park.com/attraction/water-taxi) take turns on the River Taff to ferry you to Mermaid Quay in the heart of Cardiff Bay – a pleasant and original way to discover the city. Departures are every 30 minutes from 10.30am to 5pm, and commentary cruises are available.

MORE TIME?

TINTERN ABBEY Some 48km (30 miles) east of Cardiff, the remains of this sprawling abbey on the banks of the River Wye have inspired poets, painters and lovers of romantic ruins for centuries.
BRECON BEACONS This heather-covered national park can be explored on foot or by bike and is just 50km (31 miles) north of the capital.
GOWER PENINSULA The Gower Peninsula's caramel-coloured beaches and rugged cliffs justly merit its Area of Outstanding Natural Beauty status. It's 100km (62 miles) west of Cardiff.

RUGBY MANIA

If you're lucky enough to be in Cardiff on a match day, it would be a crime not to take advantage of seeing some rugby in the country where it's almost a national religion. To see the fervour unleashed by this sport, get your ticket (between £15 and £50) and settle in for a few hours of sporting passion. In Wales, as in the south of England, rugby is a 15-a-side game, traditionally played by the middle and upper classes who are ever keen to declare that football is a gentleman's sport played by hooligans, whereas rugby is a hooligan's sport played by gentlemen.

~~~~ PRACTICALITIES ~~~~

WHEN TO GO

June and July see drier, more predictable weather than the alternating sunny spells and sudden showers that prevail from March to May. Early autumn warmth is possible in September and October.

HOW TO GET THERE

By train, it takes two hours from London's Paddington Station to reach Cardiff. The city's airport has both national and international flights.

WHERE TO STAY

Accommodation is not a problem in Cardiff. Between hotels, B&Bs and hostels, there's something for every budget. There's even a campsite (cardiffcaravanpark. co.uk) just a 15-minute walk from the city centre.

82

A taste of Scotland
IN GLASGOW & AROUND

Glasgow may not be as popular with visitors as Scotland's capital Edinburgh, but the country's largest city has a whole lot to discover. A rich industrial past dating back to Victorian times, numerous creations by architect **Charles Rennie Mackintosh**, a 15th-century cathedral, and contemporary art that has taken over the walls of former factories and shipyards (inspiring **street-art** trails) are just some of its attractions. Also on your weekend agenda should be the West End neighbourhood, home to the university (left), part of which can be visited; Kelvingrove Art Gallery and Museum (overleaf) and its adjoining park; and the city's botanic gardens. And beyond Glasgow lie some of Scotland's greatest sights. **Loch Lomond and the Trossachs National Park** (lochlomond-trossachs.org) – Scotland's first national park, created in 2002 – is only 30km (19 miles) away, accessible by public transport. Also easy to reach are **Stirling**, with a castle and Old Town that transports visitors back to medieval times; and the jagged coastline of **southern Argyll**, a ferry ride from the city.

Take a history course at Stirling

It's impossible not to fall in love with Stirling's Old Town and its beautifully preserved cobbled streets. Follow them up to the castle (stirlingcastle.scot) and inspect the refurbished Royal Palace interiors. Equally interesting is the cemetery below, surrounding the Church of the Holy Rude where James VI of Scotland (later James I of England) was crowned. Breathtaking views of the region and the Trossachs are a bonus. Descend the Back Walk to discover other historic sites, such as the Old Bridge and the Old Town Jail.

Visit the castle of Doune

If you've watched the TV show *Outlander* you'll recognise Doune Castle as soon as you see it. Although the main filming studios are located in Cumbernauld on the outskirts of Glasgow, many scenes were shot on location and in period buildings, with Doune serving as the MacKenzie clan's home for two series, hosting some memorable episodes. During your visit, you'll hear the show's lead actor, Sam Heughan, on the audio guide, alongside Monty Python member Terry Gilliam – Doune also starred in *Monty Python and the Holy Grail*.

Climb the Wallace Monument

Erected in 1869, the Wallace Monument (opposite; national wallacemonument.com) can be seen from Stirling and pays tribute to William Wallace, the hero of Scottish independence who won the Battle of Stirling Bridge in 1297 against the English (the film *Braveheart* is dedicated to him, despite taking many historical liberties). Visitors with stamina can climb the monument's 246 steps for wide-ranging views at the top.

Get away from it all in Argyll

West of Glasgow, southern Argyll and its islands is an excellent destination for exploring Scotland off the beaten track – and it's less expensive than more touristy Loch Lomond too. Dunoon on the Cowal Peninsula and Rothesay on the picturesque Isle of Bute are Victorian seaside resorts with nostalgic charm. They're within easy reach of Glasgow, less than two hours by train, bus or car and ferry. The untamed land around them, pierced by sea lochs, forms peninsulas and inlets with some of the most spectacular coastal scenery in the country.

MORE TIME?

WEST HIGHLAND WAY Scotland's legendary hiking trail runs from Milngavie, north of Glasgow, to the heart of the Highlands in Fort William, at the foot of Ben Nevis. Its 154km (96 miles) take five to seven days to complete, traversing lochs, bens (mountains) and forests.

ISLE OF ARRAN Arran is the epitome of Scotland's diverse landscapes. The mountainous north is a delight for experienced walkers, while cyclists can strike out on the coastal road that circles the island. Take the ferry at Ardrossan (about one hour from Glasgow) and disembark at Brodick (one hour, 10 minutes crossing).

MUNRO BAGGING

One of the great draws of hiking in Scotland is 'bagging the Munros', or climbing the mountains over 914m (3000ft), listed by Sir Hugh Munro in 1891. There are no fewer than 282 in all, and Ben Lomond (ben meaning 'mountain' in Gaelic) is one of the most popular. The ascent (974m/3196ft) is not too difficult and offers sweeping views of Loch Lomond and the surrounding area. Allow five hours round trip (11km/7 miles). You don't need to go far for more Munro bagging – besides Ben Lomond, Loch Lomond and the Trossachs National Park offers 20 other peaks for those up to the challenge.

~~~ **PRACTICALITIES** ~~~

🅿️ HOW TO GET THERE

Glasgow Airport is Scotland's main entry point for flights, and welcomes arrivals from around the world. From the city, you can then reach Balloch (at the southern edge of Loch Lomond) and Stirling by bus or train. A 'demand-responsive transport' system operates in parts of the national park to get visitors around, costing the same as a bus.

🍽️ WHERE TO EAT

Push open the door of the Oak Tree Inn (theoaktreeinn.co.uk) in Balmaha on Loch Lomond's eastern shore and enjoy a warm welcome and an extensive menu. Trying haggis is a must, but start with cullen skink, a thick soup blending haddock, potatoes and onions that is very Scottish and very tasty.

Loch Ness
Skye
Scottish
Highlands

Ben Nevis
Glen Coe

Loch Lomond &
The Trossachs
National Park
—— Ben Lomond
LUSS ●
EDINBURGH ●
Loch Lomond
GLASGOW ●

SCOTLAND

83

Conquer the wild heart of
SCOTLAND

Magnificent cliffs, lush green valleys, endless moorland and expansive panoramas: Scotland's most iconic landscapes are easily savoured on a road trip from its two largest cities, Glasgow and Edinburgh. Wind your way north through the splendid Scottish Highlands; marvelling at Glenfinnan Viaduct (overleaf), made famous by the Harry Potter movies; trying to spy the famous monster in Loch Ness; and exploring the Isle of Skye (left), with its powdery beaches, cute villages and whisky distilleries. Scotland also has imposing castles, ancient towns, dramatic mountains and thundering waterfalls. The UK's highest peak is here and relatively simple to climb. And for tragic history there's nowhere more heartbreaking than the valley of Glencoe. No wonder these iconic landscapes feature in so many cult films and TV series, from *Highlander* to James Bond to *Outlander*. Don't forget your walking shoes too, because while a car is the most practical way to get around, hiking is the ideal complement to driving, allowing you to really get to know the beauty of this country.

Learn the tragic history of Glencoe

Glencoe, Scotland's most famous valley, combines wonderful scenery with a terrible past. The beauty of this tranquil glen could almost make you forget that it was the scene of a bloody massacre in 1692, when soldiers of the Campbell clan murdered 38 members of the MacDonald clan. Some of the glen's prettiest walks, notably the one leading to the Lost Valley, follow the paths taken by clan members trying to escape their attackers, and where many of them perished in the snow.

Visit the famous Eilean Donan Castle

Just before crossing the bridge to the Isle of Skye, stop off at Eilean Donan Castle (opposite; eileandonancastle.com). Built in the 13th century on a rocky island on the edge of a loch, this is Scotland's most photographed fortress. After centuries of neglect, it was bought by the MacRae clan in 1911 and fully restored, creating the classic image of a Scottish castle as you'd imagine it, with its medieval towers, grand fireplaces and hunting trophies on the walls.

Explore the riches of Loch Lomond

A 'loch' in Scottish Gaelic refers to a body of water, whether fresh or salt, and can refer to a lake, an inlet or even a bay. If Loch Ness is the best-known, Loch Lomond, Britain's largest lake in the heart of the Trossachs National Park, is among the most spectacular. This haven of peace, just 32km (20 miles) north of Glasgow, is bordered by forests and surrounded by hills, including Ben Lomond, accessible on foot – its summit offers unmatched views of the lake, its islands and the mountains. The attractive village of Luss on the west bank is also worth a visit for its flower-decorated cottages and Scottish craft stores.

Getaway to the Isle of Skye

In a country renowned for show-stopping landscapes, the Isle of Skye can still wow. It's the largest island in the Inner Hebrides and provides some of Scotland's best-known wild terrain. From the brooding Cuillin range and the strange pinnacles of the Old Man of Storr to the waterfalls of the Fairy Pools, the basalt formations of Kilt Rock and the sea cliffs and lighthouse of Neist Point, a memorable photo opportunity awaits visitors at every turn.

MORE TIME?

BEN NEVIS Whether you're a hardened hiker or a nature nerd, this challenge is for you. Climbing the UK's highest peak, Ben Nevis (1345m/4413ft), is achievable for anyone with good fitness and is an unforgettable experience.
RAASAY ISLAND Stop off at Raasay Island, reached by ferry from the Isle of Skye in 25 minutes. In addition to its gorgeous beaches and walking trails, there's a whisky and gin distillery housed in a derelict Gothic hotel and the ruins of Brochel Castle.

A CELTIC LAND

From the use of tartan to make kilts to the sound of bagpipes in popular music, local Scottish culture is still very much a part of people's lives today. When it comes to gastronomy, porridge, oatcakes and haggis are a must when eating out in Scotland. As for the famous Scotch whisky, the national drink that has been distilled for at least five centuries, there are over a hundred distilleries still in operation, producing dozens of varieties of single malt that can often be tasted on guided tours.

 PRACTICALITIES

HOW TO GET THERE

Rent a car in Glasgow or Edinburgh and head north. Scottish roads are well maintained and toll-free. Drive on the left, don't forget speed limits and remember to book your ferry trips to the islands in advance (calmac.co.uk).

WHERE TO STAY

There's a wide range of accommodation in the Highlands, from hotels and campsites to quirky places and eco-friendly alternatives. Kingshouse Hotel (kingshousehotel.co.uk), in Glencoe, and Flodigarry Hotel (hotelintheskye.co.uk), on the Isle of Skye, are excellent options in idyllic settings.

EVENTS

Among Scotland's biggest events are the concerts and performances of the Edinburgh International Festival (eif.co.uk) and the Edinburgh Festival Fringe (edfringe.com) in August; the sporting competitions and cultural activities of the Highland Games in summer; and the wild street parties and dazzling torchlight processions of Hogmanay on 31 December (edinburghshogmanay.com).

SCOTLAND

84

Whisky & walking
IN THE CAIRNGORMS

Welcome to the UK's largest national park. Cairngorms (cairn-gorms.co.uk) covers twice the area of England's Lake District, and includes **five of Britain's six highest peaks** (the sixth being the highest, Ben Nevis, further west), all of which exceed 1000m (3281ft) in altitude. There are no fewer than 15 Munros (mountains over 914m/3000ft) in the Cairngorms, including **Ben Macdui**, Scotland's second highest, and **Cairn Gorm**, from which the park and range take their name. Central and easily reached from the country's major cities, the park is a paradise for nature lovers, hikers and board-sports enthusiasts. Arriving from the south, stop at **Dunkeld** to explore the Hermitage pleasure ground on a walk along the River Braan, ending in front of Ossian's Hall and the Black Linn waterfall. More experienced hikers will want to climb **Schiehallion** for a view across the national park before entering. And every visitor will want to save some time for whisky tasting in the distilleries of Speyside or seeing what the country's east coast has to offer.

Sip a dram in Speyside

Scotland's whisky is produced all over the country, but the Speyside region, on Cairngorm National Park's northern border, is especially renowned and rich in production sites (51 distilleries currently in operation), thanks to its particularly high-quality water. To discover the birthplaces of great names such as Glenfiddich (inset) and Cardhu, follow the Malt Whisky Trail (maltwhiskytrail.com). And if you're more of a gin drinker, you should know that more and more quality bottles of that are also being produced in the region.

Pay your respects at Balmoral

Balmoral Castle (opposite), between the villages of Braemar and Ballater, peeps out above its wooded surroundings. Built by Queen Victoria in 1855, it has since become the private residence of the royal family, and it was here that Queen Elizabeth II died in September 2022. You can visit some of the rooms, but not the private royal apartments. Outside, the estate is well worth a visit – a recommended walk is to Prince Albert's Cairn, erected in tribute to Victoria's husband. Its pyramid shape is a curiosity in the middle of the Scottish forest.

Pedal in the Caledonian Forest

Cycling aficionados needn't feel left out in this bit of the Highlands – numerous mountain-bike rental companies operate in the towns around the park. From Aviemore, pedal to Loch Morlich (5km/3 miles), with its beautiful sandy beach, or, for hardcore riders only, tackle the tough Cairngorm Hill Climb (16km/10 miles).

Highland life of yore

In the east of the national park, the Highland Folk Museum (highlifehighland.com/highlandfolkmuseum) invites you to travel back in time and experience Highlander life from the 1700s to the mid-20th century. The hamlet of Baile Gean recreates daily living in the 1730s and was used as a film location for the *Outlander* show. You'll also enter a number of 19th-century cottages, study in a 1930s classroom and peer inside a tweed factory. A superb immersive dive into the past.

MORE TIME?

EAST COAST Push on to the east coast from the national park, where Aberdeenshire promises some great attractions, starting with Aberdeen itself – nicknamed the Granite City because of its silver-grey buildings – which fully embraces its oil heritage. To the north, seals bask in peace on Newburgh Beach; to the south, Dunnottar Castle has a striking position on cliffs above the North Sea – and a few ghost stories to entertain you. If castles are your thing, add Fraser and Craigievar to your list while in the area.

THE HIGHLAND GAMES

The Highland Games are the Scottish Olympics. Athletes compete in disciplines such as tossing the caber (a large pole), tug-of-war and Highland dancing. These gatherings take place all summer long across the country, but the best-known are held in Braemar (braemargathering.org) – members of the royal family often attend. The rest of the year, you can roam the grounds and visit the Highland Games Centre, which traces the history of the sports and the Braemar Gathering itself. Don't miss a break at the adjoining cafe, where the pastries are exquisite.

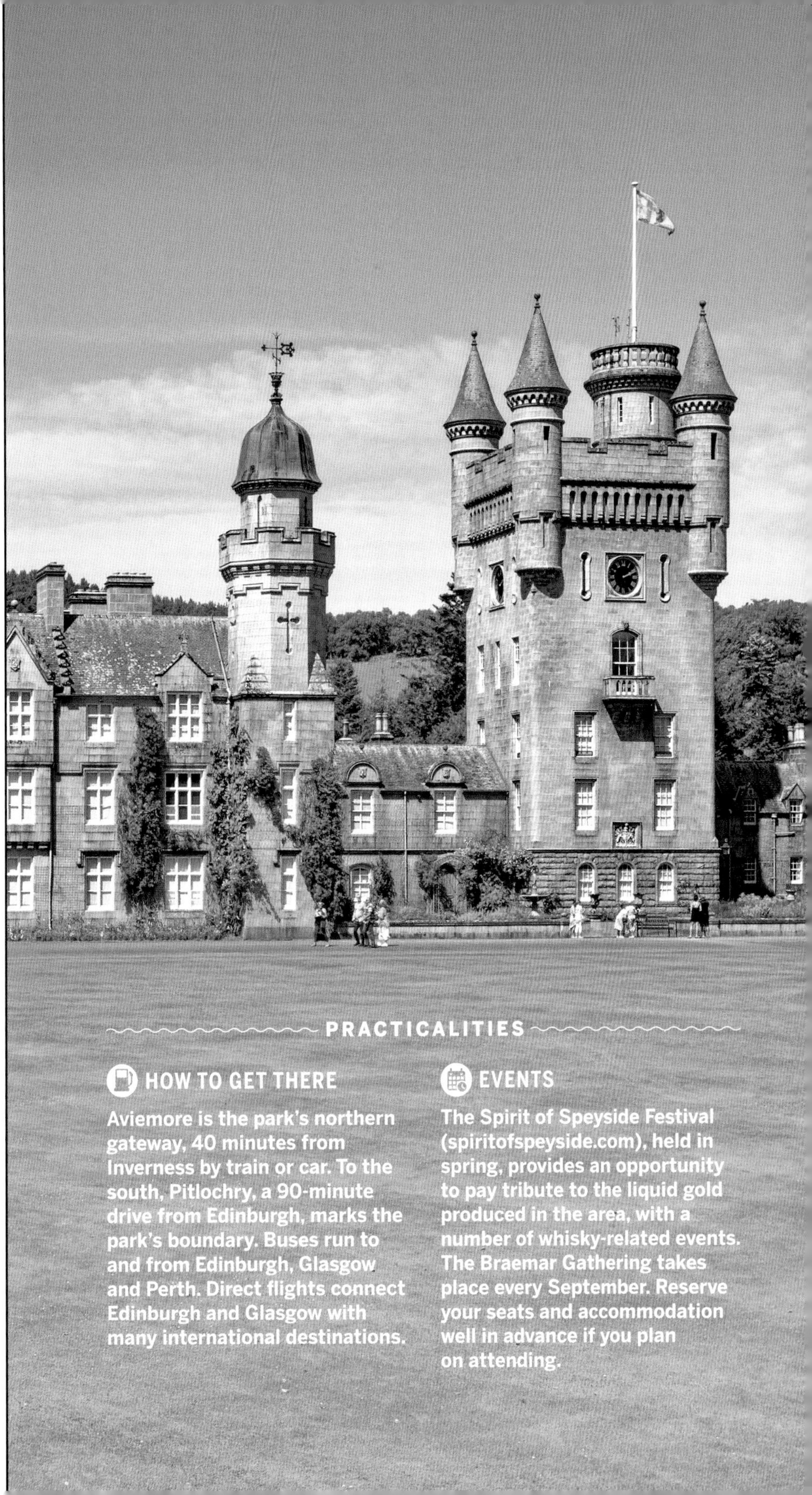

PRACTICALITIES

🚉 HOW TO GET THERE

Aviemore is the park's northern gateway, 40 minutes from Inverness by train or car. To the south, Pitlochry, a 90-minute drive from Edinburgh, marks the park's boundary. Buses run to and from Edinburgh, Glasgow and Perth. Direct flights connect Edinburgh and Glasgow with many international destinations.

📅 EVENTS

The Spirit of Speyside Festival (spiritofspeyside.com), held in spring, provides an opportunity to pay tribute to the liquid gold produced in the area, with a number of whisky-related events. The Braemar Gathering takes place every September. Reserve your seats and accommodation well in advance if you plan on attending.

HOWTH

DUBLIN

ENNISKERRY

BRAY

KILMACANOGUE

Wicklow
Mountains
National Park

IRISH SEA

GLENDALOUGH

ASHFORD

RATHDRUM

IRELAND

85

Go green
IN DUBLIN
& WICKLOW

I f you were to plan a
weekend in Dublin, you'd
imagine a city break. Maybe
gazing at the archaeological treasures of the **National Museum
of Ireland** (museum.ie), taking a
stroll around the **Trinity College**
campus (tcd.ie), having a drink
and taking in the top-floor view
at the **Guinness Storehouse**
(guinness-storehouse.com), or
listening to music in a **Temple Bar**
pub. All great Dublin experiences.
But also worth including on your
itinerary are the city's **green
spaces**: St Stephen's Green, the
most popular; Merrion Square,

an elegant public garden; Herbert
Park, full of locals enjoying outdoor
sports; and Phoenix Park, the
largest city park in Europe. And
there's much more greenery of
the less manicured variety on
Dublin's southern doorstep in
County Wicklow, a wild land
combining coastal splendour with
a mountainous interior studded
with chilly lakes, glacial valleys and
the remains of an early monastic
site. For a taste of this 'Garden of
Ireland', set off on the **Wicklow
Way** hiking trail (wicklowway.com)
from Rathfarnham on Dublin's
outskirts and see how far you get.

Be intoxicated by Powerscourt Gardens

The eminent 19th-century horticulturist Daniel Robinson, creator of the splendid Powerscourt Gardens, was allegedly sometimes too drunk to stand in the exceptional gardens he designed. You too will be intoxicated by the terraces, statues, water features and grottoes of the vast green spaces Robinson created, where over 200 varieties of trees and plants grow. Elsewhere on the estate, seek out the 121m (397ft) Powerscourt waterfall, accessed by road and footpath. From Enniskerry, 18km (11 miles) south of Dublin, it's a short walk to Powerscourt.

Hike in Glendalough

In the heart of the Wicklow Mountains National Park (inset), Glendalough (the 'valley of two lakes') is considered one of Ireland's most beautiful spots, thanks to its wild and romantic landscapes. It's also a great place to hike and to view the impressive ruins of an ancient monastic site and its famous round tower (see previous page). The valley is crisscrossed by nine trails, the longest of which is around 10km (6 miles) long. Set off from the national park information centre (nationalparks.ie/wicklow) near the upper lake car park. A bus service (St Kevin's bus; glendaloughbus. com) links Dublin to Glendalough twice a day in just under one hour, 30 minutes.

Admire Dublin from Howth Summit

The pretty port of Howth sits on a green peninsula 15km (9 miles) northeast of the Irish capital (30 minutes by train). The hill overlooking the town provides spectacular views of Dublin Bay back to the city. Howth also has a castle with grounds that contain a dolmen (ancient tomb) and medieval ruins.

Saunter through a coastal garden

Just outside Bray, a popular seaside resort with a long promenade along the beach, Killruddery House & Gardens (killruddery.com) is a mix of historic manor house (guided tour compulsory) and one of Ireland's oldest gardens, where an impressive collection of statues and plants flourishes. From Dublin, Bray is just 20km (12 miles) south and can be reached by bus in less than 45 minutes.

Buy local at Avoca Handweavers

It was in the tiny village of Avoca, located in a wooded valley in County Wicklow, that Avoca Handweavers (avoca.com), Ireland's most famous traditional clothing manufacturer, was born. To stock up on knitwear and elegant handmade souvenirs, there are two branches: 11-13 Suffolk Street, in central Dublin; or Kilmacanogue, 5km (3 miles) southeast of Enniskerry, at the company's headquarters, which occupies a 19th-century arboretum.

MORE TIME?

MT USHER GARDENS A green paradise on the edge of Ashford, 50km (31 miles) south of Dublin.
KILMACURRAGH BOTANIC GARDENS Ornamental gardens set around an 18th-century manor house, 65km (40 miles) south of Dublin.
KILMAINHAM GAOL In Dublin, this former prison (opposite) houses a remarkable museum retracing the painful process that led to Irish independence.
GREAT SUGAR LOAF The Great Sugar Loaf is County Wicklow's iconic peak (501m/1644ft), with a conical shape looming over the village of Kilmacanogue, 35km (22 miles) south of Dublin.

THE ROUND SYSTEM

It's my round! The 'getting a round in' system – paying for a drink with the person/people who bought you one – is the foundation of Irish pub culture, summed up very simply by the Irish saying: "It's impossible for two men to go to the pub for just one drink." Make sure you follow this sacred rule. And why not comply with a pint of famous Guinness, the black stout developed in 1759 by Arthur Guinness, which is said to take its flavour from the water of the Wicklow Mountains.

PRACTICALITIES

✈ HOW TO GET THERE & AROUND

Dublin Airport has flights to destinations across Europe and the rest of the world. Once in the city, in addition to buses and trams for getting around, the Dublin Area Rapid Transport (DART) provides a fast train service to the coast, as far as Howth. Enniskerry, a good base for visiting Powerscourt and Glendalough, is 45 minutes by DART, then 30 minutes by bus 185.

🏨 WHERE TO STAY

County Wicklow is a popular weekend destination for Dubliners, so book early. You'll find everything from hostels and backpacker campsites to farmhouses converted into B&Bs and manor houses transformed into luxury hotels. Among these, the Powerscourt Hotel & Spa (powerscourthotel.com) is a huge, luxury option right on the Powerscourt Estate.

📅 EVENTS

In September, the weather can be surprisingly mild, making it a good time for hiking and enjoying the Dublin Fringe Festival (fringefest.com), with over 100 shows in the streets and bars of the capital.

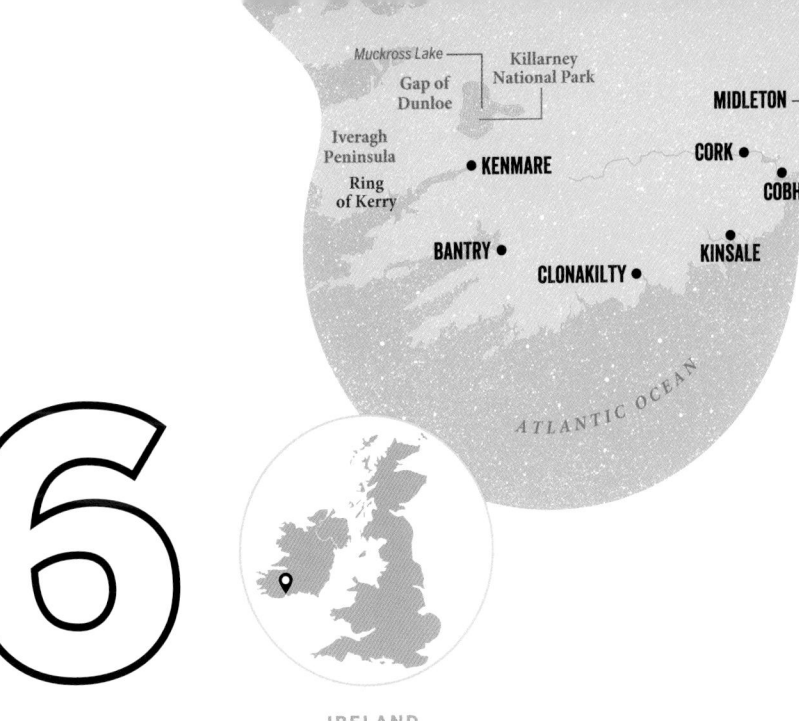

86

Admire the colours of
SOUTHERN IRELAND

I reland's second-largest city, **Cork, offers fewer attractions than capital Dublin, but has a vibrant atmosphere, strong character and is the gateway to the island's glorious south.** The landscapes in this part of the country roll out from the city like an Impressionist painting in which the dark blue of the Atlantic contrasts with the soft green of the pastures, and the mauve heather stands out from the brown peat bogs. A road trip through this artist's palette of colours begins in Cork, from where the N22 leads west to **Kenmare** and on to the celebrated **Ring of Kerry** and the coast of the **Iveragh Peninsula**. Where the land ends, Derrynane Beach spreads its white sand, and the cliffs of Kerry plunge into the surging ocean. Head southwest of Cork and stop for a cup of tea and a wander in **Bantry**, **Clonakilty** or **Kinsale**, all of which charm with their multicoloured buildings. Then keep going until you hit the coastline of **Mizen Head** or turn north and kiss the famous stone at **Blarney Castle**. Back in Cork, order a pint of Murphy's (the city's answer to Guinness) and enjoy the warm welcome of the pubs.

Find food heaven in Cork

Cork's food scene is unrivalled in Ireland, and to take the temperature of the country's gastronomic capital, there's nowhere better than the unmissable English Market (inset). One of the most beautiful markets in Europe, this place showcases the full range of local products: farmhouse cheeses, smoked fish, black pudding, corned beef, unusual vegetables and more – the perfect place to assemble a picnic lunch for your road trip. Upstairs, the Farmgate Cafe offers regional specialities based on market arrivals.

A walk in Killarney National Park

With its tall mountains, glittering lakes, dense forests and abundant wildlife, Killarney National Park (nationalparks.ie/killarney), the jewel in the crown of the Ring of Kerry (Ladies View, opposite), wins over all visitors – especially hikers. The latter can take a 16km (10-mile) loop around Muckross Lake, starting from the ruins of Muckross Abbey. The route goes over mossy undergrowth to the north of the lake and crosses first one bridge and then a second, from where the south shore section heads deep into the forest to reach bubbling Torc waterfall, before returning to the start and Muckross House.

Become a shepherd for a day

Meet a Border collie breeder and find out how these endearing sheepdogs manage to round up flocks so quickly. The Kissane Sheep Farm (kissanesheepfarm. com) has been run by the same family for almost 200 years and offers some very informative and fun demonstrations.

Visit a distillery

What would a trip to Ireland be without trying some whiskey? To discover the secrets behind the making of the amber elixir, visit the Jameson Experience (jamesonwhiskey. com) in Midleton, housed in a marvellous brick distillery restored as an Irish Whiskey Museum.

Aristocratic life in Killarney

Relive the Victorian era at Muckross House (muckross-house.ie). Nestling in the heart of Killarney National Park, this impressive residence, completed in 1843, has no fewer than 65 rooms furnished with period pieces. The elegantly decorated family bedrooms upstairs contrast sharply with the spartan servants' quarters in the basement. Cross the rhododendron-filled park to discover the estate's farms. To arrive in aristocratic style, take the horse-drawn carriage service that brings tourists from Killarney.

MORE TIME?

COBH Just 20km (12 miles) from Cork, Cobh (see previous page) was the port of departure for 2.5 million of the six million Irish who set sail for North America between 1848 and 1950. The Cobh Heritage Centre (cobhheritage.com) tells the story of the waves of Irish emigration, exacerbated by the Great Famine, through moving displays. Next door, in the former White Star Line premises from which 123 passengers boarded the *Titanic*, the Titanic Experience (titanicexperiencecobh.ie) looks back at the liner's tragic maiden voyage in 1912. Tours are partly guided, partly interactive.

THE BUTTER EXCHANGE

From the late 18th to the early 20th century, Ireland was one of the world's biggest exporters of salted butter. The arrival of margarine and the development of refrigeration changed all that, but the Butter Exchange, the world's largest butter market, continues to be held every year in Cork. It was used to categorise butters according to their quality. The astonishing Butter Museum (thebuttermuseum. com) exhibits a wide range of tools and provides an entertaining look at the methods used to make the delicious golden spread.

PRACTICALITIES

HOW TO GET THERE

Cork Airport is connected to several European destinations by direct flight. Ferries also link the city with ports in the UK, France and Spain.

WHERE TO STAY & EAT

Spend the night – or at least indulge in a grand afternoon tea – at Cork's Imperial Hotel (imperialhotelcork.com). Less elegant but just as comfortable, Hotel Isaacs (hotelisaacscork. com) has an enviable location in the centre of the city. For a pint, try the beer garden at Tom Barry's pub or the covered passageway at Arthur Mayne's Pharmacy.

EVENTS

St Patrick's Day electrifies the whole country every 17 March, and in October Cork hosts the Guinness Jazz Festival (guinnesscorkjazz.com).

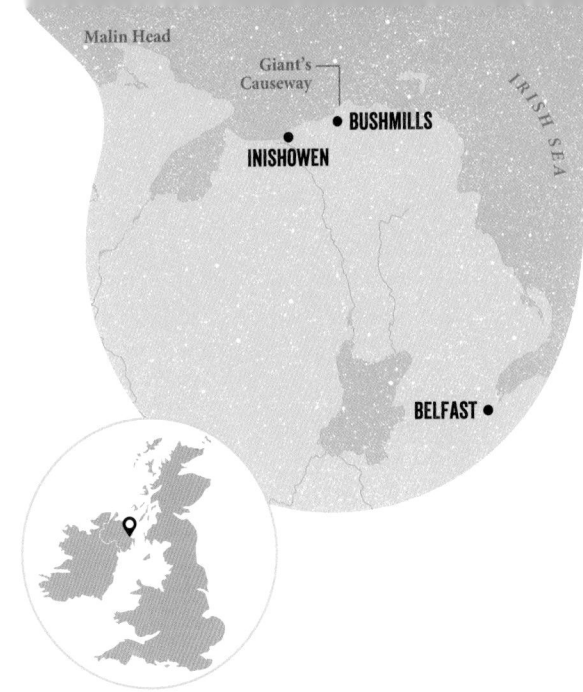

Malin Head

Giant's
Causeway

● BUSHMILLS

INISHOWEN

IRISH SEA

BELFAST ●

87

NORTHERN IRELAND

Look to the future
IN BELFAST

Belfast's transformation over the past couple of decades from no-go to must-visit destination has been remarkable. Once best known for sectarian violence between Catholics and Protestants, Northern Ireland's capital has managed to put that devastating past behind it and focus on a brighter future. So what's the appeal for visitors? First, the people. Some of the friendliest, most welcoming locals you can imagine make a trip here a treat. Then there are world-class attractions, including Titanic Belfast (titanicbelfast.com), a multimedia museum covering the famous ocean liner built in the city in 1911; and the Ulster Museum, with displays on this part of the island of Ireland. Another option is a tour of the political and religious murals of West Belfast and the Peace Line, the wall separating communities since the late 1970s. In the evening, restaurants and pubs await (Crown Liquor Saloon, left, is a favourite). So many attractions, in fact, that you might overlook – but shouldn't – the stunning Northern Irish coastline, an open-air museum of geology, just a short drive away.

Return to the time of Queen Victoria

Queen Victoria's reign (1837–1901) marked the peak of the British Industrial Revolution, during which Belfast prospered. Buildings recalling this time include the Grand Opera House (1895), Cleaver House (1888), Queen's University (founded by Victoria in 1845) and the red-brick Old Town Hall (1871). The high point of this trip back to the 19th century is a drink at the Crown Liquor Saloon – Belfast's most famous pub dates to 1885 and has an interior as elaborate as its exterior. For a bird's-eye view across Victorian Belfast, head for the glass dome in the Victoria Square shopping centre.

Connect with Titanic passengers

In dry dock next to the Titanic Belfast museum, the SS *Nomadic* (inset; nomadicbelfast.com) is the last survivor of the White Star Line and packs an emotional charge – on 10 April, 1912, this small steamer carried 172 passengers to the *Titanic* (too massive to be docked) during its stopover in Cherbourg. Equally interesting is the huge Thompson Graving Dock (titanic. memorial), an impressive vestige of the era of the great transatlantic liners, which is also located near the museum.

Tread in the footsteps of giants

Northern Ireland's only UNESCO World Heritage Site, the Giant's Causeway (opposite; nationaltrust. org.uk/visit/northern-ireland/ giants-causeway) is one of the country's most captivating spots. Wandering round this geological wonder formed of a vast expanse of hexagonal basalt columns, it's easy to understand why the ancients attributed a supernatural origin to it involving two rival giants building a stony path across the sea to fight each other. As well as the natural attractions, the coast also has dramatic castles (Dunluce), the world's oldest whiskey distillery (Bushmills) and a rope bridge that's not for the nervous (Carrick-a-Rede). The Causeway Rambler bus (translink.co.uk) and Giant's Causeway & Bushmills Railway (facebook.com/GCBRNI) provide seasonal services around the Giant's Causeway, a 90-minute drive from Belfast.

Tap your foot to some traditional music

Traditional music sessions liven up Belfast evenings all year-round. Artists perform in the city's clubs and pubs, including Kelly's Cellars (kellyscellars. co.uk), one of the city's oldest; the Duke of York (dukeofyorkbelfast. com), where band Snow Patrol started out; and White's Tavern (whitestavernbelfast.com), established in 1630. Better-known groups and singers perform at the SSE Arena (ssearenabelfast.com).

MORE TIME?

GAME OF THRONES TOURS From Belfast, companies offer tours of the filming locations of the cult show *Game of Thrones* (gameofthronestours.com; mccombscoaches.com), filmed in Northern Ireland.

CRUMLIN ROAD GAOL In the centre of Belfast, this former prison (crumlinroadgaol.com), in operation from 1846 to 1996, opens to the public its cramped cells, gruesome execution chamber and the tunnel used to transfer prisoners from the courthouse.

ULSTER TRANSPORT MUSEUM See steam locomotives, motorcycles, streetcars – and the prototype DMC DeLorean from the film *Back to the Future*, made in Belfast in 1981 (nmni.com/uftm).

THE BIRTHPLACE OF THE TITANIC

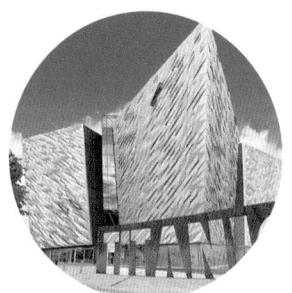

Arguably the most famous ship in history, the *Titanic* was built in Belfast at the Harland & Wolff shipyards for the White Star Line. When its keel was laid in 1909, the Belfast shipyards were at their peak. Launched from H&W's No 3 slipway on 31 May, 1911, the *Titanic* spent over a year in the Thompson Graving Dock being fitted out, before leaving Belfast on 2 April, 1912 for its maiden voyage. Three days later, the ship hit an iceberg and sank in a matter of hours, killing more than 1500 people.

PRACTICALITIES

WHEN TO GO

From May to September you can expect warmer and sunnier days – but still bring an umbrella.

HOW TO GET THERE

Belfast's two airports have flights arriving from across the UK and from many European cities. Regular trains on the Dublin–Belfast line connect the two capitals in around two hours.

WHERE TO STAY

From hostels to luxury hotels, the range of accommodation on offer is growing every year. Most of the budget addresses are to the south of the centre, in the treelined university district, a 20-minute walk from City Hall.

EVENTS

In the second half of October, the Belfast International Arts Festival (belfastinternationalartsfestival.com) attracts artists from around the world.

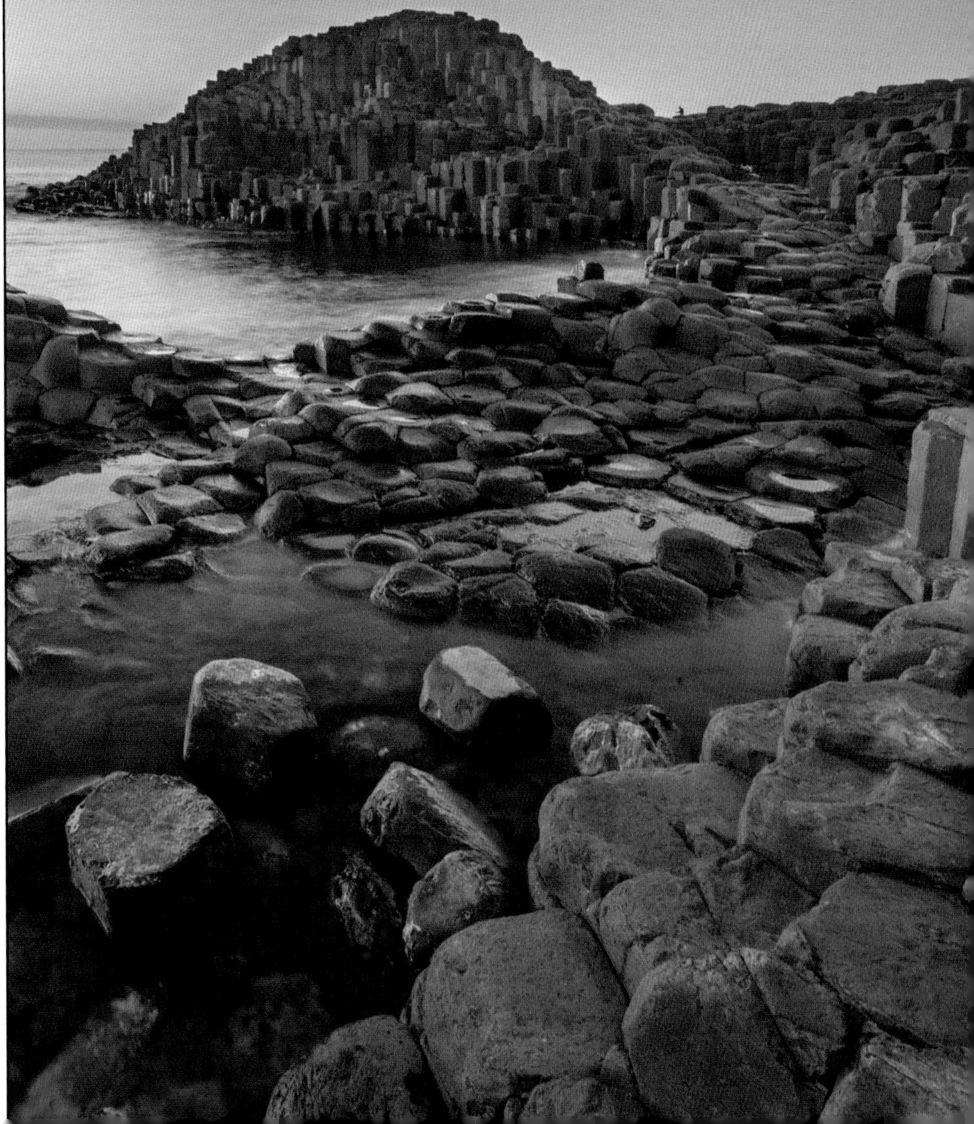

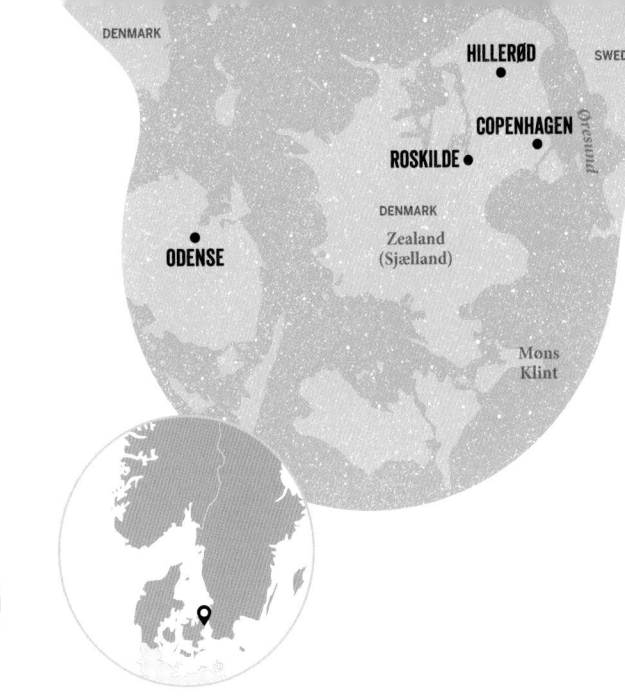

HILLERØD

SWEDEN

COPENHAGEN

ROSKILDE

Øresund

DENMARK

ODENSE

Zealand
(Sjælland)

Mons
Klint

DENMARK

88

Enjoy culture & nature
ON ZEALAND

Denmark's largest island, Zealand, is home to most of the country's population, including those in Copenhagen. Surrounded by nature in the form of beaches, forests and the Øresund Strait, the Danish capital is also a cutting-edge urban centre that attracts visitors from all over the world. **Indre By**, its charming historic centre, is best known for the famous **Nyhavn harbour** (left), where multicoloured facades, a lively atmosphere and pretty boats moored along the quays keep the crowds here all day and into the night. Stroll the scenic nearby canals, admire the splendid **Amalienborg Palace** – home to the royal family – explore the busy 'freetown' of **Christiania**, and snap a photo in front of the **Little Mermaid statue**, who watches over the waterfront. Follow the lead of locals and rent a bike for a gentle tour of this island city, cycling through the historic streets dotted with restaurants offering tasty world cuisine, trendy cafes, cool design shops and art galleries. Then get out of the capital to see what the rest of Zealand has to offer – spoiler: a lot.

Revel in the Renaissance at Frederiksborg Castle

The architecturally astounding Frederiksborg Castle (inset; dnm. dk) is a Renaissance superstar bordered by a large moat and formal gardens. Behind its 17th-century red-brick facade, built by King Christian IV, it houses important collections from the National History Museum, making for an even more captivating visit. The castle is in Hillerød, 40km (25 miles) from Copenhagen, reached either by car in 40 minutes or by train in one hour.

Visit the Louisiana Museum of Modern Art

Fans of contemporary art should make a beeline to the exhibitions at the Louisiana Museum of Modern Art (louisiana.dk). This immense gallery is home to many pieces by world-renowned artists, including priceless works by Andy Warhol, Pablo Picasso, Yves Klein and Francis Bacon. An essential part of the collection is the outdoor Sculpture Park, where 45 pieces sit in a peaceful garden looking out to sea. The museum can be visited by train from Copenhagen in around one hour.

Marvel at the Viking Ship Museum

In Roskilde, at the end of a pretty fjord, the Viking Ship Museum (opposite; vikingeskibsmuseet.dk) exhibits five extraordinary boats discovered in the nearby village of Skuldelev. The chance to see these anicent ships and learn more about Scandinavia's rich maritime culture make this place well worth the trip. The museum is 34km (21 miles) west of Copenhagen, and can be reached in 40 minutes by train.

Explore the 'Green Belt'

The huge natural spaces along Copenhagen's northern edge are called the 'Green Belt' for good reason. This paradise for fans of the outdoors has forested landscapes on one side, where you can walk and try to spot deer, and miles of beautiful coastline on the other. A place to explore on foot, by bike or even by canoe, it's accessible in just 20 minutes by train from Copenhagen.

MORE TIME?

ODENSE This appealing green city, with its historic centre, is home to many cultural attractions, including the fascinating Hans Christian Andersen House. The city is less than 90 minutes from Copenhagen by train.

MØNS KLINT This imposing chalk cliff looms over the Baltic above a pretty beach that takes on a Caribbean air in fine weather. Laze on the sand, swim in the sea or enjoy a multitude of watersports. The cliff is around two hours' drive from Copenhagen.

LIFE ON TWO WHEELS

Like every city in Denmark, Copenhagen has an extensive network of bicycle paths, stretching right to the outskirts of the capital. Cycling is an integral part of Danish culture, and residents are extremely keen on the quality of life this mode of transport brings – less stress and pollution, more physical activity. Pedalling is an excellent way for visitors to explore Zealand too; travelling at their own pace, while respecting the environment. Numerous operators offer mountain-bike and all-terrain rentals, with options suitable for all ages.

PRACTICALITIES

HOW TO GET THERE

Copenhagen Airport is connected to destinations across Europe and the world. Trains also link it to plenty of places in the rest of Europe.

WHERE TO STAY

One of the best areas to stay in Copenhagen is Indre By. Located in the heart of the city, it encompasses the famous port of Nyhavn, as well as Strøget, the capital's pedestrianised shopping hub.

EVENTS

In July, the 10-day Copenhagen Jazz Festival (jazz.dk), is a monumental gathering with a rich programme featuring internationally acclaimed musicians. At Christmas, the capital lights up and takes on a festive air, with a grand parade through the streets and a fine Christmas market in the Tivoli Gardens amusement park.

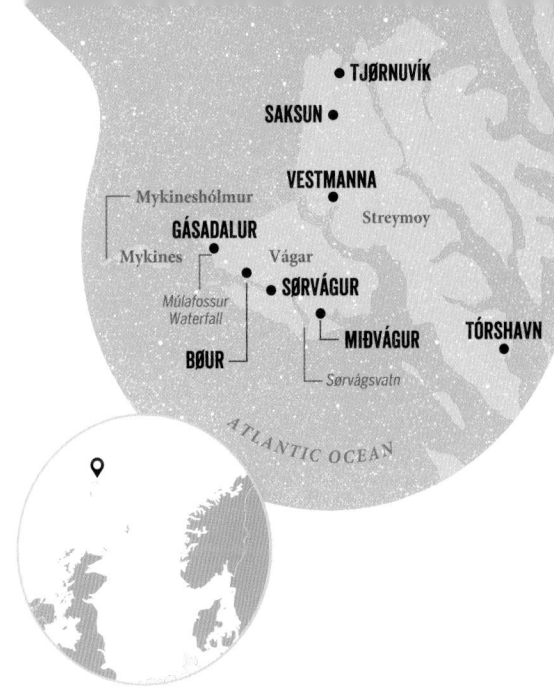

TJØRNUVÍK

SAKSUN

VESTMANNA

Mykineshólmur   GÁSADALUR   Streymoy

Mykines   Vágar

Múlafossur   SØRVÁGUR
Waterfall

MIÐVÁGUR   TÓRSHAVN

BØUR

Sørvágsvatn

ATLANTIC OCEAN

DENMARK

89

Set sail for
THE FAROE ISLANDS

Halfway between Scotland and Iceland, almost lost in the middle of the Atlantic Ocean, the Faroe Islands appeared a few years ago on the radar of adventurous travellers in search of unspoiled wilderness. This Danish territory, which has had an autonomous government since 1948, has just 52,000 human inhabitants – plus thousands of sheep grazing its immense green expanses. It would take more than a weekend to cover all 18 islands, but thanks to regular flights to Vágar – the main point of arrival – tunnels and bridges from one island to the next and a network of ferries, it's possible to get a feel for this place in just a few days. Plan your visit for the period from June to August – and bring warm clothing even then, as the weather is not always predictable or kind. Steeped in local legends and pagan myths, the islands have long maintained a traditional culture and way of life, isolated from the wider influences of the European continent they just about cling on to – making them all the more attractive as an off-the-beaten-track destination.

Horse riding on Streymoy

On the island of Streymoy, the largest and most populous of the archipelago, horse-riding excursions for all levels are organised from Tórshavn, the Faroese capital. Founded in the 10th century, the town is known for its concentration of red wooden houses with turf roofs. Some companies offer rides on a Faroese pony, a species specific to the islands. In the north of Streymoy, Tjørnuvík, also known for its typical colourful houses, and Saksun (opposite), where access is guarded by a lake encircled by mountains, are two hamlets worth a stop for their pastoral charm and peaceful atmosphere.

Hike to two water features on Vágar

Located on the island of Vágar, Lake Sørvágsvatn, the largest in the Faroe Islands, is world-famous for the mind-bending optical illusion it creates, sitting high above a cliff overlooking the Atlantic Ocean. After an hour's walk offering wonderful views, you'll arrive at the right spot to appreciate this trick of nature. Other top hikes exist on the island too, such as the one that leads from Sørvágur to the remote village of Gásadalur (see previous page), overlooking Mykines fjord (approximately six hours, round trip). Just a stone's throw from the village, mighty Múlafossur waterfall drops into the ocean. The village can now also be reached by car via a tunnel dug into the hillside near Bøur, a cute village with typical turf-roofed houses and a pretty church.

Meet the Mykines puffin

Only 20 or so inhabitants live permanently on the island of Mykines, but you'll find a wild and friendly fauna that outnumbers the people and attracts many bird-watchers. This is the home of the Atlantic puffin (inset), a protected species that should be observed from a safe distance so as not to disturb its natural habitat. Don't miss a visit to the tiny village of Mykines, before exploring further on foot and taking the Atlantic Bridge to the islet of Mykineshólmur, where you'll find a lighthouse in a location just begging to be photographed. The island of Mykines can be reached in one hour by ferry from Sorvágur on Vágar.

Discover the Vestmanna cliffs by the sea

From the port of Vestmanna, on the island of Streymoy, take a boat trip west to Vestmannabjørgini. You'll sail along steep cliffs and, weather permitting, explore rocky inlets, learning about the different species of birds that nest in the hard-to-reach nooks and crannies of this impressive natural setting.

MORE TIME?

VOLUNTOURISM Every year in April, the Faroe Islands 'close' for maintenance for a few days to help restore hiking trails, rebuild cairns and work on conservation projects. The campaign, launched in 2020, aims to prepare the chain for the peak summer tourist season while protecting its delicate landscapes.

FOOD, FAROESE-STYLE

Traditional Faroese cuisine still makes use of the island's land and sea produce: hare, lamb and fish can be found in most restaurants. Other additions to the menu are potatoes – only introduced in the 19th century – beetroots, berries and mushrooms. One notable historic speciality is *ræst*, a method of drying and fermenting fish (usually cod) and meat (often lamb), leaving it to air-dry in a wind-ventilated hut called a *hjallur*. A handful of restaurants and B&Bs have made these a signature dish, including Koks on Vágar, the archipelago's first Michelin-starred restaurant, whose young chef Poul Andrias Ziska is working hard to promote Nordic cuisine and its ancient techniques.

HOW TO GET THERE

The Faroe Islands' only airport in Vágar welcomes arrivals from a few destinations, including Copenhagen, Paris, Reykjavík, Oslo and Edinburgh. The capital Tórshavn is 56km (35 miles) from Vágar Airport and best reached by taxi or rental car (book early). For a more leisurely way to arrive (taking one to three days, depending on season/departure point), you can sail from Denmark or Iceland.

EVENTS

The islands' music scene is rooted in ancient traditions when storytelling and song were the only means of preserving the Faroese language (banned for several centuries until its rehabilitation in the 19th century). Summartónar (summartonar. fo), a festival held every year in May and June, presents over 150 concerts, performed mainly by local musicians.

UPPSALA

SIGTUNA

STOCKHOLM

Lövon

Tyresta
National Park

BALTIC SEA

Utö

SWEDEN

90

Enjoy Swedish charm

IN & AROUND STOCKHOLM

With thousands of rocky islands and a jagged coastline riddled **with lakes and forests, nature puts on quite a show in the Stockholm Archipelago.** Before heading off to hike, bike or kayak these untamed shores of the Baltic Sea though, take time to sample the delights of the Swedish capital itself. Gamla Stan (overleaf), the city's Old Town, exudes an appealing elegance, thanks to its cobbled streets, pastel-painted buildings and, topping it all, **Royal Palace** (kungligaslotten.se), one of the most beautiful in Europe.

As well as taking in the cultural highlights of several exceptional museums – try **Millesgården**, a sculpture garden and art gallery in one, or the Vasa Museum with an extraordinarily well-preserved 17th-century ship – you'll have plenty of time for shopping in the boutiques and chains of the city centre. Stockholm's 14 islands, linked by 57 bridges spanning a multitude of inlets and canals, mean you're never far from the water – or from enticing **gourmet restaurants** and bohemian bars that come alive in the evening.

Go back in time at Sigtuna

Steeped in history, lovely little Sigtuna is Sweden's oldest town. The streets here are lined with numerous reminders of its 1000-year-old past: Viking rune stones stand alongside ruined churches from later ages. After visiting the sights of this ancient place, stop for a *fika* (coffee break) in one of the chic cafes in Sigtuna's centre, before taking public transport back to Stockholm.

Dive into the past at Vasamuseet

In the heart of Stockholm, the Vasamuseet (vasamuseet.se) presents Sweden's maritime history through excellent displays. The centrepiece is an ancient warship from the 17th century, the *Vasa* (opposite), 69m (226ft) long and 48m (157ft) high, which sank in Saltsjön Bay immediately after weighing anchor for her maiden voyage. It remained underwater for three centuries before finally being raised and preserved, providing illuminating insights into the lives of sailors centuries ago.

Get lost in Tyresta National Park

Located 20km (12 miles) southeast of Stockholm, Tyresta National Park (sverigesnationalparker.se) is a wonderful green space covered with virgin forest, lakes, marshes and rocks dating back more than two billion years. This wild and peaceful spot is particularly noted for its abundant birdlife, drawing keen ornithologists and their binoculars from around the world. An on-site exhibition centre has interesting details on Sweden's other national parks, and is an ideal starting point for a fine hiking trail.

Out on the water in the Stockholm Archipelago

You can't visit Stockholm without taking a boat trip through the waters of the archipelago (see previous page; stockholmarchipelago.se). Among the various routes, one of the best is the ferry to the vast island of Utö. Here, between sea and forest, you can enjoy a wide range of outdoor activities, from hiking and mountain biking to swimming, sailing and bird-watching. Visit the striking Mine Museum, a reminder of Utö's past as home to the country's oldest salt mines, and buy some of the local speciality bread to eat on the boat back.

MORE TIME?

UPPSALA Uppsala is one of Sweden's most bewitching cities, featuring a superb cathedral, a palace, a fascinating museum on Swedish history, and ancient sites, including rune stones and pre-Viking burial mounds. It's a 40-minute journey from Stockholm on public transport.

DROTTNINGHOLM PALACE On the island of Lovön, this palace, surrounded by lovely parkland, is one of the residences of the royal family, who live here for part of the year. For insider anecdotes, opt for the guided tour. The palace is easily reached from Stockholm by bus, boat or even bicycle (13km/8 miles from the city centre).

THE 'FIKA'

In Sweden, you can't escape the *fika*, a mid-morning/ afternoon break usually consisting of a coffee and a pastry (often a *kanelbulle*, a delicious cinnamon roll) or sometimes small sandwiches or fruit. Much more than a quick bite to eat, it's a sacred social institution for Swedes, who like to have *fika* with family, friends and colleagues as often as possible. Join them.

PRACTICALITIES

HOW TO GET THERE

Stockholm has flight connections to multiple cities around the world, as well as ferry links to Finland and Estonia. Trains link the capital with the rest of Sweden and other Scandinavian destinations.

WHERE TO STAY

A little more expensive than the capital's other districts, Gamla Stan (the Old Town) is the most atmospheric place to stay in Stockholm. Here you'll find youth hostels, mid-range hotels and many upscale establishments.

EVENTS

In June, Smaka På Stockholm (smakapastockholm.se) celebrates food over five days, with dozens of stands showcasing the local culinary scene. In October, the Stockholm Jazz Festival (stockholmjazz. se) is one of Europe's biggest gatherings of this kind of music.

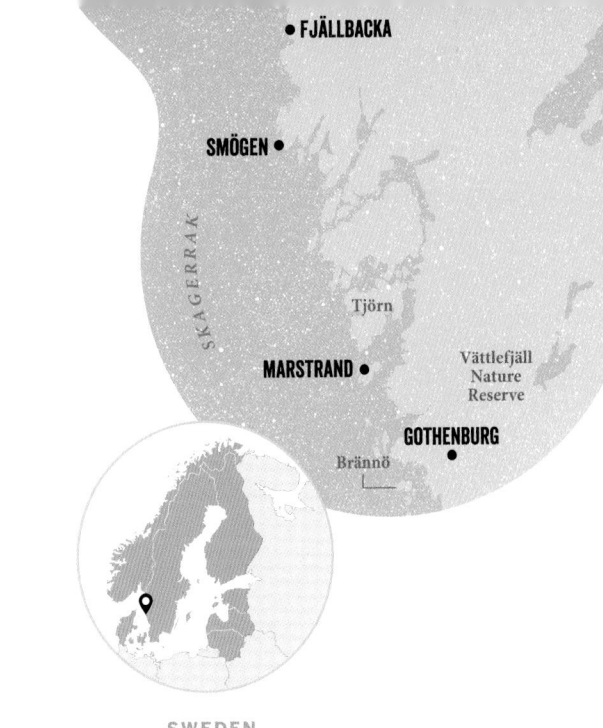

- FJÄLLBACKA
- SMÖGEN •
- SKAGERRAK
- Tjörn
- MARSTRAND •
- Vättlefjäll Nature Reserve
- GOTHENBURG
- Brännö •

SWEDEN

91

Between land & sea
IN BOHUSLÄN

T he Swedish province of **Bohuslän is perfect if you want outdoor action in beautiful surroundings.** This part of the country is nicknamed the 'sunny coast' because of its mild climate, and it's along the region's Baltic Sea shoreline that the most amazing natural gems stretch out, one after another: pink granite islands, reefs, meadows and sandy beaches, fishing villages full of brightly painted wooden huts (left) and secluded resorts. Sweden's second-largest conurbation, Gothenburg, is the point of entry to this attractive area.

The city's architecture is marked by Dutch influences, seen in the facades of its historic centre and along the banks of the large Stora HamnKanalen waterway, on which you can take a cruise. This green town, open to the sea, is a commercial port with a friendly atmosphere, and is an excellent place to spend a day taking in the culture of one of its many museums and admiring the dozens of examples of street art around the city, before heading north to enjoy Bohuslän's coastal attractions.

Take a trip to Brännö Island

Brännö, off the coast of Gothenburg, is a top destination for a day out among the region's islands. A welcome tranquillity emanates from this car-free piece of land, where wooded hills fade into the choppy sea. To enjoy the isolation the island offers, take the one-hour ferry from Gothenburg, bringing a bike along if you want to venture out on two wheels.

Life in small town Marstrand

In the middle of a natural setting of granite rock and verdant forest, quaint Marstrand attracts many summer visitors who come to walk, swim or go boating. Home to age-old maritime traditions, the small town is split in two by an arm of the sea: a ferry takes you to the western half of town and sturdy Carlsten Fort (inset), an ancient citadel built to defend Bohuslän when it became a Swedish province in 1658. The town is a 45-minute drive northwest of Gothenburg.

Take a walk on Tjörn

Cycling along winding roads, hiking in awe-inspiring landscapes, swimming in secluded coves, visiting fishing hamlets – these are just some of the experiences to be had on Tjörn, a speck of land on the Bohuslän coast. Don't miss Pilane (pilane.org), an open-air contemporary exhibition offering sculptures with a backdrop of rugged shores and grazing sheep. Connected to the mainland by a bridge, Tjörn is a 40-minute drive from Gothenburg or one hour by bus.

Canoeing in the Vättlefjäll Nature Reserve

Northeast of Gothenburg, the splendid Vättlefjäll Nature Reserve (kanotpoolen.se) is a playground for outdoor enthusiasts. Made up of moorlands, forests, hills and lakes linked by a network of canals, it's home to exceptional flora and fauna. Your stay here might include swimming, hiking, barbecuing, kayaking or even Canadian canoeing – and all this is just 20 minutes by car from Gothenburg, or 30 minutes by bus.

MORE TIME?

SMÖGEN An iconic postcard-perfect image of Sweden, this fishing village of multicoloured huts, enclosed within a granite amphitheatre, is one of the most picturesque in the country. Summer is a busy time of year, so off-season travel will allow you to make the most of this enchanting location with smaller crowds. It's a 90-minute drive north of Gothenburg.
FJÄLLBACKA Another fishing village, close to Smögen, that's full of charm, with old red wooden houses along handsome little streets. Facing Fjällbacka, the sea is speckled with rocky islets (opposite), best admired from the clifftops above the village.

STREET ART IN GOTHENBURG

Gothenburg is famous for the street art scattered throughout its various districts, brightening up buildings with vivid colours and original topics. Today, the city is home to some 100 impressive street murals, created by a plethora of talented creators. In fact, this form of expression has become such an integral part of the cultural identity of Gothenburg that the Artscape Festival, celebrating all things street art, was held here in 2016, 2019 and 2021.

~ PRACTICALITIES ~

HOW TO GET THERE & AROUND

Gothenburg Airport has direct flights to around 30 cities across Europe. Ferries and trains connect the city to Germany and Denmark. The local bus network is well-developed, and most destinations are easy to reach by public transport.

WHERE TO STAY

With its many amenities, Gothenburg's city centre is the ideal place to stay, especially around the cathedral and the Stora HamnKanalen canal.

EVENTS

Gothenburg puts on several events throughout the year. Among them is Way Out West (wayoutwest.se), a major pop and electronic music festival in August that sees crowds of visitors. In September, the Bokmässan (goteborg-bookfair. com) attracts bibliophiles to Scandinavia's most important literary event. Last but not least, the city shines brightly in December with Christmas markets and celebrations in honour of St Lucia.

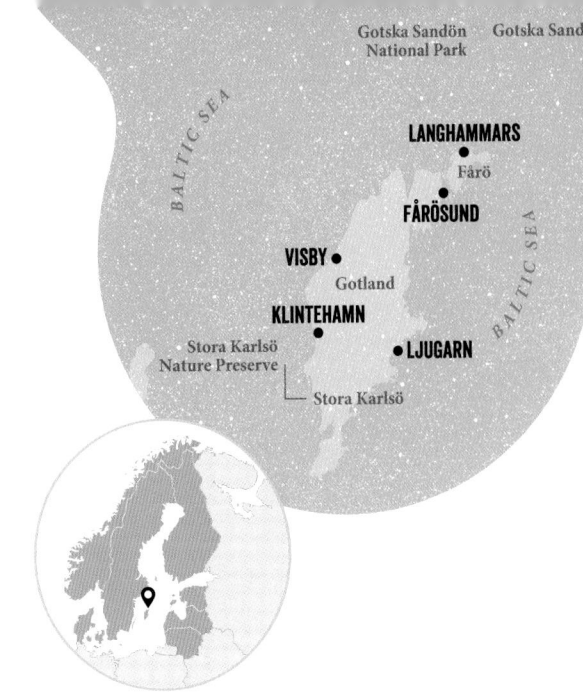

SWEDEN

92

Baltic bliss
IN GOTLAND

I f you're after wild landscapes, endless summer
days and long bike rides,
head for the island of Gotland,
halfway between Sweden and
Latvia. The largest island in
the Baltic Sea attracts quite a
few people in summer, there to
enjoy some sun (it gets more rays
than the rest of Sweden) and the
outdoor activities its forests, fields
and coastlines provide. In short,
this is an ideal place to unwind
and get away from everyday life.
Visby is the island's UNESCO
World Heritage-listed capital and
well worth the trip alone. It's a
Hanseatic port with centuries-old
architecture that's the perfect
backdrop for August's Medieval
Week events. Beyond the town,
Gotland is all about sandy shores
and old hamlets where you can feel
disconnected from time. It's also
a place where prized but elusive
truffles are found and served up on
restaurant menus. And if you want
to get even more off the beaten
track, just off Gotland sit the
islands of Fårö, indelibly linked to
one of the greatest film directors in
history, and tiny Gotska Sandön
and Stora Karlsö.

History lessons in Hanseatic Visby

The way to begin a visit to Sweden's best-preserved medieval town (inset) is with a walk along its 13th-century ramparts (3.5 km/2 miles), then smell the flowers in the botanical gardens and lose yourself in the labyrinth of picturesque alleyways with their ruined Gothic churches. Sankta Maria Domkyrka, the 12th-century cathedral, is a real eye-catcher, with its Romanesque towers, baroque domes and beautiful stained glass.

Truffle hunting in Ljugarn

Gotland's forests are rich in truffles, and 'safaris' to find them are available in October and November around Ljugarn, in the south of the island. Some packages combine a five-star dinner (with truffles, of course) with accommodation. Find out more at tryffelsafari.se.

Go back in time at Tjelvar's Grave

Traces of human occupation on Gotland date back 8000 years and are easy to see when you visit Tjelvar's Grave on the island's east coast. This Bronze Age site features a series of standing stones in the shape of a ship and is named after the legendary first settler on the island. For a look at life a few millennia later, head northeast to the Bungemuseet (bungemuseet. se), an open-air museum featuring 17th to 19th century houses, plus 7th-century rune stones.

Otherworldly landscapes in Fårö

Hop on a ferry at Fårösund, on Gotland's northeast tip, to get to Fårö – the crossing is free and takes just five minutes. This small island features some of the most beautiful beaches in the area and is famous for two things: director Ingmar Bergman, who fell in love with the place and moved here; and the astonishing rock formations called the raukar, which give part of the coastline an otherworldly appearance – the rocks near the 19th-century lighthouse contain numerous fossils. You can cycle around the island on a day trip, but if you plan on spending the night, make sure to catch the sunset show at Langhammars.

MORE TIME?

GOTSKA SANDÖN 'Sand Island', 38km (24 miles) north of Fårö, is a captivating national park where you can wander in peace and quiet through dunes and coniferous forests. Ferries run from Fårösund on Gotland and Nynäshamn on the Swedish mainland; overnight stays possible, see sandoresor.se.

STORA KARLSÖ Another teeny island, southwest of Gotland, but this one is a nature reserve with a wide variety of birds, including guillemots and razorbills. Ferries serve the island from Klintehamn.

INGMAR BERGMAN

It was while he was location-hunting for *Through a Glass Darkly* (1961) that the great Swedish director Ingmar Bergman discovered the untamed and mysterious landscapes of Fårö. The director made a total of seven films here, including the masterpieces *Persona* (1966) and *Scenes from a Marriage* (1974), lived here for 40 years and died here in 2007. If you're a fan of his movies, a visit to the Bergman Center (bergmancenter.se) on the island is akin to a pilgrimage; the centre keeps his legacy alive by organising Bergman Week every year in early summer.

WHEN TO GO

The best time to visit is between June and September, when the days are beautiful, mild and long.

HOW TO GET THERE

You'll need to connect from mainland Sweden to get to Gotland: flights operate from Stockholm-Bromma Airport (year-round) and Malmö (June to September). Ferries to the island run from Nynäshamn and Oskarshamn.

WHERE TO STAY

There are several B&Bs, hostels and lodges on the islands. For a bit more comfort and style, choose the family-run Hotell St Clemens (clemenshotell.se) in Visby, housed in five historic buildings with two gardens.

EVENTS

August's Medieval Week sees Visby put on a fantastic show with jousting, costumes, banquets and markets bringing the Middle Ages to life. Book transport and accommodation well in advance.

93

SWEDEN

In search of the Northern Lights IN SWEDISH LAPLAND

A patchwork of forests, lakes and marshes makes up Swedish Lapland, a huge region covering a quarter of the country. Its population is concentrated in three major towns: **Kiruna**, **Gällivare** and **Jokkmokk**, but it's the area's distinct scenery, outdoor pursuits and unique traditions that attract travellers: its pin-drop-quiet landscapes and Northern Lights shows, and the dogsled races and reindeer herds that are an integral part of the culture of the **Sámi**, formerly known as Lapps. Other attractions include the **King's Trail** hike, and the unsetting **midnight sun** around the summer solstice, from late May to mid-July (from mid-December to mid-January, the sun doesn't rise during the **polar night**). Swedish Lapland offers two national parks: **Sarek** and **Abisko**. In winter, the latter offers skiing and snowshoeing, as well as snowmobile and scooter excursions. In summer, activities revolve around walking and fishing. The best time to visit, though, is arguably November to March, when the land is at its icy best and the chance to see the Northern Lights is greatest.

Take a royal walk

For an unforgettable foray into the heart of Swedish Lapland, head out on the Kungsleden (the 'King's Trail'), the country's best-known walk. The signposted route stretches 450km (280 miles) between Abisko and Hemavan, and is divided into two main sections: north and south. It usually takes three weeks to complete. The northern section between Abisko and Vakkotavare is best suited to less experienced hikers. In summer, the Kebnekaise massif and the village of Nikkaluokta, near Kiruna, are home to some of the country's top shorter hikes.

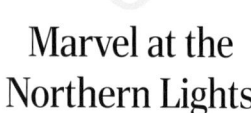

Marvel at the Northern Lights

The fabulous natural phenomenon that is the Northern Lights (opposite), when particles from the sun hit Earth's atmosphere and react with the gases, occurs regularly in Swedish Lapland. One of the best places to observe them is the Aurora Sky Station (auroraskystation.se), accessible by chairlift from the village of Abisko. From Kiruna, it's 100km (62 miles) on a winding mountain road to Abisko Turiststation, in Abisko National Park, 250km (155 miles) north of the Arctic Circle, from where you ascend to the station. Book well in advance and pray for clear skies.

Spend the night in unique accommodation

Just a 20-minute drive east of Kiruna, the village of Jukkasjärvi, population 548, has made a name for itself over the past 30-plus years by hosting, from December to April, the world's largest hotel made of ice and snow (icehotel.com). The rooms in this frozen palace are all sculpted with unique decor, renewed each season. Room temperatures vary between -3 and -8°C (27 and 17.6°F), so traditional rooms and chalets are also available for those wanting something warmer. Another hotel with an innovative design, the Treehotel (treehotel.se) in Harads is ideal for admiring the countryside, winter or summer. Its various suites perched in the trees (including a Mirrorcube, inset) were created with the help of various architectural firms.

Explore Lapland aboard the Inlandsbanan

You can travel from Gällivare to Jokkmokk on the Inlandsbanan, a historic railway line that passes through small mining towns and dense green forests. Finished in the 1930s, the 1288km (800 mile) route has enough scenic appeal to compensate for its slowness – passengers have plenty of time to appreciate the scenery and watch herds of reindeer, or even, if lucky, a moose or two.

MORE TIME?

LAPLAND REGION Listed as a UNESCO World Heritage Site since 1996, this vast region is protected by several national parks and nature reserves and crossed by hiking trails, such as Padjelantaleden, which runs from Ritsem to Kvikkjokk. The more demanding routes through Sarek National Park are only suitable for experienced, well-equipped walkers.

LULEÅ For an unusual way to discover the frozen Luleå Archipelago in winter, join a guide on board a hovercraft (luleatravel.com/activities/hovercraft) and let yourself float gently between the islands, with breaks to enjoy the scenery and spot seals and sea eagles.

THE SÁMI

Europe's last indigenous nomadic people, the Sámi historically lived from hunting and fishing, before gradually turning to reindeer herding. In Jukkasjärvi, the Nutti Sámi Siida (nutti. se) complex offers a great introduction to Sámi life, with its small open-air museum and reindeer. In Jokkmokk, Samernas utbildningscentrum (a public school open to children of Sámi parents) has been set up to pass on knowledge and skills to the next generation. Nearby, the Ájtte Museum (ajtte.com) provides perhaps the best insight into Sámi culture in the country.

∿ PRACTICALITIES ∿

🅿 HOW TO GET THERE & AROUND

Kiruna's Airport, Sweden's northernmost, has connections to European destinations via Stockholm. You can rent a car at the airport, or direct transfers to Abisko can be arranged. The road between Kiruna and Abisko is served by bus 91. Luleå Airport has several flights to Stockholm every day. Trains run between Luleå and Kiruna.

📅 EVENTS

In Jokkmokk, a large traditional market (jokkmokksmarknad.se) has been held every February since 1605. Lappish handicrafts, music and dance are all on show.

94

Get to know
OSLO & AROUND

I n southern Norway, on the edge of a fjord, sprawling Oslo stretches between sea, lakes, mountains and forests.' It's a setting conducive to outdoor fun, meaning hikers, mountain bikers and skiers are in for a treat. Although some travellers overlook the Norwegian capital, those who do make it find that along with the magical location, the city is also one of Scandinavia's leading cultural centres, with a striking opera house on the waterfront and a host of other venues keeping locals and visitors entertained. These include the Astrup Fearnley

Museum of Contemporary Art (afmuseet.no), and the National Museum (nasjonalmuseet.no), which holds the country's largest collection of art, design and architecture. In addition to this cultural appeal and the wealth of green spaces, the city also has a number of impressive historic buildings, including the cathedral, royal palace and medieval Akershus Fortress. Oslo may be a busy metropolis, but it still has a warm, friendly side, especially in the Aker Brygge neighbourhood, where you can try excellent Nordic cuisine along the pier.

Explore Nordmarka Forest

Just outside Oslo, Nordmarka Forest (opposite) is an essential destination for walkers, mountain bikers, skiers and tobogganists. A popular starting point for hikers and bikers is the Tryvannstårnet observation tower, while to the east, peaceful Lake Maridal, set in thick woods, is easily accessible by bike from the capital.

Try your hand (virtually) at ski jumping

Overlooking the Norwegian capital, the Holmenkollen ski jump (inset) offers a breathtaking view of Oslo, spreading out below between fjords and forests. Alongside the superstructure – an intimidating 134m (440ft) high – the fascinating Ski Museum (skiforeningen.no/holmenkollen) retraces 4000 years of the history of alpine and Nordic skiing, and offers a thrill ride on a ski-jump simulator – an experience you won't forget.

Visit the Viking Ship Museum

Journey through over a thousand years of history and immerse yourself in Scandinavia's Viking past at the captivating Viking Ship Museum (vikingtidsmuseet.no). Contemplate three remarkably well-preserved ships from burial sites, among them the Oseberg with a snake head adorning the bow. The museum is located on the Bygdøy Peninsula, on the outskirts of Oslo, and can be reached by ferry from the city centre.

Park life in Ekebergparken

This vast green space (ekebergparken.com), overlooking Oslo and its fjord, is home to astonishing contemporary art installations plus several trails, including a signposted Iron Age route. But, above all, it's the views, including the Munchpunktet (the panorama that inspired Edvard Munch's famous painting *The Scream*), that make spending half a day in the Ekebergparken such a delight.

MORE TIME?

FREDRIKSTAD This pretty fortified town has old wooden houses, a moat, a drawbridge and a splendid cathedral, and is topped by a massive fortress, dating from the 17th century. Fredrikstad is one hour by train from Oslo.

KOSTERHAVET NATIONAL PARK Across the border in Sweden, but just a 90-minute drive from Oslo, the Koster Islands Archipelago is a national marine park (sverigesnationalparker.se) where you can easily observe seals, go scuba diving or hike along gorgeous beaches. This protected area can be reached by boat from Strömstad in Sweden.

A CONTEMPORARY KITCHEN

Oslo's food scene offers contemporary cuisine while revisiting traditional dishes. Cod tongue, chicken giblets, blood sausage – these flavours of yesteryear have been brought up to date, surprising many a traveller. More conventional dishes, however, can be found on the menus of renowned chefs, generally involving fresh fish and local produce. And, as elsewhere, world cuisine (sushi, pizza, tapas) is becoming an increasingly important part of the Norwegian gastronomic offering.

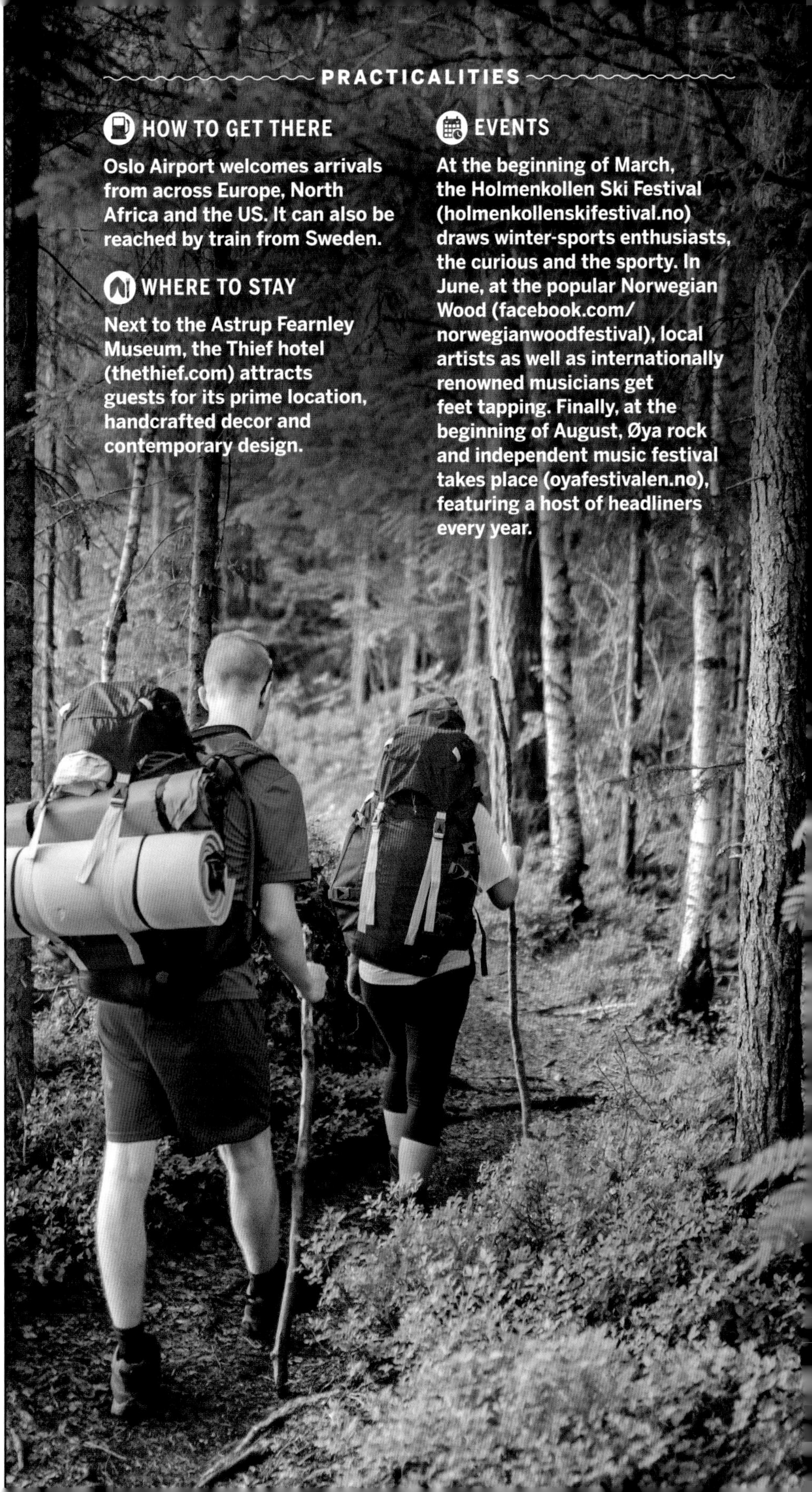

~~~~~ PRACTICALITIES ~~~~~

HOW TO GET THERE

Oslo Airport welcomes arrivals from across Europe, North Africa and the US. It can also be reached by train from Sweden.

WHERE TO STAY

Next to the Astrup Fearnley Museum, the Thief hotel (thethief.com) attracts guests for its prime location, handcrafted decor and contemporary design.

EVENTS

At the beginning of March, the Holmenkollen Ski Festival (holmenkollenskifestival.no) draws winter-sports enthusiasts, the curious and the sporty. In June, at the popular Norwegian Wood (facebook.com/ norwegianwoodfestival), local artists as well as internationally renowned musicians get feet tapping. Finally, at the beginning of August, Øya rock and independent music festival takes place (oyafestivalen.no), featuring a host of headliners every year.

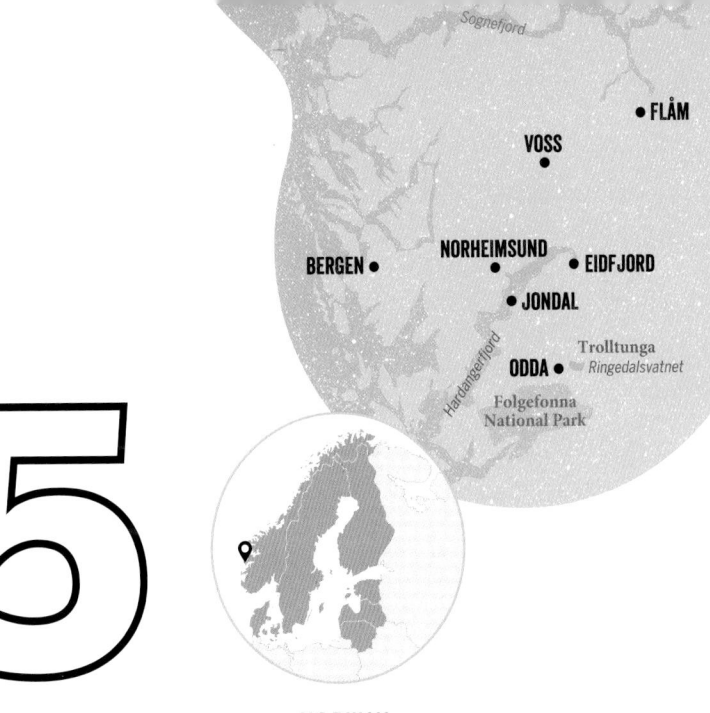

Sognefjord

• FLÅM

VOSS

NORHEIMSUND • • EIDFJORD

BERGEN • • JONDAL

Trolltunga
Ringedalsvatnet
ODDA •

Hardangerfjord

Folgefonna
National Park

NORWAY

95

*Experience the
drama of the fjords*
IN WESTERN NORWAY

There's no better place to spend a memorable weekend than in the maritime maze of Norway's western fjords, where you can enjoy a wide range of outdoor activities on foot, bike, kayak or boat. Along scenic roads linking the highlights of this dazzling Scandinavian region, you'll pass grinding glaciers, azure lakes, perpetually snowcapped mountains, orchards in bloom on spring days and a rough coastline sprinkled with islands. At the heart of this enchanting picture lies Bergen (see page 395). The country's former capital and one of the first Hanseatic trading posts, Bergen promises a charming city break in a laid-back atmosphere. Its pretty narrow streets, multi-coloured houses and old port, bordered by the unmissable Bryggen wharf lined with picturesque wooden boathouses, are the stuff that holiday dreams are made of. In summer, off the coast of the city, treat yourself to an unforgettable cruise on the waters of the North Sea, getting a fish-eye's view of the fjords. Then test your head for heights with a visit to the legendary Trolltunga rock.

Explore Hardangerfjord

You'll fall hard for Hardangerfjord (hardangerfjord.com), a stunningly beautiful inlet with emerald waters surrounded by high mountains; sparkling glaciers; waterfalls; woods; orchards full of strawberries, plums and apples; and quaint villages. From Bergen, take the bus to Norheimsund and then the ferry that sails through the heart of Hardangerfjord to Eidfjord, a village at the bottom of a vast glacial valley.

Hiking on Mt Fløyen

From downtown Bergen, the Fløibanen cable car (floyen.no) takes you up Mt Fløyen, one of seven mountains rising above the city, in just a few minutes. A number of walking trails at the top offer splendid views, including a route to nearby Mt Ulriken, another natural viewpoint overlooking Bergen and the fjords (three-hour walk). To save retracing your steps, the Ulriksbanen cable car can take you back down to the Bergen area (3km/2 miles from the centre, served by a bus to Bryggen).

Take a trip to Sognefjord

At 204km (127 miles) long, Sognefjord (see previous page and page 310) is Norway's largest and deserves a full day to appreciate it. From Bergen, the Sognefjord in a Nutshell tour is offered from May to September by Fjord Tours (norwaynutshell.com). The boat cruises from the city and then along the length of the fjord, with its turquoise waters and snowcapped mountains, all the way to the village of Flåm, before you return to the city by train along a scenic railway line.

Push your limits in Voss

A resort on the shores of Lake Vangsvatnet, Voss is renowned throughout Norway for extreme sports. Mountain biking, hiking, climbing, skiing, rafting and, above all, kayaking are just some of the activities you can enjoy around and on the water here. To get to Voss from Bergen, follow the E16 for 100km (62 miles) – an excellent road trip along fjords and lakes.

MORE TIME?

FOLGEFONNA Accessible from Jondal village, two hours, 30 minutes' drive east of Bergen, Folgefonna National Park (folgefonna.info) is perfect for walkers and skiers. The immense glacier here is best explored in summer with a guide.
TROLLTUNGA The famous rocky prow that is the 'Troll's Tongue' (inset; trolltunga.com) offers an unparalleled if daunting view of Ringedalsvatnet lake, 700m (2297ft) below. Start the strenuous hike to get there (10 hours) at Tyssedal, near the lovely town of Odda.

THE RIGHT TO NATURE

Norway's *Allemannsretten* ('everyone's right') is a law that guarantees free access for all to the great outdoors. To enjoy the unrivalled beauty of the country's nature, there is one restriction, though – stay on uncultivated or unfenced land. You can also pitch your tent for the night, as long as it's at least 150m (492ft) from any dwelling. In return, ensure you leave no trace of your visit, don't disturb wildlife and walk on paths to limit your impact.

～～～～～ PRACTICALITIES ～～～～～

🅿 HOW TO GET THERE

Bergen is easily reached by flights from dozens of international destinations, including cities in the UK, France, Germany, Italy and Spain.

⛺ WHERE TO STAY

The Bryggen district, adjacent to the old harbour, is home to a number of attractive accommodation options in the city's most scenic spot.

📅 EVENTS

In May, the Bergen International Festival (fib.no) puts on a variety of concerts, plays and exhibitions. Norway's Constitution Day on 17 May is also a major event, with brass bands and parades in traditional costume. Gourmets will prefer to visit in September, though, for the Matfestival (matfest.no), a food and cider festival featuring local produce.

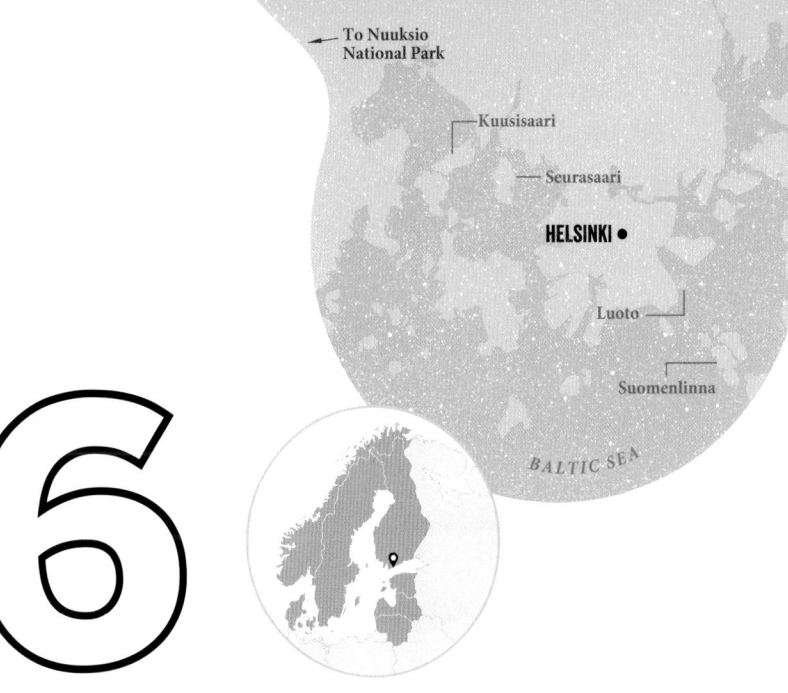

To Nuuksio
National Park

Kuusisaari

Seurasaari

HELSINKI ●

Luoto

Suomenlinna

BALTIC SEA

FINLAND

96

Find Finnish cool
AROUND HELSINKI

A port city and capital of a country where water is everywhere, Helsinki's location on the Baltic Sea couldn't be more apt. The twists and turns of its ragged coastline conceal numerous bays, coves and hundreds of islands worth exploring, including Suomenlinna with its imposing fortress. And the city itself has plenty of land-based appeal too. In addition to splendid Art Nouveau architecture, heritage museums and century-old cafes and restaurants, there's a cool contemporary artistic culture, with more than 50 museums and galleries, including Kiasma (kiasma.fi), an icon of modern Helsinki, housed in a dazzling metal building. The stark white Tuomiokirkko (Lutheran cathedral; left) and the red-brick and gold-domed Uspenskin Katedraali (Orthodox cathedral) can be added to the list of top sights. Nature is also very present in Helsinki, and a stroll through the Kaisaniemi Botanic Garden or Esplanadi Park is a must. For an overview of the capital and surrounding region, take a spin on the SkyWheel, a Ferris wheel by the port.

Shop in the Design District

Helsinki is an international capital of design, from ready-to-wear to the latest furniture and home decor. The Design District (designdistrict.fi) stretches from Esplanadi in the east, Punavuori in the south and Kamppi to the west and is home to hundreds of boutiques, workshops and galleries, including stalwart Artek (artek. fi) and relative newcomer Lokal (lokalhelsinki.com). Round off your design day out with a visit to the Design Museum (designmuseum. fi), which traces the origins of Finnish design, its links with nature and its continuing evolution.

Explore the island fortress of Suomenlinna

Suomenlinna, the 'Fortress of Finland' (inset), is a UNESCO World Heritage Site on an island just southeast of Helsinki. Built by the Swedes in the 18th century, it covers an archipelago of six islands linked by bridges. Ferries run between downtown Helsinki and Suomenlinna, where you can visit museums, old casemates and fortifications, and a WWII submarine. From the main quay, a blue signposted path links the main sights.

A nature trip in Nuuksio National Park

Close enough to Helsinki – just 35km (22 miles) northwest – for a half-day getaway, Nuuksio National Park (opposite) opens the doors to the wonders of Finland's nature. Two trails offer walks through glacier-eroded wooded valleys, home to elk, lynx and nocturnal flying squirrels. You can stay on-site too, in one of the campsites, chalets or refuges.

Discover the Finnish way of life

On the wooded island of Seurasaari, an open-air museum founded in 1909 offers a complete change of scenery from the capital. It features 87 homes imported from every province in Finland – the Niemelä farmhouse (1844) features a smoke sauna – plus guides in traditional costume demonstrating folk dancing and handicrafts. Bring a picnic and make a day out of your visit.

MORE TIME?

ISLAND OF THE ARTS The island of Kuusisaari, accessible by bus or ferry from Helsinki, is home to two private museums housed in opulent villas: the Didrichsen Art Museum (didrichsenmuseum. fi) and the Villa Gyllenberg (villagyllenberg.fi), which exhibit the collections of their former owners, mainly focusing on the Finnish Golden Age (roughly 1880–1910) and the 20th century.
DINNER AT SAARISTO The most famous restaurant in the Helsinki Archipelago, Saaristo (ravintolasaaristo.fi) occupies an Art Nouveau villa on the island of Luoto and serves seasonal produce – crayfish is a summer treat. Access is by private boat.

LÖYLY SAUNA

What could be more closely linked to Finnish culture than the sauna, a place to purify body and mind? There are hundreds of them in Helsinki, but Löyly (loylyhelsinki.fi), built in 1916, stands out as one of the best. This sauna-restaurant complex has 4000 custom-cut natural wood planks, a Scandinavian birch interior and is powered entirely by water and wind. The two electric saunas and the traditional wood-fired sauna offer direct access to the waterfront – which becomes a hole in the ice in winter – for cooling off.

PRACTICALITIES

⛽ HOW TO GET THERE

Helsinki is extremely well connected to cities around the world. For a different way to arrive, take the ferry from Tallinn (Estonia) or Stockholm (Sweden).

🏨 WHERE TO STAY

The accommodation on offer is dominated by chain hotels, but there are a few boutique and design options, plus a campsite. Central Hotel Klaus K (klauskhotel.com) has cool minimalist decor. On Suomenlinna, Hostel Suomenlinna (hostelhelsinki.fi) makes an excellent base.

📅 EVENTS

Things to plan a trip around in the city include September's Helsinki Design Week (helsinkidesignweek.com), the largest design festival in the Nordic countries; and June's St John's Day, celebrated on the longest day of the year.

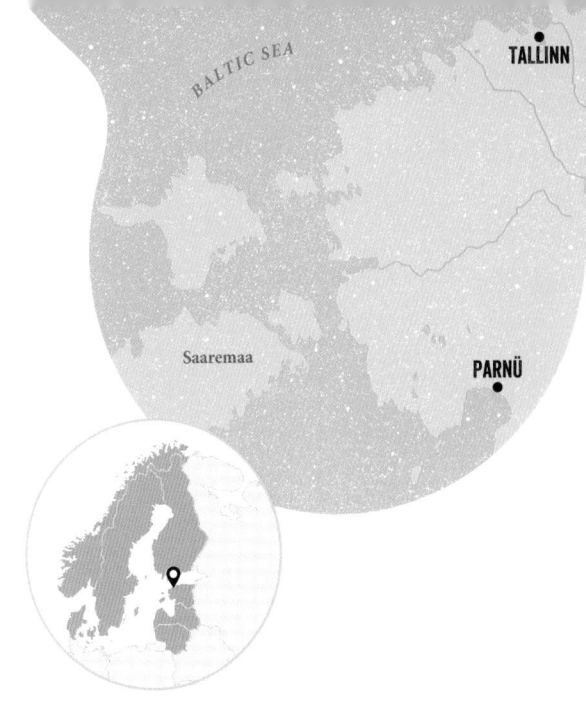

TALLINN

PARNÜ

Saaremaa

ESTONIA

97

Ease into Estonia
IN THE BAY OF TALLINN

Estonia's capital Tallinn offers a glimpse back in time to the Middle Ages, with its 13th-century historic centre enclosed by ramparts and filled with brightly painted houses lining cobblestone streets. The city's Old Town recalls the days when Hanseatic merchants controlled the Baltic Sea and this was one of their most important ports. The museum at Kiek in de Kök (linnamuuseum. ee/kiek-in-de-kok), one of the 26 watchtowers of the original fortifications, allows visitors to explore underground passages once used to defend the city. The Church of the Holy Spirit houses treasures of sacred art. And St Catherine's Passage is home to a guild of craftspeople still working the old-fashioned way. The same goes for the Masters' Courtyard, an ivy-covered haven of peace where you can visit the workshops and enjoy a coffee on the terrace. For a postcard-worthy panorama, climb Toompea Hill (left), lorded over by a castle housing the Estonian Parliament. For a breath of that invigorating Baltic Sea air, head to the sandy beaches of Pärnu and the wild, wooded islands south of the capital and easily reached by car or public transport.

Bohemian Kalamaja

With its abandoned canneries and multicoloured wooden houses, the former fishing district of Kalamaja now cultivates a bohemian atmosphere. After some shopping at the Balti Jaam farmers' market, climb aboard the *Lembit*, a 1936 submarine, at the Estonian Maritime Museum. Then it's off to the Telliskivi warehouses, converted into an artistic hub full of cool cafes, street art, galleries and concept stores. Discover the work of Estonia's up-and-coming creators and sit on a terrace with a beer brewed in the neighbourhood.

Swim in Pärnu

Pärnu (opposite) was a pioneer of Baltic seaside resorts and today is *the* place to be seen for Estonia's elite. After a refreshing dip in the sea and a walk along the beach, head into the town centre, where beautiful, old pastel-coloured buildings still operate as shops or homes. Visit baroque St Catherine's Church and the medieval Red Tower, before lunch at elegant Mon Ami (facebook.com/restoranmonami) or quirky Supelsaksad (supelsaksad. ee). Finish with a visit to the spa in the unique Mud Baths (hedonspa. com), built on the beach in the 19th century.

Unwind in a sauna

Saunas are a way of life in Estonia, and one of the best and oldest is Kalma Saun (kalmasaun.ee), built in 1928 and hidden behind an Art Deco facade. Men and women bathe separately. Fancy combining a hot sauna with a beer to cool off? Visit Bar Heldeke! (heldeke. ee), a former brothel converted into a bar and club, which opens its sauna two days a week (Wednesday and Sunday).

Estonian life in the 1700s

In the Rocca al Mare district, the Estonian Open-Air Museum (evm.ee) displays an astonishing life-size reconstruction of a typical 18th-century Estonian village. This huge exhibition features dozens of buildings, including an inn, mills, farms, a school, a military barracks and a church. To complete the illusion, craftspeople work with period tools, and visitors can sample traditional Estonian products.

See a tsar's palace

To the east of Tallinn's Old Town, the suburb of Kadriorg is home to a graceful pink-and-white palace built by Tsar Peter the Great in the early 18th century. After a tour of the apartments, spend time smelling the blooms in the vast flower-filled garden that surrounds it.

MORE TIME?

SAAREMAA During the Soviet era, the island of Saaremaa (inset; visitsaaremaa.ee) housed a missile reserve and was strictly off-limits – which meant the whole place was frozen in time, with its mills, villages, pine forests and attractive beaches left undisturbed. These days you can cycle around the island before enjoying a plate of smoked fish.
KUMU In the Kadriorg neighbourhood, KuMu museum (kumu. ekm.ee) exhibits the country's finest collection of modern art.

E-ESTONIA

Since the 2000s and the early pioneering digitisation of its government services, Estonia has been a global digital role model. Whether it's voting, paying taxes, setting up a business, picking up medication or keeping track of your children's schooling, everything is now done online. The use of 4G and 5G is widely available across the country, even in the most remote forests. Targeted by nationwide cyberattacks in 2007, the country now also excels in cybersecurity.

~ PRACTICALITIES ~

HOW TO GET THERE

Tallinn has direct flights to destinations across Europe, plus a ferry linking it to Helsinki (Finland) in just a couple of hours.

WHERE TO STAY & EAT

Enjoy the cool Scandinavian design of Citybox Tallinn City (cityboxhotels.com) or Hektor Container Hotel (hektorstay.com), occupying a former Telliskivi railway depot. To discover Estonian cuisine, try the gourmet plates at Rataskaevu 16 (rataskaevu16.ee) or the innovative cuisine at Lee (leeresto.ee), which features local farm produce. In Pärnu, magnificent Villa Ammende (ammende.ee) has preserved its sublime Art Nouveau features.

EVENTS

In June, the Craft Beer Weekend (tcbw.ee) livens up the streets of Tallinn with countless street bars and concerts. For the festive season, a Christmas market lights up the old square.

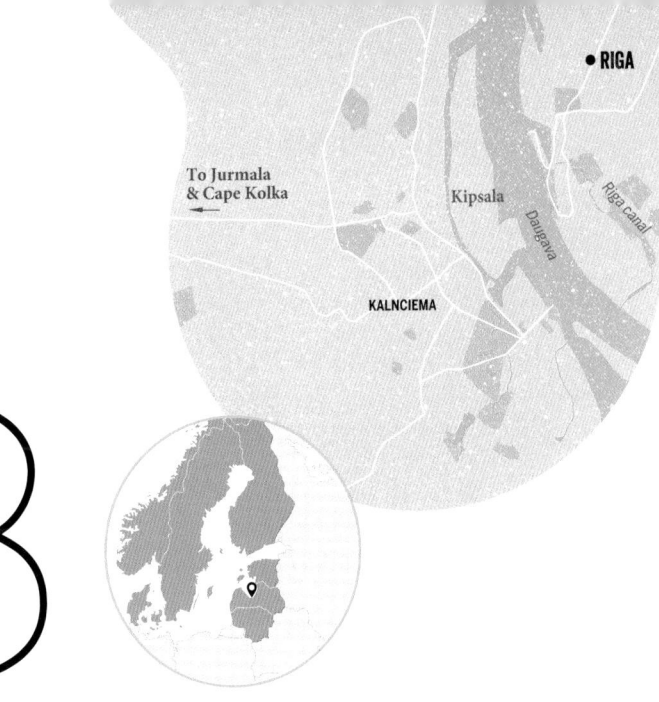

LATVIA

98

Sign up for an architecture course
IN RĪGA

Latvia's capital Rīga presents visitors with a wonderfully eclectic architectural heritage, ranging from medieval to Art Nouveau. On Town Hall Sq in old Rīga, Blackheads House (see page 407) shows off its 14th-century brick facade adorned with statues. To the north, the Three Brothers – dressed in green, yellow and white – are the city's oldest dwellings. After a walk through the Middle Ages in the Old Town, head for the Central District to discover the curves and quirks of its Art Nouveau buildings – Strēlnieku and Elizabetes streets have plenty of examples of the style, while Alberta St displays a symphony of pastel tones and sculpted motifs alternating between grimacing masks, sphinxes, winged lions, peacocks and centaurs. To complete your education, visit the Art Nouveau Museum – its interior has been restored as a typical 1900s apartment; then the futuristic National Library, all glass and steel. For beyond-architecture activities, canoe on the canal, swim in resort town Jūrmala or grab a bite to eat at the Central Market.

The high life in Rīga

It's best to go up to look down on Rīga's architectural diversity, and the Gothic tower of St Peter's Basilica provides the ideal opportunity – the city's tallest building has a spire reaching 124m (407ft) with unsurprisingly impressive views from its 72m (236ft) lookout. Other spots from which to admire the capital include the 15th floor of the Stalinesque Academy of Science (panoramariga.lv/) or, more glamorous, sipping a drink at the Skyline Bar (skylinebar.lv), on the top floor of the Radisson Blu Latvija hotel.

Spread your towel on the beach at Jūrmala

Just 30 minutes by train from Rīga, the seaside resort of Jūrmala is great for a break by the Baltic Sea. The white sand of its 30km (19 miles) of beach bordered by pine forest, the old-fashioned charm of its 19th-century wooden houses and the spas of its luxury hotels have been seducing Latvians for centuries. Avoid the overpriced tourist restaurants and opt instead for the simple dishes and warm ambience of Jomas Terase, the Georgian cuisine of Halipapa or the elegant terrace of Noi.

Relax on the water

Rīga's Old Town is surrounded by the Daugava River and a belt of canals lined with parks. Enjoy a relaxing ride on one of the small wooden tourist boats (inset) or rent a pedalboat and discover the city from an aquatic perspective (rigabycanal.lv).

Meander through Little Moscow

Located behind the Central Market, Little Moscow is known for its ramshackle wooden houses. Once a best-avoided neighbourhood, it's now the Spīķeri cultural hub, where former warehouses are home to art galleries, restaurants and cafes popular with the cool crowd. Collectors will love the Latgale Tirgus flea market with its stalls full of vintage items.

Taste local specialities at the Central Market

Meat pies, homemade honey, rye bread, smoked fish, sauerkraut, blueberries – Europe's largest indoor market, built in former Zeppelin hangars from WWI, is a first-rate introduction to delicious regional products and the specialities of Latvian cuisine.

MORE TIME?

CAPE KOLKA In the days of the USSR, a military base was set up on this cape northwest of Rīga and the area was off-limits. The long, white sandy beaches are now open and form an unspoiled natural landscape with an end-of-the-world feel.
KALNCIEMA Located across the Daugava, Kalnciema is Rīga's bohemian heart, with its epicentre being the market and its stalls of farm produce, designer boutiques and concerts.
ĶĪPSALA This island offers a bubble of calm in the middle of the busy city, thanks to its green spaces and pretty houses on the water's edge.

RĪGA BLACK BALSAM

Created in 1752 by a pharmacist, Black Balsam is Latvia's national drink. The recipe for this bitter liqueur is kept secret, but it's known to contain around 20 ingredients, including oak bark, honey and cranberries. Older Latvians claim that a glass a day will help you reach a venerable age and keep all illnesses at bay. Legend has it that the elixir cured Empress Catherine the Great of Russia, who fell ill during a visit to Latvia.

~ PRACTICALITIES ~

HOW TO GET THERE

Rīga has flight connections to several European cites. To reach Jūrmala by train from the Latvian capital, get off at Majori.

WHERE TO STAY & EAT

In the historic centre, the Wellton Riverside SPA Hotel (wellton.com) overlooks the Daugava.

The dishes at John restaurant (johnrestaurant.com) embody new Latvian cuisine, while at Zivju Lete (zivjulete.lv), you can feast on fish and seafood. For brunch, Anna's Därzs (annasdarzs.lv) is ideal, with its gargantuan buffet and pretty garden.

EVENTS

During Re Riga! (reriga.lv), in August, street arts and contemporary circus take over the city. In December, Christmas markets fill the Old Town's squares.

MATER VILNENSIS

99

LITHUANIA

Hunt for historical treasures
IN VILNIUS

Between its Old Town, a UNESCO World Heritage Site, and its New Town, home to interesting museums, the Lithuanian capital has plenty of sights that add up to an exciting weekend visit. With its twisting streets, hidden courtyards and baroque churches, the Lithuanian capital's historic core is just the start of the fun – sunny terraces, top-rated restaurants and quiet cafes, craft workshops and design stores all contribute to the city's appeal, best experienced on foot. A potential route takes you up Gediminas Hill, where the remains of the castle stand, reached either on two legs or by historic funicular; aim for the end of the day when this high point is the best place to admire the sun setting behind Vilnius' spires. Down below, the cathedral and belfry adjoin the Palace of the Grand Dukes of Lithuania, a vibrant museum of art and history, a must for anyone with an interest in the history of the country and Baltic States in general. Another treasure not to be missed is St Anne's Church, which, legend has it, Napoleon wanted moved to Paris because he found it so beautiful.

Remembering the tragedies of the 20th century

Nicknamed the 'Jerusalem of the East', Vilnius was a major centre of Jewish learning before WWII. The Holocaust Exhibition and Tolerance Centre (jmuseum.lt) tell the story of the extermination of the Litvaks, Lithuania's thriving Jewish community, during the conflict, while the Samuel Bak Museum exhibits the bold works of this artist, whose early life was marked by being forced into Vilnius' ghetto. Paneriai pine forest, 11km (7 miles) from the city, was the scene of around 100,000 murders between 1941 and 1944 – a memorial and small museum recount that horrific story. Finally, located in the former KGB and Gestapo headquarters, the Museum of Genocide Victims (genocid.lt/muziejus) remembers those murdered and deported by the Soviet Union after 1945.

Consider the merits of contemporary art

MO Museum (mo.lt), the country's first private museum, brings together contemporary Lithuanian art and photography. Designed by Daniel Libeskind, the visionary architect of Berlin's Jewish Museum, the ultramodern building also hosts cultural events. The Contemporary Art Centre (cac.lt) displays photos, videos and installations. For a trip to somewhere more alternative, visit Užupis (inset), a veritable artistic incubator.

Venture into rebel territory

Tucked away in a loop of the Vilnia River, 1.5km (1 mile) from the city centre, the capital's bohemian community created its own independent state in 1998 – the Republic of Užupis (uzhupisembassy.eu), complete with a president, a national anthem, a 41-point constitution and a public holiday on 1 April. A victim of its own success, the area is now home to a growing number of workshops, restaurants and galleries, attracting free spirits and creators of all kinds, and making Užupis feel like an open-air gallery with works by local artists on the riverbanks, including a grand piano and a giant rocking horse.

Sample the flavours of Lithuanian chefs

With inventive cuisine inspired by the whole of Europe, Lithuania's food scene is on the up, particularly in Vilnius, where a new generation of talented chefs is making a name for themselves. Three strongholds of this reinvented Baltic cuisine are worth seeking out: Nineteen18 (nineteen18.lt), Šturmų Švyturys (sturmusvyturys.lt) and Sweet Root (sweetroot.lt).

MORE TIME?

TELEVISION TOWER Accessible by trolleybus, this 326m (1070ft) tower (tvbokstas.lt) contains the Milky Way observation platform and a revolving restaurant.
TRAKAI This pretty village, 28km (17 miles) west of Vilnius in Trakai Historical National Park (tinp.lrv.lt), is home to a fairy-tale castle (opposite).
EUROPOS PARKAS SCULPTURE PARK Just 21km (13 miles) north of Vilnius, this outdoor museum (europosparkas.org/lt) displays contemporary works, including the world's largest sculpture – made of 3000 television sets – and a labyrinth leading to an upside-down statue of Lenin.

SOLSTICE FUN

The Northern Hemisphere's summer solstice in late June marks the start of the harvest season in the agricultural calendar and the start of the biggest celebration in Lithuania's calendar of events, in a country where winters are long and summers short. On the night of the 23/24 June, the festival of Joninės features bonfires being lit and jumped over, folk songs and dances performed, traditional stories told to excited crowds, bathing in the morning dew and not going to bed until the sun has risen.

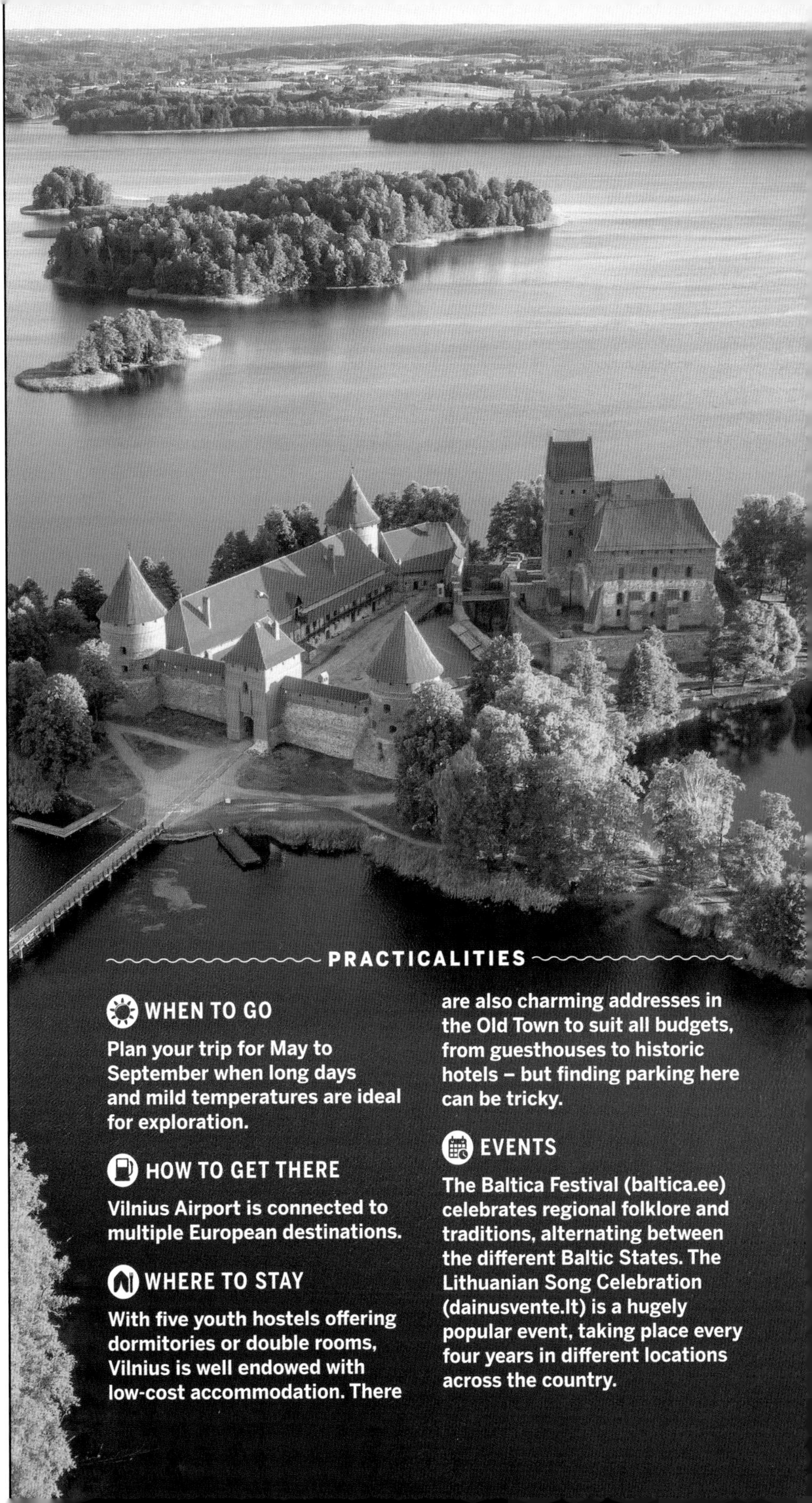

∼∼∼∼ PRACTICALITIES ∼∼∼∼

☀ WHEN TO GO

Plan your trip for May to September when long days and mild temperatures are ideal for exploration.

⛽ HOW TO GET THERE

Vilnius Airport is connected to multiple European destinations.

🏠 WHERE TO STAY

With five youth hostels offering dormitories or double rooms, Vilnius is well endowed with low-cost accommodation. There are also charming addresses in the Old Town to suit all budgets, from guesthouses to historic hotels – but finding parking here can be tricky.

📅 EVENTS

The Baltica Festival (baltica.ee) celebrates regional folklore and traditions, alternating between the different Baltic States. The Lithuanian Song Celebration (dainusvente.lt) is a hugely popular event, taking place every four years in different locations across the country.

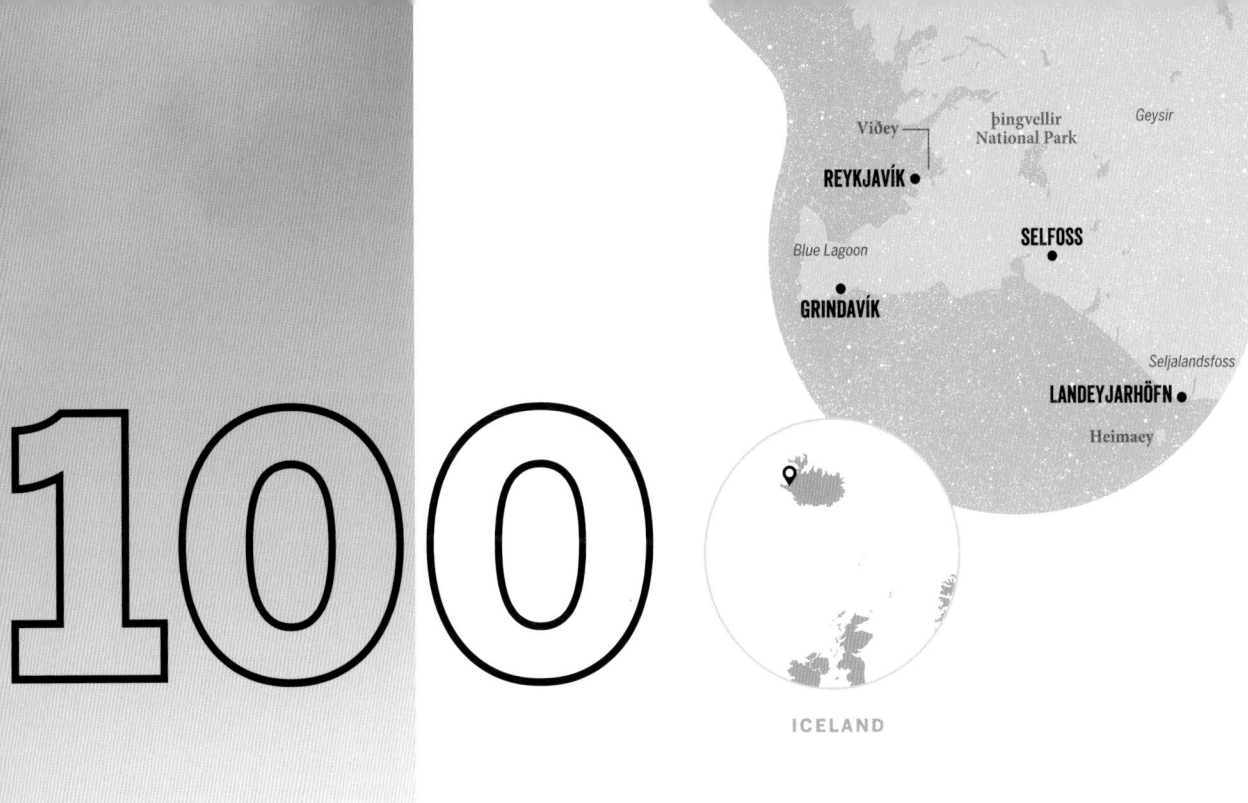

ICELAND

100

Icelandic adventures
AROUND REYKJAVÍK

ocated in a spectacular setting, with a coastline of bays and peninsulas, vast stretches of wilderness and snowcapped mountains, Reykjavík is a small city built on a human scale in the grandest of natural surroundings. Even with limited time, the Icelandic capital and the region around it offer a satisfying taster of this fascinating land of fire and ice. Reykjavík itself is a lively and dynamic place. With its busy Laugavegur shopping street, huge, rocket-ship-like Hallgrímskirkja (left), picturesque harbour, beloved Lake

Tjörnin, remarkable street art and colourful old houses, 'Smokey Bay', as the city's name translates, is an inviting, compact place to stroll. But save some energy for its nightlife – in addition to welcoming bars and excellent restaurants, fun festivals are held regularly too. And if you have a bit of time to spare, plan an excursion to the nearby island of Viðey, a top spot for hikers and bird-watchers; and a tour of some of the nearby highlights, notably those along the famous Golden Circle.

Swim in the waters of the Blue Lagoon

An essential stop on the outskirts of Reykjavík, the Blue Lagoon (bluelagoon.com) is renowned the world over for the benefits of its thermal waters, rich in algae, silica mud and mineral salts. Nestled in a dark, captivating rocky landscape, this open-air wellness centre is the prime place to recharge your batteries in water at 38°C (100°F), whatever the outside temperature. It's easy to get there by bus from Reykjavík.

Discover the jewels of the Golden Circle

The Golden Circle is a 300km (186-mile) itinerary checking off some of Iceland's most magical spots. Gasp at the deafening roar of Gullfoss waterfall, wait expectantly at Geysir geothermal site for the impressive Strokkur geyser (opposite) to shoot into the air (every 4–10 minutes), and walk between continents at þingvellir National Park, full of historic significance and where two tectonic plates meet.

Hunt the Northern Lights

What could be more enchanting than seeing the mesmerising Northern Lights in the heart of unspoiled nature on a clear, cold winter's night? Many tour operators run aurora-borealis-seeking trips from Reykjavík between September and April, but you can also try to look on your own, consulting the en.vedur.is website on the probability of seeing them.

Around the Reykjanes Peninsula

In the southwest of the country, the Reykjanes Peninsula (home to Keflavík Airport, the country's main entry point) is home to astonishing landscapes of lichen-covered lava fields and fascinating geothermal zones with boiling mud pools and hot springs. Numerous marked trails allow you to explore these remote areas, reached by several bus routes or by car – check for updates on volcanic activity in the area before setting out, though, as there's been significant disruption in recent years after eruptions.

Walk on the heights of the Kerið Crater

Situated north of the town of Selfoss on the Golden Circle route, Kerið (inset; kerid.is), an ochre-coloured volcanic crater, is the result of an eruption that took place over 6000 years ago. An easy path leads around the rim before descending to the crater floor, filled by a small emerald-green lake.

MORE TIME?

VESTMANNAEYJAR ARCHIPELAGO A 30-minute boat ride from Landeyjarhöfn, on the south coast, brings you to Heimaey island in the Vestmannaeyjar Archipelago, where you can observe puffins on the rocky cliffs and visit the fascinating Eldheimar volcano museum (eldheimar.is).

SELJALANDSFOSS This waterfall is one of the most beautiful in the country and very popular because, along with being wowed by its 65m (213ft) drop, you can also walk behind it.

NATURAL ENERGY

Iceland is home to some unique geothermal phenomena, thanks to intense volcanic activity and the omnipresence of water on the island. From one end of the country to the other, you'll find hot springs and rivers, pools of bubbling mud, fumaroles and a few geysers. Many of these natural marvels have been turned by Icelanders into great outdoor relaxation spots, but they've proved equally useful for domestic use – the country's energy supplies are close to 100% renewable, with roughly 70% coming from hydro and 30% from geothermal sources.

HOW TO GET THERE & AROUND

Reykjavík is well connected to both North America and Europe, and is a popular stopover between the two. Once there, rent a car, though many of the most popular sights can be reached by public transport or organised tour.

WHERE TO STAY

Iceland's capital offers a wide range of accommodation, from budget hostels to luxury hotels.

If you want to sleep right in the heart of the city, check that the address shows post code 101.

EVENTS

In August, Reykjavík shines during Culture Night (Menningarnótt; culturenight. is), which highlights many cultural and artistic venues, while in November the city rocks to the rhythms of Iceland Airwaves (icelandairwaves.is), a major contemporary music festival showcasing local and international acts.

INDEX

PHOTO CREDITS

Marcel /Adobe Stock; p216 julia700702 / Adobe Stock; p218 Juriaan / Adobe Stock; p219 Birol Bali / Adobe Stock; (inset) AR / Adobe Stock; p220 acnaleksy / Adobe Stock; p222 john / Adobe Stock; p223 Pablo Debat / Shutterstock; (inset) Alessia / Adobe Stock; p224, p226 Boris Stroujko / Adobe Stock; p227 itravelshot / Adobe Stock; (inset) Lotharingia / Adobe Stock; p228 Mike Mareen /Shutterstock; p230 Ryszard Filipowicz / Shutterstock; p231 Composer / Adobe Stock; (inset) York / Adobe Stock; p232, p234 Sina Ettmer / Adobe Stock; p235 Westend61 / Getty Images; (inset) senteliaolga / Adobe Stock; p236 Simon Dux Media / Shutterstock; p238 leoks / Shutterstock; p239 J rgen Wackenhut / Getty Images; (inset) kab-vision / Adobe Stock; p240 Harald Tedesco / Adobe Stock; p242 Manuel Schönfeld / Adobe Stock; p243 dudlajzov / Adobe Stock; (inset) Johannes Öhl / Adobe Stock; p244 Daniel Pahmeier / Shutterstock; p246 Thomas / Adobe Stock; p247 egon999 / Adobe Stock; (inset) Jesus Fernandez / Shutterstock; p248 Marina Datsenko / Shutterstock; p250 gevision / Shutterstock; p251 xbrchx /Shutterstock; (inset) Roberto Moiola / Sysaworld /Getty Images; p252 Pete Seaward for Lonely Planet; p254 Boris Stroujko / Adobe Stock; p255 Pete Seaward for Lonely Planet; (inset) Ron Sumners / Alamy Stock Photos; p256 skam-pypictures / Adobe Stock; p258 Elenarts / Adobe Stock; p259 FenlioQ / Shutterstock; (inset) Julien Viel / Adobe Stock; p260 Francesco Bergamaschi / robertharding / Getty Images; p262 SimonMichael / Adobe Stock; p263 Marcial Gamma / Shut-terstock; (inset) Taljat David / Shutterstock; p264 ecstk22 / Adobe Stock; p266 krivinis / Adobe Stock; p268 fotorince / Adobe Stock; p269 vivooo / Shutterstock; (inset) Xavier Allard / Adobe Stock; p270 Only Fabrizio / Adobe Stock; p272 kanu-man / Adobe Stock; p 273 mikolajn / Getty Images; (inset) martin-dm / iStock; p274 Anna Lurye / Adobe Stock; p276 oksanamedvedeva / Adobe Stock; p277 Layue / Shutterstock; (inset) Valerie2000 / Adobe Stock; p278 Nikolay N. Antonov / Adobe Stock; p280 Andrey Shevchenko / Adobe Stock; p281 DaLiu / Shutterstock; (inset) Lipe / Adobe Stock; p282 Sarah Coghill for Lonely Planet; p284 Shchipkova Elena / Adobe Stock; p285 Jan / Adobe Stock; (inset) Blickfang / Adobe Stock; p286 Andreas Karnholz / Adobe Stock; p288 Roman Babakin / Adobe Stock; p289 Izim M. Gulcuk / Shutterstock; (inset) johnmerlin / Adobe Stock; p290 Jonathon Stokes for Lonely Planet; p292 Peter Widmann / Adobe Stock; p293 Jonathon Stokes for Lonely Planet; (inset) Yingko / Adobe Stock; p294 k5hu / Adobe Stock; p296 Fabio Lotti / Adobe Stock; p297 adisa / Adobe Stock; (inset) fottoo / Adobe Stock; p298 xbrchx / Adobe Stock; p300 kasto / Adobe Stock; p301 Justin Foulkes for Lonely Planet; (inset) Miljan Živković / Adobe Stock; p302 Balate Dorin / Adobe Stock; p304 Claudiu / Adobe Stock; p305 Iulius Agency /Shutterstock; (inset) adellyne /Adobe Stock; p306 dudlajzov / Adobe Stock; p308 MilaDrumeva / iStock; p309 Julian Popov / Shutterstock; (inset) Kostadin Petkov / iStock; p310 Simon Dannhauer / Adobe Stock; p312, p314 ElenaChayki-naPhotography / Shutterstock; p315 CK Travels / Shutterstock; (inset) ElenaChaykinaPhotography / Shutterstock; p316 NDLR PHOTONONSTOP / Shutterstock; p318 Alexey Fedorenko / Adobe Stock; p319 Nicola Pulham / Shutterstock; (inset) JohnGK / Shutterstock; p320 Aeypix / Shutterstock; p322 Alicia G. Monedero / Shutterstock; p323 S-F / Shutterstock; (inset) Sakura / Adobe Stock; p324 Alberto Manuel Urosa Toledano / Getty Images; p326 Valdis Skudre / Shutterstock; p327 Gordon-BellPhotography / Getty Images; (inset) coward_lion / Adobe Stock; p328 Valdis Skudre / Shutterstock; p330 dronemybusiness / Shutterstock; p331 chrisatpps / Shutterstock; (inset) travellight / Shutterstock; p332 Michael Runkel / Getty Images; p334 allard1 / Adobe Stock; p335 Michael Heffernan for Lonely Planet; (inset) Ulrike Uhlig / Adobe Stock; p336 muratart / Adobe Stock; p338 GarethWilley / Shutterstock; p339 Matt Trommer / Shutterstock; (inset) Becky Stares / Shutterstock; p340 Martin Gaal / Shutterstock; p342 Anton Ivanov Photo / Adobe Stock; p343 Guillaume / Adobe Stock; (inset) David C Tomlin-son / Getty Images; p344 elxeneize / Shutterstock; p346 miroslav_1 / Getty Images; p347 Leighton Collins / Shutterstock; (inset) Carol_Ann_Peacock / Getty Images; p348 Sandra GS fotos / Shutterstock; p350 Martin M303 / Shutterstock; p351 adfoto / Adobe Stock; (inset) JASPERIMAGE / Shutterstock; p352 JiriCastka / Shutterstock; p354 GPM / Adobe Stock; p355 Rodrigo Garrido / Shutterstock; (inset) Tyler W. Stipp / Shutterstock; p356 susanne2688 / Adobe Stock; p358 D. Ribeiro / Shutterstock; p359 Pete Seaward for Lonely Planet; (inset) D. Ribeiro / Shutterstock; p360 Sergei Afanasev / Shutterstock; p362 Anton_Ivanov / Shutterstock; p363 Kanuman / Shutterstock; (inset) Atmosphere1 / Shutterstock; p364 jankost / Adobe Stock; p366 Arndale / Shutterstock; p367 Jon Davison for Lonely Planet; (inset) Dreamer Company / Shutterstock; p368 evenfh / Adobe Stock; p370 Justin Foulkes for Lonely Planet; p371 Nick Fox / Adobe Stock; (inset) Justin Foulkes for Lonely Planet; p372 valerie_v /Adobe Stock; p374 Mistervlad / Adobe Stock; p375 Boumen Japet / Shutterstock; (inset) Lola Akinmade Akerstrom for Lonely Planet; p376 Johner Images /Getty Images; p378 Jonas Tufvesson / Shutterstock; p379 Johner Images / Getty Images; (inset) Trygve / Adobe Stock; p380 It4All / Adobe Stock; p382 Isabelle Nyrot / Shutterstock; p383 David Sahlberg / Shutterstock; (inset) Rolf_52 / Shutterstock; p384 LouieLea / Shutterstock; p386 Kedardome / Shut-terstock; p387 Justinreznick /Getty Images; (inset) Johner Images / Getty Images; p388 xbrchx / Adobe Stock; p390 nanisimova / Adobe Stock; p391 Morten Falch Sortland / Getty Images; (inset) Jamesbox / Adobe Stock; p392 Apostolis Giontzis / Adobe Stock; p394 Simon Dannhauer / Adobe Stock; p395 Zarnell / Getty Images; (inset) Dmitry Naumov / Adobe Stock; p396 Mistervlad / Shutterstock; p398 Pauliina / Adobe Stock; p399 yari2000 / Shutterstock; (inset) Karis48 / Shut-terstock; p400 KavalenkavaVolha / iStock; p402 Jelana M / Adobe Stock; p403 LordRunar / iStock; (inset) SeanPavonePhoto /Adobe Stock; p404 Nikolay N. Antonov / Adobe Stock; p406 dimbar76 / Adobe Stock; p407 Sarah Coghill for Lonely Planet; (inset) voloshin311 / Adobe Stock; p408 Roman Babakin / Adobe Stock; p410 agephotography / Adobe Stock; p411 dzmi-trock87 / Adobe Stock; (inset) Anna Jurkovska /Adobe Stock; p412 RPBaiao / Shutterstock; p414 Thomas Heitz / Adobe Stock; p415 Wojtek Chmielewski / Shutterstock; (inset) zicksvift / Adobe Stock

100 WEEKENDS IN EUROPE 1st edition

© Lonely Planet Global Limited 2025
© Lonely Planet and Édi8 2023
92 avenue de France - 75013 Paris

Printed in Malaysia

Published by Lonely Planet Global Limited
January 2025
CRN 554153
www.lonelyplanet.com
10 9 8 7 6 5 4 3 2 1

ISBN 978 1 83758 310 2

Photographs © as shown 2025

STAY IN TOUCH
lonelyplanet.com/contact

Lonely Planet Global Limited
Digital Depot, Roe Lane (off Thomas St),
Digital Hub, Dublin 8,
D08 TCV4
Ireland

Authors Angélique Adagio, Claire Angot, Rodolphe Bacquet, Mathilde Benezet, Jean-Bernard Carillet, Thérèse de Cherisey, Astrid Duvillard, Julie Hainaut, Caroline Hattiger, Élodie Lecadieu, Alexandre Lenoir, Coralie Modschiedler

Editorial management Dominique Bovet

Publishing director Piers Pickard

Gift & illustrated publisher Becca Hunt

Senior editor Robin Barton

Editors Polly Thomas & Cliff Wilkinson

Proofreader Karyn Noble

Design Caroline Donadieu & Emily Dubin

Layout design Jo Dovey

Cartography Caroline Sahanouk & Wayne Murphy

Print production Nigel Longuet

Cover image: Sicily, Italy: Andrew Montgomery for Lonely Planet

Back cover clockwise from top: Sandra GS fotos/Shutterstock; Sarah Coghill for Lonely Planet; Justin Foulkes for Lonely Planet; Justin Foulkes for Lonely Planet

Cover flap: PHOTOERICK/stock.adobe.com